DA?

MAR 9 2011

GLOBAL ISSUES

ADOPTION
AND
SURROGATE
PREGNANCY

GLOBAL ISSUES

ADOPTION AND SURROGATE PREGNANCY

Faith Merino

Foreword by Pamela Anne Quiroz
Professor of Policy Studies and Sociology, University of Illinois

Facts On File
An imprint of Infobase Publishing

GLOBAL ISSUES: ADOPTION AND SURROGATE PREGNANCY

Facts On File, Inc.
An imprint of Infobase Publishing
132 West 31st Street
New York NY 10001

Library of Congress Cataloging-in-Publication Data
Merino, Faith.
    Adoption and surrogate pregnancy / Faith Merino ; foreword by Pamela Anne Quiroz.
        p. cm. — (Global issues)
    Includes bibliographical references and index.
    ISBN 978-0-8160-8087-8
    1. Adoption—Case studies. 2. Surrogate motherhood—Case studies. I. Title.
    HV875.M44 2010
    362.734—dc22   2009036453

Facts On File books are available at special discounts when purchased in bulk quantities for businesses, associations, institutions, or sales promotions. Please call our Special Sales Department in New York at (212) 967-8800 or (800) 322-8755.

You can find Facts On File on the World Wide Web at http://www.factsonfile.com

Text design by Erika K. Arroyo
Tables and graphs by Dale Williams
Composition by Mary Susan Ryan-Flynn
Cover printed by Art Print, Taylor, Pa.
Book printed and bound by Maple Press, York, Pa.
Date printed: May 2010
Printed in the United States of America

10 9 8 7 6 5 4 3 2 1

This book is printed on acid-free paper.

CONTENTS

List of Tables and Graphs   **vii**

Foreword by Pamela Anne Quiroz   **viii**

PART I: AT ISSUE

Chapter 1:
Introduction   **3**
  Adoption   **6**
  Surrogate Pregnancy   **16**
  Ethical Concerns   **21**
  Conclusion   **23**

Chapter 2:
Focus on the United States   **28**
  History and Law   **28**
  Characteristics of Participants   **39**
  Conclusion   **42**

Chapter 3:
Global Perspectives   **48**
  Introduction   **48**
  China   **53**
  India   **61**
  Great Britain   **68**
  Guatemala   **75**
  Conclusion   **81**

PART II: PRIMARY SOURCES

Chapter 4:
United States Documents   **93**

Chapter 5:
International Documents   **117**
  China   **138**
  India   **152**
  Great Britain   **162**
  Guatemala   **171**

PART III: RESEARCH TOOLS

Chapter 6:
How to Research Adoption and Surrogacy   **185**
  Becoming Familiar with the Topic   **185**
  Perspectives and Angles   **190**
  Sources   **193**

Chapter 7:
Facts and Figures   **199**

Chapter 8:
Key Players A to Z   **216**

Chapter 9:
Organizations and Agencies   **229**

Chapter 10:
Annotated Bibliography   **250**
  Adoption and the Issues   **250**
  Surrogate Pregnancy and the Issues   **255**
  Adoption and Surrogate Pregnancy
    Worldwide   **261**
  Adoption and Surrogate Pregnancy in the
    United States   **269**
  Adoption and Surrogate Pregnancy in
    China   **275**
  Adoption and Surrogate Pregnancy in
    India   **278**
  Adoption and Surrogate Pregnancy in
    Great Britain   **281**
  Adoption and Surrogate Pregnancy in
    Guatemala   **284**

Chronology   **287**

Glossary   **312**

Index   **323**

List of Tables and Graphs

1.	International Adoptions to the United States, 1998–2009	**199**
2.	International Adoptions to the United States by Sending Country, 2004–2009	**200**
3.	International Adoptions to the United States and Europe, 1995–2006	**201**
4.	International Adoptions to the United States by Sex and Age, 2002	**202**
5.	U.S. Adoptions in 1992 and 2001	**203**
6.	Preferences for Adopted Children in the United States, 2002	**204**
7.	Adoption Demand in the United States, 2002	**206**
8.	Children Born to Single Mothers Relinquished for Adoption in the United States, 1973–2002	**208**
9.	Perceptions of Adoptive Parents in the United States, 2002	**209**
10.	Racial Differences in Views of Birth Parents in the United States, 1997	**210**
11.	Total World Fertility Rates, 1998	**211**
12.	Percentage of Women in Developing Countries Who Have No Say in Their Own Health Care Needs	**212**
13.	Millennium Development Goals on Maternal and Child Health, 2005	**213**
14.	U.S. State Laws on Surrogacy, 2005	**214**
15.	International Laws on Surrogacy, 2004	**215**

Foreword

Despite undergoing many changes in the past several decades, the family remains an important institution of social organization. The family is the first opportunity children have to realize their role as part of a larger group (e.g., neighborhoods, racial groups, nation-states). Therefore, it is important to understand how the creation of families intersects with social, economic, and ethical issues, and what types of changes must occur for families and societies to thrive.

While the motivations for pursuing adoption and surrogate pregnancy vary, those who seek adoption and surrogate pregnancy undeniably represent cultures of privilege; they can afford to use other people's children or other women's bodies as a means to their ends. The practices surrounding adoption account for millions of dollars in local and global economies, which is often exchanged between countries with asymmetric economic and power relations. Independent adoption lawyers, for-profit adoption agencies, and a variety of businesses profit from the commercialization of adoption by selling dolls, clothes, books, and other cultural artifacts. Some agencies specialize in organizing roots trips or culture camps for adoptive families.

In the process, adoption has stimulated the growth of illegal activities and abuses of human rights. The practices of private adoption (i.e., adoptions handled by a privately funded and licensed agency that places infants or young children) prompted UNICEF to assess it as a high risk activity and one that required an international framework to reduce the abuses of children. The result was the 1993 Hague Convention on Intercountry Adoption. The goals of the Hague Convention were to serve as an international governing structure for adoptions, encourage domestic adoption of children as a priority over intercountry adoption, create neutral authorities to regulate and provide information on transnational adoption, and prevent the abduction, sale, or trafficking of children. In short, its purpose was to promote civil society, global equity, and respect for human rights.

Introduction

The debate continues as to whether transnational adoption represents a global humanitarian effort or a neocolonial project that allows countries with more economic resources to exploit, either directly or indirectly, those with few resources. In my own work on adoption I have argued that institutional and interpersonal relations are now often viewed and conducted from the position of extreme individualism, and adoption and surrogate pregnancy are no exceptions. Parent selection among sending countries involves individual preferences, historical and current relations with a particular country, views of children from sending countries, and the marketing of programs by private adoption agencies. Does the "rescue" of some children occur at the expense of others? How does rescue work? Do policies that support adoption and surrogacy impede policies that would have a broader impact on a larger number of children? How does surrogate pregnancy operate and what is the impact on women of color and women from poor countries? In short, are adoption and surrogate pregnancy simply neocolonialism at its worst, purchasing, absorbing, and transforming the bodies of the less fortunate? Or does the fact that financial incentives for participating women are comparatively greater than what many women could hope to gain through alternative labor support a humanitarian view?

In the past 15 years, researchers and activists have addressed the issues of adoption and reproduction by refocusing our attention beyond questions involving the integration of individuals, identity development, or even the morality of fertility treatment and surrogate pregnancy, to ask other questions, such as, how do children and women come to occupy particular social spaces in the first place (i.e., adoptive status or surrogate)? How do we create just policies and link these policies to systemic changes so that women and children can occupy other spaces? Regardless of good intentions or factors beyond participants' control, it is still the case that these activities are situated within unequal contexts, and participants have varying degrees of control. Therefore, any resolution to these issues needs to include the voices of all participants.

Adoption and surrogate pregnancy have become part of the conversation on social responsibility, global human rights, and justice, and Faith Merino's book assists us in understanding these issues. Merino provides the history of adoption and surrogate pregnancy and situates these activities in rich case studies that encourage us to delve deeper into the social, ethical, and moral implications of building families. More important, she allows us to draw our own conclusions on these important matters.

Adoption and Surrogate Pregnancy provides an excellent starting point for examining the history, the alternative ways in which family-building is framed, and the current debates surrounding adoption and surrogate pregnancy. As Merino illustrates, the implications of adoption and surrogate pregnancy speak to issues of immigration, citizenship and nationality, culture, race, gender, and social class. *Adoption and Surrogate Pregnancy* is fundamentally about providing information necessary to reframe issues of family-building in the 21st century and thus encourages us to address important social and ethical issues. Merino also subtly reminds us that our solutions to these complex issues will affirm our commitment to families, society, and our conception of global justice.

—Pamela Anne Quiroz
Professor, Policy Studies and Sociology
University of Illinois, Chicago

PART I

At Issue

1

Introduction

Few elements of human life are so protected and difficult to govern politically as the family unit. This is due, in part, to the prevailing belief that human life is bifurcated into two separate domains: public life (work) and private life (family). Historically, the two have been maintained as distinct areas of human existence that do not (or should not) overlap. But with increasingly rapid developments in reproductive technology, the family unit is being thrust into the public eye as politicians, the legal system, the media, and scientific and religious communities are asked to determine what constitutes a family. In the practice of surrogate pregnancy, as many as five people can lay claim to a child: the contracting parents, the surrogate mother, and the egg and sperm donors (if used). How are courts to define and decide kinship bonds? Is kinship defined through biological relatedness or intent to love? Is it both, and if so, what takes precedence?

The goal of this book is to address family formation through adoption and surrogate pregnancy and its global effects. For most people choosing to have children, the question of *when* to start a family is difficult to answer, as career, financial stability, and the support of family and friends must be taken into account. But for those suffering from infertility, the question of *how* is even more difficult to answer. According to the Centers for Disease Control and Prevention (CDC), in 2002 11.8 percent of U.S. women (both married and unmarried) were unable to get pregnant or carry a baby to term.[1] The wealth of media attention devoted to issues of infertility and childlessness over the last four decades has led many to wonder about a possible infertility epidemic. Though infertility rates have remained stable since the 1950s,[2] and even dropped among married couples between 1965 and 1982 from 11.2 percent to 8.5 percent, many social factors have contributed to the perception of a higher infertility rate, particularly the number of women who delay childbearing in favor of career development.[3] In 1950, approximately one in three women in the United States participated in the workforce. By 1998, three in five women were participating in the workforce. Among women between the ages of 34 to 45, labor force participation doubled from 34 percent in 1950 to 76.3 percent in 1998.[4] Coinciding with this increase was a rise in the number of women who chose to delay childbearing. Between 1969 and 1994, the median age at first birth rose from 21.3 years to 24.4 years, and the proportion of first births for women in their 30s rose from 4.1 percent in 1969 to 21.2 percent in 1994. This percentage spike is even higher for college-educated women: 45.5 percent of first births were to female graduates in their 30s in 1994, compared with 10.2 percent in 1969.[5] By 2002, the average age of U.S. mothers at first birth was 25.1 years, an all-time national high.[6] Among European women, the average age at first birth rose from 27.1 years in 1980 to 28.6 years in 1993. In Italy and the Netherlands, the median age at first birth has remained stable, at 29 years, since 1960.[7]

Worldwide alarm over infertility was catalyzed in 1973, when a French sperm bank found that a patient's chances of achieving a successful pregnancy after artificial insemination directly corresponded with her age. While women under the age of 31 had a 74 percent chance of becoming pregnant following artificial insemination, that number dropped to 61 percent for women between the ages of 31 and 35, and to 54 percent for those over the age of 35.[8] Thus, because a woman's fertility decreases with age, more women today are faced with the possibility of suffering from infertility than they were 50 years ago. Though one-third of all cases of infertility among couples are male-related, age does not affect male fertility as dramatically as it does female fertility.[9] Furthermore, a rise in voluntary childlessness may contribute to an overall worldwide perception of failing reproductive health among women. Women in developed nations are having fewer children, with an average of 1.5 births for western European women and two births for North American women. Discussions of an infertility epidemic rarely mention developing nations, however, where birth rates have remained consistently high. In sub-Saharan Africa, the average woman gives birth to six children, while in the Middle East and North Africa the average birthrate is four per woman.[10]

New developments in reproductive technology, including the advent of birth control and legalized abortion in the 1960s and 1970s, have given women and men more control over career and family planning. Nevertheless, judging from the media attention the topic has received, the accompanying redefinition of the family has also caused collective anxiety over the future of the traditional family unit. In the decade between 1968 and 1978, a total of 18 articles on infertility were published; since 1978, however, an average of 13 articles on infertility have been published every year. In 1978 alone, the year that Louise Brown became the first baby to be born through the use of in vitro fertilization (IVF), a total of 16 articles were published.[11] The private family unit has become a highly politicized and publicly debated facet of human existence. In the mid-1980s, the U.S. war on drugs and increasing public and political concern over prenatal drug exposure led to discussions of fetal rights and fetal abuse. Throughout the 1980s and 1990s, several U.S. bills were introduced that would have defined the use of drugs during pregnancy as child neglect, and one bill would have mandated forcible sterilization for women convicted of fetal abuse.[12] Many pro-choice activists have argued against such legislation, as indeed the concept of fetal abuse does not legally coincide with women's reproductive rights. While to date no fetal abuse laws have been passed in the United States the introduction of such legislation was an explicit manifestation of public fear for its future citizens.

The family, while seemingly objective and self-defined, cannot be separated from issues of gender, race, class, and commerce, and it is for this reason that adoption and surrogate pregnancy remain hotly contested topics. As alternative means of creating families, both adoption and surrogate pregnancy are rife with debates over their potential for exploitation, as well as their capacity to magnify existing social injustices. Many argue, for example, that while international adoption has flourished within the last decade as more adoptive parents look overseas for healthy infants, hundreds of thousands of children await placement in the United States. These children tend to be harder to place due to age, minority status, and possible health problems. Thus, international adoption, while altruistic in appearance, is considered by some a social injustice. Similarly, when individuals turn to surrogate pregnancy as a means of becoming parents, the question of why they choose not to adopt inevitably arises. One director of a surrogacy center addressed the issue with biting clarity: "It is not, nor should it be the sole responsibility of the infertile to remedy this particular societal problem. Every one of you in the audience should ask yourself why you haven't adopted one of these children. You don't have to be infertile to adopt."[13]

What role does fertility play in addressing social injustice, and do infertile couples have an obligation to be color-blind and politically correct when creating their families? How imperative is the biological drive to reproduce and have a genetic child of one's own?

There is a plethora of angles from which to view adoption and surrogate pregnancy, as well as a wealth of ideological rhetoric when arguing for or against reproductive alternatives. To successfully research this topic, one must be able to identify the rhetorical frames that are so often used when debating such a controversial issue.

As technology continues to develop and global regulations become more standardized, both adoption and surrogate pregnancy will become increasingly accessible and more provocative as topics of discourse. At present, both reproductive alternatives challenge basic, deeply held beliefs regarding kinship bonds and family relationships, and as these reproductive alternatives continue to evolve, so too will the face of the family unit.

ADOPTION

The earliest known example of a written adoption law can be traced back to the Babylonian Code of Hammurabi around 1780 B.C.E., in which child welfare and parent-child bonding are viewed as legitimate concerns.[14] In many other ancient societies, such as Greece and Rome, adoption was less a matter of placing orphaned children with families than it was about establishing an heir. In ancient Athens, for example, the need to have an heir meant that adult men often adopted other adult men rather than children.[15]

Adoption refers to the matching of a parentless child with a family that wants him or her. In most cases, this serves a humanitarian purpose, but historically it has also been true that some children have been adopted for purposes of labor and exploitation. Today, in most developed countries, adoption is perceived as a matter of love and child well-being.

Adoption can be a complicated process, and it is important for both adoptive and birth parents to understand the different types of adoption from which to choose, as well as the language of adoption. Various terms exist to designate sensitively the different individuals involved in the adoption process. Because of the delicate and highly emotional nature of adoption, language must be employed carefully and respectfully. The following list of terms relates to the participants in the adoption process.

- Adoption triad: Refers to the relationship of the birth parents, adoptive parents, and adoptee.
- Birth/biological parent: The individual who is terminating his or her parental rights; formerly referred to as the real/natural parent.
- Adoptive parent: The individual who is awarded parental rights. At a certain point in the process, the parties involved are encouraged to refer to the adoptive parent simply as the parent.
- Waiting child: A child in foster care who has been legally released for adoption; formerly referred to as an available or adoptable child.
- Special needs child: A child who is difficult to place. This term does not refer exclusively to children with disabilities, but rather includes older children, children of mixed race, children who are part of a sibling group that should not be separated, children with developmental delays, and African-American boys over the age of eight.

- Child with special needs: Refers exclusively to a child with physical disabilities or developmental delays; formerly referred to as handicapped or feebleminded.
- Transracial adoption: An adoption in which the adoptive parents and the adoptee are of different ethnic backgrounds; formerly referred to as cross-racial or mixed-race.
- Intercountry/international adoption: Refers to the adoption of a child from another country; formerly referred to as a foreign adoption.

Language is a subtle but useful framing device for emotionally charged topics like adoption, in which certain terms may be used to connote positive or negative meanings. The terms above are considered positive adoption language and developed out of a movement to create adoption-friendly language. Positive adoption language emerged in 1972 in an effort to afford birth parents and adoptive parents the "maximum respect, dignity, responsibility, and objectivity" possible in the decision-making process.[16] Some individuals and organizations, however, object to the use of positive adoption language. The First Mothers Action Group asserts that such language has been developed to prioritize adoptive parents at the expense of birth parents. In her rebuttal to an article on positive adoption language, Diane Turski of the First Mothers Action Group argued that the term *birth parent* is dehumanizing and equates the role of the birth parent to that of an incubator or breeder.[17] For purposes of clarity, this book uses the terms *birth parent* and *adoptive parent* to distinguish between the two parties.

Types of Adoption

Adoption is not a uniform process. Every situation is unique, and various types of adoption exist to meet the needs of all individuals. They include the following.

OPEN ADOPTION

In an open adoption, the birth parents maintain a relationship with the child and continue to play a role in his or her life. In some cases, other relatives may also visit the child, including grandparents and siblings. Open adoption became popular in the United States in the 1970s and continues to gain momentum as a viable alternative to what many feel is a process that has been unnecessarily shadowed in secrecy and shame. Proponents of open adoption believe it to be emotionally healthier than closed adoption. Birth parents are allowed to know their child's future and find closure in knowing that they did not abandon their child, but rather devised an alternative plan for his or her care. Adoptive parents are said to find security in receiving official permission from the birth parents to adopt their child and have greater access to information regarding their new child's genetic health history. The adopted child has a complete and accurate history to refer to and may develop a better comprehension of the circumstances that led to his or her adoption, rather than suffer from a feeling of abandonment. Open adoption may also help facilitate easier identity formation for the child as he or she matures. The overall experience of open adoption as described by many participants is that of knowledge, communication, and security.

Open adoption can also have disadvantages. The various parties involved may not agree on the appropriate amount of contact between the birth parents and a child, leading to disappointment for some and frustration for others. In some situations, the birth parents and adoptive families may find themselves in unstable or unhealthy relationships, which can disrupt both families' lives and cause possible confusion for the adopted child. And while some claim that open adoption aids in a child's identity formation, it may also contribute to confusion and uncertainty in this regard.

The United Kingdom became one of the first countries to make a national move toward open adoption by unsealing birth records in 1975, thereby granting adoptees the right to access identifying information. While no mandate regarding relationships between birth and adoptive parents exists, the nation has formally prohibited social workers and adoption agencies from making any promises of anonymity to birth mothers.

CLOSED ADOPTION

When birth parents and adoptive parents choose closed adoption, they agree to anonymity and the severance of all communication. No identifying information is shared between the parties and no contact is made prior to or after the adoption. The process of a closed adoption was originally developed to protect birth mothers from the stigma of being unmarried and pregnant, as well as adoptive parents from the stigma of being infertile. Proponents of closed adoption emphasize the importance of privacy (not secrecy), which they believe to be beneficial to the birth parents, the adoptive parents, and the adopted child. Many assert that closed adoption allows adoptive parents to establish their family without the possibly intimidating influence of the birth parents, while allowing the birth parents to heal from a difficult and perhaps traumatic situation. Furthermore, the child may benefit by being able to assimilate into the family with greater ease.

Some of the possible disadvantages associated with closed adoption include, for birth parents, a lack of information about their child, which may intensify feelings of grief and guilt. As the very nature of closed adoption was designed to allow the birth parents to continue their lives "as if nothing happened," this may lead to an unhealthy state of denial in which the biological parents do not cope with their decision to relinquish their parental rights, but rather deny that the child was ever born. For adoptive parents, the lack of information in a closed adoption may allow them to imagine their child as a parentless orphan with no history or background. As with the birth parents, this may lead to a state of denial in which the adoptive parents deny that the child has any identity beyond the insulated family unit.

In many countries, closed adoption has been the norm for thousands of years. In ancient India, kinship and intimacy within the family unit was considered so important that an adopted son who openly declared his status as an adoptee could be punished by having his tongue cut out. To announce one's status as an adoptee was to shame the family by announcing its deviation from normative familial structures.

SEMI-OPEN ADOPTION

Generally speaking, open adoption is the norm in most industrialized nations today, but many consider the entire adoption process to be on a spectrum between open and closed. Kathleen Silber, associate and clinical director of the Independent Adoption Center (which arranges only open adoptions), avers that in the future the very term *closed adoption* will be rendered obsolete as today virtually all adoptions involve some level of openness.[18]

For families who desire some degree of physical and emotional distance, semi-open adoption is a viable alternative to fully open adoption. In a semi-open adoption, birth parents and adoptive parents may meet, but do not exchange identifying information, and while the two families may maintain contact throughout the years as the child grows, all contact is facilitated and monitored by a mediating party, such as a lawyer or adoption agency. The families may exchange cards and letters, but all items are screened to censor identifying information. Both families have the option of discontinuing contact at any time, at which point the third party mediator will keep all letters and cards on file to be claimed when desired.

SEMI-CLOSED ADOPTION

Semi-closed adoption exists for families who do not want any future contact, but nevertheless desire some information about one another. Birth parents are allowed to choose from previously screened and approved couples to decide who will raise their child but may not contact the prospective couples. This type of adoption may be beneficial to birth parents who desire confidentiality and anonymity but do not want to feel as though they are abandoning their child. By choosing semi-closed adoption, they may feel empowered by the fact that they are deciding on their child's future while also having the freedom to put the experience behind them and move on with their lives when the process is over.

DOMESTIC INFANT ADOPTION

Infant adoption is the most widely pursued form of adoption for many adoptive parents, who, if successful, may take the baby home soon after its birth. Couples interested in adopting an infant generally begin by making a profile with an adoption agency and writing a "Dear birth mother" letter that describes them and their reasons for wanting to adopt.[19]

Infant adoption is riddled with controversy, as this form of adoption tends to incite questions regarding child desirability and the commodification of infants. While there were some 130,000 children in the public foster care system awaiting adoption in the United States in 2007,[20] there were 40 or more prospective adoptive parents competing to adopt every one healthy white infant.[21] The number of white infants voluntarily relinquished for adoption has dropped by nearly 20 percent since 1973, and many couples are willing to pay vast sums of money for services to procure such an infant.[22] According to the authors Kim Clarke and Nancy Shute of *U.S. News & World Report*, the total rate of spending on infant adoption is rising at a rate of 15 percent a year.[23] The same article reports that many hopeful adoptive parents prefer infant adoption to foster care adoption because most foster care children are over five years of age and are more likely to be physically disabled or emotionally disturbed.[24] While more than one-fourth of American women have considered adoption, only 4 percent of the total female population has ever taken steps to adopt, with only 1.3 percent ever actually completing an adoption, and studies indicate that the dramatic discrepancy between women who consider adopting and women who actually do adopt may be due in part to the shortage of healthy white infants.[25] The adoption of an unrelated child in the United States is most common among white women, who tend to prefer healthy, white infants, while women from ethnic minority communities are more likely to adopt a related child. Virtually every developed nation in which reliable methods of contraception are available and in which tolerance toward unwed parenthood and legalized abortion has increased has seen a precipitous drop in the number of adoptable infants. In some countries, like the United Kingdom, this has resulted in a decrease in adoption overall, as many are reticent to adopt from public care. In Norway, it has resulted in greater numbers of overseas adoptions. When pursuing infant adoption, adoptive parents often pay for the birth mother's living and medical expenses, which can cost many thousands of dollars, with no guarantee that they will actually adopt the infant once it is born, as some birth mothers change their minds and choose to keep their babies. On the other side of this matter is the pressure that monetary reimbursement places on the birth mother to give up her child. As she struggles with the choice of whether or not to relinquish her parental rights, she may come to feel that the adoptive family has already paid and that she is thus obligated to produce a baby for them.

The dilemmas that may arise from monetary reimbursement produce a parallel between infant adoption and surrogate pregnancy, in which a woman receives money to gestate a child for a contracting couple or individual. Between the two situations, the only distinguishing characteristic is intention. The process of an infant adoption involves finding parents for a child who is the product of an unintended pregnancy, while the process of a surrogate pregnancy involves the contractual conception of a child for infertile parents.

Most states allow a period of time after the birth of the baby for birth mothers to revoke their consent to the adoption and reclaim their babies. In the United States, revocation periods vary by state and can be anywhere from four to 90 days. A 2006 report by the Evan B. Donaldson Adoption Institute suggests that birth mothers should be allowed several weeks after birth to revoke their consent to the adoption.[26] Revocation periods are generally based on the belief that during pregnancy and shortly after birth, a woman's decision-making process is jeopardized by hormonal imbalances, and thus she should have a specified amount of time to recover in order to make a sound decision.

INTERNATIONAL ADOPTION

Many individuals today choose to adopt internationally for a number of reasons. Many opt for international adoption for humanitarian reasons, while others do so to increase their chances of adopting an infant or toddler. International or intercountry adoption increased by 42 percent worldwide between 1998 and 2004.[27] In the United States, the rate of international adoption rose by 180 percent between 1989 and 2005, at which point it leveled off to around 25,000 overseas adoptions per year.[28] Some adoptive parents believe that international adoption is easier than domestic adoption. One couple, Candy and Bob Murdoch, complained to reporters that after paying $11,000 to a Mississippi adoption agency and waiting for two years, the agency never found a child for them, and they have since filed a civil suit to reclaim their money. After enduring their disappointment and legal ordeal, Candy Murdoch stated, "I would tell anyone considering adoption to go international."[29]

Those who have adopted internationally, however, contend that the process is not easier, but in fact more difficult as one needs to meet the standards of two national governments instead of one. The sending country's regulations must be implemented in order to obtain legal approval for the adoption, which can require that adoptive parents be married and of a particular religion. China, for example, has recently tightened its requirements regarding who may adopt, which include a rigid mandate for mental and physical fitness. Individuals with health complications ranging from AIDS and schizophrenia to facial deformity and obesity are now ineligible to adopt from China.[30]

The Hague Convention on Protection of Children and International Adoption was approved in 1993 by 66 member countries to police intercountry adoption and protect the rights of children, birth parents, and adoptive parents, as well as prevent child abuse and trafficking. The United States signed the treaty on March 31, 2004, and ratified it on December 12, 2007. The act now requires, among other things, that international adoption agencies be accredited by the Department of State.

SPECIAL NEEDS ADOPTION

As mentioned earlier, a special needs child awaiting adoption is not necessarily a child with a physical or mental disability, but rather one who is difficult to place. The reasons for this include that the child is part of a sibling group that should not be separated, belongs to an ethnic minority, or is older. Children *with* special needs are also classified as special needs children.

While it would be a mistake to suggest that every child in foster care has special or unusual needs, most have ended up in the foster care system because they have been removed from their homes due to abuse and neglect and thus may suffer from emotional or psychological problems.

Despite the discrepancy between the adoption demand for infants versus foster care children, the adoption rate of children in foster care has risen from 17,000 adoptions in 1990 to 51,000 adoptions in 2007.[31] This may be a result of the decrease in the number of voluntarily relinquished children, as well as increased efforts to ensure better support for families that adopt special needs children, such as providing subsidies for medical treatment and counseling services.

FOSTER ADOPTION

Children are placed in foster care when the state deems their parents unfit to care for them. The ultimate goal of foster care is to provide a safe home for a child until he or she can be reunited with his or her parents, and the state must pursue all efforts to reunite children with their families. In 2007, there were approximately 496,000 children in foster care in the United States, 130,000 of whom were eligible for adoption.[32] On average, a child placed in foster care spends roughly 12.2 months in the public care system and may experience several home placements.[33] Because movement from one home to another can be emotionally traumatizing for a child, the Adoption and Safe Families Act of 1997 was passed to fast-track children who cannot be reunited with their birth parents to permanent homes as quickly as possible.[34] Fast tracking is used only for children whose parents have chronically abused them or abandoned them or have lost parental rights to the child's sibling. If a child has been removed for other reasons, his or her parents can regain custody by complying with a court-ordered treatment plan. If the parents do not comply with the plan, their parental rights may be terminated, at which point the child becomes eligible for adoption.

In efforts to find other ways to reduce the number of times a child is shifted, social workers are now asking hopeful adoptive families if they would be interested in a foster care child with the eventual goal of adopting if and when the child becomes available for adoption. Some may consider this a conflict of interest, however, when the primary goal of foster care is to eventually reunite children with their birth parents. For some families, the prospect of growing attached to a child only to have to return him or her to birth parents is very difficult to bear.

KINSHIP/RELATIVE ADOPTION

Kinship or relative adoption occurs when a child is adopted by a family member due to the birth parents' voluntary or involuntary termination of parental rights. Kinship care can be arranged formally, through a social service agency, or informally, through private family arrangements that do not involve a public service agency. Some 76 percent of all kinship care arrangements are private. Kinship care arrangements, whether formal or informal, can follow two possible scenarios. In one case, a mother facing an unplanned pregnancy may arrange for a relative to care for and possibly adopt her infant, though this is rare; less than 2 percent of all children in kinship care are under one year of age.[35] The other, more frequent scenario is one in which the birth parents are deemed unfit to care for their child, either by child welfare services or by other family members. Family members may attempt to intercede before social service agencies become involved, or social services may remove the child from the home and place him or her with relatives.

In many parts of the world, kinship care is the most common form of informal adoption. In Namibia, Zimbabwe, and South Africa, 60 percent of all parentless children live with grandparents. In Cambodia, 90 percent of orphaned children reside with relatives. The reasons for kinship placements vary from nomadic tribal lifestyles that may result in a child being placed with relatives to attend school, to poverty, illness, war, and inadequate social services. In matrilineal cultures, orphaned children are more often placed with the mother's relatives, while in patrilineal cultures, children are more commonly placed with the father's relatives.[36]

In the United States, kinship care is most prevalent in the southern states, and two-thirds of all children in kinship care belong to ethnic minorities. Kinship adoption is most common among African-American families and families with low incomes and lower levels of education. Because the percentage of African-American women who voluntarily relinquish their children for adoption dropped from 1.5 percent in 1973 to nearly 0 percent in 1995, some speculate that many African-American families privately handle their own kinship care arrangements.

According to the Urban Institute, half of all children in kinship care arrangements in the United States live below the poverty line, often with a caregiver who is over 50 years of age and/or does not have a high school education.[37] Because these children often face greater hardship than others, they are in need of services, particularly if they have been abused or neglected. If the kinship care arrangement was made through social services or the child has been adopted, he or she is likely to receive needed services. However, as fully three-quarters of all kinship care arrangements are private, the vast majority of these children do not receive the help and counseling they need.

This is true for other countries, as well. In Cambodia, though 90 percent of orphaned children live with relatives, only 25 percent receive financial assistance. As in the United States, children in formal kinship care placements worldwide are significantly more likely to receive government support, while children in informal kinship care arrangements are unlikely to receive financial assistance.[38]

STEPPARENT ADOPTION

Stepparent adoption accounts for the highest rate of adoptions in the United States. A study by the National Center for State Courts estimates that 42 percent of all adoptions in 1992 involved a stepparent adopting his or her spouse's child.[39] This could account for the reason why men are more than twice as likely as women to have adopted.[40]

In a stepparent adoption, the biological parent must consent to the adoption and voluntarily terminate his or her parental rights and responsibilities to the child, including child support. State laws vary, and while most do not require a homestudy for stepparent adoption as they do in a typical adoption case, some require a criminal background check and others require that the adopting stepparent be married to the child's parent for at least one year.[41] Most states also require the child's consent if he or she is over a certain age.

INDEPENDENT ADOPTION

Independent adoption (also called private adoption) consists of the birth parents and adoptive parents arranging the adoption of a child without the use of an agency. The parties may locate each other in a newspaper or on a Web site and usually employ the help of a facilitator, which may be an attorney who makes sure that all individuals meet the associated legal requirements. The primary difference between independent adoption and agency adoption lies in the birth parents' relinquishment of parental rights. In agency adoption, the birth parents relinquish their child to an agency, which then consents to an adoption by a prospective couple, whereas in an independent adoption, the birth parents relinquish their child directly to the adoptive parents of their choice.

Independent adoption is illegal in some states, and experts note several problems with the practice. One is the lack of counseling (both legal and personal) for birth parents, who may not be aware of their rights or the full implications of their decision. Another is the matter of legal representation: While an attorney may act as a facilitator, he or she exclusively represents the interests of the adoptive parents. According to one adoption attorney, independent adoptions have an unusually high rate of failure. Approximately half of all birth parents change their minds before the baby is adopted and another 20 percent revoke consent shortly after the baby is born.[42] This number speaks to a high risk of failure in independent adoption.

Nevertheless, birth parents and adoptive parents are drawn to independent adoption for a number of reasons, one of which is the freedom and openness with which all parties are able to participate in the decision-making process. In choosing independent adoption, birth parents cite reasons such as a desire to play a more active role in deciding a future for their child, as well as a generally negative perception of adoption agencies, while adoptive parents are drawn to the reduced waiting periods and the ability to choose their prospective child's birth parents.

NO GUARANTEE OF SUCCESS

While most adoptions follow the possible arrangements discussed here, each adoption experience is different, and the process varies from case to case. No method of adoption is guaranteed to be successful, and sometimes birth parents and adoptive parents are traumatized by the loss of a child. For birth parents, the trauma of regret can last a lifetime, particularly in cases of closed adoption or where they were pressured or coerced into relinquishing their parental rights. For adoptive parents, the loss of a child through revocation of consent or the birth parents' inability to carry out the adoption plan can be equally devastating. Some adoptive parents care for an infant or child for two months or longer before consent is revoked.

Many experts agree that increased support is necessary for both birth parents and adoptive parents in the adoption process. As studies reveal that thorough counseling and better access to services increases the chances of success when adopting, it is easier now for birth parents and adoptive parents to plan an adoption that will benefit all parties.

SURROGATE PREGNANCY

Surrogate pregnancy shares many similarities with adoption, and, like adoption, it has a long and varied past that stretches back to antiquity. One of the earliest and most recognizable accounts of a surrogate pregnancy is the Old Testament story of Abraham and Sarah. When Sarah cannot conceive a child, she arranges for her handmaid Hagar to conceive a child with her husband, Abraham, and thereby produce a child for them. This story also accounts for one of the earliest known controversies surrounding surrogate pregnancy: The boundaries of propriety between the three individuals are blurred, the contracting wife becomes jealous, the surrogate is exploited, and eventually the arrangement ends in the surrogate keeping the child and being ejected from the household.

In more recent years, surrogate pregnancy has ignited a maelstrom of controversy in which scholars, politicians, judges, scientists, and religious authorities debate the definition of family and kinship. Like adoption, surrogate pregnancy is not an isolated phenomenon but rather overlaps with myriad other social issues, such as wealth distribution, race and color-blindness, gender equality, and children's rights, all of which come into play when defining family bonds and relationships.

Unlike adoption, surrogate pregnancy is not federally regulated in the United States, and thus there are few if any statistics from which to achieve a better understanding of surrogate pregnancy and its occurrence in the United States. In 2002, India became one of the first countries to legalize commercial surrogacy, and while official statistics are not yet available, trends are beginning to emerge that provide a clearer picture of the circumstances of such pregnancies, surrogate mothers, and the individuals and couples who contract the pregnancies.

New developments in assisted reproductive technology have led to a relative boom in surrogate pregnancy arrangements, and surrogacy centers have been cropping up all over the world since the 1970s. The birth of the first test-tube baby in 1978 opened numerous doors for parents facing infertility, one of which was the possibility that they could, indeed, have their own genetic child through the use of a surrogate mother. While this type of surrogacy remains the exception and not the rule, it has sparked the interest of the media and a plethora of individuals who might not have previously considered surrogacy.

Types of Surrogacy

Like adoption, each surrogacy arrangement is unique, and there are several types of surrogacy from which to choose. Due to the delicate nature of surrogacy, it is vitally important that all parties are comfortable and confident with one another and the process in order to achieve success.

TRADITIONAL SURROGACY

Traditional surrogacy is the most widely used method of surrogate pregnancy, as well as the most historically prevalent. Before the era of assisted reproductive technology and IVF, traditional surrogacy was the only form of surrogacy available.

Traditional surrogacy consists of the artificial insemination of the surrogate mother with the sperm of the contracting father or donor sperm. Because it is her own egg that is being fertilized, the surrogate mother is genetically related to the fetus that she conceives. The fetus may or may not be related to the contracting father, depending on whether or not he supplied his own sperm. Typically, insemination is performed by a doctor within a clinical setting, although some centers allow surrogates to perform their own insemination in the privacy of their homes based on the belief that the surrogate's comfort level should be respected. During this time, the surrogate mother agrees to refrain from sexual intercourse with any man, including her husband if she is married, from the point of signing the contract until a pregnancy is confirmed, which can take up to a year.

Because the surrogate mother will be the genetic mother of the child conceived, traditional surrogacy presents a unique opportunity for contracting couples to choose the genetic heritage of their child—an opportunity that is not afforded to adoptive parents. Often this means contracting couples can specify phenotypic characteristics that they desire in a surrogate mother and can screen for undesirable traits, such as a genetic history of mental illness or disease. Many couples look for a surrogate that resembles either of them.

When a surrogate is selected, she will be medically evaluated and tested for venereal diseases, such as HIV. In some cases, the surrogate's husband is also tested for such diseases. When the surrogate has met contractual requirements for physical and mental fitness, she will be inseminated when fertile.

Traditional surrogacy, though complicated by ethical uncertainty over the relationship between biological relatedness and kinship bonds, remains the most popular form of surrogacy in the United States due to its high success rates and its low fees. Traditional surrogacy has a success rate of

95 percent,[43] and because couples are not paying for in vitro cycles, which can take several cycles and cost thousands of dollars, the cost of a traditional surrogate pregnancy is relatively inexpensive.

There is division in the surrogacy community regarding the ethics of traditional surrogacy. Some surrogates are willing to be either traditional or gestational surrogates, while others will not consider traditional surrogacy at all. In some countries, such as India, traditional surrogacy is considered highly taboo, while in others, such as China, traditional surrogacy is the only legal surrogacy arrangement.

GESTATIONAL SURROGACY

Gestational surrogacy is preferred by couples who desire a biological connection to their child, assuming the husband and/or wife have viable gametes. The process of gestational surrogacy consists of a surrogate being impregnated via IVF with one or more embryos with which she is not genetically linked. In most cases, the contracting couple supplies the ova and sperm, which means the child conceived will be biologically related to them. However, in the event that one or both members of the contracting couple do not have viable gametes, the process may require donor eggs or sperm. Thus, in a gestational surrogacy, as many as five adults—not including physicians or attorneys—may be involved in the conception of a child.

Due to the lower success rates and the number of individuals involved, gestational surrogacy is often more expensive than traditional surrogacy. In an interview with Helena Ragoné, an anthropologist and the author of *Surrogate Motherhood: Conception in the Heart,* one surrogacy center director referred to gestational surrogacy and IVF procedures as a "rip-off that simply prolongs the couple's infertility while charging them outrageous sums of money per attempt."[44] Success rates of surrogate pregnancy via IVF are difficult to gauge, as most statistics for IVF procedures typically refer to women who are infertile. According to the U.S. Department of Health and Human Services (HHS), in 2004 the success rate per cycle at the average fertility clinic was 33.7 percent, using nonfrozen, non-donor eggs and embryos.[45] Surrogacy centers, however, tend to claim higher success rates. The Reproductive Science Center of the Bay Area, in California, claims a success rate of more than 50 percent.[46] The discrepancy between the two rates can be explained by the fact that women who approach a fertility clinic have an average age of 36 years and are unable to conceive on their own,[47] while surrogates using IVF are almost always fertile, with an average age of 27 years and proven success in carrying a pregnancy to term.[48]

Nevertheless, several IVF cycles may be required to produce a pregnancy, which can be costly. A single IVF cycle consists of preliminary tests, fertility drugs to stimulate egg growth, ultrasounds and lab work, egg retrieval, fertilization in a lab, embryo transfer (the point at which one or more embryos are placed in the uterus via a catheter through the vagina), and progesterone injections to aid implantation.[49] The average cost of a single IVF cycle is $10,000 in the United States, which means that if a surrogate undergoes a minimum of two IVF cycles, the total cost of the IVF procedure can be $20,000.[50] If three or more cycles are needed, the total cost could be doubled.[51] If donor eggs or sperm are used, this cost can be even higher. Ragoné estimates the total cost of a gestational surrogacy to be $44,800 if only one IVF cycle is needed and the ova and sperm are supplied by the contracting couple, while the total cost of a traditional surrogacy is estimated at $43,544.[52]

Types of Surrogacy Programs
OPEN PROGRAM

Like adoption, surrogacy can take place in an open or a closed program or somewhere in between. In an open program, the contracting couple and the surrogate choose one another based on feelings of compatibility and mutual requirements. Some surrogates state the desire to work exclusively with married, religious, or heterosexual couples with no other children, while others seek to work with gay couples or single men and women. Similarly, contracting parents may seek a surrogate who is married with a completed family (she may then have no desire to have any more children of her own) and a stable income. Surrogates and couples may find one another through a surrogacy center or ads in newspapers and on Web sites. In his book *A Gay Couple's Journey through Surrogacy: Intended Fathers*, Michael Menichiello describes his frustration at receiving e-mails from surrogates who appeared to be driven by money, surrogates who were living in poverty and desperate for money, and surrogates who refused to work with a gay, non-Christian couple.[53] Similarly, surrogates may be driven by the desire to provide a child for an infertile couple and may experience disappointment in dealing with couples who are not infertile or who have had previous pregnancies that ended in abortion.

Contracting couples and surrogates are expected to develop a relationship in an open program, and it is considered necessary for both parties to exchange information such as telephone numbers, addresses, and e-mail addresses. Some programs mandate a minimum amount of contact that a contracting couple must make with their surrogate before a pregnancy can be attempted. Open program directors often stress the importance of developing a relationship between a couple and their surrogate, and, indeed, Ragoné's research has shown higher rates of success, satisfaction, and repeat business in open programs as opposed to closed ones. Furthermore, Ragoné

19

theorizes that the relationship that develops between a surrogate and a couple is crucial in transferring the feelings of bonding and closeness that a pregnant woman normally develops toward a child onto the couple, thereby reducing the likelihood that she will want to keep the child.[54]

The primary difference between open and closed programs is generally characterized by the way in which a center approaches and views its surrogates. In open programs, surrogates are not viewed as employees, but rather as partners who are providing a valuable and unique service. Surrogate Mothers, Inc., a surrogacy center that has been operating since 1984, claims to encourage open programs because their surrogates "are not doing this for the money; they want (and have every right) to know the types of people for whom they are doing this."[55] Open programs emphasize the surrogacy contract as an altruistic act of love, in which the surrogate and contracting couple are equal participants in the process and exchange gifts out of respect and affection for one another (the surrogate gives the gift of a child and the contracting parents give the gift of remuneration). The relationship that develops between the surrogate and couple can range from weekly phone calls to outings. If the surrogate lives far away, the couple may initiate a slightly more distant relationship based on phone calls, e-mails, and occasionally flights out to attend doctor's appointments. If she lives nearby, however, the couple and surrogate are encouraged to meet often and partake in family activities together, such as going to the movies or having dinner. Upon the birth of the child, the couple and surrogate are encouraged to limit their contact to yearly Christmas cards and photos.

CLOSED PROGRAM

A closed program, by contrast, approaches surrogacy as a transaction, an exchange of money for a service. In her anthropological study of surrogacy, Helena Ragoné interviewed 28 surrogates and 17 contracting individuals, and from those interviews she determined that closed programs are designed to give priority to the contracting couple (the client), while approaching the surrogate as an employee.[56] In a closed program, the contracting couple selects their surrogate from a sample of photos and biographical profiles, and while some contact is permitted, such as heavily screened phone calls and letters, there is minimal or no face-to-face contact. One reason a contracting couple may opt for a closed program is a desire or need for anonymity. This can lead to a host of problems, including denial that a surrogate was ever used and the refusal to accept one's own inability to produce children.

In addition to the potential for psychological harm, a greater likelihood of abuse has been found among closed programs. Because such programs view surrogacy as a business transaction, surrogate and couple screening is often less rigorous and psychological counseling and support for the surrogate is often not a high priority, which may increase the chances that a surrogate will refuse to part with the child. It thus comes as no surprise that surrogates have reported feelings of negativity and regret more often with closed programs than with open ones.[57] Ragoné also found that surrogates who participated in closed programs often did so because they did not know that open programs existed.[58]

Many of the stories picked up by the U.S. media in the past in which a surrogate mother refused to relinquish the child were based on closed contracts. Seven out of 10 legal disputes in the 1980s and early 1990s—including the infamous Baby M case—were closed contracts that had been arranged by the attorney Noel Keane.[59] Keane is renowned for having arranged the first legal contract between a surrogate mother and a contracting couple in the United States.[60] One of Keane's many surrogacy programs, Frick, was also renowned among other surrogacy centers for its lax screening process and profit-driven motives. While the directors of some programs have claimed to screen surrogates so thoroughly that they accept fewer than 5 percent of applicants, the Frick program openly acknowledged that it accepted 95 percent of applicants.[61] Such lax policies sometimes ended in disaster, which prompted lawmakers in some states to enact anti-surrogacy legislation.

ETHICAL CONCERNS

Unconventional family formation naturally invites controversy, and many social and ethical debates have arisen in response to potentially exploitative adoption and surrogate pregnancy arrangements. The desirability of some children over others fuels many arguments and indeed is a chief concern of many child welfare organizations. The overwhelming demand among adoptive parents for white infants has turned adoption into what many see as a commercial enterprise, with higher fees for some children and lower fees for others. These fees tend to be in direct proportion to a child's race, as the sociology professor Pamela Anne Quiroz found in her study of racialized adoption trends and practices. While it is illegal to exchange money for a child, many adoption agencies charge operation costs, which can range from $4,000 to more than $40,000. Quiroz found that many private adoption agencies categorize their programs into separate divisions that include Caucasian, minority, and special needs, however, racialized language is only used in reference to minority and special needs children; white infants are generally not referred to as white or Caucasian but as "healthy infants."[62] Adoption fees and requirements vary by division. The Love Basket adoption agency lists fees of $20,000 for a white infant, $16,000 for a biracial infant, and $9,000 for an African-American infant.[63] Similarly, the American Adoptions agency offers three programs: Traditional I, Traditional II, and Minority. Both Traditional programs refer to the adoption of all non–African-American children, including white, Hispanic, Asian, and Native American, while the Minority program refers exclusively to the adoption of African-American or any mixed-race African-American infants. In addition to disparate fees, requirements for adoptive parents vary by program. The Evangelical Child and Family Agency explicitly states that single adoptive parents may apply for adoption of African-American infants (full or biracial) but will not be considered for adoption of white, Latino, or Asian infants. Similarly, Quiroz found that the American Adoptions agency allows adoptive parents in its Minority program to be 10 years older than the age limit for parents in the Traditional programs, and while it does not allow single parents to adopt from the Traditional programs, it does allow singles to adopt from the Minority program.[64]

Though many private adoption agencies justify their relaxed requirements and lower fees on the established fact that African-American children are more difficult to place than non–African-American children, such policies expose an unpalatable racial hierarchy in which a child's value is determined by the lightness of his or her skin. Miriam Reitz and Kenneth W. Watson, the authors of *Adoption and the Family System,* theorize that the demand for lighter skinned babies could account for the meteoric rise in international adoptions: As white babies became increasingly scarce in the United States, many parents turned to overseas adoptions, and private agencies began arranging intercountry adoptions to meet demand.[65] The beginning of the rapid rise in international adoptions coincides with the collapse of the Soviet Union in 1991, at which point the adoption market was suddenly flooded with adoptable white infants and children from eastern European countries. That same year saw the primary sending country shift suddenly from Korea, which had dominated the international adoption market from 1980 to 1990, to Romania.[66] Since the rising popularity of international adoption began, the top sending countries have consistently come from eastern Europe, Asia, and Latin America. The demand for infants and young children from these sending countries has resulted in a number of social and ethical problems, including baby-buying and child trafficking.

Child desirability and commerce also play a significant and often overlooked role in the phenomenon of surrogate pregnancy. Advertisements for surrogate mothers invite women to help an infertile couple have a child by becoming a surrogate. Little mention is made of the fact that more than 100,000 children in the United States are awaiting adoption, as many are hesitant to judge couples who turn to surrogate pregnancy to have a child. For many people, the need to have a child of one's own is a powerful biological drive, but how is family formation affected when commerce becomes a means of obtaining a child? Even more provocative is the question of how this path to parenthood changes when biology is not a factor. In most cases, a surrogate pregnancy involves only one parent's genetic contribution, and in some cases neither parent is genetically related to the child. What, then, is the driving force behind a couple's decision to pursue surrogacy other than to commission the creation of a white baby to adopt when none can be found within the adoption market? As Ragoné found in her study, one-third of the parents she interviewed had considered adoption but were discouraged by what they considered flaws in the system. According to Ragoné: "A major obstacle posed by an adoption solution is the length of the waiting period, which can be as long as five to six years."[67] The unstated reality of this fact is that a waiting period can be as long as five to six years for couples who seek to adopt only a healthy white infant. Couples who are open to minority infants generally wait less than a year. Another deterrent is cost: Michael Menichiello laments in his book *A Gay Couple's Journey through Surrogacy: Intended Fathers* that the cost of adopting is too high—between $50,000 and $100,000—and that surrogacy by comparison is simply more economically sensible.[68] Again, the unstated reality of the problem of high cost is that it is reserved for those who wish to adopt a healthy white infant.

CONCLUSION

The desire to have children and create a family is not one that many are comfortable questioning, and indeed it seems inappropriate to suggest that social inequity should be addressed through family formation. Rather, family formation trends can serve as a means of highlighting societal trends and perspectives. It is also worth noting that adoption and surrogate pregnancy often challenge normative family structure, not only in terms of race, but in terms of age, pregnancy and motherhood, gender roles, and sexuality. Adoption and surrogate pregnancy allow for the creation of families that may include same-sex parents and older parents, while disconnecting motherhood from pregnancy and childbearing. Surrogate pregnancy allows women to exercise greater control over their bodies either by choosing to get pregnant as a means of employment and self-fulfillment or, conversely, by choosing to become a mother without experiencing pregnancy (contracting mothers). As alternative paths to family formation continue to develop, these discussions will intensify on both a national and global level.

---

[1] U.S. Department of Health and Human Services, Centers for Disease Control and Prevention. "Key Statistics from the NSFG." Available online. URL: http://www.cdc.gov/nchs/about/major/nsfg/abclist_i.htm#infertility. Accessed December 13, 2008.

[2] Susan Markens. *Surrogate Motherhood and the Politics of Reproduction.* Berkeley: University of California Press, 2007, p. 14.

[3] *Washington Post.* "Research Refutes Perceived 'Infertility Epidemic'; Study Suggests Social, Not Physical Causes Are Affecting Women's Ability to Have Children." (12/7/90).

[4] United States Department of Labor: Bureau of Labor Statistics. "Changes in Women's Labor Force Participation in the 20th Century" (2/16/00). Available online. URL: http://www.bls.gov/opub/ted/2000/feb/wk3/art03.htm. Accessed April 9, 2009.

[5] Katherine E. Heck, Kenneth C. Schoendorf, Stephanie J. Ventura, and John L. Kiely. "Delayed Childbearing by Education Level in the United States, 1969–1994." *Maternal and Child Health Journal* 1 (June 1997): 81–88.

[6] National Center for Health Statistics. "Average Age of Mothers at First Birth, by State— United States, 2002" (5/20/05). Available online. URL: http://www.cdc.gov/mmwr/preview/mmwrhtml/mm5419a5.htm. Accessed April 10, 2009.

[7] Gerard Breart. "Delayed Childbearing." *European Journal of Obstetrics & Gynecology and Reproductive Biology* 75 (December 1997): 71–73.

[8] Gina Maranto. "Delayed Childbearing." *Atlantic Monthly* 275 (June 1995): 55–66.

[9] U.S. Department of Health and Human Services: The National Women's Health and Information Center. "Infertility: Frequently Asked Questions" (5/1/06). Available online. URL: http://womenshealth.gov/faq/infertility.cfm#c. Accessed April 9, 2009.

[10] "U.S. Census Bureau: Total Worldwide Fertility Rates in 1998." *Women's International Network News* 25 (1999): 26.

[11] Arthur Greil. *Not Yet Pregnant: Infertile Couples in Contemporary America.* New Brunswick, N.J.: Rutgers University Press, p. 197.

[12] Susan Markens. *Surrogate Motherhood and the Politics of Reproduction,* p. 53.

[13] Helena Ragoné. *Surrogate Motherhood: Conception in the Heart.* Boulder, Colo.: Westview Press, 1994, p. 94. The director of the Allen surrogacy program was speaking at an American Civil Liberties Union (ACLU) meeting.

[14] L. W. King. "Ancient History Sourcebook: Code of Hammurabi, c. 1780 B.C.E." (1998). Available online. URL: http://www.fordham.edu/halsall/ancient/hamcode.html. Accessed April 10, 2009. And Barbara A. Moe. *Contemporary World Issues: Adoption, Second Edition.* Santa Barbara, Calif.: ABC–CLIO, 2007, p. 1.

[15] Nigel Guy Wilson. *Encyclopedia of Ancient Greece.* New York: Routledge, 2005, p. 10.

[16] Adoption.com. "Adoption Language." Available online. URL: http://international.adoption.com/foreign/adoption-language-2.html. Accessed December 15, 2008.

[17] Diane Turski. "'Respectful' Adoption Language—Rebuttal." First Mothers Action Group (2004). Available online. URL: http://www.exiledmothers.com/speaking_out/respectful_adoption_language.html. Accessed December 15, 2008.

[18] Kathleen Silber. "Open Adoption History." Independent Adoption Center. Available online. URL: http://www.adoptionhelp.org/about/history.html. Accessed December 17, 2008.

[19] Barbara A. Moe. *Contemporary World Issues: Adoption, Second Edition,* p. 4.

[20] Child Welfare Information Gateway. "Persons Seeking to Adopt" (2005). Available online. URL: http://www.childwelfare.gov/pubs/s_seek.cfm. Accessed December 20, 2008. And, U.S. Department of Health and Human Services, Children's Bureau. "Trends in Foster Care and Adoption—FY 2002–FY 2007" (2008). Available online. URL: http://www.acf.hhs.gov/programs/cb/stats_research/afcars/trends.htm. Accessed April 30, 2009.

[21] Darlene Gerow. "Infant Adoption Is Big Business in America." Concerned United Birth Parents. Available online. URL: http://www.birthmothers.info/infant.pdf. Accessed December 20, 2008.

[22] Pamela Anne Quiroz. *Adoption in a Color-Blind Society.* Lanham, Md.: Rowman & Littlefield Publishers, 2007, p. 63.

[23] Kim Clarke and Nancy Shute. "The Adoption Maze." *U.S. News & World Report* (3/4/01), p. 1. Available online. URL: http://www.usnews.com/usnews/culture/articles/010312/archive_004508_1.htm. Accessed December 20, 2008.

[24] Kim Clarke and Nancy Shute. "The Adoption Maze," p. 2.

[25] Child Welfare Information Gateway. "Persons Seeking to Adopt" (2005). Available online. URL: http://www.childwelfare.gov/pubs/s_seek.cfm. Accessed December 20, 2008.

[26] Associated Press. "More Adoption Rights Urged for Birth Mothers" (11/20/06). Available online. URL: http://www.msnbc.msn.com/id/15801325/. Accessed December 21, 2008.

[27] Peter Selman. "Trends in Intercountry Adoption: Analysis of Data From 20 Receiving Countries, 1998–2004." *Journal of Population Research* 23 (2006): 183–204.

[28] Child Welfare League of America. "National Data Analysis System Issue Brief: International Adoption: Trends and Issues" (November 2007). Available online. URL: http://www.ccainstitute.org/pdf/international_adoption/International%20Adoption%20Trends%20and%20Issues.pdf. Accessed April 30, 2009. And, Child Welfare Information Gateway. "How Many Children Were Adopted in 2000 and 2001?" (2004). Available online. URL: http://www.childwelfare.gov/pubs/s_adoptedhighlights.cfm. Accessed December 21, 2008.

[29] Kim Clarke and Nancy Shute. "The Adoption Maze," p. 3.

[30] Office of Children's Issues, United States Department of State. "Intercountry Adoption" (April 2008). Available online. URL: http://adoption.state.gov/country/china.html#who1. Accessed December 22, 2008.

[31] National CASA Association. "Foster Care and Adoption Statistics" (1997). Available online. URL: http://www.casanet.org/library/foster-care/fost.htm. Accessed April 30, 2009. And, U.S. Department of Health and Human Services, Children's Bureau. "Trends in Foster Care and Adoption—FY 2002–FY 2007" (2008).

[32] U.S. Department of Health and Human Services, Children's Bureau. "Trends in Foster Care and Adoption—FY 2002–FY 2007."

[33] U.S. Department of Health and Human Services, Children's Bureau. "AFCARS Report: Preliminary FY 2006 Estimates as of January 2008" (2008). Available online. URL: http://www.acf.hhs.gov/programs/cb/stats_research/afcars/tar/report14.htm. Accessed April 30, 2009.

[34] Administration for Children and Families. "Report to Congress on Adoption and Other Permanency Outcomes for Children in Foster Care: Focus on Older Children." U.S. Department of Health and Human Services, Children's Bureau (9/18/06). Available online. URL:

http://www.acf.hhs.gov/programs/cb/pubs/congress_adopt/leadership.htm. Accessed December 22, 2008.

35 The Urban Institute. "Children in Kinship Care" (10/9/03). Available online. URL: http://www.urban.org/publications/900661.html. Accessed December 23, 2008.

36 Save the Children UK. "Kinship Care: Providing Positive and Safe Care for Children Living Away from Home" (2007). Available online. URL: http://www.crin.org/docs/kinship_care.pdf. Accessed April 30, 2009.

37 The Urban Institute. "Children in Kinship Care."

38 Save the Children UK. "Kinship Care: Providing Positive and Safe Care for Children Living Away from Home."

39 Cynthia R. Mabry. *Adoption Law.* Buffalo, N.Y.: William S. Hein & Co., 2006, p. 231.

40 U.S. Department of Health and Human Services, Centers for Disease Control and Prevention, National Center for Health Statistics. "Adoption Experiences of Women and Men and Demand for Children to Adopt by Women 18–44 Years of Age in the United States, 2002" (August 2008). Available online. URL: http://www.cdc.gov/nchs/data/series/sr_23/sr23_027.pdf. Accessed December 23, 2008.

41 Child Welfare Information Gateway. "Stepparent Adoption" (2008). Available online. URL: http://www.childwelfare.gov/pubs/f_step.cfm. Accessed December 23, 2008.

42 *Adoptive Families.* "Risks and Benefits of Independent Adoption" (2008). Available online. URL: http://www.adoptivefamilies.com/articles.php?aid=1017. Accessed December 26, 2008.

43 Helena Ragoné. *Surrogate Motherhood: Conception in the Heart,* p. 35.

44 Helena Ragoné. *Surrogate Motherhood: Conception in the Heart,* p. 33.

45 U.S. Department of Health and Human Services, Centers for Disease Control and Prevention. "2004 Assisted Reproduction Technology Success Rates: National Summary and Fertility Clinic Reports" (2004). Available online. URL: http://ftp.cdc.gov/pub/Publications/art/2004ART508.pdf. Accessed December 31, 2008.

46 Reproductive Science Center of the Bay Area. "In Vitro Fertilization/Surrogacy Services" (2008), p. 17. Available online. URL: http://www.rscbayarea.com/donors_invitro_fertilization_ivf/surrogacy_program.html. Accessed December 31, 2008.

47 Reproductive Science Center of the Bay Area. "In Vitro Fertilization/Surrogacy Services," p. 15.

48 Helena Ragoné. *Surrogate Motherhood: Conception in the Heart,* p. 54.

49 Meg Lundstrom. "What to Expect during IVF." WebMD, Infertility and Reproductive Health Center (2005–2007). Available online. URL: http://www.webmd.com/infertility-and-reproduction/features/what-to-expect-during-ivf. Accessed December 31, 2008.

50 Roxanne Nelson. "Financing Infertility." WebMD (1999). Available online. URL: http://www.cnn.com/HEALTH/women/9905/19/financing.infertility. Accessed December 31, 2008.

51 Helena Ragoné. *Surrogate Motherhood: Conception in the Heart,* p. 34.

52 Helena Ragoné. *Surrogate Motherhood: Conception in the Heart,* p. 34.

Introduction

[53] Michael Menichiello. *A Gay Couple's Journey through Surrogacy: Intended Fathers.* New York: The Haworth Press, 2006, p. 15.

[54] Helena Ragoné. *Surrogate Motherhood: Conception in the Heart,* p. 44.

[55] Surrogate Mothers, Inc. "General Information" (6/18/03). Available online. URL: http://www.surrogatemothers.com/info.html. Accessed January 1, 2009.

[56] Helena Ragoné. *Surrogate Motherhood: Conception in the Heart,* p. 46.

[57] Olga B. A. van den Akker. "Psychological Aspects of Surrogate Motherhood." *Human Reproduction Update* 1 (2007). Available online. URL: http://humupd.oxfordjournals.org/cgi/reprint/13/1/53. Accessed January 2, 2009.

[58] Helena Ragoné. *Surrogate Motherhood: Conception in the Heart,* p. 28.

[59] Helena Ragoné. *Surrogate Motherhood: Conception in the Heart,* p. 26.

[60] Lawrence van Gelder. "Noel Keane, 58, Lawyer in Surrogate Mother Cases, Is Dead." *New York Times* (1/28/97). Available online. URL: http://query.nytimes.com/gst/fullpage.html?res=9400E7D8113AF93BA15752C0A961958260. Accessed January 2, 2009.

[61] Helena Ragoné. *Surrogate Motherhood: Conception in the Heart,* p. 26.

[62] Pamela Anne Quiroz. *Adoption in a Color-Blind Society,* p. 68.

[63] Pamela Anne Quiroz. *Adoption in a Color-Blind Society,* p. 72.

[64] Pamela Anne Quiroz. *Adoption in a Color-Blind Society,* pp. 71–73.

[65] Miriam Reitz and Kenneth W. Watson. *Adoption and the Family System.* New York: Guilford Press, 1992, p. 311.

[66] Gretchen Miller Wrobel and Elsbeth Neil. *International Advances in Adoption Research for Practice.* Malden, Mass.: John Wiley & Sons, 2007, p. 46.

[67] Helena Ragoné. *Surrogate Motherhood: Conception in the Heart,* p. 93.

[68] Michael Menichiello. *A Gay Couple's Journey through Surrogacy: Intended Fathers,* p. 6.

2

~~~

Focus on the United States

Adoption and surrogate pregnancy have undergone a multifaceted evolution in the United States. Adoption has developed from a practice in which suitable children were found for childless couples to one in which suitable parents are found for parentless children. Surrogate pregnancy has grown from an exotic pursuit between infertile couples and voluntary, unpaid surrogates to a thriving market that matches paying clients with phenotypically similar surrogates. Both reproductive alternatives have met with varied responses from the media, medical community, and lawmakers to create policies and practices in the United States that differ dramatically from those of other developed nations.

HISTORY AND LAW
Adoption
Massachusetts passed the Adoption of Children Act in 1851, which stipulated that adoptive parents must be sufficiently capable of raising a child and providing a nurturing and educational environment for that child. This act was the first adoption law to be passed in the United States, and by 1925 all the other states had enacted such laws.[1] Though progressive in its emphasis on child welfare, the Massachusetts act did little to sway popular opinion on adoption.

Illegitimacy
Much of the historical controversy surrounding adoption has stemmed from the concept of illegitimacy and its moral and psychological implications. At best, illegitimacy was considered a social taint, and at worst it was believed to be a genetic defect that threatened to pollute the white American gene pool. In the 19th and early 20th centuries, out-of-wedlock pregnancy was considered by many to be a visual indicator of moral degradation. An unmar-

ried woman who became pregnant was quickly associated with promiscuity and lasciviousness—traits that she could theoretically pass on to her child. Thus, orphaned children in early America were traditionally seen as the by-products of moral failure and thus were themselves likely to be morally flawed. Many believed that the adoption of such children threatened the future of a stable, moral society. Such attitudes toward orphans can be traced back to earlier British perspectives on illegitimate children, portrayed in popular novels such as Henry Fielding's *The History of Tom Jones, a Foundling* (1749) and Daniel Defoe's *Moll Flanders* (1722). Both books portray the illegitimate main characters as destructive forces on well-mannered upper-class society, producing numerous illegitimate children themselves and even dabbling in incest.

Orphan Trains

One response to the suspicion of moral depravity among illegitimate children came from Reverend Charles Loring Brace, who established the New York Children's Aid Society in 1853. Brace differed from his contemporaries in his belief that immorality among illegitimate children was not the result of heredity, but rather environment. Brace came to the conclusion that urban slums were the breeding ground of future criminals and that if this "happy race of little heathens and barbarians" could simply be removed from such environments and placed in the homes of rural, Protestant families, they could be reformed.[2] He likened the effect to "withdrawing the virus from one diseased limb and diffusing it through an otherwise healthy body. It seems to lose its intensity."[3] In 1854, Brace established the orphan trains, which took children from crowded urban centers to the farms and open air of midwestern states. Ironically, most of these children were not in fact orphans, with many even maintaining contact with their birth families. By 1929, as many as 250,000 children had been relocated.[4] The trains would stop at rural towns, where children would be displayed on the platform for selection by local farmers. The term *put up* for adoption literally refers to the children who were put up on the station platform. Children who were not selected boarded the train once more to travel to the next stop.[5] Brace's objective, however, was not simply to remove children from urban centers, but to remove them from their birth parents, many of whom were immigrant Catholics or Jews. By placing the children of these immigrants in the homes of white Protestant farmers, Brace realized the potential for a mass Americanization of an entire population of children.

Despite his good intentions, Brace's placement methods were dangerously haphazard, and no investigation was made into those adopting. Nevertheless, while adoption reformers decried Brace's methods, the practice of placing out was soon established as an offshoot of the orphan trains. In 1868, the Massachusetts Board of State Charities began placing orphaned children in the homes of local families who could care for them, rather than in orphanages. It was not unusual for older children to be placed in foster homes as indentured servants, even into the 20th century. Foster care would not become the norm until the 1950s.

Eugenics

A very different response to adoption came from eugenicists. With the popularization of eugenics in the early 20th century, many people feared the repercussions of Brace's attempt at "diffusion," arguing that families should remain intact so as not to intermix genetically flawed individuals with the genetically fit. Out-of-wedlock pregnancy, they argued, was a symptom of mental retardation and the mother's genetic inferiority. Furthermore, it was argued that parents who could not take care of their children were genetically flawed, and thus their children were likely to be genetically inferior. The terms *feebleminded* and *moron* arose from this movement, as eugenicists sought to define the genetically unfit. Henry Herbert Goddard, an authority on eugenics, intelligence, and children in the first two decades of the 20th century, was outspoken in his opposition to the adoption of feebleminded children and his support of institutionalization for the mentally unfit. Believing feeblemindedness to be the result of a recessive gene, Goddard warned of the dire consequences of allowing such individuals to reproduce in his 1913 book, *The Kallikak Family: A Study in the Heredity of Feeble-Mindedness*, which argued that feeblemindedness as well as criminality and immorality were genetically inherited traits. In addition to proposing permanent sterilization for these individuals, Goddard founded the Vineland Training School for Backward and Feeble-minded Children in Vineland, New Jersey, in a personal effort to colonize and institutionalize the genetically weak.[6] Advocating for the administration of intelligence tests for all children (whether or not they were orphans), Goddard translated the Binet Scale in 1908, which was revised in 1916 to become an I.Q. test widely used in determining an orphan's suitability for adoption.[7] Though the I.Q. test was used to weed out feebleminded children from normal children (feeblemindedness could even serve as grounds to annul an adoption), Goddard, like many eugenicists of his time, believed that simply being an orphan was an admission of the parents' genetic weakness and thus the child's own.[8]

Sealed Records

Around this time, secrecy and sealed records became the norm in adoption procedures, and in 1917 Minnesota passed the first sealed records law, which prevented the disclosure of an adoptee's natal identity as well as that of the birth parents.[9] By sealing birth records, adoption professionals hoped to protect adopted children from the stigma of illegitimacy, birth mothers from the stigma of out-of-wedlock pregnancy, and adoptive parents from the stigma of infertility. Though not as openly condemned as unmarried pregnant women or illegitimate children, infertile couples—particularly women—felt the stigma of childlessness in a Judeo-Christian culture that equated fertility with femininity. Historical accounts of infertility often link childlessness with sinful behavior and divine retribution. One popular theory in medieval England proposed a connection between infertility and lascivious behavior, arguing that conception cannot take place in a "slippery" womb. Prostitutes were also associated with childlessness, contraception, abortion, and thus infertility.[10] Freudian theories of frigidity and psychological resistance to conception arose in the early 20th century and did little to ease the suffering of childless couples. Some, however, theorized that if psychological resistance to being a parent could prevent conception, then adoption could break down such resistance.

While adoption was believed to promote pregnancy in infertile women, sealed records were believed to facilitate assimilation and reconstitute as closely as possible a natural family. Matching children physically, intellectually, and religiously with adoptive parents consequently became a popular practice. By simply replacing the "old" family, the adoptive family was legitimized as being no different from the natal family. The child's sealed records allowed for the legal creation of a fantasy family, outside of which the child had never existed. Similar physical characteristics also allowed the adoptive parents to appear to outsiders to be the child's biological parents, thereby creating the illusion of normal fertility and thus normal masculine and feminine gender roles.[11]

Sealed records were of vital importance in protecting birth mothers from any association with adoption. Women who acted against the patriarchal family structure by becoming pregnant out of wedlock were given a chance to be assimilated back into the community once they had given up their child for adoption. Many feminists today liken this process to an act of patriarchal social control: As punishment for getting pregnant, unwed mothers were to give their children to middle-class married couples and forgo any future contact with those children.[12]

Psychoanalysis

Between 1938 and 1958, out-of-wedlock births leapt from 88,000 per year to 201,000 per year. As growing numbers of unmarried mothers were coming from the middle class—girls from good families and the daughters of prominent members of the community—theories of bad genes and feeblemindedness could no longer be applied. Further, eugenicist theories became suspect after the United States' confrontation with the atrocities of World War II, and adoption professionals ended the practice of assessing a child's genetic fitness. Orphaned and relinquished children were no longer believed to be of low-grade genetic stock, and sentimental hopes for a return to traditional family life following World War II led to increased demand for adoptable children. The development of infant formula in the 1920s made it possible for birth mothers to relinquish infants shortly after birth, which led to a rise in demand specifically for infants.[13]

The stigmatization of illegitimacy, however, continued to necessitate confidentiality and sealed records, particularly as other theories emerged to explain the causes of unwed motherhood. Psychoanalysis offered a new perspective on pregnant, unmarried women: Rather than attributing out-of-wedlock pregnancy to sexual deviance and loose morals, Freudian theorists diagnosed unmarried women who became pregnant as neurotic and suffering from a subconscious desire to become pregnant.[14] While such a theory shifted the central focus on out-of-wedlock pregnancy from uncontrolled female sexuality to mental illness, thereby easing social condemnation somewhat, it nevertheless provided adoption professionals with a firm justification for removing an infant from an unmarried mother. Neurotic women could not function properly as mothers; thus the fact that the pregnancy occurred at all served as a diagnosis and reason for removal.

Race

For African-American women, out-of-wedlock pregnancy was not diagnosed as a product of neurosis but rather was viewed as a result of natural racial inferiority and an overactive libido.[15] African-American families were denied adoption services, and many states refused to place African-American children, even as late as the 1940s.[16] When the field of adoption expanded during World War II, the Child Welfare League of America began to press for the placement of minority children, and in 1939 the New York State Charities Aid Association began placing African-American children, although slowly. While states such as Florida and Louisiana still refused to place any African-American children, New York began placing approximately 18 to 20 children a year.[17] African-American parents who could not care for their children may have arranged informal adoptions within their own families and communities, which may account for the high rate of informal adoptions among African-American families today.

Transracial Adoption

Transracial adoption became the subject of heated debate at this time, as families began adopting children from overseas. The Doss family became famous when they were featured in *Life* magazine in the late 1940s with their 12 transracially adopted children. Helen and Carl Doss had adopted Hawaiian, Chinese, Mexican, Indian, Native American, Balinese, Filipino, and Malayan children, as well as children with physical and mental handicaps—together they became known as the one-family U.N.[18] In 1954, Helen Doss wrote *The Family Nobody Wanted*, in which she detailed the unique challenges of raising a multiethnic family at a time when fears of global communism and racial tensions led many to decry transracial adoption. Throughout the book, Doss champions racial equality and cultural tolerance, often mocking cruel and insensitive remarks made by family and friends. Optimistic dreams of color-blindness reached a breaking point, however, when the Dosses considered adopting a mixed-race African-American child. Protests from family and friends effectively convinced Helen and Carl Doss to forgo the adoption, and they chose instead to locate an African-American family to adopt the girl.[19]

The Dosses were not the only family to adopt across racial lines. The first adoption of an African-American infant by a white couple took place in 1948 in Minnesota, despite advice to the contrary from social workers.[20] A lack of minority families seeking to adopt eventually pushed social workers to begin placing minority children with white families. An important feature to note in the development of transracial adoption is the fact that *transracial* has generally referred to the placement of children of minority groups in white homes.

Indian Adoption Project

The use of adoption as an Americanizing mechanism is not new. In the 1860s, droves of Native American children were taken from their families to be educated in boarding schools, where they were far removed from their tribal cultures and rituals and taught to assimilate into Anglo-American culture. In 1958, the Bureau of Indian Affairs and the Child Welfare League of America developed the Indian Adoption Project, which recruited white families to adopt Native American children. The project was short lived; nevertheless, by its end in 1971 one in four Native American infants in Minnesota had been placed with white families. Cultural confusion and misunderstanding led to the removal of children based on hazy charges of abuse, such as social deprivation.[21] As the U.S. government has long since agreed to recognize Native American tribes as sovereign nations, the act of systematically removing children from their tribes and placing them with white Judeo-Christian families amounted to what many Native Americans considered cultural genocide. The Indian Child Welfare Act was developed in 1978 to address the right of tribes to regulate the adoption of Native American children.[22] Shortly before the Indian Child Welfare Act was signed, the National Association of Black Social Workers also openly opposed the adoption of black children by white families, without success. An overrepresentation of African-American children in the foster care system combined with disproportionately higher numbers of white parents seeking to adopt made transracial adoption virtually inevitable. In 1994, the Multiethnic Placement Act (MEPA) explicitly barred the practice of race matching among non–Native American children and adoptive parents and denied federal funds to agencies that participated in race matching. Furthermore, MEPA stipulated a new requirement for agencies to recruit foster and adoptive families of diverse ethnic backgrounds.[23]

Reproductive Rights Movement

A number of social revolutions and upheavals took place throughout the 1960s and 1970s that permanently altered the face and politics of adoption in the United States. Possibly the most significant was the reproductive rights movement. The accessibility of the birth control pill in 1960 drastically reduced the number of out-of-wedlock pregnancies, and, with the legalization of abortion in 1973, women who did become pregnant unintentionally had the option of terminating the pregnancy. In addition to changing legislation, a new sense of social acceptance emerged for single mothers who chose to keep and raise their children on their own.[24] In 1960, 24 percent of African-American infants and 3.1 percent of white infants were born to unwed mothers, whereas by 1990, those numbers had ballooned to 64 percent for African-American infants and 18 percent for white infants.[25] While the number of infants born to single mothers skyrocketed, the number of infants relinquished for adoption by unmarried mothers plunged from nearly 20 percent prior to 1973 to 1.7 percent in 1995.[26] This sudden shortage of infants (namely, healthy white infants) proved to be a devastating blow to the adoption industry, which now had to deal with a dramatic imbalance between supply and demand. Parents seeking to adopt a healthy white infant now faced a waiting period of five years or more.[27] Competition among adoptive parents increased as well, particularly as agencies developed stricter requirements to distinguish the more deserving from the less deserving.

Assisted Reproductive Technology

The pressure that the reproductive rights movement placed on the adoption industry produced significant changes. Discouraged by lengthy waiting periods and inflated fees, many couples became open to transracial and special needs adoption, and, despite continuing racial disparities within the adoption industry, more transracial adoptions occur today than ever before. Equally significant is the pressure that the shortage of adoptable white infants placed on the field of assisted reproductive technology. In 1944, a Harvard medical professor named John Rock became the first person to fertilize ova outside the womb, and, while his research was groundbreaking, he discontinued his work despite pleas from parents desperate to conceive. Whether due to lack of market pressure or funding, research on in vitro fertilization (IVF) became dormant for nearly 20 years.[28] In the 1960s, the Cambridge researchers Robert Edwards and Patrick Steptoe took up IVF, and in 1978 the first test tube baby, Louise Brown, was born, igniting a maelstrom of controversy.[29]

During this period, a number of commercial fertility enterprises were established, including the first fertility drugs in the 1960s and the first commercial sperm bank in 1970.[30] Shortly after the birth of Louise Brown, Robert Edwards and Patrick Steptoe opened their own fertility clinic, which specialized in IVF and embryo transfer, and found themselves treating clients within days of opening their doors. Though many developments in reproductive technology began as nonprofit endeavors—typically using unpaid, altruistic donors—increasing demand soon necessitated monetary exchange to boost supply. Thus, commerce and fertility became deeply intertwined. The market for fertility became impossible to ignore, and Edwards and Steptoe's efforts to join commerce with fertility with the opening of their clinic paved the way for a global IVF market.[31]

Surrogate Pregnancy

The issue of monetary reimbursement proved to be a complicated obstruction to the development of a surrogate pregnancy market. In his book *The Surrogate Mother*, the Michigan lawyer Noel Keane discussed the first couples to ask for his help in finding a surrogate mother. Both couples had concluded that their only means of having a child was to find a woman who would agree to be artificially inseminated with the contracting husband's semen and then relinquish the infant at birth.[32] Under Michigan law, it is illegal to exchange money for a baby, which initially was an insurmountable obstacle in finding a surrogate mother. While Keane emphatically denies any monetary reimbursement to the first Michigan surrogate mothers, it would have been possible (and probable) for the couples to pay their surrogates under the table.

Noel Keane became known for drafting the first surrogacy contract in 1980. According to Keane: "There is a simple reason why people prefer finding a surrogate to adopting: the child will bear the genetic imprint of the man . . . People want this blood tie."[33]

Without the promise of payment, few women were willing to conceive and gestate a child for other people. While Keane managed to find unpaid surrogates for his Michigan couples, legal strictures on the process prompted him to move his practice to Florida, which had no laws on the exchange of money for infants.

The progression of surrogate pregnancy from an unusual and even taboo means of obtaining a child to a thriving market can be traced to several factors. First, the emergence of artificial insemination not only separated procreation from intimacy but allowed for anonymity. Rather than finding a mate, a woman could simply purchase genetic material to create a child. For infertile couples, this allowed for the possibility of using a surrogate to produce a child without involving sexual intercourse. Many of the first surrogate pregnancy contracts involving artificial insemination attempted to replicate the anonymity involved in sperm donation, which led to the creation of closed programs.

Noel Keane went on to establish the Frick surrogacy center, which specialized in closed programs and was involved in several lawsuits between surrogates and couples. The Frick program became renowned among competitors and the general public for its high failure rate due to its lax surrogate screening process and an unusually high acceptance rate of 98 percent among surrogate applicants. Another surrogacy program director remarked that Keane's top priority was "money, pure and simple. He makes no excuses about it."[34] Nevertheless, Keane was integral in establishing a surrogacy market, and by 1982, some 100 children had been born via surrogate pregnancy.[35]

Others followed Keane's lead and established surrogacy centers of their own in the 1980s. A Kentucky doctor Richard Levin began his surrogacy business in 1979, which still operates as a closed program, and by 2000 he had been directly involved in more than 1,200 surrogate pregnancies.[36] Unlike other program directors, Dr. Levin has made no attempt at disguising the commercial nature of his business as altruism. With a Web site URL of www.babies-by-levin.com and a license plate reading "Baby 4 U," Levin has made very clear that his center takes a business-oriented product and consumer perspective to surrogate pregnancy.[37]

Baby M

Little legislative action was taken on surrogate pregnancy until the late 1980s, when the explosive Baby M custody battle forced the issue into the public eye. Mary Beth Whitehead was employed as a surrogate mother by the Frick program despite the program psychologist's concern that she may have had an unresolved desire to have another child of her own, suggesting that "it would be important to explore with her in somewhat more depth whether she will be able to relinquish the child at the end."[38] Despite concerns about her emotional stability, Whitehead was hired as a surrogate for William and Elizabeth Stern. William Stern was a biochemist and Elizabeth Stern was a pediatrician with self-diagnosed multiple sclerosis. Fearing that pregnancy would aggravate Elizabeth's condition, the Sterns decided to hire a surrogate. Mary Beth Whitehead was a mother of two who had not completed high school and was married to an alcoholic sanitation worker. The Sterns and Mary Beth Whitehead agreed to artificially inseminate Mary Beth with William's sperm for a fee of $10,000 on relinquishment of the infant. Whitehead was inseminated and became pregnant but began to express anxiety in her third trimester over whether she could relinquish the baby. In March 1986, Whitehead gave birth to Melissa Stern, whom the Sterns took home. However, after a week of intense depression, Mary Beth Whitehead went to the Sterns' house, returned the money, and reclaimed the infant.

A heated custody battle ensued, in which the Sterns sought legal enforcement of the surrogacy contract, which would require Mary Beth Whitehead to terminate her parental rights and relinquish the child to the Sterns. After fleeing to Florida with Melissa and making phone calls to William Stern threatening to kill herself and the baby if he continued to pursue custody, the trial court upheld the surrogacy contract and terminated Whitehead's parental rights, allowing Elizabeth Stern to adopt the infant. The case later went to the New Jersey Supreme Court, which determined that the surrogacy contract was not legally enforceable as money cannot be exchanged for a baby and a pregnant mother cannot be contractually forced to terminate her parental rights on the birth of her baby. While the trial court decision was reversed, the Supreme Court agreed that the Sterns should maintain custody of Melissa under the condition that Mary Beth Whitehead be recognized as the infant's legal mother and have broad visitation rights. The case was a highly emotional one in which the Supreme Court acknowledged: "If we go beyond suffering to an evaluation of the human stakes involved in the struggle, how much weight should be given to [Mrs. Whitehead's] nine months of pregnancy, the labor of childbirth, the risk to her life, compared to the payment of money, the anticipation of a child and the donation of sperm?"[39] Melissa Stern evidently had a normal childhood, and at the age of 18 she initiated the adoption process that would make Elizabeth Stern her legal mother.[40]

Legislation

The Solomon-like dilemma of deciding which mother should get the child prompted many lawmakers to introduce legislation that would regulate the burgeoning surrogacy business. On a federal level, surrogacy is not explicitly banned as illegal; however, a legal distinction is made between altruistic surrogacy and commercial surrogacy. While surrogacy itself is not illegal, the payment of a fee for a baby is illegal. The surrogacy market has addressed this hindrance over the years by reframing the transaction to that of payment for a service. Many programs (typically open programs) pay a monthly fee instead of a lump sum upon the birth and relinquishment of the baby, as was the case in the Baby M situation. If the surrogate miscarries, the payments are discontinued, but she has nevertheless been compensated for her time.[41]

State laws generally frame surrogacy within an adoption context. Fees paid to the surrogate must be disclosed, along with their specific purposes. Monetary reimbursement may not exceed reasonable expenses, such as medical bills and emergency room fees.[42] In some cases, however, reasonable expenses may include rent payments, maternity clothes, daycare, and food. Surrogates can charge as much of $50,000, and more for multiple births and cesarean sections.[43]

Because procreation and family formation tend to fall under the constitutional right to privacy, much of the legislation that has been introduced to regulate surrogacy has been rejected.[44] Nevertheless, most states have enacted laws that prohibit the contractual selling or transfer of parental rights, thereby rendering surrogacy contracts legally unenforceable.[45]

Gestational Surrogacy

The advent of gestational surrogacy complicated surrogacy legislation. Following the birth of Louise Brown, the possibilities that IVF and embryo transfer presented for surrogacy prompted many contracting couples to seek "gestational carriers." The first successful gestational surrogacy was documented in 1985, in which one woman's ova were extracted and fertilized, with the resulting zygote transplanted into another woman's uterus during her own natural cycle.[46] The implications of IVF for surrogacy meant that couples no longer had to seek out a phenotypically similar surrogate or even a surrogate of the same ethnicity. As the surrogate did not donate genetic material, tensions over ethics and parental rights were somewhat eased. The relationship between the surrogate and the fetus was disconnected from traditional notions of biological mother and child unity.

In 1990, the *Calvert v. Johnson* case once again brought surrogacy to public attention and forced many to reconsider notions of kinship and family. In 1989, Mark and Crispina Calvert contracted for gestational surrogacy with Anna Johnson, in a process to retrieve Crispina's ova, fertilize them with Mark's sperm, and transfer the resulting embryos to Anna's uterus. Anna agreed to carry the child for Mark and Crispina and terminate her parental rights upon giving birth in exchange for $10,000, to be paid in monthly installments. Several months into her pregnancy, however, Anna Johnson demanded the balance of the money, threatening to refuse to relinquish the child. The Calverts sued for custody, and on the birth of the baby a blood test confirmed that the Calverts were the child's genetic parents. A 1990 trial determined that Anna Johnson had no parental claim to the child, concluding that "She who intended to procreate the child—that is, she who intended to bring about the birth of a child that she intended to raise as her own—is the natural mother under California law."[47] In this case, intention became the deciding factor. Finding the surrogacy contract legal and enforceable, the court granted full custody to the Calverts and terminated Anna's visitation rights.

Worth noting is the fact that Anna Johnson was African American, while Mark Calvert was white and Crispina Calvert was Filipino. Despite the fact that the baby boy was half Filipino, he was frequently referred to in the media as white, while Johnson was black. This ethnic disparity likely played a role in the public perception of the case, as it was a visual indicator of the nonbiological relationship between Johnson and the infant.

CHARACTERISTICS OF PARTICIPANTS

While there is no uniform type of birth or adoptive parent, studies have found statistical averages that reveal what type of women are more likely to relinquish their parental rights, as well as what type of individuals are more likely to choose adoption in the formation of their family.

Birth Parents

Voluntary relinquishment of an infant is rare. According to the 1995 National Survey of Family Growth, less than 1 percent of infants born to unmarried women were relinquished for adoption. The majority of unmarried teenage women who voluntarily relinquish are white, with more years of education and have parents who are married and have higher levels of education.[48]

A 1986 study by Dr. Christine Bachrach for the National Survey of Family Growth suggests that young women who choose to keep their children instead of relinquishing them tend to complete fewer years of education and earn lower incomes than women who do not give birth before marriage. Of all unmarried women aged 15 to 44 who experienced an unintended pregnancy, those who relinquished their children for adoption were more likely to complete high school, earn higher incomes, and get married; whereas women who chose to keep their children were more likely to live below the poverty line, receive public assistance, and drop out of high school.[49]

It is important to note that the relationship between premarital childbearing and poverty is not necessarily a causal one. While it remains true that a single-parent household is more likely to live below the poverty line and receive public assistance, young women who choose to relinquish typically come from upper-middle-class backgrounds and have future plans and goals.[50] Women who do not relinquish, as Bachrach points out, generally do not come from educated, high-income backgrounds and thus may not have goals that would be hindered by the presence of a child.[51]

Adoptive Parents

According to a 2002 study conducted by the U.S. Department of Health and Human Services (HHS), one-third of all polled U.S. women 18 to 44 years of age had considered adoption. Only 1.6 percent of all women had actually sought to adopt. Women who had taken steps toward adopting were likely to be between the ages of 30 and 44, to be currently married, and to have used infertility services.[52] Non-related adoption is more common among white women and women with higher levels of income and education, while related adoption is more common among African-American families and families with lower levels of income and education.[53] As the Adoption Assistance and Child Welfare Act of 1980 has mandated that all efforts be undertaken to keep families intact and reunite children with their birth parents when possible, related adoption has become more prevalent.[54] Despite lower levels of income and financial stability, studies have found high success rates among related adoptions, while some studies have found higher rates of disruption among adoptive parents with higher levels of education and income.[55]

Also worth noting are the types of children that adoptive parents seek. The majority of parents seeking to adopt would prefer a female child under the age of two, with no disability or siblings. While most would accept a child that does not match the preferred characteristics, two-thirds of seeking parents would not accept a child over the age of 13 or with a disability.[56]

Surrogate Mothers

No government statistics or studies exist that reveal shared characteristics among surrogate mothers, although several researchers have conducted studies from which patterns among surrogate mothers emerge. One study found that surrogate mothers are, on average, working-class women with high school educations, families, and a mean age of 27. The average income of married surrogates at the time of the study (1994) was $38,700, and while many were full-time homemakers, those that worked outside the home were often employed in the service sector.[57] As one surrogacy director remarked, the average surrogate "won't be a high-powered executive making two hundred and fifty thousand dollars a year."[58]

The motivation of surrogates has been a hotly contested issue among researchers. As many have found, money alone is usually not the primary motivational factor in a woman's choice to become a surrogate. Nor do most surrogates exhibit characteristics of psychopathology. Some have suggested that surrogates are attempting to atone for past mistakes, such as a previous adoption or abortion, or to mend childhood trauma such as abuse, but such theories have been largely disqualified. The vast majority of surrogates (more than 99 percent) do not bond with the infants they relinquish, report high levels of satisfaction upon relinquishment, and claim to experience no psychological damage as a result of relinquishment.[59]

Most surrogates cite two main reasons for choosing to become pregnant for another couple: one is the desire to give a child to an infertile couple, and the other is the pleasure they experience in being pregnant.[60] Such explanations seem obvious enough, but they do not satisfactorily explain the director's remark that a surrogate will not be a high-powered executive. Nor do they explain why most surrogates have no more than a high-school education and work in the service sector.

Helena Ragoné theorizes that women who become surrogates do so because they view surrogacy as a vocation to which they can provide a unique skill. This type of paid employment allows women to "transcend the limitations of their roles as wives/mothers and homemakers while concomitantly attesting to the satisfaction they derive from these roles."[61] In other words, surrogacy as a type of employment provides working-class women with a sense of independence and autonomy from their families that, simultaneously, reinforces traditional notions of femininity, maternity, and what it means to be a "good wife and mother."

Contracting Parents

The majority of U.S. couples who commission a surrogate pregnancy are white, with an average family income of $100,000 or more. Similar to mothers seeking to adopt, contracting mothers tend to be older, with higher levels of education.[62]

Contracting couples' motivations to commission a surrogate pregnancy tend to stem from a desire not only to produce a child, but to produce a child that is genetically related to one or both parents.[63] During the Baby M custody battle, William Stern stated a desire to continue his family line due to the fact that most of his family had been killed in the Holocaust.[64]

While many couples who enter into surrogacy contracts do so out of a desire for their own biological child, many others do consider adoption but are discouraged by lengthy waiting periods, high costs, and the fact that the birth mother may change her mind once the baby is born. Furthermore, many contracting couples are older, having discovered their infertility later in life or having spent several years undergoing fertility treatments before giving up.[65]

The relationship that develops between the contracting couple and the surrogate has also been studied extensively, notably for the fact that surrogates tend to become intimately attached to their contracting couples, which can become problematic after the surrogate gives birth and the couple begins to distance themselves from her. One study found that surrogates who reported a negative experience typically did so due to dissatisfaction with their relationship with the contracting couple, often citing the fact that their couples were distant or detached.[66] Ragoné's study found that couples took either a pragmatic or an egalitarian approach toward their surrogates. Pragmatists typically adhered strictly to the program's guidelines, eventually terminating their relationship after the birth of the child, while egalitarians favored a more intimate relationship that would continue after the surrogate gave birth. Pragmatists claimed to fear of the effects of a continuing relationship with their surrogate, particularly on their child, and preferred some amount of confidentiality, while egalitarians preferred openness and honesty, though not always without some reservations.[67]

CONCLUSION

Efforts to standardize both adoption and surrogate pregnancy are continually developing, but there are many challenges due to the highly sensitive nature of family formation and its regulation.

The primary concerns within adoption center around hard-to-place children, and legislation has been enacted to provide incentives for parents who may be open to adopting a special needs child. Older children, African-American children, and children with disabilities are the hardest to place. To facilitate the adoption of special needs children, Congress passed legislation through the Adoption Assistance and Child Welfare Act of 1980 to provide subsidies to families that adopt hard-to-place children. The amount of financial assistance that a family may receive depends on the needs of the child, thereby supporting families that may need to acquire new skills to raise a physically or developmentally disabled child.[68]

The concept of financial incentive has also been used by agencies specializing in infant adoptions, to the dismay of many who view it as a form of baby pricing. While hopeful parents may pay upward of $30,000 for a white infant, the cost of adopting a black infant is only a fraction of that fee. Many agencies explain that the high fees for white infants pay for overhead costs, while the low fees for African-American infants are a financial incentive for prospective parents. Such discrepancies in cost have prompted many to campaign against discriminatory practices within adoption, likening adoption fees to baby-selling.[69]

Commercial surrogacy has also been a highly problematic practice to regulate, and many states take vastly different approaches to it. New York banned commercial surrogacy and rendered surrogacy contracts illegal and unenforceable, while California passed a bill that would have allowed for state regulation of surrogacy, but this was vetoed by Governor Pete Wilson.[70] The vast majority of states have no laws addressing surrogacy.[71] The researchers Jennifer Damelio and Kelly Sorensen argue that states should neither flatly approve nor ban commercial surrogacy but should create legislation that regulates surrogacy and protects surrogate mothers from exploitation. Damelio and Sorensen advocate a "soft law" that would mandate several hours of education for surrogates before they can be approved, thereby ensuring that a surrogate is fully informed of her legal rights.[72]

Education as a means of standardizing adoption and surrogacy will enable all parties to make informed decisions that take into account child welfare, as well as ethical practices.

[1] Katarina Wegar. *Adoption, Identity, and Kinship: The Debate Over Sealed Records.* New Haven, Conn.: Yale University Press, 1997, p. 3.

[2] Charles Loring Brace. *The Dangerous Classes of New York, and Twenty Years Among Them.* (1880). Reprinted: Chestnut Hill, Mass.: Adamant Media Corporation, 2005, p. 97.

[3] Charles Loring Brace. *The Dangerous Classes of New York, and Twenty Years Among Them,* p. 26.

[4] Ellen Herman. "Adoption History: Orphan Trains." The Adoption History Project, University of Oregon (7/11/07). Available online. URL: http://darkwing.uoregon.edu/~adoption/topics/orphan.html. Accessed January 10, 2009.

[5] Michelle Kahan. "'Put Up' on Platforms: A History of Twentieth Century Adoption Policy in the United States." *Journal of Sociology & Social Welfare* 33 (Sept. 2006). Boston: McCormack School of Policy Studies, University of Massachusetts, Boston, p. 55.

[6] Henry Herbert Goddard. *The Kallikak Family: A Study in the Heredity of Feeble-Mindedness.* In *Classics in the History of Psychology,* edited by Christopher D. Green. York University, Toronto, Ontario, p. 107. Available online. URL: http://psychclassics.

yorku.ca/Goddard/chap5.htm. Accessed January 11, 2009. [This reference is unclear. Is Classics in the History of Psychology a series? If so, it can be deleted. We also need the publisher and place and date of publication.]

[7] Ellen Herman. "Adoption History: 'Feeble-Minded' Children." The Adoption History Project, University of Oregon (7/11/07). Available online. URL: http://darkwing.uoregon. edu/~adoption/topics/orphan.html. Accessed January 11, 2009.

[8] Henry Herbert Goddard. "Wanted: A Child to Adopt" (1911). The Adoption History Project, University of Oregon (7/11/07). Available online. URL: http://darkwing.uoregon. edu/~adoption/topics/orphan.html. Accessed January 11, 2009.

[9] Katarina Wegar. Adoption, Identity, and Kinship: The Debate over Sealed Birth Records, p. 25.

[10] Debora L. Spar. The Baby Business: How Money, Science, and Politics Drive the Commerce of Conception. Boston: Harvard Business School Press, 2006, p. 8.

[11] Ellen Herman. "Adoption History: 'Feeble-Minded' Children."

[12] Katarina Wegar. Adoption, Identity, and Kinship: The Debate Over Sealed Birth Records, p. 38.

[13] Debora L. Spar. The Baby Business: How Money, Science, and Politics Drive the Commerce of Conception, pp. 170–171.

[14] Ann Fessler. The Girls Who Went Away: The Hidden History of Women Who Surrendered Children for Adoption in the Decades Before Roe v. Wade. New York: Penguin, 2006, pp. 147–148.

[15] Katarina Wegar. Adoption, Identity, and Kinship: The Debate Over Sealed Birth Records, p. 38.

[16] Ellen Herman. "Adoption History: African-American Adoptions." The Adoption History Project, University of Oregon (7/11/07). Available online. URL: http://darkwing.uoregon. edu/~adoption/topics/AfricanAmerican.htm. Accessed January 13, 2009.

[17] E. Wayne Carp. Adoption in America: Historical Perspectives. Ann Arbor: University of Michigan Press, 2002, p. 14.

[18] Mary Battenfeld. "Introduction." The Family Nobody Wanted. Boston: Northeastern University Press, 2001, p. xxii.

[19] Helen Doss. The Family Nobody Wanted. Boston: Northeastern University Press, 2001, pp. 187–191.

[20] Ellen Herman. "Adoption History: Transracial Adoptions." The Adoption History Project, University of Oregon (7/11/07). Available online. URL: http://darkwing.uoregon. edu/~adoption/topics/transracialadoption.htm. Accessed January 13, 2009.

[21] Dorothy E. Roberts. Shattered Bonds: The Color of Child Welfare. New York: Basic Civitas Books, 2002, pp. 249–250.

[22] Billy Joe Jones. The Indian Child Welfare Act Handbook: A Legal Guide to the Custody and Adoption of Native American Children. Chicago: Section of Family Law, American Bar Association, 1995, p. 7.

[23] U.S. Department of Health and Human Services, Administration for Children and Families. "A Guide to the Multiethnic Placement Act of 1994 as Amended by the Interethnic Adoption Provisions of 1996" (2/16/06). Available online. URL: http://www.acf.hhs.gov/ programs/cb/pubs/mepa94/mepachp1.htm. Accessed January 16, 2009.

[24] Deborah L. Spar. *The Baby Business: How Money, Science, and Politics Drive the Commerce of Conception,* p. 173.

[25] George A. Akerlof and Janet L. Yellen. "An Analysis of Out-of-Wedlock Births in the United States." Washington, D.C.: The Brookings Institution, 1996. Available online. URL: http://www. brookings.edu/papers/1996/08childrenfamilies_akerlof.aspx. Accessed January 15, 2009.

[26] Child Welfare Information Gateway. "Voluntary Relinquishment for Adoption" (2005). Available online. URL: http://www.childwelfare.gov/pubs/s_place.cfm. Accessed January 15, 2009.

[27] Deborah L. Spar. *The Baby Business: How Money, Science, and Politics Drive the Commerce of Conception,* p. 173.

[28] Deborah L. Spar. *The Baby Business: How Money, Science, and Politics Drive the Commerce of Conception,* p. 25.

[29] Martin Hutchinson. "Edwards: The IVF Pioneer." BBC News (7/24/03). Available online. URL: http://news.bbc.co.uk/1/hi/health/3093429.stm. Accessed January 17, 2009.

[30] Deborah L. Spar. *The Baby Business: How Money, Science, and Politics Drive the Commerce of Conception,* pp. 24–35.

[31] Kay Elder, Julie Ribes, and Doris Baker. *Infections, Infertility, and Assisted Reproduction.* Cambridge: Cambridge University Press, 2005, p. 9.

[32] Noel P. Keane and Dennis L. Breo. *The Surrogate Mother.* New York: Everest House Publishers, 1981, pp. 27–45.

[33] Noel P. Keane and Dennis L. Breo. *The Surrogate Mother,* p. 15.

[34] Helena Ragoné. *Surrogate Motherhood: Conception in the Heart.* Boulder, Colo.: Westview Press, 1994, p. 26.

[35] Noel P. Keane and Dennis L. Breo. *The Surrogate Mother,* p. 12.

[36] Richard M. Levin, M.D. "Frequently Asked Questions." Available online. URL: http://www. babies-by-levin.com/spa_5.htm. Accessed January 18, 2009.

[37] Richard M. Levin, M.D. "Frequently Asked Questions." Available online. URL: http://www. babies-by-levin.com/spa_5.htm. Accessed January 18, 2009. And, Deborah L. Spar. *The Baby Business: How Money, Science, and Politics Drive the Commerce of Conception,* p. 76.

[38] Helena Ragoné. *Surrogate Motherhood: Conception in the Heart,* p. 19.

[39] New Jersey Supreme Court. *In the Matter of Baby M, a Pseudonym for an Actual Person,* 537 A.2d 1227, 109 N.J. 396 (N.J. 02/03/1988). Available online. URL: http://biotech.law.lsu. edu/cases/cloning/baby_m.htm. Accessed January 18, 2009.

[40] Jennifer Weiss. "Now It's Melissa's Time." *New Jersey Monthly Magazine* (March 2007). Available online. URL: http://www.reproductivelawyer.com/news/babym.asp. Accessed January 18, 2009.

[41] Helena Ragoné. *Surrogate Motherhood: Conception in the Heart,* p. 26.

[42] Mark A. Johnson, Corporate Holdings, LLC. "Some Observations of Laws of Surrogacy in the U.S." TASC: The American Surrogacy Center (2/26/05). Available online. URL: http:// www.surrogacy.com/Articles/news_view.asp?ID=88. Accessed January 19, 2009.

[43] Michael Menichiello. *A Gay Couple's Journey through Surrogacy: Intended Fathers.* Binghampton, N.Y.: Haworth Press, 2006, p. 14.

[44] Rachel Cook, Shelley Day Sclater, and Felicity Kaganas. *Surrogate Motherhood: International Perspectives.* Oxford: Hart Publishing, 2003, p. 27.

[45] Larry Ogalthorpe Gostin. *Surrogate Motherhood: Politics and Privacy.* Bloomington: Indiana University Press, 1990, p. 263.

[46] William F. Ziegler and Jeffrey B. Russell. "Clinical Assisted Reproduction: High Success with Gestational Carriers and Oocyte Donors Using Synchronized Cycles." *Journal of Assisted Reproduction and Genetics* 5. Dordrecht, the Netherlands: Springer, 1995, pp. 297–300.

[47] *Johnson v. Calvert,* 5 Cal. 4th 84, 851 P.2d 776 (1993). Available online. URL: http://faculty. law.miami.edu/zfenton/documents/Johnsonv.Calvert.pdf. Accessed January 19, 2009.

[48] Child Welfare Information Gateway. "Voluntary Relinquishment for Adoption" (2005). Available online. URL: http://www.childwelfare.gov/pubs/s_place.cfm. Accessed January 19, 2009.

[49] Christine Bachrach. "Adoption Plans, Adopted Children, Adoptive Mothers." *Journal of Marriage and Family* 48 (May 1986): 249–250.

[50] Child Welfare Information Gateway. "Voluntary Relinquishment for Adoption" (2005). Available online. URL: http://www.childwelfare.gov/pubs/s_place.cfm. Accessed January 19, 2009.

[51] Christine Bachrach. "Adoption Plans, Adopted Children, Adoptive Mothers," p. 250.

[52] U.S. Department of Health and Human Services, Centers for Disease Control. "Adoption Experiences of Men and Women and Demand for Children to Adopt by Women 18–44 Years of Age in the United States, 2002." (August 2008), p. 2. Available online. URL: http://www.cdc.gov/nchs/data/series/sr_23/sr23_027.pdf. Accessed January 20, 2009.

[53] Child Welfare Information Gateway. "Persons Seeking to Adopt" (2005). Available online. URL: http://www.childwelfare.gov/pubs/s_seek.cfm. Accessed January 20, 2009.

[54] U.S. Department of Health and Human Services, Centers for Disease Control. "Adoption Experiences of Men and Women and Demand for Children to Adopt by Women 18–44 Years of Age in the United States, 2002," p. 2.

[55] James A. Rosenthal and Victor K. Groze. *Special-Needs Adoption: A Study of Intact Families.* New York: Praeger, 1992, pp. 8–47.

[56] U.S. Department of Health and Human Services, Centers for Disease Control. "Adoption Experiences of Men and Women and Demand for Children to Adopt by Women 18–44 Years of Age in the United States, 2002," p. 2.

[57] Helena Ragoné. *Surrogate Motherhood: Conception in the Heart,* pp. 8–55.

[58] Michael Menichiello. *A Gay Couple's Journey Through Surrogacy: Intended Fathers,* p. 11.

[59] Elly Teman. "The Social Construction of Surrogacy Research: An Anthropological Critique of the Psychosocial Scholarship on Surrogate Motherhood." *Social Science and Medicine* 67 (June 2008): 1,104–1,108.

[60] R. J. Edelmann. "Surrogacy: The Psychological Issues." *Journal of Reproductive and Infant Psychology* 22 (May 2004): 128.

[61] Helena Ragoné. *Surrogate Motherhood: Conception in the Heart,* pp. 55–63.

[62] Helena Ragoné. *Surrogate Motherhood: Conception in the Heart*, p. 91.

[63] R. J. Edelmann. "Surrogacy: The Psychological Issues," p. 128.

[64] *In the Matter of Baby M, a Pseudonym for an Actual Person*, 537 A.2d 1227, 109 N.J. 396 (N.J. 02/03/1988). Available online. URL: http://biotech.law.lsu.edu/cases/cloning/baby_m.htm. Accessed January 18, 2009.

[65] Helena Ragoné. *Surrogate Motherhood: Conception in the Heart*, p. 93.

[66] Melinda B. Hohman and Christine B. Hagan. "Satisfaction with Surrogate Mothering: A Relational Model." *Journal of Human Behavior in the Social Environment* 4. Binghamton, N.Y.: Haworth Press, 2001, p. 68.

[67] Helena Ragoné. *Surrogate Motherhood: Conception in the Heart*, pp. 102–107.

[68] North American Council on Adoptable Children. "Adoption Subsidy" (Sept. 2008). Available online. URL: http://www.nacac.org/adoptionsubsidy/stateprofiles/montana.html. Accessed January 23, 2009.

[69] Dean Schabner. "Why It Costs More to Adopt a White Baby." ABC News. Available online. URL: http://abcnews.go.com/US/Story?id=91834&page=1. Accessed January 23, 2009.

[70] Susan Markens. *Surrogate Motherhood and the Politics of Reproduction*. Berkeley: University of California Press, 2007, p. 4.

[71] TASC: The American Surrogacy Center, Inc. "Legal Map" (2002). Available online. URL: http://www.surrogacy.com/legals/map.html. Accessed January 23, 2009.

[72] Jennifer Damelio and Kelly Sorensen. "Enhancing Autonomy in Paid Surrogacy." *Bioethics* 22 (Feb. 2008): 269–277.

3

Global Perspectives

INTRODUCTION

An increasingly globalized community has allowed for the possibility of family formation on a worldwide scale. A high demand for infants has led to the prevalence of intercountry adoption, and flexible surrogacy laws in some countries have lured couples desperate for a baby.

As has been noted, the topics of adoption and surrogate pregnancy are rife with complex ethical and legal issues that are in need of further discussion. These topics become even more complicated when they involve an exchange between two nations and their differing legal codes, cultures, family structures, and beliefs regarding child psychology and development. An inequitable distribution of power can also become problematic when an exchange is made between an industrialized nation and a developing country, prompting discussions of exploitation, corruption, and fraud.

In recent years, innovations in technology and global communications have had a profound impact on family formation around the world. Rapidly increasing rates of international adoption have altered the economies and populations of some third world countries while changing the face of the average family in some developed countries. The legalization of commercial surrogacy in some countries has resulted in new business opportunities and a means of survival for some, while providing new opportunities for parenthood to others.

When discussing the complex issues involved in international adoption and surrogate pregnancy, certain terms frequently arise, including *sending* and *receiving* countries, child abandonment, the Hague Convention, and reproductive tourism. A basic understanding of such terms and definitions will enable easier navigation of discussions of international adoption and surrogacy.

Sending and Receiving Countries

These terms refer to international adoption exchanges between two countries: the country that sends the child and the country that receives the child. In broader terms, a sending country is typically, though not always, a poorer nation in which circumstances such as poverty and weak social programs prevent families from being able to house and feed their children. As such, sending countries often have high numbers of homeless and/or orphaned children in need of adoption.

The top three countries that sent children to the United States from 2004 to 2008 were Russia, China, and Guatemala.[1] The three countries have shifted positions throughout the years due to internal legislative changes but have nevertheless remained the top senders. While the high number of children placed for adoption in Russia and Guatemala is primarily due to widespread poverty, China differs in that it has a relatively stable economy. The number of Chinese children placed for adoption is almost exclusively the result of China's singular population control efforts. China's one-child policy has resulted in unprecedented levels of child abandonment and infanticide, and each year thousands of Chinese children are adopted by families overseas.

Other sending countries include Ethiopia, South Korea, India, Haiti, Kazakhstan, Vietnam, Ukraine, and Cambodia. In many of these countries, overseas adoptions have become necessary for the survival of countless children. Without intercountry adoption, not only would many children lose the opportunity to be part of a loving family, but orphanages and institutions would become overcrowded, resulting in myriad related problems. In the early 1990s, Romania opened its doors to international adoption, and the world saw the appalling conditions in its overcrowded orphanages.

Efforts to adopt from impoverished nations are not without controversy, however. Some 46 percent of children adopted internationally are under one year of age, and 90 percent are under the age of five, despite the fact that most children in institutional care are over the age of five.[2] Virtually all intercountry adoptions involve the adoption of a child from an impoverished, developing nation into a wealthy, developed country, which necessarily leads to questions about the ultimate purpose of international adoption: finding homes for poor children or finding babies for wealthy couples?

Between the 1980s and 2004, international adoption rates increased exponentially. The United States currently holds the position of top receiving country. In 2004, the United States adopted 22,884 children internationally, more than triple the number of any other receiving country. The second-highest receiving country in 2004 was Spain, which adopted 5,541 children, and third was France, which adopted 4,079 children.[3]

Other receiving countries include Italy, Canada, Australia, Norway, Denmark, and Sweden. While the United States accounts for the highest numbers of international adoptions, Norway has consistently held the highest annual international adoption rate. In 2004, there were 15.4 international adoptions for every 100,000 people in Norway, compared with 7.8 in the United States. Spain came in second, with 13 adoptions per 100,000 people, and Sweden was third, with 12.3. In terms of international adoption rates, the United States ranks eighth out of 15 countries. The United Kingdom came in last, with 0.6.[4]

Marked differences between receiving and sending countries can be observed in terms of economy, population, health, and education levels.

Child Abandonment

Few children in institutional care throughout the world are true orphans, meaning both of their parents are dead. In many countries, such as India and China, the majority of children in orphanages have been abandoned, meaning that one or both of their parents abandoned them without going through legal adoption proceedings. In most cases this is due to a combination of poverty, social stigma, and political climate. In India, a poor economy combined with the heavy stigmatization of unwed motherhood leads many women to leave their villages to give birth and abandon their babies in front of orphanages or hospitals. In China, poverty as well as the government's efforts to reduce the population by allowing only one child per family has led countless numbers of couples to travel to major urban areas to abandon their infants, namely girls.

Infant abandonment primarily affects girls and occurs frequently in patriarchal and patrilocal cultures such as India and China. Both Indian and Chinese cultures practice patrilocality, which consists of a woman's relocation to her husband's family upon marriage. Often, the family is headed by the eldest male who serves as the family authority, whether a father or an elder brother. A new bride has little to no power within the family but rather acts as a servant who takes orders from her mother-in-law until she bears her first son. This cultural custom makes female children a liability. Giving birth to and raising a girl not only means having to invest resources into an individual who will not reinvest in the family but often means having to produce a dowry, particularly in India. For poor families, this can be financially devastating and may mean that a daughter cannot be married off due to limited family resources. Some recent accounts report of men taking dowry money to leave the country or start a business, and then abandoning their wives.

Infant abandonment differs from official relinquishment in that it may also act as a form of infanticide. While the relinquishment of a child ensures that the child will be cared for, abandonment may result in the child's death if it is not found. In China, though a female infant may be left in plain view on a busy street, passersby may avoid taking the girl to authorities for fear of being accused of having given birth to the child and being punished for an over-quota birth. Every year, many baby girls die of exposure due to abandonment. Abandonment and direct infanticide of female children have resulted in imbalanced sex ratios in both China and India. Historically, the killing of female children in China and India has been culturally sanctioned, and, while both countries have implemented legislation to curtail this, the entrenched custom of abandoning or killing a second-born daughter nevertheless continues. Today, the use of fetal diagnostic technology, such as ultrasounds and amniocentesis, has ushered in the problem of sex-selective abortion, or what is referred to as female feticide.

One of the challenges involved in the adoption of an abandoned child is his or her unofficial status as an orphan. Because the parents have not officially terminated their parental rights, years may go by before the child is deemed legally adoptable.

The Hague Convention

In response to the rapidly increasing rates of international adoption and the complexities involved, a number of both sending and receiving countries convened on May 29, 1993, to develop a unified system of adoption that would protect the rights of children, birth parents, and adoptive parents. The mission of the Hague Convention on Protection of Children and Co-operation in Respect of Intercountry Adoption is to "ensure that intercountry adoptions are made in the best interests of the child and with respect for his or her fundamental rights, and to prevent the abduction, the sale of, or traffic in children."[5] Cases of child-trafficking and fraud have been reported in several countries, including countries that are party to the Hague Convention. Cambodia, for example, is party to the Hague Convention, but reports of baby buying, fraud, and money laundering have led to many countries suspending adoptions from that country. Similar reports have led to the suspension of adoptions from Guatemala by many receiving countries; Guatemala is also a signatory to the Hague Convention. Similar abuses have been reported in Nepal, Nigeria, and Sierra Leone.[6]

In an attempt to curb such abuses, the Hague Convention established flexible adoption guidelines that could be adapted to various governments and child welfare systems. These guidelines include the establishment of a central authority in each country to oversee and approve adoption regulations. In the United States, the central authority over international adoption regulations is the Department of State. Other guidelines include the accreditation of acceptable adoption agencies and their compliance with reporting requirements, proper screening of prospective parents, proper counseling of prospective parents, assurance by authorities that a child may enter and live in a particular state, the determination that no unauthorized money has been exchanged for a child, and the conclusion by authorities that an adoption has followed Hague standards.[7] While many countries became members of the Hague Convention in 1993, some have neglected to implement legislation that would help ensure adherence to the standards it set down. Guatemala, for example, has not established a central authority to regulate and approve adoptions. The United States became a member in 1994 but did not ratify the treaty until December 2007.

In addition to the established Hague guidelines, the United States has created a Hague Complaint Registry for individual cases, as well as a registry to track adoption cases called the Adoptions Tracking Service (ATS). The ATS tracks individual cases involving the United States and the accreditation of adoption service providers and the contact information of adoption service providers and the accrediting entity.

Reproductive Tourism

Reproductive tourism, also known as fertility tourism or procreative tourism, consists of an infertile couple from one country or region traveling to another country or region where they can obtain the reproductive assistance they desire, whether that is in vitro fertilization (IVF), eggs, sperm, embryos, or surrogates. The reasons for reproductive tourism are many and include high costs and banned procedures in one's home country, more liberal laws in other countries, or a desire for anonymity.

Since the passage of the Assisted Human Reproductive Act in 2004 in Canada, which banned the sale of human ova, many Canadian couples have traveled to the United States and overseas to buy eggs from fertility clinics.[8] Similarly, in many European countries the fertility industry is heavily regulated and does not allow for the donation of eggs or embryos. In 2004, the Italian parliament banned the destruction or cryopreservation of embryos, limited the number of embryos created for implantation to three, banned surrogacy and the use of donated eggs and sperm, and barred gay couples and single people from receiving reproductive assistance.[9] Prior to the passage of these new fertility regulations, no laws existed to regulate assisted reproduction in Italy.

By contrast, Spain, another largely Catholic nation, is well known as a reproductive tourism destination because of its liberal fertility laws. Many women undergo fertility procedures using donated embryos, which are banned in most other European countries. In 2005, approximately 15 to 20 percent of the 42,000 IVF procedures were performed on foreign women.[10] Thousands of women travel to Spain each year to avoid restrictive fertility laws in their home countries. In France, gay couples and single women are denied fertility treatments, and in the United Kingdom, recent passage of a law that has banned anonymity in gamete donation has resulted in a shortage of available eggs and sperm.

The United States differs from Canada and Europe in that its fertility laws are relatively relaxed. Most American couples who travel abroad for fertility treatments do so not to avoid strict regulations but cripplingly high costs. A single egg retrieval cycle can cost $30,000, and, with a roughly 30 percent success rate, many women must undergo several IVF cycles to achieve a pregnancy.

Countries with low costs and liberal regulations are attracting couples from around the world. As one of the first countries to legalize commercial surrogacy, India has become a major reproductive tourism site as couples from the United States and elsewhere look for surrogate mothers whose services will cost a fraction of what they would in their home country. In the United States, an IVF procedure can cost $30,000, while in India it costs $6,000. Such a dramatic price difference has many couples traveling to India, where the total cost of the surrogacy, IVF procedure, plane flights, and accommodation is still less than the cost of a surrogate pregnancy in the United States.

Many are critical of the reproductive tourism movement as historically most countries have been slow to keep pace with developments in reproductive technology. With so many couples arriving in countries like India, Guatemala, Romania, and Russia in search of eggs, embryos, and surrogates, critics fear that too little protection is being afforded to poor women who may have been forced to become surrogates and donors due to poverty, lack of education, and family pressure. Those in favor of reproductive tourism argue that surrogate mothers from poverty-stricken countries have the unprecedented opportunity to make five years' worth of money in less than a year and thereby provide not only for themselves, but for their families and their children's education. As debates wage on, many can agree that increased regulation is necessary to ensure that all involved parties are protected.

CHINA

Historically, family and kinship formation in China has been identified with continuation of the family name, as well as a type of social security for aging parents. The ancient Chinese practice of ancestor worship exemplifies the importance of heritage, kinship, and roots, as well as the debt that is owed to the past.

Adoption and surrogacy as alternative means of family formation have gained popularity in recent decades, though with many challenges that are unique in China's current political climate and cultural views of kinship. Unusually strict reproductive laws, an authoritarian government, and a cultural preference for male children have led to high rates of child abandonment, infanticide, and exploitation of women. After criticism from the international community, China has reformed many of its social programs to achieve increased protection for the socially vulnerable. However, the international community still believes that the Chinese government has much to do to protect basic human rights. Others argue that China's ethically questionable reproductive laws have led to improvements in the lives of women and children, allowing women the opportunity to get an education and providing children with stable home environments. An analysis of adoption and surrogacy will help illuminate governmental and cultural views of women and children in China.

Global Role in Adoption and Surrogate Pregnancy

In 1992, China allowed the first overseas adoptions of its orphans, and that year 206 Chinese children were adopted by American couples and brought to the United States. In 1995, more than 2,500 Chinese orphans were adopted internationally. High demand for healthy infants in Western countries led to higher numbers of internationally adopted Chinese children, and in 2005 more than 14,500 children were adopted overseas. Nearly three-quarters of these children were adopted by American couples.[11] In 1998, some 4,243 Chinese children were adopted and brought to the United States and that number almost doubled, to 7,903, by 2005.[12]

Until 2008, China consistently accounted for the majority of internationally adopted children in the United States, often in close competition with Russia. The collapse of the Soviet Union in 1989 led many former Soviet bloc countries to open up their orphanages to overseas adoptions, and in the early 1990s China, Russia, and Romania became the primary sending countries in international adoption. Romania was prominently featured in exposés and documentaries as a nation that did not protect its weak and vulnerable, and the deplorable conditions of the Romanian orphanages led many U.S. couples to adopt for humanitarian reasons. The case was similar for China. Overpopulation combined with policies that valued the rights of the community over those of the individual led to the neglect of unwanted and abandoned children in understaffed orphanages.

Global Perspectives

China's one-child policy, implemented in 1978, has been blamed for the nation's markedly high rate of infanticide and infant abandonment. Under Mao Zedong, Chinese families were encouraged to produce many children to work on the collective farms, and the nation's fertility rate rose to an average of 5.8 children per woman. Though infant abandonment and infanticide had been practiced for nearly 3,000 years, both decreased sharply during the collective era.[13] Shortly after the death of Mao in 1976, the one-child policy was enacted and the national birthrate fell to 2.9 children per woman in 1979, and then to 1.98 children per woman in 2001.[14] As birthrates fell, cases of infant abandonment and infanticide rose. In an attempt to work around cultural preferences for male children in China's rural areas and decrease the number of infant girls who are abandoned or killed, exceptions to the one-child policy were made for families whose first child was a girl.[15] Nevertheless, countless numbers of female infants continue to be abandoned or killed each year. The 1994 worldwide sex ratio for infants was 101.5 boys for every 100 girls. In China, this figure was 116 boys for every 100 girls.[16] The vast majority of children in Chinese orphanages are girls who were abandoned by their parents.

While many of China's orphaned girls are adopted internationally every year, this rate has dropped precipitously in recent years. In 2007, China implemented new regulations regarding who may adopt—now excluded are individuals under the age of 30, homosexual couples, and people who have been divorced more than twice. Furthermore, individuals are disqualified from adopting if they have ever taken medication prescribed for mental illness, have paralysis of a limb, have a facial deformity, are overweight, or are blind in either eye. Such restrictions have caused the rate of U.S. adoptions of Chinese children to drop from 7,903 in 2005 to 3,911 in 2008.[17]

China's global role in surrogacy is limited due to the fact that many forms of assisted reproduction are illegal. While sperm banks are allowed to operate out of hospitals under government approval, the selling of eggs and embryos is illegal. In 2001, gestational surrogacy was officially banned after a deliberation by eight sessions of experts and scholars determined that the social and ethical consequences were too serious to allow it to continue. Many agencies continue to operate, however, with virtual offices on the Internet.

History and Law

Adoption in China has been historically identified with abandonment. An account from 145 B.C.E. details one woman's decision to abandon her infant for fear that his illegitimacy would bring her bad luck. Another woman found the child and named him Ji, which means "abandonment."[18]

Confucian patriarchy promotes the Chinese cultural preference for boys and maintains that a husband and wife who cannot have a son are unfortunate. Sons have been traditionally seen as necessary for the continuation of the family name, caring for aging parents, and performing sacred ancestral rituals.[19] Historical texts refer to the practice of *ni ying*, in which a midwife would drown a second-born daughter in a bucket of water.[20] Though sons were highly valued, traditional Chinese law banned adoption outside of one's family name. Ironically, one means of obtaining a son was through a sort of surrogacy arrangement whereby a concubine would produce a child in place of the infertile wife.[21]

Today, the overwhelming majority of children in Chinese orphanages are girls, but many are adopted nevertheless. To avoid being penalized for an over-quota birth, many birth parents will leave their infant daughters in public places, such as a hospital or a busy street, to be discovered by strangers. Research reveals that the majority of families that adopt abandoned children do so before the child even enters an orphanage; however, legal challenges may prevent them from officially adopting. If a couple already has one child, the adoption of a second child will be penalized as an over-quota birth. The adoptive parents may face a fine of more than double their annual income and one or both will be forced to undergo a sterilization procedure. If they cannot pay the fine or undergo sterilization, the child may be removed from their home and placed in a state-run orphanage.[22] In some cases, however, ministry officials will not enforce the law, viewing the family's adoption of a child as a humanitarian act.

Though it would seem counterproductive if not unreasonable to remove children from willing adoptive parents to be placed in an orphanage at the government's expense, penalizing over-quota adoptions is aimed at curbing the number of parents who attempt to hide over-quota births through informal and often false adoption arrangements. Unfortunately, such punishments have led to many cases of double abandonment. In some cases, a child who has lived with a family for years and is found to have been illegally adopted may be seized and placed in an orphanage as a means of punishing parents. Another side effect of such prohibitive and stringently enforced reproductive laws is the fact that some infants die because passersby refuse to take them to hospitals or orphanages for fear that they may be suspected of having given birth to an over-quota child themselves.[23]

Because population control is so heavily emphasized by the Chinese government, it is hardly surprising that many forms of assisted reproduction are also illegal. In 2001, the Chinese Ministry of Health issued a regulation that effectively banned gestational surrogacy, citing the fact that it gives rise to unavoidable social and ethical questions that cannot yet be answered, such as what type of woman should act as a surrogate, what actions should be taken if a surrogate refuses to relinquish a child, and who is to assume responsibility if a child is born with genetic defects. The ban met with mixed responses. In a society where children are a parent's only hope for security and well-being in old age, an inability to produce children can be potentially devastating. Some doctors agreed with the ban, while others questioned why infertile couples should be deprived of the right to have children.[24] Though gestational surrogacy is illegal, the practice continues with relative openness in certain areas.

Characteristics of Birth Parents and Adoptive Parents

Though not exclusive to any one area, infant abandonment and infanticide have been most widely practiced in the southern and southeastern regions of China, particularly in areas along the Yangzi River.[25] A 1995–96 study on infant abandonment and adoption in China found that the majority of people who abandon are married, live in rural areas where they work in agriculture, and have lower levels of education or are illiterate. The patriarchal social structure not only affects the lives of infant girls but also extends to parental decision-making and how much say a mother has in infant abandonment. Of the 237 families that were interviewed fully 50 percent admitted that the decision to abandon was made exclusively by the father, while 40 percent involved an agreement between both parents. Many of the women interviewed continued to suffer from feelings of guilt and remorse years later.[26]

Studies reveal that infant abandonment is most prevalent during times of famine, economic hardship, and war, which suggests that the practice of discarding infant girls is not strictly due to a preference for male children but coincides with poverty and economic instability.[27] The rate of infant abandonment also coincides with the degree of enforcement of the one-child policy. In the late 1990s, with the 2000 census approaching, a rigid birth planning campaign was enforced throughout various areas of China, which led to ever greater numbers of discarded infants.[28] Today, the average abandoned infant is a healthy newborn girl with one or more older sisters and no brothers.[29] First-born daughters are rarely abandoned, which suggests that parents are reluctant to abandon but do so when they believe their chances of having a son are threatened. Parents who abandon their infants are rarely caught, but when they are, they are almost always punished for bearing an over-quota child rather than for abandoning and endangering their child.[30]

In contrast to birth parents, adoptive parents tend to come from urban areas, where infants are most often abandoned. As the overwhelming majority of Chinese orphans are healthy newborn girls, the average adopting family is one in which a son is already present and the parents desire a daughter to complete their family. Chinese adoption law, however, reflects the one-child policy and mandates that adoptive parents be childless and over the age of 30 (which was reduced from 35 in 2001).[31] The Chinese government claims that the one-child adoption policy is meant to protect orphaned girls from adults who wish to adopt future servants or future daughters-in-law. The China scholar Kay Johnson contends that such practices have not been in existence for several years and argues that the one-child adoption law is meant to reinforce population control policies rather than protect the rights of children.[32]

As there are far more orphaned girls than there are childless couples over the age of 30, most Chinese adoptions are informal and occur before a child falls into government hands. Depending on the level of enforcement of the one-child policy in a particular area, however, many adoptive parents face fines and possible sterilization, if not the removal of the child altogether. Contrary to many Western notions of Chinese attitudes toward children, many adoptive parents are willing to go to great and admirable lengths to keep their children.[33]

Characteristics of Surrogate Mothers and Contracting Parents

As in the United States, China has no statewide law regarding surrogacy, other than a ban on gestational surrogacy. Nevertheless, both forms of surrogacy are still in practice, and no official studies or statistics on Chinese surrogacy exist.

In 2006, a female journalist contacted several surrogacy agencies posing as a potential surrogate mother. Her findings revealed that Chinese surrogates are classified according to their appearance, educational background, and other features and are paid accordingly between 40,000 and 100,000 yuan. An attractive young woman with a junior college education can expect to be paid 100,000 yuan, or about 12,000 U.S. dollars. One woman was paid 120,000 yuan, or $14,500, as she was a university graduate and attractive.[34]

The process of contracting a surrogate pregnancy is much less rigorous in China than it is in the United States. Contracting parents can expect to be matched with a surrogate within a day or two of applying. While fees for a surrogate pregnancy in the United States can range upward of $30,000, Chinese contracting parents can expect to pay between 130,000 and 140,000 yuan, or about $16,000 to $17,000. Surrogacy center directors cited altruistic reasons for becoming involved in surrogacy, but here, too, altruism is overshadowed by the gender inequalities entrenched in Chinese culture. Two surrogacy directors claimed that they knew women who had been abandoned by their husbands for their inability to produce children, and such stories inspired them to establish surrogate pregnancy agencies.[35]

Unique Circumstances of Adoption
and Surrogate Pregnancy in China

Chinese women and children's rights are a matter of great concern to the international community as their social status renders them relatively powerless. In the case of adoption, a child's right to be recognized as a Chinese citizen can be tenuous. If an adoptive parent is charged with an over-quota adoption and is unable to pay the fine but refuses to relinquish the child, the child may simply be denied a *hukou*, or household registration, which amounts to a child being denied legal status and basic legal rights. Without a *hukou*, an "illegal" child, or *heihaizi*, may not receive basic childhood immunizations or access to education. Most parents manage to win a *hukou* for their child only after many years of struggling with birth planning officials and expending vast sums of money, but many others eventually find themselves unable to care for a child without a *hukuo* and are forced to hand the child over to an orphanage. In effect, these "illegal" children are denied basic acknowledgement that they exist.[36]

Such an attitude toward children's rights would appear to have obvious ramifications for a child's emotional development, especially when his or her peers are going to school. The development and social acceptance of child psychology has been particularly problematic in China. In the early 1990s, the country came under intense criticism from the international community for the deplorable state of its orphanages. Many Chinese infants and toddlers were diagnosed by foreign psychologists as suffering from a failure to thrive due to a lack of human contact. Statistics revealed that half of all children placed in orphanages died within a few months of arrival, and in 1996 an investigation was conducted by Human Rights Watch. Even today, reports reveal that children's emotional needs are rarely taken into consideration in orphanages, where staff members may openly characterize a child to researchers as pretty or stupid in front of the child.[37] This lack of sensitivity to a child's emotional needs is likely symptomatic of the contemporary communistic climate, in which the rights of the individual are rejected in favor of the well-being of the community.

Women's rights have long been overlooked in China, and the effects of surrogate pregnancy on women's rights and social status are being debated. The Confucian feminist Julia Tao Lai, Po-Wah, rejects the notions that surrogacy enhances female autonomy by allowing women to freely enter into contracts and reduces essentialized notions of femininity and childbearing. Rather, she argues, a woman's status in Chinese culture is defined by her ability to produce children, thus to deprive her of that token of social power is to render her valueless and replaceable. Chinese women have long been exploited as domestic laborers at the bottom of the familial hierarchy. For centuries, a girl could expect to get married and serve her husband's family, remaining relatively powerless within the household until she gave birth to a son. Therefore, to reduce pregnancy and childbearing to an act of commercialized productivity not only strips a Chinese woman of the only power she may be entitled to but reinforces the female role as that of a producer and bearer of children.[38]

Nevertheless, compelling arguments are made regarding surrogacy and women's autonomy. Perhaps if pregnancy were successfully disconnected from notions of motherhood and femininity, women would be less likely to be defined exclusively by their ability to give birth. Further, if women are able to contract a pregnancy, they may likely have more say in matters of decision-making. As long as surrogacy remains unregulated, however, women have little assurance that their rights will be protected.

Conclusion: Efforts to Standardize Adoption and Surrogate Pregnancy in China

The Adoption Law of the People's Republic of China passed in 1992 was the first law designed to regulate domestic and international adoption. Prior to the establishment of this law, adoptions were arranged privately, with little government oversight. In 1996, the China Center of Adoption Affairs (CCAA) was established to regulate international adoption by screening overseas adoption agencies, examining applications from foreign adopters, and matching Chinese children with applicants.[39] International adoption is generally perceived positively by the Chinese, who view foreign adopters as being very wealthy because they can travel to China, and thus they are considered capable of providing material well-being for Chinese children. Additionally, international adoption is viewed by many Chinese as a bridge to the west.[40] Nevertheless, priority is given to domestic adoption.

Despite reports in the 1990s that found Chinese orphanages to be unmindful of children's emotional needs, Luo and Bergquist's 2004 study on Chinese perceptions of international adoption found that many orphanage directors and staff members believe that institutionalized care cannot substitute for family and love and that the ultimate goal of the orphanage is to find a family for each child.[41]

Current Chinese legislation prioritizes population control over children's rights, as exemplified by the fact that when families are caught abandoning their children, they are punished not by the courts, but by birth planning officials. In a statement made in March 2008, the nation's family planning minister announced that China would not be relinquishing reproductive controls as of yet but expects to maintain the one-child policy for another 10 years.[42]

Until legislation accurately addresses embedded cultural beliefs, as well as trends within assisted reproductive technology, the rights of women, children, and families will not be guaranteed.

INDIA

As the fourth-largest economy in the world, India is home to more than 1 billion people and is the site of a number of complex political struggles for freedom. British colonial rule came to an end in 1947, and a violent partition ensued, resulting in the creation of contemporary India and Pakistan. Today, India is 80 percent Hindu, with minority communities of Shia Muslims and Christians.

Family and community are heavily emphasized in modern Indian culture, and the research of the ethnographer Susan C. Seymour indicates that children are raised to be members of an interdependent community that consists of immediate and extended family.[43] Joint-family homes are the norm and may include grandparents, aunts, uncles, and cousins, so that a child may be raised by several caregivers. Such joint-family homes are often patrilocal and structured on a set of brothers or a father and son, with the eldest male wielding the most authority. Wives are brought into the family from outside and gain authority as they bear children.

The intimacy and interdependence of the Indian family unit pose a challenge to alternative methods of family formation, such as adoption and surrogate pregnancy. In the past, adoption outside of the family was viewed with distrust as orphaned children were often assumed to be illegitimate or from bad genetic stock. While this attitude remains prevalent in many rural communities, adoption is becoming more common throughout India, particularly among more educated urban couples. Nevertheless, many Indian families have historically preferred to keep adoption and even assisted reproduction within the family.[44]

Despite cultural beliefs in the intimacy of the family unit, commercial surrogacy was legalized in India in 2002 and has since become a thriving international enterprise, with Indian surrogacy agencies overwhelmed with requests from Western couples for surrogate mothers. Though not yet widely accepted by Indian families, many poor Indian women who act as surrogates have found economic security that otherwise would not have been available to them.

Indians' cultural views of family formation through adoption and surrogate pregnancy are influenced by many other cultural complexities, such as views of family, gender, caste status, and fertility. Through an analysis of such cultural perspectives, one can reach a better understanding of adoption and surrogate pregnancy in India.

Global Role in Adoption and Surrogate Pregnancy

The adoption of an unrelated child has historically been viewed negatively, and prior to the 1982 Indian Supreme Court decree mandating that all adoption agencies be registered with the government, orphaned children often suffered from malnutrition and languished in overcrowded orphanages and even prisons if space could not be found elsewhere.[45] Today, the conditions of orphanages in India have improved, although child homelessness remains pervasive.

Domestic adoption is now gaining popularity, but in the past startlingly few adoptions took place within India. Furthermore, the Hindu Adoption and Maintenance Act of 1956 prohibited all non-Hindus (including foreign nationals) from adopting Indian children in India. This changed in the 1970s when the Indian government introduced a provision that would allow foreign couples to apply for legal guardianship of a child with the intention of adopting in their own home countries.[46] The first Indian children to be placed abroad went to Norway, Sweden, Denmark, Switzerland, Holland, and the United States. In 1988, there were 1,661 overseas adoptions of Indian-born children and only 398 domestic adoptions.[47]

Opposition to international adoption has remained strong, however. While many Indians agree that international adoption is a preferable option for special needs children and less desirable tribal children, many others remain distrustful of overseas adoption. Such sentiments may arise in part from India's troubled relationship with the West due to its former status as a British colony. More likely, though, is an essentialist view of genetics as the primary determinant of an individual's identity.[48] Tendencies to believe that Indian children must be raised by Indian parents have been observed among adoption authorities in India, and reports have suggested that Indians abroad are given priority over non-Indians seeking to adopt.

Government efforts to reduce overseas adoptions of Indian children have resulted in the 50/50 rule, which stipulates that for every child that is adopted by a foreign couple, another must be adopted by an Indian couple. Concerted efforts are being made to encourage Indian couples to adopt, and in 1998 there were 1,746 domestic adoptions and 1,406 international adoptions.[49] Of the 17,433 children who were adopted internationally in the United States in 2008, 307 came from India.[50]

Since 2002, prospective parents who cannot or choose not to adopt from India now have the option of hiring an Indian surrogate mother. What began as a commercial endeavor in Gujarat, western India, has expanded into a $445 million reproductive tourism enterprise.[51] Many couples from around the world travel to India each year to hire a surrogate, lured by few legal restrictions, highly educated doctors and medical staff, and low costs. Virtually no laws exist to regulate the fertility industry, and fees are often a fraction of the normal cost for surrogacy in developed nations such as the United States and the United Kingdom. For middle- and working-class Western couples who cannot afford the exorbitant costs of surrogacy in their home countries, the low costs of hiring an Indian surrogate provide a doorway to having children that would not otherwise be available. Many critics, however, are concerned with the economic inequity of a process in which relatively well-off Westerners rent the wombs of poor Indian women, many of whom have few options for survival in a country that is wracked by poverty. As of 2007, 220 million people, or more than 35 percent of the population, were living below the poverty line.[52] Debates continue to be waged over the ethics of creating a business of surrogacy in such a poverty-stricken nation. While some argue that the process exploits poor women who have no other means of survival, others contend that the surrogacy provides these women with food, shelter, and the financial stability that they desperately need, and is thus a form of philanthropy.

History and Law

The importance of children, particularly sons, is directly emphasized in the Yogatattava Upanisad, which states: "The husband, after conception by his wife, becomes an embryo and is born again of her; for that is the wifehood of a wife, that he is born again by her."[53] Sons are also believed necessary for the performance of sacred rituals that will rescue dead relatives from Put, or hell. Children thus play an integral role in the sacred family triad, which can only be completed through the process of marriage, conception, and childbirth. In India, an inability to conceive can be highly problematic, and the legal codes of Vishnu indicate 11 other kinds of sons that can be absorbed into the family unit in the event that a newly married couple cannot conceive. The next most desirable option, according to the legal codes, is the son born of a male surrogate or the use of one man to impregnate another man's wife. The sons are listed in order of preference, with the adopted son being eighth on the list.[54]

Resistance to adoption in India is prevalent, particularly in rural communities. Many infertile couples have rejected the notion of adopting based on the assumption that orphaned children are the products of illicit unions and are therefore genetically tainted.[55] Interestingly, however, Aditya Bharadwaj, a professor of medical sociology at the University of Edinburgh, found that the majority of the infertile couples he studied would choose IVF using donor gametes before considering adoption. In this light, one can surmise that the stigma of adopting has less to do with the problem of genetics than the visibility of infertility: to adopt an unrelated child is to make known one's inability to conceive. Nevertheless, genetics and relatedness remain highly important and many couples will use donor gametes from siblings and other relatives if possible. In most cases, however, the use of donor gametes, whether from relatives or strangers, is shrouded in secrecy. Many couples will not disclose to family members their use of donated sperm or ova but will maintain that the resulting child is genetically their own.[56] Similarly, many Indian communities still consider surrogate pregnancy taboo, despite the recent rise in surrogate pregnancies in the country.

At present, no uniform law regulating adoption or the fertility industry exists in India. The Hindu Adoption and Maintenance Act of 1956 (HAMA) made non-Hindus ineligible to adopt and restricted families to the adoption of only one child of each sex. If a family already has a biological son or daughter, they may not legally adopt another. Without uniform laws and codes, many adoption agencies have created their own guidelines. Agencies receiving large donations of money from foreign agencies find international adoption financially attractive and make little or no attempt to place children domestically. Some agencies do not approve of single parents, while others want documented proof of infertility. In 2000, the Juvenile Justice Act was implemented—it allows non-Hindus to adopt and allows for the adoption of more than one child of each sex. Many states, however, have simply not yet enacted the legislation. In 2004, the Central Adoption Resource Authority (CARA) proposed a set of uniform regulations for all adoption agencies, which included the encouragement of Indian couples to adopt homeless and orphaned children.[57]

Characteristics of Birth Parents and Adoptive Parents

Abandonment remains more common in India than official relinquishment of parental rights. The two main causes of abandonment are illegitimacy and poverty.[58] One 1993 study found that of 4,526 orphaned children, 74 percent were abandoned by their birth mothers because they were born out of wedlock.[59] When one considers the heavy stigmatization of premarital pregnancy, as well as the lack of resources available to single mothers, it is little wonder that so many abandon their children. Many cultural practices, such as arranged marriage and sex segregation, are intended to maintain male-based hierarchical systems, leaving women with little freedom, even in the event of widowhood or desertion. Arranged marriage remains popular, particularly in rural regions, and typically a girl is married off at a relatively young age to ensure her virginity and protect the family from the dishonor of out-of-wed-lock pregnancy. As one Indian man commented to a researcher, "American girls are given too much independence. A girl should marry young, before she has a chance to develop independent ideas."[60] In many cases of arranged marriage, girls are married off with only a few years of schooling and are allowed few if any options for the development of vocational skills, thereby ensuring their dependence and obedience. Such views of gender and female sexuality obviously make pregnancy outside of marriage a tremendous risk. Further, research reveals that even when a woman becomes a single mother through the death of her husband or desertion, she has few if any resources to rely on. In most cases, the family income drops precipitously and children are forced to become wage earners, in which case they may have to abandon their schooling.[61]

As the adoption of an illegitimate or lower-caste child is unacceptable to many Indians, adoptive parents will often go to great lengths to maintain appearances in order to appease disapproving family members. One study found that the vast majority of parents adopting from an agency had told their families that they were adopting from a distant relative or a friend within their caste.[62]

Though adoption is rare, its occurrence is often treated as being no different from a biological parent-child relationship. Indeed, in ancient India, complete assimilation into the new family was vital and necessitated the total severance of all ties to one's biological family. Four thousand years ago, an adoptee who publically declared that he was not born to his parents would have been punished by having his tongue cut out. An actual search for birth parents was punishable by blinding.[63] Today, many families and adoption authorities insist that there is no difference between adoptive and biological parenting.

Characteristics of Surrogate Mothers and Contracting Parents

The total cost of hiring an Indian surrogate can range anywhere from $12,000 to $25,000. This includes the cost of airfares, IVF procedures, and payment to the clinic and surrogate mother. The surrogate mother typically pockets between $3,000 and $7,000, which is more money than most Indians make in several years, especially when one considers the fact that over one-third of the population survives on less than $1 a day.[64] Many of the women who become surrogates do so to provide for their families, particularly the education of their children. In many cases, they are single mothers or are seeking to supplement their husbands' meager earnings.[65]

Like surrogacy centers in the United States and the United Kingdom, Indian surrogacy clinics have differing standards and practices. Some clinics house surrogates in dormitory-like settings, while others leave surrogates to find their own housing. Some clinics allow surrogates and clients to meet, while others do not give surrogates any information about the couples for whom they are carrying a baby, although the couples may have information about the surrogate. In almost all surrogacy cases, donor eggs (or the contracting mother's eggs) are used in the IVF process. Unlike in the United States, where the most common form of surrogacy (traditional) uses the surrogate mother's own eggs to conceive an embryo, an Indian surrogate's eggs are not used in order to protect against the possibility of the surrogate becoming attached to the baby. In this way, clinic directors are able to more effectively train the surrogates to view the baby as someone else's.[66]

Despite the skyrocketing numbers of surrogate pregnancies, many Indian communities frown upon surrogacy, leading many surrogates to live elsewhere during their pregnancies.[67] Some move with their husbands and children to neighboring villages, while those who choose to stay in their villages may pretend that the child is theirs and, upon giving birth, tell family and friends that the baby was stillborn.

Contracting parents in India are almost exclusively foreign. At one clinic, 75 percent of the clientele consists of nonresident Indians who live in the United States, the United Kingdom, and elsewhere.[68] Contracting parents are required to travel to India only twice: once to participate in the IVF process and once more to collect the infant, making the whole process as convenient and comfortable for the contracting couple as possible.[69] Furthermore, because the fertility industry is not regulated, doctors can take risks that they cannot in more developed countries, such as implanting multiple embryos to increase the chances of producing a live birth. Such possibilities can reduce the total costs of surrogacy even more.

Unique Circumstances of Adoption and Surrogate Pregnancy in India

As India is a highly patriarchal society with patrilocal family structures similar to Chinese family units, female infant abandonment, feticide, and reproductive coercion of women remain problems. The United Nations Children's Fund (UNICEF) has estimated that over 50 million Indian females have simply "gone missing," referring to the severely imbalanced sex ratio and the number of female births that are unreported each year. In 2007, there were 927 girls per 1,000 boys in India. In some areas, this ratio is even lower: 845 to 1,000 in the southwest district of Delhi. It has also been estimated that 70 percent of all abortions performed in India are a direct result of the fetus being female.[70]

In India, sons are looked upon as wage earners, preservers of the family name, and caretakers for aging parents. Similar to Chinese custom, sons traditionally remain with their parents their whole lives, while daughters are married out to other families. For this reason, girls are often viewed as a drain on family resources, as they are essentially being raised to become part of another family. The practice of dowry-giving makes girls even more of an economic hardship for their families. Easy access to prenatal diagnostic techniques has made it possible for even low-income families to seek a sex-selective abortion if necessary, despite the recent implementation of the Prenatal Diagnostic Techniques Act, which outlaws the practice. The penalty for performing or requesting a sex-selective abortion is a three-year jail sentence and a fine of 10,000 rupees, or U.S. $250. To date, there have been two convictions under the Prenatal Diagnostic Techniques Act, in which one individual was fined 300 rupees ($7) and another 4,000 rupees ($98).[71]

The preference for sons mean that girls are less likely than boys to be adopted. Some estimates have posited that 90 percent of abandoned infants are girls. Dark-skinned girls have even less of a chance of being adopted.[72] While couples who seek to adopt a child of either sex often receive a child within months, couples who specifically request a son often wait up to two years due to the high demand for male infants.[73]

While the Indian government has made some efforts to curb the severity of gender inequality, cultural norms and practices remain firmly rooted and will take time to eradicate. Oppressive patriarchal traditions become even more volatile when combined with modern technologies, such as ultrasound technology and reproductive alternatives, like surrogate pregnancy. Some critics question how much autonomy surrogate mothers really have in a culture in which women tend to take orders from their husbands and in-laws and therefore may be offering their surrogacy services under pressure from their families to bring in money.[74]

Indian cultural views of women and girls have led to skewed sex ratios and an oppressive imbalance in women's reproductive rights. Ethnographers maintain, however, that many such antifeminist tendencies are slowly disappearing with increasing urbanization and the gradual breakdown of the patrilocal joint-family in many regions of the country.

Conclusion: Efforts to Standardize Adoption and Surrogate Pregnancy in India

In response to pressure from the international community and the mounting numbers of destitute children in its orphanages, the Indian government in 2007 announced plans to allow more children to be adopted overseas and to speed up the adoption process. Thousands more children will be sent to Europe, the United Kingdom, and the United States. While in the past the process could take more than a year, it will now take only 45 days.[75]

Such legislative action will likely result in greater numbers of adoptions of special needs and dark-skinned children. Most Indian couples who seek to adopt domestically prefer fair-skinned, healthy newborns and will not take "tribal children." One researcher found that even individuals who were openly hostile to the concept of international adoption agreed that foreigners could serve a useful purpose by taking older, physically or mentally disabled, and dark-skinned children.[76]

The topic of surrogate pregnancy is still widely debated. Though legislation has been proposed to regulate the practice of commercial surrogacy, no official action has been taken. The Indian Medical Council does issue surrogacy guidelines however.[77] Reproductive tourism businesses have already reported marked increases in the number of inquiries into Indian surrogacy, and it will be necessary to implement a uniform set of regulations in the near future to protect all the parties involved.

GREAT BRITAIN

As one of the great world powers, Britain has historically been highly influential in global trends. At its zenith in the early 20th century, the British Empire ruled over one-quarter of the world's population, shaping everything from linguistic and cultural developments to educational and business structures. Many of the Western world's laws and legal perspectives come from the British tradition, which has been no less influential in family formation trends.

Britain is an ethnically diverse nation with varying views on family formation, gender, and children. Ethnic groups in Britain include people from Pakistan, India, Bangladesh, Africa, China, the Caribbean Islands, and Ireland. The various religious groups include Christians, Muslims, Sikhs, Hindus, Buddhists, and Jews.[78] With such wide-ranging cultural traditions and perspectives, it is not surprising that adoption and surrogate pregnancy are viewed with little uniformity.

As in the United States, adoption and surrogacy in England are viewed in light of the introduction of a third party to the process of procreation and family formation. While studies in the 1980s found that the vast majority of British respondents were not open to the concept of egg and sperm donation, later studies revealed a gradual rise in positive responses. A 2005 study found that nearly half of female respondents would be willing to donate eggs. This study also found that a positive view of egg donation and a willingness to be an egg donor correlated directly with a person's ethnic and religious background. Asian women and women who practiced a religion were found to be least likely to donate eggs.[79]

Just as public responses to adoption and surrogate pregnancy are not uniform, the laws that regulate such practices are not always uniform either. This has been particularly problematic in the areas of intercountry adoption and commercial surrogacy, and many adoption and surrogacy professionals are urging for increased standardization.

Global Role in Adoption and Surrogate Pregnancy

Britain's role in international adoption came to light most vividly in 2006 when the celebrities Guy Ritchie and Madonna attempted to adopt a 14-month-old boy from Malawi. The adoption was thwarted by human rights groups that claimed the couple had not followed the proper procedure to adopt, and studies are finding that many countries are now refusing to send children to Britain because of its reputation for disorganization and lack of regulation.[80]

As a developed nation, Britain is in much the same situation as most other "receiving" countries. A stable economy, accessible birth control and abortion services, and accepting attitudes toward unmarried parents have drastically reduced the numbers of infants available for adoption. Many British couples have turned to overseas adoption in their quest to have a child but have met with frustrating roadblocks. Researchers report fluctuating views of intercountry adoption that vary among adoption agencies and social workers, whose negative views of overseas and transracial adoption may lead them to deliberately block the adoption process. Weak central government control has done nothing to resolve this problem, leading many to pursue unauthorized adoptions.[81] One such case involved an American-born infant who was adopted by a British couple through a private Texas adoption agency in 2000. British adoption authorities later learned that the independent social worker the couple had contracted to conduct their home study had fraudulent credentials, and the infant was subsequently returned to the United States.[82] In other cases, British couples have been known to simply travel overseas, adopt a child in his or her own home country, and legalize his or her status on their return to England.[83] Such practices have likely contributed to the negative opinion that many sending countries hold of British adopters.

Another option for British couples is surrogacy. Though commercial surrogacy and advertisements for surrogates are illegal in England, altruistic surrogacy is legal, assuming no other reimbursement is paid to the surrogate other than what is necessary to cover reasonable expenses. There exists, however, no legal definition of "reasonable expenses." Thus, surrogacy in England mirrors surrogacy in the United States, in that a lack of regulation leaves room for problematic loopholes.

On a global scale, many cases of surrogacy in Britain have become widely known. One surrogate, Carole Horlock, is known as England's most prolific surrogate mother, having given birth to 12 children through surrogate pregnancy. In her most recent pregnancy, in 2008, she carried a set of triplets for a couple in Greece.[84] Other cases of surrogacy involving British couples commissioning overseas surrogates have come to international attention due to unforeseen legal problems. One such case involved an Indian couple living in England who went to India and conceived a set of twins in vitro, which were then gestated by the wife's mother. Shortly after the twins' birth, however, the new parents found themselves unable to return to England with their children. Under British law, a child born to a surrogate takes on the nationality of the surrogate mother. In this case, British law considered the twins citizens of India, and the only way for the new parents to take custody of them was to initiate official adoption proceedings.[85]

Adoption and surrogate pregnancy practices in Britain are plagued by haphazard standards of regulation and poor central oversight, leaving many people in a state of legal uncertainty and discouraging many others from pursuing these avenues.

History and Law

Family formation in Britain parallels that seen in much of the Western world. Adoption was traditionally practiced as a means of obtaining an heir, but illegitimacy remained highly stigmatized and orphans were often excluded from such arrangements. Child placement in Britain can be traced back to 1562. In 1601, the Elizabethan Poor Laws were created, which established poorhouses and almshouses for impoverished families and destitute orphans. The conditions of such dwellings were often deplorable, and children were typically beaten, forced to labor, and given little food. Under the indenture system, many orphans were placed with craftsmen and artisans to learn a trade.[86]

Similar to the pattern seen in the United States, attitudes toward children's rights and adoption began to shift with the rising popularity of psychology and the large number of infants and children orphaned during World War II. Adoption was not officially legalized in Britain until 1926, and even then the Adoption Act did not allow adopted children to inherit from their adoptive parents.[87]

Today, few infants are placed for adoption. Despite the shortage of available infants, adoption from public care remains uncommon. While there were 59,500 children in public care in March 2008, only 2,600 were placed for adoption. Some 70 percent of those adopted were under the age of four, and 92 percent were under the age of nine.[88]

In 2007, UNICEF released a report that placed Britain at the bottom in a table of child well-being among industrialized nations. The report assessed such areas as material well-being, family and peer relationships, health and safety, behavior and risks, and a child's own sense of well-being. The report's findings revealed that child poverty in Britain had doubled since 1979, with 16 percent of children coming from families that earn less than half the national average income, while 31 percent of children polled admitted to having been drunk on two or more occasions.[89] The report was released at a time of high tensions between Britain and many sending countries that refused to place children for adoption with British couples.

Traditional notions of family formation were revolutionized in 1985 with the birth of "Baby Cotton," which opened new channels of discussion on assisted reproduction and ethics. In January 1985, Kim Cotton, a 28-year-old surrogate mother, gave birth to a healthy baby girl who had been conceived via artificial insemination as per a £6,500 contract. The commissioning couple had hired Cotton anonymously through the Surrogate Parenting Centre of Great Britain. Because Cotton had sold her story to a British newspaper, authorities were alerted to the transaction, which was deemed baby selling, and Cotton was legally blocked from handing over the baby. When she refused to take the child home with her, a judge eventually ruled that the child should be given to the commissioning couple, who soon after left the country with the baby.[90] Immediately following the much-publicized case, the Surrogacy Arrangements Act of 1985 was drafted, which specified that no money may be exchanged in a surrogate pregnancy arrangement.

Characteristics of Birth Parents and Adoptive Parents

Approximately 200 infants are voluntarily relinquished for adoption by their birth parents every year in England and Wales. One study of birth mothers in Britain found that 97 percent of respondents desired basic information about the children they had placed for adoption, while 3 percent desired continued anonymity.[91] While the number of birth parents who voluntarily relinquish parental rights remains miniscule, a disproportionately high number of infants who are voluntarily relinquished have parents of South Asian origin.[92] This is likely due to cultural views of marriage and family and the stigmatization of unwed motherhood.

The Children Act of 1975 and the Adoption Act of 1976 revoked any guarantee of anonymity to birth parents and made it possible for adopted adults to obtain access to their original birth records. No provision was made for birth parents seeking information on the children they relinquished however. Some birth mothers attempted to establish their own organization, known as Jigsaw, the goal of which was the creation of a mutual consent registry whereby birth parents and adopted children could agree to contact one another. Demands from birth parents for information led to the establishment of an adoption contact register in 1989.[93]

While 14 percent of all U.S. adoptions are by relatives, the vast majority of adoptions in Britain are by people previously unknown to the child.[94] In 2007, 91 percent of the 3,200 children who were adopted from public care were adopted by married couples, while 9 percent were adopted by single individuals.[95]

While there is no upper age limit to adopting in England, those looking to adopt must be over the age of 21 and in relatively good health. In the recruitment process, social workers tend to favor adopters with certain personality characteristics, such as flexibility, determination, and patience. To much controversy, many British adoption agencies still practice race matching under the belief that "children do best when brought up in a family that reflects their ethnic and racial identity as closely as possible."[96] Luckily for children of ethnic origin, many same-race placements are now available due to increasing numbers of ethnic minority families seeking to adopt.

Characteristics of Surrogate Mothers and Contracting Parents

There are an estimated 40 surrogate births each year in England and Wales.[97] One 2003 study found that the majority of surrogate mothers who were recruited by a British surrogacy agency were approximately 34 years of age and of unskilled working-class status with families of their own; 94 percent had children at home and 67 percent were married at the time of the surrogate pregnancy. The majority of respondents (56 percent) were traditional surrogates who had been artificially inseminated and therefore were the genetic mothers of the children they carried. Twenty-one percent of the respondents were previously known to the contracting couple as a friend, sister, or relative, while 79 percent were previously unknown to the couple.[98]

Current data on the psychological effects of surrogate pregnancy and the motives of surrogate mothers suggest that women who offer to be surrogate mothers tend to be well adjusted and have positive experiences with surrogacy. An altruistic desire to help childless couples is often cited as the primary reason for becoming a surrogate.[99] Like U.S. surrogates, many British surrogates report their enjoyment of pregnancy as another motivating factor. While most U.S. surrogacy centers have a policy of providing psychological counseling both before and after pregnancy, the Vasanti Jadva et al. study of

34 British surrogate mothers found that in Britain 91 percent of respondents received no psychological counseling prior to becoming surrogates and only 12 percent received counseling after they gave birth.[100]

Contracting couples are generally motivated by infertility and a desire to have a genetically related child. This may be the case more often in Britain than elsewhere, as both domestic and international adoptions are becoming increasingly difficult, thus couples may be more likely to rely on assisted reproductive technology to achieve conception. It is estimated that between 72 and 95 percent of British couples who experience infertility seek medical assistance in conceiving.[101]

The Vasanti Jadva et al. study found that the majority of contracting parents were very involved in the pregnancy and 79 percent maintained contact with the surrogate mother following the birth of the child. Some critics have expressed concern about the possible psychological effects that may carry over into the contracting parents' ability to raise a child born through a surrogacy arrangement, but research has shown such concerns to be unwarranted. Data from one 2003 study in England suggests that families created through surrogacy arrangements may be more psychologically well adjusted and attached than families created by natural means. This same study found that mothers and fathers in surrogacy families showed greater levels of warmth and attentiveness to their children, as well as a greater overall enjoyment of parenting than non-surrogacy parents. In addition, contracting parents exhibited lower levels of stress in relation to parenting, and contracting mothers had lower levels of depression than non-surrogacy mothers.[102]

Unique Circumstances of Adoption and Surrogate Pregnancy in Britain

Britain has long been at the forefront of assisted reproductive technology. The British researchers Patrick Steptoe and Robert Edwards pioneered reproductive technology with the first successful IVF pregnancy in 1978, the results of which made it possible for couples around the world to conceive. Sentiments regarding traditional family values and structures have not necessarily kept pace with rapidly developing technologies, however, which may account for the haphazard regulation of adoption and surrogate pregnancy.

Though surrogacy contracts are not legally binding in Britain, a 2007 court battle between a surrogate mother and contracting parents over a child conceived via artificial insemination led a high court judge to uphold the surrogacy contract and remove the 18-month-old child from the surrogate mother, who was also his genetic mother, and hand him over to the contracting parents.[103] The judge's decision poses a contradiction in British law, which does not legally recognize surrogacy agreements, thereby further complicating surrogacy regulation.

Poor central oversight has also led to many irregularities within adoption practice, particularly where children of ethnic origin are involved. While Britain is an ethnically diverse nation and has made many advancements in race relations in recent years, minority children are frequently underserved in terms of adoption. Black infants under six months of age tend to wait an average of 10 months for placement, as opposed to three months for white infants, and older black children are more often placed in long-term fostering situations, while white children are more often placed for adoption.[104] Many are hopeful that such irregularities will be remedied in the future as greater uniformity develops among adoption and surrogate pregnancy regulation.

Conclusion: Efforts to Standardize Adoption and Surrogate Pregnancy

In response to concerns over the high numbers of children in foster care who are unlikely to be adopted and the psychological damage that may result from long-term public care, former prime minister Tony Blair made adoption reform one of his priorities. In 2005, Britain passed legislation that would make it possible for single people and gay couples to adopt, hoping to reduce the number of children waiting to be adopted. The act provoked ire from Catholic adoption agencies, which demanded exemption from the new law, but were denied. Reports show, however, that gay couples often wait significantly longer than heterosexual couples for foster children, as they are at the bottom of an "unspoken hierarchy" of foster care providers.[105] Jonathan Pearce, director of Adoption UK, blamed the slow rate of adoption among gay couples on a tendency among social workers to make child placement decisions based on their personal belief systems rather than the child's best interests.[106]

Little change has been made in surrogacy legislation since the Surrogacy Arrangements Act of 1985, which banned commercial surrogacy and advertisements for surrogates and contracting couples. The Adoption and Children Act of 2002, which came into effect in 2005, made it more difficult for women in Britain to act as surrogate mothers for overseas couples, as it is now illegal for anyone to take a child out of the country with the intention of adopting it in a non-British country.

As greater uniformity is achieved within adoption and surrogacy regulation, it is expected that hopeful parents and children in need of families will find greater access to information and resources.

GUATEMALA

Devastated by the longest civil war in Latin American history (1960–96), in which countless numbers of indigenous Maya were systematically massacred, Guatemala is now looking to create social stability and economic growth. Though the war ended in 1996, its effects continue to reverberate throughout the country, particularly among the thousands of orphans who are now old enough to leave the orphanage system but have few skills and no family on which to rely.

Poverty remains a persistent problem in Guatemala, which has one of the most unequal income distributions in the Western Hemisphere.[107] The wealthiest 10 percent of the population accounts for nearly half of the total income in the country, and over 30 percent of the population lives on less than two dollars a day. Some 50 percent of the population works in agriculture at the subsistence level.

In addition to crippling poverty, health and education are areas of grave concern in Guatemala, which has an infant mortality rate of 32/1,000 and a life expectancy of 69 years. Though education is compulsory, only 41 percent of children attend school and 70 percent of the total population is literate.

Such economic and social instability plays a critical role in family formation in Guatemala, which is also heavily influenced by the Catholic Church and its teachings on contraception, abortion, assisted reproduction, and same-sex relationships. The Guttmacher Institute estimates that 32 percent of all pregnancies in Guatemala are unplanned and 24 of every 1,000 pregnancies are illegally aborted. Every year, some 65,000 women seek illegal abortions, and 21,600 are hospitalized due to complications from them.[108]

Attitudes toward adoption and surrogate pregnancy are influenced by traditional gender roles and family structures. One study found a correlation between these roles (particularly male dominance and female submissiveness) and a negative perception of adoption. While most of the women studied were found to have more egalitarian attitudes toward gender roles and positive views of adoption, men who embraced traditional attitudes of masculinity and machismo were found to have negative views of adoption.[109]

Complex interactions between the culture, the political climate, and the economy have a direct influence on family formation. In 2007, human rights groups around the world protested the government's consideration of the Integral Protection for Marriage and Family Act, which would legally define a family as originating "exclusively, from the conjugal union between a man and a woman," thereby excluding single parents, same-sex parents, and children conceived through reproductive technology.[110] As of 2009, this act had not been voted on.

ADOPTION AND SURROGATE PREGNANCY

Global Role in Adoption and Surrogate Pregnancy

In 2008, Guatemala became the leading sending country for international adoptions in the United States, having long been the third to Russia and China.[111] This shift was primarily due to restrictions placed on international adoption by the Russian and Chinese governments, but Guatemala nevertheless remains unique in that fully 98 percent of all of its adoptions are international.[112] Until 2009, it was estimated that one out of every 100 children born in Guatemala was adopted by an American couple.[113]

The primary reason for such high rates of overseas adoption is the fact that there is virtually no government regulation of international adoption in Guatemala. All adoptions are privately arranged and in most cases the mother is paid anywhere from $200 to $2,000 to relinquish her infant. The private international adoption system in Guatemala consists of lawyers, baby brokers, *notarios*, pediatricians, and foster mothers. No judges or courts are involved in the process, therefore it is a self-regulating system.[114]

International adoption from Guatemala has long been riddled with controversy. Following the country's accession to the Hague Convention in November 2002, its adoption practices have come under much criticism by other signatory countries. Canada, the Netherlands, Spain, Germany, and Great Britain all discontinued international adoptions with Guatemala following its accession to the Hague Convention, claiming that its adoption practices are inconsistent with Hague standards.[115]

Concerns regarding child trafficking surfaced in 2007 when the Guatemalan government, UNICEF, and Holt International Children's Services conducted a survey of the children in Guatemalan orphanages. A total of 5,600 children were counted, 4,600 of whom were older than four. Fewer than 400 of the children were under the age of 12 months. Meanwhile, 270 infants under the age of one were adopted from Guatemala every month by American families in 2006.[116]

In 2006 and 2007, kidnapping charges began to emerge from mothers who claimed their infants had been stolen. Several kidnapped children were later found to be en route to being adopted by American families, and in September 2008 the United States discontinued international adoptions with Guatemala.

Nevertheless, hopeful parents may still consider surrogacy in Guatemala. As in India, reproductive tourism enterprises are now offering to take couples to Guatemala, where they can hire a surrogate mother at a fraction of the cost in the United States. Also similar to India, surrogate pregnancy in Guatemala is advertised as a charitable exchange: A woman in poverty with few options for survival can live in comfort with food and shelter and make more money than she ordinarily would, in return for producing a baby for a childless couple.

History and Law

In 1989, 208 Guatemalan children were adopted by American families. By 2003, this number had risen to 2,328.[117] By 2007, the number of children adopted from Guatemala into the United States more than doubled, to 4,728.[118] By 2008, international adoption was one of the largest economic sectors in Guatemala, bringing in $50 million in 2001.[119]

As concerns over trafficking began to emerge in the mid-1990s, the Guatemalan government instituted a law mandating signed statements of relinquishment as well as DNA testing to prove the parent-child relationship. To safeguard against the possibility of forged documents, the U.S. Bureau of Citizenship and Immigration Services will occasionally interview birth mothers.[120] Despite such precautions, some children have been returned to their birth mothers, who claimed to have been pressured into relinquishing their children by lawyers and baby brokers. In some cases, mothers are told that they will have monthly visitations with their children.

Recent examination of social welfare documents revealed the existence of child trafficking dating back to the early days of the nation's 36-year civil war. During the war, many children "disappeared" and were in fact sent to government-run orphanages and later sold to adoptive parents.[121]

While most Guatemalans reportedly approve of international adoption as a means of providing a family for a parentless child as well as relief for overcrowded Guatemalan orphanages, many also report rumors of organ trafficking and child abduction by gangs that roam the country. In May 2007, a mob killed two women in Camotan on suspicion that they had kidnapped and killed a young girl for her heart and kidneys.[122] Other incidents of adoption-related violence point to legal and political corruption. The disappearance of a well-known professor in April 2000 is believed to be linked to her research on illegal adoption, and some individuals report having been threatened for attempting to reclaim their children.[123]

In 2007, the U.S. embassy in Guatemala began mandating two DNA tests to verify parent-child relation, but corruption within the adoption trade prompted U.S. and Guatemalan officials to discontinue adoptions altogether in September 2008.[124] The decision left 2,286 pending adoptions in uncertainty as Guatemalan officials applied themselves to the task of examining each case to ensure that the exchange was ethical.

The status of surrogacy in Guatemala is as uncertain as that of adoption. As business Web sites advertise cheap surrogacy arrangements with Guatemalan surrogate mothers, the fertility industry in Guatemala and much of Latin America remains both unregulated and highly restrictive. In keeping with the philosophy of criminalized abortion, an embryo is legally considered an independent person and is therefore entitled to the same rights as the mother. In fertility clinics, the destruction of unused embryos and selective reduction (the act of aborting one or more fetuses in the event that too many have implanted) is punishable by imprisonment. Thus, women who undergo IVF in many Latin American countries must either use all of the embryos that have been created or donate the remainder.[125] Homosexual couples and single women face greater restrictions, as many Latin American countries prohibit assisted reproductive technologies for all but married, heterosexual couples.

A Latin American network of fertility specialists convened in Chile in 1994 to come to a consensus regarding the ethical and legal status of assisted reproductive technology. The community of specialists came to an agreement that assisted reproductive technologies would be reserved only for infertile heterosexual couples and that all cryogenically preserved embryos must be donated for adoption by other infertile couples.[126] Though there is little evidence that such guidelines are commonly enforced in Guatemala, they may prove to be a hindrance to foreign couples seeking a Guatemalan surrogate.

Characteristics of Birth Mothers and Adoptive Parents

The average child relinquished for adoption in Guatemala is the third or fourth child born into a family with other children who have not been relinquished, suggesting that the decision to terminate parental rights is often based on a lack of resources.[127] While this is a striking contrast to voluntary relinquishment in developed nations, where a relinquished child is typically a first pregnancy, it is unsurprising in a nation in which the majority of people subsist on less than two dollars a day.

Other factors may also influence a Guatemalan woman's decision to relinquish her child, such as social pressure and the stigma of single motherhood. Described as one of the most collectivist cultures in the world, Guatemalan family and community life is highly intimate, which likely complicates the decision to relinquish. As in many other cultures, a mother's decision to give up her child is an emotionally difficult one, but this may be even more difficult in Latin American cultures, where women are encouraged to embrace motherhood and nurturing roles.[128] Research suggests that the families of women who choose to relinquish, particularly in rural areas, are aware of the pregnancy and relinquishment.

Common characteristics of Guatemalan birth mothers include a life of poverty and a lack of sexual education. Pervasive religious sentiment and taboos surrounding premarital sex mean that little information on sexual health and contraception is available to Guatemalan women.

Sixty-two percent of adopted Guatemalan children go to the United States, while most of the remaining 38 percent go to Canada.[129] The vast majority of these adoptions are transracial, involving white parents, and as the average Guatemalan adoption costs between $20,000 and $30,000, most adoptive parents are probably upper middle class. This has prompted recent discussions about neocolonialism, in which wealthy white North Americans adopt and assimilate the children of poor South Americans. Until 2008, adoption from Guatemala was a highly attractive option for North American parents seeking to adopt infants, as the adoption process in Guatemala was often speedy and accommodating. While most international adoptions take upward of a year to finalize, Guatemala has been known for finalizing adoptions in as little as five months.[130] Furthermore, so many North Americans were traveling to Guatemala each year to pick up their adopted children that hotels had opened exclusively for such travelers.

Some American families have searched for their children's birth mothers to provide them with pictures and information on the children they relinquished years earlier. In some cases, the adoptive families have been able to gain knowledge about their children's medical histories while birth mothers have gained a sense of closure in the knowledge that their children are alive, healthy, and loved.[131]

Characteristics of Surrogate Mothers and Contracting Parents

As in many other countries, little information exists on surrogacy in Guatemala. Nevertheless, evidence suggests that some Guatemalan women may simply be blurring the line between adoption and surrogacy by getting pregnant and relinquishing successive children for adoption in exchange for money. In 2006, one Guatemalan birth mother was interviewed by a *Buffalo News* reporter and admitted to having relinquished the last five of her 10 children for adoption to American families. In light of such cases, one Guatemalan adoption official remarked: "When you look at the time between pregnancies and the number of children they have given up, you have to conclude they are doing it for money. What we're witnessing is a baby factory or farm, dealing with children who should not have been born or put up for adoption."[132] While situations like this are clearly not the norm, Guatemala's unstable adoption system allows for their occurrence.

Reproductive tourism businesses advertising Guatemalan surrogates guarantee medical and psychological screening of surrogates, as well as savings of tens of thousands of dollars, anonymity, and the potential for leisure and travel in a beautiful country. The Surrogacy and Fertility Law Center, which operates a Guatemalan surrogacy program, claims to serve hopeful parents who desire a genetic child of their own but simply cannot afford the high costs of surrogacy in the United States.[133]

Unique Circumstances of Adoption and Surrogate Pregnancy in Guatemala

While it is not the only country to face criticism and scrutiny over its adoption practices, Guatemala is responsible for prompting worldwide discussions over the ethics of international adoption and the exchange of money for children. While international adoption has long been perceived as a humanitarian solution to global poverty and war violence, questions are now arising as to the truth of that perception. Critics of international infant adoption point out the fact that most orphans in need of adoption are older than five, disabled, and/or victims of abuse, while healthy infants can easily be adopted within their own countries. However, because international adoption is a lucrative business, they say that little effort is made to keep families intact or to find adoptive families within a child's own culture and community. Nigel Cantwell, a consultant on child protection policy in Geneva, has openly stated that it is unlikely that international adoptions would continue to take place at all if no money was exchanged.[134]

The exchange of money for children has illuminated a number of ethical and social issues specific to Guatemala. Allegations of women being paid to get pregnant and relinquish their children to American couples prompt questions regarding the line between adoption and surrogate pregnancy. The only clear difference between a case in which a Guatemalan woman has received money to get pregnant and relinquish her child and a traditional surrogate pregnancy is social context.

As Guatemala's adoption system undergoes further examination by the global community, discussions of adoption, surrogacy, and the exchange of money may lead to more legislative action in other countries.

Conclusion: Efforts to Standardize Adoption and Surrogate Pregnancy

Following the United States' ratification of the Hague Convention in 2007, international adoptions from Guatemala were suspended to allow for a complete governmental overhaul of the adoption system. Thousands of pending cases are being systematically reexamined and birth mothers are being asked to verify their consent to the relinquishment of their children. This has also followed pressure from other Hague countries to implement Hague-consistent standards of adoption within Guatemala. If the Guatemalan government chooses to enact Hague-consistent regulations, future adoptions will be approved with judicial oversight, relatives will be given priority when placing children with families, and birth mothers will be allowed more time to change their minds.

Many have expressed concern over a complete cessation of international adoptions within Guatemala however. With so many Guatemalan children being adopted overseas, some researchers worry that a discontinuation of international adoption will leave thousands of children to languish in over-crowded orphanages. Critics of the plan to discontinue adoptions, such as Laura Beth Daly, suggest that the U.S. government establish a structured framework to assist in reforming the Guatemalan adoption system while continuing to allow adoptions of Guatemalan children by American families. Past international adoption closures by countries such as Romania and Cambodia serve as examples of the grave implications for orphans in those countries. In both cases, the cessation of international adoptions resulted not only in greater rates of child homelessness, but also a sudden degradation of living conditions for orphans residing in institutions. Unsanitary living conditions, malnourishment, and safety hazards in orphanages increased sharply in Romania and Cambodia when overseas adoptions were discontinued, which has led many to fear for the future of Guatemalan children.[135]

Though international adoptions from Guatemala have been suspended, the move is by no means permanent, and many are hopeful that the system will be reformed quickly and efficiently so that Guatemalan children can be placed with new families, whether domestically or internationally.

CONCLUSION

The countries discussed here share many connections and similarities, while maintaining distinct differences shaped by their unique cultural heritages. The ways in which adoption and surrogate pregnancy are approached in each country reveal the interconnections between family formation, culture, politics, and economy. Even more revealing are the effects that the laws and ideologies of one country have on another.

International adoption gained popularity in the United States shortly after World War II, when Harry and Bertha Holt saw a film about orphans in Korea and decided to adopt eight Korean children. Their decision was revolutionary not only because legislation had to be changed to allow them to adopt internationally (and interracially), but because their actions set a precedent: As healthy, comfortable white Americans, they accepted the responsibility of saving other countries' orphans from lives of poverty and hunger.[136] Soon after they adopted their own children from Korea, they applied themselves to the task of helping others adopt internationally.

The rise of international adoption in the United States was founded on the humanitarian desire to help the children of poverty-stricken and war-torn countries. Children were brought to the United States from other countries at war, such as Greece and Germany, and the Holts credited their Christian faith with their desire to provide families for these children.

The humanitarian legacy of international adoption continued into the 1970s, during the last days of the Vietnam War. As North Vietnamese troops invaded South Vietnam and Saigon was overtaken, thousands of South Vietnamese fled and an emergency evacuation was ordered for American troops. Shortly before the evacuation was complete, however, Operation Babylift was approved and several thousand orphaned Vietnamese infants and children were loaded onto planes and flown out of the country. Approximately 2,000 were taken to the United States and another 1,300 were flown to Canada, Australia, and Europe, where they were adopted.[137] Thus, the Vietnamese diaspora became ideologically enmeshed with international adoption and the desires of Western parents for infants and children.

As money has become an integral part of international adoption, humanitarian groups are concerned about the commercialization of adoption and the global effects of wealthy Western couples paying for infants from impoverished nations. As the demand for infants increases, more cases of baby-buying and fraud are being uncovered among sending countries, many of which have founded a thriving economic sector in international adoption. When adoptions from such countries are suspended due to human rights abuses, trends reveal that adoption agencies and hopeful parents simply shift their focus to a new "hot spot" country.[138]

As international adoption is still relatively innovative, having experienced its most profound surge in popularity only in the mid-1990s, children's rights groups and adoption authorities are hopeful that a global standardization of international adoption can be achieved. The Hague Convention was the first worldwide effort to regulate intercountry adoption, and since its creation in 1993 it has established global standards that have provided protection and safety to countless numbers of children, birth parents, and adoptive parents. At present, the choice to implement Hague standards is left to the discretion of individual countries, and as international adoption continues to thrive and expand, international pressure to comply with Hague regulations will likely lead to greater global standardization.

---

[1] U.S. Department of State. "Total Adoptions to the United States" (2008). Available online. URL: http://adoption.state.gov/news/total_chart.html. Accessed April 7, 2009.

[2] Evan B. Donald Adoption Institute. "International Adoption Facts" (2002). Available online. URL: http://www.adoptioninstitute.org/FactOverview/international.html. Accessed April 7, 2009.

[3] Peter Selman. "Trends in Intercountry Adoption: Analysis of Data from 20 Receiving Countries, 1998–2004." *Journal of Population Research* 23 (2006): 183–204.

[4] ———. "Trends in Intercountry Adoption: Analysis of Data from 20 Receiving Countries," p. 189.

[5] HCCH: Hague Conference on Private International Law. "Intercountry Adoption Section" (2009). Available online. URL: http://www.hcch.net/index_en.php?act=text. display&tid=45#parties. Accessed April 7, 2009.

[6] Annette Schmit. "The Hague Convention: The Problems with Accession and Implementation." *Indiana Journal of Global Legal Studies* 15 (winter 2008): 375–395.

[7] ———. "The Hague Convention: The Problems with Accession and Implementation," p. 380.

[8] Sara Cherian-Thomas. "Americans and Reproductive Tourism." University of Houston Law Center (2006). Available online. URL: http://www.law.uh.edu/healthlaw/perspectives/2006/ (SC-T)InfertilityAbroad.pdf. Accessed April 8, 2009.

[9] OBGYN.net: The Universe of Women's Health. "Assisted Reproduction: Tough Law on Fertility Treatments Approved by Italian Lawmakers" (3/4/04). Available online. URL: http://www. obgyn.net/newsheadlines/womens_health-Assisted_Reproduction-20040304-7.asp. Accessed April 8, 2009.

[10] Monica Lel Pais Ferrado. "Spain's Thriving 'Reproductive Tourism.'" *El Pais* (8/18/08), p. 3.

[11] The Schuster Institute for Investigative Journalism. "Adoption: China." Brandeis University, 2008–2009. Available online. URL: http://www.brandeis.edu/investigate/gender/adoption/china.html. Accessed February 3, 2009.

[12] United States Department of State. "China: Country Information" (Jan. 2009). Available online. URL: http://adoption.state.gov/country/china.html#statistics. Accessed February 3, 2009.

[13] Nili Luo and Kathleen Ja Sook Bergquist. "Born in China: Birth Country Perspectives on International Adoption." *Adoption Quarterly* 8 (2004): The Haworth Press, p. 24.

[14] Hong Zhang. "China's Rural Daughters Coming of Age: Downsizing the Family and Firing Up Cash-Earning Power in the New Economy." *Signs: Journal of Women in Culture and Society* 32 (2007): 675.

[15] Nili Luo and Kathleen Ja Sook Bergquist. "Born in China," p. 24.

[16] Anne F. Thurston. "In a Chinese Orphanage." *Atlantic Monthly* (April 1996). Available online. URL: http://www.theatlantic.com/issues/96apr/orphan/orphan.htm. Accessed February 3, 2009.

[17] United States Department of State. "China."

[18] Nili Luo and Kathleen Ja Sook Bergquist. "Born in China," p. 23.

[19] Signe Howell. *The Kinning of Foreigners: Transnational Adoption in a Global Perspective.* New York: Berghahn Books, 2006, p. 211.

[20] Nili Luo and Kathleen Ja Sook Bergquist. "Born in China," p. 24.

[21] Signe Howell. *The Kinning of Foreigners*, p. 211.

[22] Kay Johnson. "Chaobao: The Plight of Chinese Adoptive Parents in the Era of the One-Child Policy." *Cultures of Transnational Adoption*, edited by Tony Alice Volkman. Durham: Duke University Press, 2005, pp. 117–138.

[23] ———. "Chaobao," pp. 126–127.

[24] China Internet Information Center. "Gestational Surrogacy Banned in China" (June 2001). Available online. URL: http://www.china.org.cn/english/2001/Jun/15215.htm. Accessed February 5, 2009.

[25] Nili Luo and Kathleen Ja Sook Bergquist. "Born in China," p. 24.

[26] Kay Johnson, Huang Banghan, and Wang Liyao. "Infant Abandonment and Adoption in China." *Population and Development Review* 24 (Sept. 1998): 473.

[27] Nili Luo and Kathleen Ja Sook Bergquist. "Born in China," p. 24.

[28] Kay Johnson. "Chaobao," p. 130.

[29] Singe Howell. *The Kinning of Foreigners*, p. 212.

[30] Kay Johnson, Huang Banghan, and Wang Liyao. "Infant Abandonment and Adoption in China," p. 480.

[31] Singe Howell. *The Kinning of Foreigners*, p. 212.

[32] Kay Johnson, Huang Banghan, and Wang Liyao. "Infant Abandonment and Adoption in China," p. 482.

[33] ———. "Chaobao," p. 121.

[34] Zhang Tingting. "China Grapples with Legality of Surrogate Motherhood" (June 2006). Available online. URL: http://www.china.org.cn/english/2006/Jun/170442.htm. Accessed February 8, 2009.

[35] ———. "China Grapples with Legality of Surrogate Motherhood."

[36] Kay Johnson. "Chaobao," p. 130.

[37] Singe Howell. *The Kinning of Foreigners*, pp. 212–214.

[38] Julia Tao Lai Po-Wah. "Right-Making and Wrong-Making in Surrogate Motherhood: A Confucian Feminist Perspective." In *Linking Visions: Feminist Bioethics, Human Rights, and the Developing World*. Lanham: Rowman & Littlefield Publishers, 2004, p. 166.

[39] Singe Howell. *The Kinning of Foreigners*, p. 212.

[40] Nili Luo and Kathleen Ja Sook Bergquist. "Born in China," pp. 28–32.

[41] ———. "Born in China," p. 31.

[42] CNN.com. "China to Keep One-Child Policy" (March 2008). Available online. URL: http://www.cnn.com/2008/WORLD/asiapcf/03/10/china.onechild/index.html. Accessed February 9, 2009.

[43] Susan C. Seymour. *Women, Family, and Childcare in India: A World in Transition.* Cambridge: Cambridge University Press, 1999, p. 79.

Global Perspectives

[44] Aditya Bharadwaj. "Why Adoption Is Not an Option in India: the Visibility of Infertility, the Secrecy of Donor Insemination, and Other Cultural Complexities." *Social Science and Medicine* 56 (May 2003): 1,873.

[45] Cheri Register. *"Are Those Kids Yours?" American Families with Children Adopted from Other Countries.* New York: The Free Press, 1991, p. 20.

[46] Consulate General of the United States, Chennai, India. "Adoption: Introduction." Available online. URL: http://chennai.usconsulate.gov/intro.html. Accessed February 28, 2009.

[47] Signe Howell. *The Kinning of Foreigners*, p. 191.

[48] ———. *The Kinning of Foreigners*, p. 191.

[49] ———. *The Kinning of Foreigners*, p. 191.

[50] U.S. Department of State. "Total Adoptions to the United States" (2008). Available online. URL: http://adoption.state.gov/news/total_chart.html. Accessed February 28, 2009.

[51] Yoo Jin Jung. "Outsourcing Pregnancy?" *The Illinois Business Law Journal* (Feb. 2008). Available online. URL: http://iblsjournal.typepad.com/illinois_business_law_soc/2008/02/outsourcing-pre.html. Accessed February 28, 2009.

[52] EconomyWatch. "Poverty in India." Available online. URL: http://www.economywatch.com/indianeconomy/poverty-in-india.html. Accessed March 1, 2009.

[53] Aditya Bharadwaj. "Why Adoption Is Not an Option in India," p. 1,870.

[54] ———. "Why Adoption Is Not an Option in India," p. 1,875.

[55] Signe Howell. *The Kinning of Foreigners*, p. 191.

[56] Aditya Bharadwaj. "Why Adoption Is Not an Option in India," pp. 1,870–1,872.

[57] Vinita Bhargava. *Adoption in India: Policies and Experiences.* New Delhi: Sage Publications India, 2005, pp. 48–49.

[58] Signe Howell. *The Kinning of Foreigners*, p. 191.

[59] Aditya Bharadwaj. "Why Adoption Is Not an Option in India," pp. 1,876–1,877.

[60] Susan C. Seymour. *Women, Family, and Child Care in India: A World in Transition.* Cambridge: Cambridge University Press, 1999, p. 55.

[61] N. Indira Rani. "Child Care by Poor Single Mothers: Study of Mother-Headed Families in India." *Journal of Comparative Family Studies* 37 (2006): 1.

[62] Vinita Bhargava. *Adoption in India*, p. 95.

[63] ———. *Adoption in India*, p. 24.

[64] Sudha Ramachandran. "India's New Outsourcing Business: Wombs." *Asia Times Online* (June 2006). Available online. URL: http://www.atimes.com/atimes/south_asia/hf16df03.html. Accessed March 3, 2009.

[65] Amelia Gentleman. "India Nurtures Business of Surrogate Motherhood." *New York Times* (May 2008). Available online. URL: http://www.nytimes.com/2008/03/10/world/asia/10surrogate.html. Accessed March 2, 2009.

[66] ———. "India Nurtures Business of Surrogate Motherhood."

[67] Anuj Chopra. "Childless Couples Look to India for Surrogate Mothers." *Christian Science Monitor* (April 2006). Available online. URL: http://www.csmonitor.com/2006/0403/p01s04-wosc.html. Accessed March 3, 2009.

[68] ———. "Childless Couples Look to India for Surrogate Mothers."

[69] Amelia Gentleman. "India Nurtures Business of Surrogate Motherhood."

[70] S. Garg and A. Nath. "Female Feticide in India: Issues and Concerns." *Journal of Postgraduate Medicine* 54 (2008): 276–277.

[71] ———. "Female Feticide in India," p. 278.

[72] Dean Nelson. "India Pleads: Adopt Our Orphan Girls." *Sunday Times* (April 2007).

[73] Vinita Bhargava. *Adoption in India*, p. 96.

[74] Sudha Ramachandran. "India's New Outsourcing Business: Wombs."

[75] Dean Nelson. "India Pleads: Adopt Our Orphan Girls."

[76] Signe Howell. *The Kinning of Foreigners*, p. 195.

[77] Yoo Jin Jung. "Outsourcing Pregnancy?"

[78] National Statistics. "Census 2001: Ethnicity and Religion in England and Wales" (Feb. 2003). Available online. URL: http://www.statistics.gov.uk/pdfdir/ethnicity0203.pdf. Accessed March 9, 2009.

[79] S. Purewal and O. B. A. van den Akker. "British Women's Attitudes Towards Oocyte Donation: Ethnic Differences and Altruism." *Patient Education and Counseling* 64 (Nov. 2005): 43–49.

[80] Amelia Hill. "Adoption Agencies Shun UK: Developing Countries Brand British Safeguards as 'Unsuitable' for Children Who Need a Family." *Observer* (Oct. 2006). Available online. URL: www.guardian.co.uk/society/2006/oct15/adoptionandfostering.childrensservices. Accessed September 27, 2009.

[81] Peter Hayes. "Deterrents to Intercountry Adoption in Britain." *Family Relations* 49 (Oct. 2000): 465.

[82] Joanne Selinske, Dana Naughton, Kathleen Flanagan et al. "Ensuring the Best Interest of the Child in Intercountry Adoption Practice: Case Studies from the United Kingdom and the United States." *Child Welfare* 80 (2001): 660–661.

[83] Peter Hayes. "Deterrents to Intercountry Adoption in Britain," p. 465.

[84] James Mills. "Britain's Most Prolific Surrogate Mum Will Risk Her Life to Have Triplets." *Mail Online* (Jan. 2008). Available online. URL: http://www.dailymail.co.uk/news/article-505557/Britains-prolific-surrogate-mum-risk-life-triplets.html. Accessed March 10, 2009.

[85] A. Nakash and J. Herdiman. "Surrogacy." *Journal of Obstetrics and Gynaecology* 27 (April 2007): 246–247.

[86] Lonnie R. Helton and Mieko Kotake Smith. *Mental Health Practice with Children*. Binghamton, N.Y.: Haworth Press, 2004, pp. 24–25.

[87] Anthony Douglas and Terry Philpot. *Adoption: Changing Families, Changing Times*. New York: Routledge, 2003, p. 2.

[88] British Association for Adoption and Fostering. "Fostering and Adoption Statistics (England)" (2008). Available online. URL: http://www.baaf.org.uk/info/stats/england.shtml. Accessed March 9, 2009.

[89] BBC News. "UK Accused of Failing Children" (Feb. 2007). Available online. URL: http://news.bbc.co.uk/2/hi/uk_news/6359363.stm. Accessed March 14, 2009.

[90] Robert J. Edelmann. "Psychological Assessment in 'Surrogate' Motherhood Relationships." In *Surrogate Motherhood*, eds. Rachel Cook, Shelley Day Sclater, and Felicity Kaganas. Portland, Ore.: Hart Publishing, 2003, p. 146.

[91] Evan B. Donaldson Adoption Institute. "Safeguarding the Rights and Well-Being of Birthparents in the Adoption Process" (November 2006). Available online. URL: www.adoption institute.org/publications/2006Birthparentstudyrevised07.pdf. Accessed March 14, 2009.

[92] June Thoburn. "Home News and Abroad." In *Adoption: Changing Families, Changing Times*, eds. Anthony Douglas and Terry Philpot. New York: Routledge, 2003, p. 228.

[93] E. Wayne Carp. "Does Opening Adoption Records Have an Adverse Social Impact? Some Lessons from the U.S., Great Britain, and Australia, 1953–2007." *Adoption Quarterly* 10. Binghamton, N.Y.: Haworth Press, 2007, p. 41.

[94] Anthony Douglas and Terry Philpot. *Adoption: Changing Families, Changing Times*, p. 1.

[95] British Association for Adoption and Fostering. "Fostering and Adoption Statistics."

[96] ———. "First Questions: Adoption" (2009). Available online. URL: http://www.baaf.org.uk/info/firstq/adoption.shtml#whocan. Accessed March 14, 2009.

[97] Martin Hutchinson. "Surrogate Mothers Happy in Their Role." BBC News (July 2003). Available online. URL: http://news.bbc.co.uk/2/hi/health/3037912.stm. Accessed March 15, 2009.

[98] Vasanti Jadva, Clare Murray, Emma Lycett et al. "Surrogacy: The Experiences of Surrogate Mothers." *Human Reproduction* 8 (2003): 2,197.

[99] R. J. Edelmann. "Surrogacy: The Psychological Issues." *Journal of Reproductive and Infant Psychology* 22 (May 2004): 128.

[100] Vasanti Jadva, Clare Murray, Emma Lycett et al. "Surrogacy: The Experiences of Surrogate Mothers," p. 2,199.

[101] R. J. Edelmann. "Surrogacy: The Psychological Issues," p. 124.

[102] Susan E. Golombok, Clare E. Murray, Vasanti Jadva et al. "Families Created Through Surrogacy: Parent-Child Relationships in the First Year of Life." *Developmental Psychology* 40 (May 2004): 400.

[103] Clare Dyer. "Judge Warns Agencies after Surrogate Mother Dupes Couples to Keep Babies." *Guardian* (October 2007). Available online. URL: http://www.guardian.co.uk/uk/2007/oct/31/law.world. Accessed March 15, 2009.

[104] Anthony Douglas and Terry Philpot. *Adoption: Changing Families, Changing Times*. New York: Routledge, 2003, pp. 11–19.

[105] Helen Cosis Brown and Julie Cooke. "Lesbian and Gay Carers Are Kept Waiting, Experts Say." *Community Care* (May 2008): 7.

[106] Amy Taylor. "Gay Couples Overlooked in Adopters Shortage." *Community Care* (Nov. 2008). Available online. URL: http://www.communitycare.co.uk/Articles/2008/11/05/109856/gay-couples-overlooked-in-adopters-shortage.html. Accessed March 15, 2009.

[107] U.S. Department of State: Bureau of Western Hemisphere Affairs. "Guatemala." (Feb. 2009). Available online. URL: http://www.state.gov/r/pa/ei/bgn/2045.htm. Accessed March 21, 2009.

[108] Susheela Singh, Elena Prada, and Edgar Kessler. "Induced Abortion and Unintended Pregnancy in Guatemala." *Family Planning Perspectives* 32 (Sept. 2006). Available online. URL: http://www.guttmacher.org/pubs/journals/3213606.html. Accessed March 22, 2009.

[109] Judith L. Gibbons, Samantha L. Wilson, and Christine A. Rufener. "Gender Attitudes Mediate Gender Differences in Attitudes towards Adoption in Guatemala." *Sex Roles* 54 (Jan. 2006): 139–145.

[110] Scott Long. "Letter to the Guatemalan Congress Regarding Marriage and Family Law." Human Rights Watch (Sept. 2007). Available online. URL: http://www.hrw.org/en/news/2007/09/30/letter-guatemalan-congress-regarding-marriage-and-family-law. Accessed March 21, 2009.

[111] U.S. Department of State. "Total Adoptions to the United States" (2008). Available online. URL: http://adoption.state.gov/news/total_chart.html. Accessed March 21, 2009.

[112] Judith L. Gibbons, Samantha L. Wilson, and Christine A. Rufener. "Gender Attitudes Mediate Gender Differences in Attitudes Towards Adoption in Guatemala," pp. 139–145.

[113] Laura Beth Daly. "To Regulate or Not to Regulate: The Need for Compliance with International Norms by Guatemala and Cooperation by the United States in Order to Maintain Intercountry Adoptions." *Family Court Review* 45 (Oct. 2007): 621.

[114] ———. "To Regulate or Not to Regulate," p. 624.

[115] ———. "To Regulate or Not to Regulate," p. 624.

[116] E. J. Graff. "Foreign Policy: The Lie We Love." *Foreign Policy* (November/December 2008). Available online. URL: http://www.foreignpolicy.com/story/cms.php?story_id=4508&page=0. Accessed March 22, 2009.

[117] Laurie C. Miller. *The Handbook of International Adoption Medicine: A Guide for Physicians, Parents, and Providers.* New York: Oxford University Press, 2005, p. 59.

[118] U.S. Department of State. "Total Adoptions to the United States" (2008). Available online. URL: http://adoption.state.gov/news/total_chart.html. Accessed March 25, 2009.

[119] Ann Laura Stoler. *Haunted by Empire: Geographies of Intimacy in North American History.* Durham, N.C.: Duke University Press, 2006, p. 356.

[120] Laurie C. Miller. *The Handbook of International Adoption Medicine*, pp. 59–61.

[121] EFE News Service. "Files Show Guatemalan War Orphans Were Sold" (3/23/09).

[122] Rory Carroll. "Child-Trafficking Fears as Guatemalan Police Rescue 46 from House: Mothers Pressured to Put Babies up for Adoption, Illegal Agencies Target Sales to Western Parents." *Guardian* (August 2007).

[123] Ann Laura Stoler. *Haunted by Empire*, pp. 356–359.

[124] Rory Carroll. "Child-Trafficking Fears as Guatemalan Police Rescue 46 from House."

[125] Claudia Lima Marquez. "Assisted Reproductive Technology (ART) in South America and the Effect on Adoption." *Texas International Law Journal* 35 (2000): 65–91.

[126] Florencia Luna. "Assisted Reproduction in Latin America: Some Ethical and Sociocultural Issues." In *Infertility and Assisted Reproductive Technologies from a Regional Perspective*. World Health Organization (July 2006): 31–40.

[127] Laurie C. Miller. *The Handbook of International Adoption Medicine*, pp. 59–61.

[128] Judith L. Gibbons, Samantha L. Wilson, and Christine Rufener. "Gender Attitudes Mediate Gender Differences in Attitudes Towards Adoption in Guatemala." *Sex Roles* 54 (January 2006): 142.

[129] Ann Laura Stoler. *Haunted by Empire*, p. 356.

[130] Juan Carlos Llorca. "Guatemala's Poverty Breeds a Mecca for Adoptions." *Buffalo News* (7/30/06).

[131] Ellen Guettler. "Finding the Birth Mother." American RadioWorks, American Public Radio (2009). Available online. URL: http://americanradioworks.publicradio.org/features/adoption/g1.html. Accessed March 28, 2009.

[132] Juan Carlos Llorca. "Guatemala's Poverty Breeds a Mecca for Adoptions."

[133] Surrogacy and Fertility Law Center. "Surrogacy in Guatemala Infertility Options: IVF, Surrogate, Egg Donation, Embryo, Outsourcing, ICSI." Available online. URL: http://fertility surrogacy.com/default.htm. Accessed March 28, 2009.

[134] E. J. Graff. "Foreign Policy: The Lie We Love."

[135] Laura Beth Daly. "To Regulate or Not to Regulate," pp. 620–637.

[136] Holt International. "Introduction to Holt: Historical Perspective" (2009). Available online. URL: http://www.holtinternational.org/historical.shtml. Accessed April 9, 2009.

[137] Allison Martin. "Legacy of Operation Babylift." *Adoption Today* 2 (March 2000). Available online. URL: http://www.adoptvietnam.org/adoption/babylift.htm. Accessed April 9, 2009.

[138] E. J. Graff. "Foreign Policy: The Lie We Love," p. 1.

PART II

Primary Sources

4

~

United States Documents

The primary sources in this chapter are arranged in chronological order. Documents that have been excerpted are identified as such; all others are reproduced in full.

Massachusetts Adoption of Children Act (1851)

As the first adoption law passed in the United States, the Massachusetts Adoption of Children Act was drafted and implemented not only to regulate adoption, but to protect children. Prior to the Adoption of Children Act, adoptions were contractual and privately arranged, and virtually no laws existed to govern the termination or transfer of parental rights. Birth parents had unmitigated power to sell or transfer parental rights, regardless of the adoptive parents' intentions or motives. With the passage of the Adoption of Children Act, not only were both birth parents required to consent to the adoption, but the qualifications and fitness of the adoptive parents had to be reviewed and approved by a court judge, who was required to act in the best interests of the child. The Act was revolutionary for a number of reasons, the first being the basic structural shift in legislative perspectives on adoption. No longer was adoption to be considered a means of providing a fit and suitable child for a childless couple, but rather it was to be viewed as providing a family for a parentless child. Furthermore, the Act was innovative as one of the first adoption laws in the industrialized world. Many other developed nations were much slower to consider adoption legislation. Britain did not pass any adoption legislation until 1922. Some researchers have attributed progressive American laws on adoption to a general national identity based on immigration and allegiance rather than race or blood relation.

ADOPTION AND SURROGATE PREGNANCY

BE it enacted by the Senate and House of Representatives, in General Court assembled, and by the authority of the same, as follows:

Sect. 1. Any inhabitant of this Commonwealth may petition the judge of probate, in the county wherein he or she may reside, for leave to adopt a child not his or her own by birth.

Sect. 2. If both or either of the parents of such child shall be living, they or the survivor of them, as the case may be, shall consent in writing to such adoption: if neither parent be living, such consent may be given by the legal guardian of such child; if there be no legal guardian, no father nor mother, the next of kin of such child within the State may give such consent; and if there be no such next of kin, the judge of probate may appoint some discreet and suitable person to act in the proceedings as the next friend of such child, and give or withhold such consent.

Sect. 3. If the child be of the age of fourteen years or upwards, the adoption shall not be made without his or her consent.

Sect. 4. No petition by a person having a lawful wife shall be allowed unless such wife shall join therein, and no woman having a lawful husband shall be competent to present and prosecute such petition.

Sect. 5. If, upon such petition, so presented and consented to as aforesaid, the judge of probate shall be satisfied of the identity and relations of the persons, and that the petitioner, or, in case of husband and wife, the petitioners, are of sufficient ability to bring up the child, and furnish suitable nurture and education, having reference to the degree and condition of its parents, and that it is fit and proper that such adoption should take effect, he shall make a decree setting forth the said facts, and ordering that, from and after the date of the decree, such child should be deemed and taken, to all legal intents and purposes, the child of the petitioner or petitioners.

Sect. 6. A child so adopted, as aforesaid, shall be deemed, for the purposes of inheritance and succession by such child, custody of the person and right of obedience by such parent or parents by adoption, and all other legal consequences and incidents of the natural relation of parents and children, the same to all intents and purposes as if such child had been born in lawful wedlock of such parents or parent by adoption, saving only that such child shall not be deemed capable of taking property expressly limited to the heirs of the body or bodies of such petitioner or petitioners.

Sect. 7. The natural parent or parents of such child shall be deprived, by such decree of adoption, of all legal rights whatsoever as respects such child; and such child shall be freed from all legal obligations of maintenance and obedience, as respects such natural parent or parents.

Sect. 8. Any petitioner, or any child which is the subject of such a petition, by any next friend, may claim and prosecute an appeal to the supreme judicial court from such decree of the judge of probate, in like manner and with the like effect as such appeals may now be claimed and prosecuted in cases of wills, saying only that in no case shall any bond be required of, nor any costs awarded against, such child or its next friend so appealing.

Approved by the Governor, May 24, 1851.

Source: "An Act to Provide for the Adoption of Children." *Acts and Resolves Passed by the General Court of Massachusetts.* Ellen Herman. "The Adoption History Project." Department of History, University of Oregon (2007). Available online. URL: http://darkwing.uoregon.edu/~adoption/archive/CwlaMSA.htm. Accessed April 19, 2009.

Charles Loring Brace. *The Dangerous Classes of New York and Twenty Years' Work Among Them* (1872) (excerpts)

The founder of the New York Children's Aid Society in 1853, Charles Loring Brace was an early innovator in the development of social welfare work and child advocacy at a time when the only options for an orphaned or abandoned child were institutional care or an almshouse. After studying and working with street children and orphans for several years, however, Brace concluded that institutional care was not only an unsatisfactory environment for a child's development but was actually harmful and inhibitive. Brace structured his advocacy efforts around his own revolutionary notion that the most effective method of developing street children into functional and dependable members of society was to provide them with loving families, educations, and employment. Thus, the orphan trains were created. A controversial project that sought to emphasize placing out rather than institutionalizing children, the orphan trains relocated nearly 250,000 children from eastern states to the west between 1854 and 1930. The trains followed a schedule of stops, where children were placed on the platform to be claimed by families who needed extra farmhands or genuinely wanted a child. The term "put up for adoption" is derived from the act of placing a child "up" on a train platform for adoption.

Brace's work was controversial because he often targeted the children of Catholic and Jewish parents for relocation. Trained as an evangelical minister, he sought to remove children from urban Catholic and Jewish households

95

and place them in rural Protestant homes. Despite the project's title, the vast majority of the children on the Orphan Trains were not, in fact, orphans, but rather street children who Brace and his colleagues sought to separate from their parents, thereby removing them from their degenerate home environments and resettling them into more wholesome and healthy circumstances. Most of the children were eventually reunited with their parents.

We shall speak more particularly of the causes of crime in future chapters, but we may say in brief, that the young ruffians of New York are the products of accident, ignorance, and vice. Among a million people, such as compose the population of this city and its suburbs, there will always be a great number of misfortunes; fathers die, and leave their children unprovided for; parents drink, and abuse their little ones, and they float away on the currents of the street; step-mothers or step-fathers drive out, by neglect and ill-treatment, their sons from home. Thousands are the children of poor foreigners, who have permitted them to grow up without school, education, or religion. All the neglect and bad education and evil example of a poor class tend to form others, who, as they mature, swell the ranks of ruffians and criminals. So, at length, a great multitude of ignorant, untrained, passionate, irreligious boys and young men are formed, who become the "dangerous class" of our city. They form the "Nineteenth-street Gangs," the young burglars and murderers, the garroters and rioters, the thieves and flash-men, the "repeaters" and ruffians, so well known to all who know this metropolis.

. . .

The Causes of Crime.

THE great practical division of causes of crime may be made into preventible and non-preventible. Among the preventible, or those which can be in good part removed, may be placed ignorance, intemperance, over-crowding of population, want of work, idleness, vagrancy, the weakness of the marriage-tie, and bad legislation.

Among those which cannot be entirely removed are inheritance, the effects of emigration, orphanage, accident or misfortune, the strength of the sexual and other passions, and a natural weakness of moral or mental powers.

Ignorance.

There needs hardly a word to be said in this country on the intimate connection between ignorance and crime.

The precise statistical relation between them in the State of New York would seem to be this: about thirty-one per cent. of the adult criminals cannot read or write, while of the adult population at large about six (6.08) per cent. are illiterate; or nearly one-third of the crime is committed by six-hundredths of the population. In the city prisons for 1870, out of 49,423 criminals, 18,442 could not write and could barely read, or more than thirty-three per cent.

. . .

Orphanage.

Out of 452 criminal children received into the House of Refuge in New York during 1870, only 187 had both parents living, so that nearly sixty per cent. had lost one or both of their parents, or were otherwise separated from them.

According to Dr. Bittinger, of the 7,963 inmates of the reformatories in the United States in 1870, fifty-five per cent. were orphans or half orphans.

. . .

Emigration.

There is no question that the breaking of the ties with one's country has a bad moral effect, especially on a laboring class. The Emigrant is released from the social inspection and judgment to which he has been subjected at home, and the tie of church and priesthood is weakened. If a Roman Catholic, he is often a worse Catholic, without being a better Protestant. If a Protestant, he often becomes indifferent. Moral ties are loosened with the religious. The intervening process which occurs here, between his abandoning the old state of things and fitting himself to the new, is not favorable to morals or character.

. . .

Of the 49,423 prisoners in our city prisons, in prison for one year before January, 1870, 32,225 were of foreign birth, and, no doubt, a large proportion of the remainder of foreign parentage. Of the foreign-born, 21,887 were from Ireland; and yet at home the Irish are one of the most law-abiding and virtuous of populations—the proportion of criminals being smaller than in England or Scotland.

. . .

Want of a Trade.

It is remarkable how often, in questioning the youthful convicts in our prisons as to the causes of their downfall, they will reply that "if they had had a trade, they would not have been there." They disliked drudgery, they found places in offices and shops crowded; they would have enjoyed the companionship and the inventiveness of a trade, but they could not obtain one, and therefore they were led into stealing or gambling, as a quick mode of earning a living.

There is no doubt that a lad with a trade feels a peculiar independence of the world, and is much less likely to take up dishonest means of living than one depending on manual labor, or chance means of living.

. . .

Of course, if such a lad would walk forth to the nearest country village, he would find plenty of healthy and remunerative employment in the ground, as gardener or farmer. And to a country-lad, the farm offers a better chance than a trade. But many city boys and young men will not consent to leave the excitements of the city, so that the want of a mechanical occupation does expose them to many temptations.

. . .

The effort to place the city-children of the street in country families revealed a spirit of humanity and kindness, throughout the rural districts, which was truly delightful to see. People bore with these children of poverty, sometimes, as they did not with their own. There was—and not in one or two families alone—a sublime spirit of patience exhibited toward these unfortunate little creatures, a bearing with defects and inherited evils, a forgiving over and over again of sins and wrongs, which showed how deep a hold the spirit of Christ had taken of many of our countrywomen.

. . .

Having found the defects of our first plan of emigration, we soon inaugurated another, which has since been followed out successfully during nearly twenty years of constant action.

We formed little companies of emigrants, and, after thoroughly cleaning and clothing them, put them under a competent agent, and, first selecting a village where there was a call or opening for such a party, we dispatched them to the place.

The farming community having been duly notified, there was usually a dense crowd of people at the station, awaiting the arrival of the youthful travelers. The sight of the little company of the children of misfortune always touched the hearts of a population naturally generous. They were soon billeted around among the citizens, and the following day a public meeting was called in the church or town-hall, and a committee appointed of leading citizens. The agent then addressed the assembly, stating the benevolent objects of the Society, and something of the history of the children. The sight of their worn faces was a most pathetic enforcement of his arguments. People who were childless came forward to adopt children; others, who had not intended to take any into their families, were induced to apply for them; and many who really wanted the children's labor pressed forward to obtain it.

In every American community, especially in a Western one, there are many spare places at the table of life. There is no harassing "struggle for existence." They have enough for themselves and the stranger too. Not, perhaps, thinking of it before, yet, the orphan being placed in their presence without friends or home, they gladly welcome and train him. The committee decide on the applications. Sometimes there is almost a case for Solomon before them. Two eager mothers without children claim some little waif thus cast on the strand before them. Sometimes the family which has taken in a fine lad for the night feels that it cannot do without him, and yet the committee prefer a better home for him. And so hours of discussion and selection pass. Those who are able, pay the fares of the children, or otherwise make some gift to the Society, until at length the business of charity is finished, and a little band of young wayfarers and homeless rovers in the world find themselves in comfortable and kind homes, with all the boundless advantages and opportunities of the Western farmer's life about them.

Source: Charles Loring Brace. *The Dangerous Classes of New York and Twenty Years' Work Among Them.* New York: Wynkoup & Hallenbeck, 1872, pp. 28–38, 230.

Child Welfare League of America. "Minimum Safeguards in Adoption" (1938)

Concerns over haphazard adoption regulations led many to demand minimum standards within the adoption process. As social work was still a developing professional field at the beginning of the 20th century, adoptions could be arranged by virtually anyone. Private adoptions were often arranged by baby farmers, whose aim to turn a profit led to the abuse and malnourishment of many of the children in their care. Advocates of minimum standards petitioned for the certification of individuals placing children, as well as investigation into the adoptability of a child and the suitability of adoptive parents.

In 1917, Minnesota passed legislation that implemented minimum standards of adoption by requiring the assessment of parents' and children's suitability to adopt and be adopted before adoptions could be finalized. Under Minnesota law, an adoption could be annulled within the first five years if one of these minimum standards was not met, such as the later discovery of a child's "feeblemindedness" or disease.

Soon after Minnesota enacted minimum standards legislation, other states followed suit, and within a few years nearly all 50 states had implemented legislation that required certification of individuals placing children and investigation into child and parent suitability prior to adoptions being finalized. Minimum standards of adoption paved the way for better record-keeping and supervision of adoptive families after placement. In endeavoring to protect children and families, child advocates and adoption reformers sought to standardize child welfare on a nationwide scale.

I. The safeguards that the child should be given are:

1. That he be not unnecessarily deprived of his kinship ties.

2. That the family asking for him have a good home and good family life to offer and that the prospective parents be well adjusted to each other.

3. That he is wanted for the purpose of completing an otherwise incomplete family group, in which he will be given support, education, loving care, and the feeling of security to which any child is entitled.

II. The safeguards that the adopting family should expect are:

1. That the identity of the adopting parents should be kept from the natural parents.

2. That the child have the intelligence and the physical and mental background to meet the reasonable expectations of the adopting parents.

3. That the adoption proceedings be completed without unnecessary publicity.

III. The safeguards that the state should require for its own and the child's protection are:

1. That the adopting parents should realize that in taking the child for adoption they assume as serious and permanent an obligation as do parents rearing their own children, including the right to inherit.

2. That there be a trial period of residence of reasonable length for the best interests of the family and the child whether there be a legal requirement for it or not.

3. That the adoption procedure be sufficiently flexible to avoid encouragement of illegitimacy on the one hand and trafficking in babies on the other.

4. That the birth records of an adopted child be so revised as to shield him from unnecessary embarrassment in case of illegitimacy.

These safeguards are best provided to the natural parents and also to those asking adoption if they turn to a well established children's organization which has a reputation in this field for good advice and good results.

Source: Child Welfare League of America. "Minimum Safeguards in Adoption" (1938). Ellen Herman. "The Adoption History Project." Department of History, University of Oregon (2007). Available online. URL: http://darkwing. uoregon.edu/~adoption/archive/CwlaMSA.htm. Accessed April 19, 2009.

Noel P. Keane and Dennis L. Breo. *The Surrogate Mother* (1981) (excerpts)

The lawyer Noel Keane became famous in the late 1970s for drafting the first official contract between a surrogate mother and a commissioning couple. In his book, The Surrogate Mother, *Keane discusses not only how he began his surrogacy practice, but the fact that surrogate pregnancies were being arranged outside of legal definition or regulation for years before he drafted a surrogacy contract. Prior to Keane's work, several couples and surrogate mothers in the United States had already arranged surrogate pregnancies without legal or medical help by performing their own artificial inseminations. It was not until one couple came to him for legal help in procuring a surrogate mother that Keane became involved.*

One of the first obstacles to Keane's surrogacy enterprise was the issue of payment. It was illegal to pay a woman to carry a child and terminate her parental rights in Michigan, where his offices were located, and while many women were willing to be surrogate mothers for a fee, very few were willing to do so as unpaid volunteers. Keane moved his practice to Florida, which had no laws regarding the payment of money for a baby, and went on to establish surrogacy centers in California, Indiana, New York, and Nevada. By the mid-1980s, Keane's surrogacy practice was grossing $600,000 a year.

ADOPTION AND SURROGATE PREGNANCY

Keane arranged the surrogate pregnancies in his offices, where surrogates were brought together with infertile couples. The commissioning couple was assigned to an office, through which hopeful surrogates and their own babies (proof of their fertility) were rotated for the couple's assessment. Couples could expect to pay a $10,000 fee to the surrogate, another $10,000 fee for Keane's services, and an additional $5,000 for the surrogate's medical expenses. Never shy of public attention, Keane and several of his surrogates and couples made the talk show circuit, appearing on shows like the Phil Donohue Show *to bring attention to surrogacy. Noel Keane died of melanoma in 1997.*

Introduction
"Noel, you're onto something really big."

Before the celebrity and the cause, there were simply people who needed help.

A woman sat across from my desk and cried. That's how it started, my strange career as the legal champion of "surrogate mothers," a revolutionary new source of hope for infertile couples.

The woman had been everywhere and tried everything, but nothing had changed. She was now thirty-eight, her husband thirty-six, and still, the experts told her, they could not have children. She cried and he squirmed, and they asked for help in curing their infertility.

Incredibly, though, they not only asked for help, but they also had an idea, an idea that at the time I thought very weird.

We'll call them Tom and Jane. They had been married eleven years, and they were living a life of agony. This was their last chance for happiness. They asked me this question:

"Can you help us find a very rare woman? A woman who will legally agree—perhaps for a fee, perhaps for medical expenses only—to be artificially inseminated with Tom's sperm, conceive and carry a child, give birth, and surrender the child for adoption?"

I did not believe it possible then, but I tried. We did find such a woman and today, Tom and Jane have a life enriched by Tommy Jr., their adopted child born to surrogate mother Carol.

At that time, we had never heard of the term "surrogate mother." The news media would later force that phrase upon us. We found Carol through a classified newspaper ad asking for a "female donor for test-tube baby." We placed a newspaper ad because that was the way it had been done in the past. It was the only precedent we had ever heard about, a precedent that occurred in, where else but, California.

102

That was five years ago. Today, that "weird" idea is the basis of a powerful new option that may replace adoption as the major hope for the infertile: the surrogate mother.

Surrogate parenting means finding a woman who will legally contract with a married couple to be artificially inseminated with the husband's sperm, conceive and carry a child, give birth, and surrender custody for adoption. Exactly what Tom and Jane and Carol did years ago to bring Tommy, Jr. into the world.

By the end of 1981, there will be about a hundred children born to surrogate mothers and adopted by others. Ordinary people, extraordinary births, brave new children. These are children who are truly wanted.

This book represents the first comprehensive look at surrogate parenting, its promise and potential perils. It fully discusses the dimensions of the controversy and outlines recommendation for state regulation of the phenomenon.

. . .

Carol carried Tom's baby for Tom and Jane out of love. She was not paid a fee and she never entered into a legal contract. Neither was necessary. Their experience started what has become a movement. Some things have changed from that time, though. Now most people pay fees and almost all sign contracts. The basic elements of the surrogate mother situation, however, remain the same.

Despair. One of every six American couples is infertile. That's roughly twenty million Americans unable to bring a child into the world. And those who want children but cannot have them are often desperate. There are thousands of people out there like Tom and Jane; the question they ask is whether there are other people out there to help them like Carol helped Tom and Jane. My answer is yes.

. . .

But as we proceed with the story, try to understand why I got started in this new field of law. Because it is really very simple. Desperate people came to me in pain with their problems and I decided to try to help.

Our potential clients are the 15 percent of the population who cannot have children. Those who want to take life can turn to abortion. Those unfortunate people who want to create life yet cannot do not have such a simple solution. The waiting list to adopt is often seven years or more, and even then there is not guarantee that a child will be available. Surrogate mothers provide another source of children for the infertile.

. . .

Obviously, there is a demand for the surrogate mother. But how about the supply? Why would a woman want to become a surrogate mother? There are many reasons.

Money, of course, is one. We are paying many of our surrogate mothers $10,000, which we think is a reasonable fee for the time and hardship of pregnancy. In Michigan, however, where I practice law, the payment of a fee to a surrogate mother is currently illegal if there is to be an adoption. So most of my cases so far have involved volunteer surrogate mothers, women who have done it simply for medical expenses. The exceptions have been single men, who, of course, are already the child's father and therefore do not need to adopt.

. . .

Money, however, is not the only reason. Women are volunteering to be surrogate mothers—without a fee—for all the reasons women want to have babies. Among my early clients, one did it out of sincere love for a friend, another as a private protest against abortion, a third to have the experience of giving birth.

With surrogate mothers, we are talking about giving life. Those who want to deny life can practice contraception or obtain an abortion. Previously, barren couples and single people have had few places to turn. Now, for the first time, the childless have the opportunity of hiring a surrogate mother.

Source: Noel P. Keane and Dennis L. Breo. *The Surrogate Mother.* New York: Everest House, 1981, pp. 11–17.

Multiethnic Placement Act, Title V, Part E, Subpart 1 of P.L. 103-382 (1994) (excerpt)

The topic of transracial adoption has frequently met with controversy as advocates and opponents debate its social, political, and emotional effects. Around the middle of the century, families like the Holts and the Dosses began adopting internationally and transracially, directly flouting sensitive notions of silence and secrecy, and boldly announcing their families' adoptive status. Such actions incited debate over the merits of transracial adoption, in particular the adoption of African-American children by white parents. Today, advocates of transracial adoption argue that transracial adoption should be encouraged to reduce the

*length of time minority children spend in foster care awaiting permanent place-
ment, and the Multiethnic Placement Act (MEPA) supports the same. In 2004,
African-American children spent an average of three years in foster care, while
white children waited for an average of two years. Prior to the MEPA, minority
children could wait even longer while adoption agencies searched for parents
of the same race, of which there was often a shortage as many agencies focused
their efforts on recruiting white families.*

*Opponents of transracial adoption argue that the placement of minority
children with white parents is an act of cultural genocide and an attempt to
"anglicize" ethnic minority groups. Such a claim is not made lightly or without
historical evidence of such efforts. In the 19th century, droves of Native American children were forcibly removed from their families and tribes and sent
to boarding schools to be "Americanized." In 1978, the Indian Child Welfare
Act put an end to the adoption of Native American children by white families
under the claim that Native children are cultural resources. Other minority
groups have attempted to make the same claim, without success.*

*MEPA was designed to reduce the length of time children spent in foster
care awaiting adoption, eliminate discriminatory race-matching practices,
and recruit more ethnic minority families to adopt. The most socially significant aspect of MEPA is the prohibition of denying, delaying, or making a
placement based on race or national origin of the child or adoptive parents.
The act also made a violation of MEPA a violation of Title VI of the Civil
Rights Act.*

Part E—Multiethnic Placement
Subpart 1—Multiethnic Placement
[*551] Sec. 551. <42 USC 5115a note> SHORT TITLE.

This subpart may be cited at the "Howard M. Metzenbaum Multiethnic
Placement Act of 1994".

[*552] Sec. 552. FINDINGS AND PURPOSE.

(a) Findings.—The Congress finds that—
(1) nearly 500,000 children are in foster care in the United States;
(2) tens of thousands of children in foster care are waiting for
adoption;
(3) 2 years and 8 months is the median length of time that children
wait to be adopted;
(4) child welfare agencies should work to eliminate racial, ethnic, and
national origin discrimination and bias in adoption and foster care recruitment, selection, and placement procedures; and

(5) active, creative, and diligent efforts are needed to recruit foster and adoptive parents of every race, ethnicity, and culture in order to facilitate the placement of children in foster and adoptive homes which will best meet each child's needs.

(b) Purpose.—It is the purpose of this subpart to promote the best interests of children by—
 (1) decreasing the length of time that children wait to be adopted;
 (2) preventing discrimination in the placement of children on the basis of race, color, or national origin; and
 (3) facilitating the identification and recruitment of foster and adoptive families that can meet children's needs.

[*553] Sec. 553. <42 USC 5115a> MULTIETHNIC PLACEMENTS.

(a) Activities.—
 (1) Prohibition.—An agency, or entity, that receives Federal assistance and is involved in adoption or foster care placements may not—
 (A) categorically deny to any person the opportunity to become an adoptive or a foster parent, solely on the basis of the race, color, or national origin of the adoptive or foster parent, or the child, involved; or
 (B) delay or deny the placement of a child for adoption or into foster care, or otherwise discriminate in making a placement decision, solely on the basis of the race, color, or national origin of the adoptive or foster parent, or the child, involved.
 (2) Permissible consideration.—An agency or entity to which paragraph (1) applies may consider the cultural, ethnic, or racial background of the child and the capacity of the prospective foster or adoptive parents to meet the needs of a child of this background as one of a number of factors used to determine the best interests of a child.
 (3) Definition.—As used in this subsection, the term "placement decision" means the decision to place, or to delay or deny the placement of, a child in a foster care or an adoptive home, and includes the decision of the agency or entity involved [**4057] to seek the termination of birth parent rights or otherwise make a child legally available for adoptive placement.

(b) Equitable Relief.—Any individual who is aggrieved by an action in violation of subsection (a), taken by an agency or entity described in subsection (a), shall have the right to bring an action seeking relief in a United States district court of appropriate jurisdiction.

(c) Federal Guidance.—Not later than 6 months after the date of the enact-ment of this Act, the Secretary of Health and Human Services shall publish guidance to concerned public and private agencies and entities with respect to compliance with this subpart.

(d) Deadline for Compliance.—

(1) In general.—Except as provided in paragraph (2), an agency or entity that receives Federal assistance and is involved with adoption or fos-ter care placements shall comply with this subpart not later than six months after publication of the guidance referred to in subsection (c), or one year after the date of enactment of this Act, whichever occurs first.

(2) Authority to extend deadline.—If a State demonstrates to the satis-faction of the Secretary that it is necessary to amend State statutory law in order to change a particular practice that is inconsistent with this subpart, the Secretary may extend the compliance date for the State a reasonable number of days after the close of the first State legislative session beginning after the date the guidance referred to in subsection (c) is published.

(e) Noncompliance Deemed a Civil Rights Violation.—Noncompliance with this subpart is deemed a violation of title VI of the Civil Rights Act of 1964.

(f) No Effect on Indian Child Welfare Act of 1978.—Nothing in this section shall be construed to affect the application of the Indian Child Welfare Act of 1978 (25 U.S.C. 1901 et seq.).

Source: Child Welfare Information Gateway. "Multiethnic Placement Act of 1994, P.L. 103-382." Available online. URL: basis.caliber.com/cwig/w:library/docs/gateway/Blob/56379.pdf?rpp-10&upp-&m=1&w+NATIVE%28%2TRE CNO%3D56379%27%29&r=1. Accessed September 27, 2009.

New Jersey Supreme Court. "In the Matter of Baby M, a Pseudonym for an Actual Person" (1988) (Excerpts)

In 1986, A New Jersey housewife and mother Mary Beth Whitehead gave birth to a healthy baby girl who would later become the center of a sensational-ized court battle that would not only call into question the rights of surrogate mothers and contracting parents, but the ethics of surrogate pregnancy and the legal status of surrogacy contracts.

Mary Beth Whitehead was employed as a surrogate by one of Noel Keane's surrogacy centers in New Jersey, where she met William and Elizabeth Stern, a moderately wealthy couple who did not want to conceive on their own for fear that pregnancy would aggravate Elizabeth's self-diagnosed multiple sclerosis. Mary Beth Whitehead was artificially inseminated with William Stern's sperm, conceived, and later gave birth to a baby girl. Intense misgivings and second thoughts led to Mary Beth's refusal to relinquish the baby, and the Sterns pursued legal action. The trial court decided the dispute in favor of the Sterns, and the judge ordered that the contract be enforced and Mary Beth Whitehead's parental rights be terminated against her will. The case later went to the New Jersey Supreme Court, which reversed the trial court's decision based on the illegal nature of exchanging money for an infant. The Sterns were found to be more capable parents, and custody of baby Melissa remained with them, while Mary Beth Whitehead was awarded visitation rights.

The case of Baby M brought worldwide attention to the complexity of surrogate pregnancy and the problem of advanced reproductive technology coupled with an outdated legal system. The definition of motherhood is also called into question, particularly when considering the language of surrogate pregnancy. In this case, the media, the trial court, and the surrogacy community gave the natural mother the misnomer of "surrogate," a term that framed the entire court battle and gave Mary Beth Whitehead the predetermined definition of substitute or stand-in mother, when she was, in fact, the natural mother.

The problems encountered in the Baby M case prompted many lawmakers to introduce legislation that would regulate, if not outright prohibit, the practice of surrogacy, but to date few surrogacy laws have been implemented due to the private and sensitive nature of family formation.

In this matter the Court is asked to determine the validity of a contract that purports to provide a new way of bringing children into a family. For a fee of $10,000, a woman agrees to be artificially inseminated with the semen of another woman's husband; she is to conceive a child, carry it to term, and after its birth surrender it to the natural father and his wife. The intent of the contract is that the child's natural mother will thereafter be forever separated from her child. The wife is to adopt the child, and she and the natural father are to be

[109 NJ Page 411]

regarded as its parents for all purposes. The contract providing for this is called a "surrogacy contract," the natural mother inappropriately called the "surrogate mother."

[32] We invalidate the surrogacy contract because it conflicts with the law and public policy of this State. While we recognize the depth of the yearning of infertile couples to have their own children, we find the payment of money

to a "surrogate" mother illegal, perhaps criminal, and potentially degrading to women. Although in this case we grant custody to the natural father, the evidence having clearly proved such custody to be in the best interests of the infant, we void both the termination of the surrogate mother's parental rights and the adoption of the child by the wife/stepparent. We thus restore the "surrogate" as the mother of the child. We remand the issue of the natural mother's visitation rights to the trial court, since that issue was not reached below and the record before us is not sufficient to permit us to decide it de novo.

[33] We find no offense to our present laws where a woman voluntarily and without payment agrees to act as a "surrogate" mother, provided that she is not subject to a binding agreement to surrender her child. Moreover, our holding today does not preclude the Legislature from altering the current statutory scheme, within constitutional limits, so as to permit surrogacy contracts. Under current law, however, the surrogacy agreement before us is illegal and invalid.

[34] I.

[35] FACTS

[36] In February 1985, William Stern and Mary Beth Whitehead entered into a surrogacy contract. It recited that Stern's wife, Elizabeth, was infertile, that they wanted a child, and that Mrs. Whitehead was willing to provide that child as the mother with Mr. Stern as the father.

[109 NJ Page 412]

The contract provided that through artificial insemination using Mr. Stern's sperm, Mrs. Whitehead would become pregnant, carry the child to term, bear it, deliver it to the Sterns, and thereafter do whatever was necessary to terminate her maternal rights so that Mrs. Stern could thereafter adopt the child. Mrs. Whitehead's husband, Richard, was also a party to the contract; Mrs. Stern was not. Mr. Whitehead promised to do all acts necessary to rebut the presumption of paternity under the Parentage Act. N.J.S.A. 9:17 -43a(1), -44a. Although Mrs. Stern was not a party to the surrogate agreement, the contract gave her sole custody of the child in the event of Mr. Stern's death. Mrs. Stern's status as a nonparty to the surrogate parenting agreement presumably was to avoid the application of the baby-selling statute to this arrangement. N.J.S.A. 9:3-54.

[37] Mr. Stern, on his part, agreed to attempt the artificial insemination and to pay Mrs. Whitehead $10,000 after the child's birth, on its delivery to him. In a separate contract, Mr. Stern agreed to pay $7,500 to the Infertility

Center of New York ("ICNY"). The Center's advertising campaigns solicit surrogate mothers and encourage infertile couples to consider surrogacy. ICNY arranged for the surrogacy contract by bringing the parties together, explaining the process to them, furnishing the contractual form, and providing legal counsel.

. . .

[41] Both parties, undoubtedly because of their own self-interest, were less sensitive to the implications of the transaction than they might otherwise have been. Mrs. Whitehead, for instance, appears not to have been concerned about whether the Sterns would make good parents for her child; the Sterns, on their part, while conscious of the obvious possibility that surrendering

[109 NJ Page 414]

the child might cause grief to Mrs. Whitehead, overcame their qualms because of their desire for a child. At any rate, both the Sterns and Mrs. Whitehead were committed to the arrangement; both thought it right and constructive.

[42] Mrs. Whitehead had reached her decision concerning surrogacy before the Sterns, and had actually been involved as a potential surrogate mother with another couple. After numerous unsuccessful artificial inseminations, that effort was abandoned. Thereafter, the Sterns learned of the Infertility Center, the possibilities of surrogacy, and of Mary Beth Whitehead. The two couples met to discuss the surrogacy arrangement and decided to go forward. On February 6, 1985, Mr. Stern and Mr. and Mrs. Whitehead executed the surrogate parenting agreement. After several artificial inseminations over a period of months, Mrs. Whitehead became pregnant. The pregnancy was uneventful and on March 27, 1986, Baby M was born.

[43] Not wishing anyone at the hospital to be aware of the surrogacy arrangement, Mr. and Mrs. Whitehead appeared to all as the proud parents of a healthy female child. Her birth certificate indicated her name to be Sara Elizabeth Whitehead and her father to be Richard Whitehead. In accordance with Mrs. Whitehead's request, the Sterns visited the hospital unobtrusively to see the newborn child.

[44] Mrs. Whitehead realized, almost from the moment of birth, that she could not part with this child. She had felt a bond with it even during pregnancy. Some indication of the attachment was conveyed to the Sterns at

the hospital when they told Mrs. Whitehead what they were going to name the baby. She apparently broke into tears and indicated that she did not know if she could give up the child. She talked about how the baby looked like her other daughter, and made it clear that she was experiencing great difficulty with the decision.

[45] Nonetheless, Mrs. Whitehead was, for the moment, true to her word. Despite powerful inclinations to the contrary, she

[109 NJ Page 415]

turned her child over to the Sterns on March 30 at the Whiteheads' home.

[46] The Sterns were thrilled with their new child. They had planned extensively for its arrival, far beyond the practical furnishing of a room for her. It was a time of joyful celebration—not just for them but for their friends as well. The Sterns looked forward to raising their daughter, whom they named Melissa. While aware by then that Mrs. Whitehead was undergoing an emotional crisis, they were as yet not cognizant of the depth of that crisis and its implications for their newly enlarged family.

[47] Later in the evening of March 30, Mrs. Whitehead became deeply disturbed, disconsolate, stricken with unbearable sadness. She had to have her child. She could not eat, sleep, or concentrate on anything other than her need for her baby. The next day she went to the Sterns' home and told them how much she was suffering.

[48] The depth of Mrs. Whitehead's despair surprised and frightened the Sterns. She told them that she could not live without her baby, that she must have her, even if only for one week, that thereafter she would surrender her child. The Sterns, concerned that Mrs. Whitehead might indeed commit suicide, not wanting under any circumstances to risk that, and in any event believing that Mrs. Whitehead would keep her word, turned the child over to her. It was not until four months later, after a series of attempts to regain possession of the child, that Melissa was returned to the Sterns, having been forcibly removed from the home where she was then living with Mr. and Mrs. Whitehead, the home in Florida owned by Mary Beth Whitehead's parents.

· · ·

[58] Mrs. Whitehead contends that the surrogacy contract, for a variety of reasons, is invalid. She contends that it conflicts with public policy since it

guarantees that the child will not have the nurturing of both natural parents—presumably New Jersey's goal for families. She further argues that it deprives the mother of her constitutional right to the companionship of her child, and that it conflicts with statutes concerning termination of parental rights and adoption. With the contract thus void, Mrs. Whitehead claims primary custody (with visitation rights in Mr. Stern) both on a best interests basis (stressing the "tender years" doctrine) as well as on the policy basis of discouraging surrogacy contracts. She maintains that even if custody would ordinarily go to Mr. Stern, here it should be awarded to Mrs. Whitehead to deter future surrogacy arrangements.

[59] In a brief filed after oral argument, counsel for Mrs. Whitehead suggests that the standard for determining best interests where the infant resulted from a surrogacy contract is that the child should be placed with the mother absent a showing of unfitness. All parties agree that no expert testified that Mary Beth Whitehead was unfit as a mother; the trial court expressly found that she was not "unfit," that, on the contrary, "she is a good mother for and to her older children," 217 N.J. Super. at 397; and no one now claims anything to the contrary.

[60] One of the repeated themes put forth by Mrs. Whitehead is that the court's initial ex parte order granting custody to the Sterns during the trial was a substantial factor in the ultimate

[109 NJ Page 420]

"best interests" determination. That initial order, claimed to be erroneous by Mrs. Whitehead, not only established Melissa as part of the Stern family, but brought enormous pressure on Mrs. Whitehead. The order brought the weight of the state behind the Sterns' attempt, ultimately successful, to gain possession of the child. The resulting pressure, Mrs. Whitehead contends, caused her to act in ways that were atypical of her ordinary behavior when not under stress, and to act in ways that were thought to be inimical to the child's best interests in that they demonstrated a failure of character, maturity, and consistency. She claims that any mother who truly loved her child might so respond and that it is doubly unfair to judge her on the basis of her reaction to an extreme situation rarely faced by any mother, where that situation was itself caused by an erroneous order of the court. Therefore, according to Mrs. Whitehead, the erroneous ex parte order precipitated a series of events that proved instrumental in the final result.

[61] The Sterns claim that the surrogacy contract is valid and should be enforced, largely for the reasons given by the trial court. They claim a constitutional right of privacy, which includes the right of procreation, and

the right of consenting adults to deal with matters of reproduction as they see fit. As for the child's best interests, their position is factual: given all of the circumstances, the child is better off in their custody with no residual parental rights reserved for Mrs. Whitehead.

. . .

[65] INVALIDITY AND UNENFORCEABILITY OF SURROGACY CONTRACT

[66] We have concluded that this surrogacy contract is invalid. Our conclusion has two bases: direct conflict with existing

[109 NJ Page 422]

statutes and conflict with the public policies of this State, as expressed in its statutory and decisional law.

[67] One of the surrogacy contract's basic purposes, to achieve the adoption of a child through private placement, though permitted in New Jersey "is very much disfavored." Sees v. Baber, 74 N.J. 201, 217 (1977). Its use of money for this purpose—and we have no doubt whatsoever that the money is being paid to obtain an adoption and not, as the Sterns argue, for the personal services of Mary Beth Whitehead—is illegal and perhaps criminal. N.J.S.A. 9:3–54. In addition to the inducement of money, there is the coercion of contract: the natural mother's irrevocable agreement, prior to birth, even prior to conception, to surrender the child to the adoptive couple. Such an agreement is totally unenforceable in private placement adoption. Sees, 74 N.J. at 212–14. Even where the adoption is through an approved agency, the formal agreement to surrender occurs only after birth (as we read N.J.S.A. 9:2–16 and –17, and similar statutes), and then, by regulation, only after the birth mother has been offered counseling. N.J.A.C. 10:121A–5.4(c). Integral to these invalid provisions of the surrogacy contract is the related agreement, equally invalid, on the part of the natural mother to cooperate with, and not to contest, proceedings to terminate her parental rights, as well as her contractual concession, in aid of the adoption, that the child's best interests would be served by awarding custody to the natural father and his wife—all of this before she has even conceived, and, in some cases, before she has the slightest idea of what the natural father and adoptive mother are like.

[68] The foregoing provisions not only directly conflict with New Jersey statutes, but also offend long-established State policies. These critical

terms, which are at the heart of the contract, are invalid and unenforceable; the conclusion therefore follows, without more, that the entire contract is unenforceable.

[109 NJ Page 423]

A. Conflict with Statutory Provisions

[69] The surrogacy contract conflicts with: (1) laws prohibiting the use of money in connection with adoptions; (2) laws requiring proof of parental unfitness or abandonment before termination of parental rights is ordered or an adoption is granted; and (3) laws that make surrender of custody and consent to adoption revocable in private placement adoptions.

[70] (1) Our law prohibits paying or accepting money in connection with any placement of a child for adoption. N.J.S.A. 9:3-54a. Violation is a high misdemeanor. N.J.S.A. 9:3-54c. Excepted are fees of an approved agency (which must be a nonprofit entity, N.J.S.A. 9:3-38a) and certain expenses in connection with childbirth. N.J.S.A. 9:3-54b.

[71] Considerable care was taken in this case to structure the surrogacy arrangement so as not to violate this prohibition. The arrangement was structured as follows: the adopting parent, Mrs. Stern, was not a party to the surrogacy contract; the money paid to Mrs. Whitehead was stated to be for her services—not for the adoption; the sole purpose of the contract was stated as being that "of giving a child to William Stern, its natural and biological father"; the money was purported to be

[109 NJ Page 424]

"compensation for services and expenses and in no way . . . a fee for termination of parental rights or a payment in exchange for consent to surrender a child for adoption"; the fee to the Infertility Center ($7,500) was stated to be for legal representation, advice, administrative work, and other "services." Nevertheless, it seems clear that the money was paid and accepted in connection with an adoption.

[72] The Infertility Center's major role was first as a "finder" of the surrogate mother whose child was to be adopted, and second as the arranger of all proceedings that led to the adoption. Its role as adoption finder is demonstrated by the provision requiring Mr. Stern to pay another $7,500 if he uses Mary Beth Whitehead again as a surrogate, and by ICNY's agreement to "coordinate arrangements for the adoption of the child by the wife." The surrogacy agreement requires Mrs. Whitehead to surrender Baby M for the

114

purposes of adoption. The agreement notes that Mr. and Mrs. Stern wanted to have a child, and provides that the child be "placed" with Mrs. Stern in the event Mr. Stern dies before the child is born. The payment of the $10,000 occurs only on surrender of custody of the child and "completion of the duties and obligations" of Mrs. Whitehead, including termination of her parental rights to facilitate adoption by Mrs. Stern. As for the contention that the Sterns are paying only for services and not for an adoption, we need note only that they would pay nothing in the event the child died before the fourth month of pregnancy, and only $1,000 if the child were stillborn, even though the "services" had been fully rendered. Additionally, one of Mrs. Whitehead's estimated costs, to be assumed by Mr. Stern, was an "Adoption Fee," presumably for Mrs. Whitehead's incidental costs in connection with the adoption.

[73] Mr. Stern knew he was paying for the adoption of a child; Mrs. Whitehead knew she was accepting money so that a child might be adopted; the Infertility Center knew that it was being paid for assisting in the adoption of a child. The actions of all three worked to frustrate the goals of the statute. It strains

[109 NJ Page 425]

credulity to claim that these arrangements, touted by those in the surrogacy business as an attractive alternative to the usual route leading to an adoption, really amount to something other than a private placement adoption for money.

[74] The prohibition of our statute is strong. Violation constitutes a high misdemeanor, N.J.S.A. 9:3-54c, a third-degree crime, N.J.S.A. 2C:43-1b, carrying a penalty of three to five years imprisonment. N.J.S.A. 2C:43-6a(3). The evils inherent in baby-bartering are loathsome for a myriad of reasons. The child is sold without regard for whether the purchasers will be suitable parents. N. Baker, Baby Selling: The Scandal of Black Market Adoption 7 (1978). The natural mother does not receive the benefit of counseling and guidance to assist her in making a decision that may affect her for a lifetime. In fact, the monetary incentive to sell her child may, depending on her financial circumstances, make her decision less voluntary. Id. at 44. Furthermore, the adoptive parents may not be fully informed of the natural parents' medical history.

[75] Baby-selling potentially results in the exploitation of all parties involved. Ibid. Conversely, adoption statutes seek to further humanitarian goals, foremost among them the best interests of the child. H. Witmer, E.

Herzog, E. Weinstein, & M. Sullivan, Independent Adoptions: A Follow-Up Study 32 (1967). The negative consequences of baby-buying are potentially present in the surrogacy context, especially the potential for placing and adopting a child without regard to the interest of the child or the natural mother.

Source: New Jersey Supreme Court. *In the Matter of Baby M, a Pseudonym for an Actual Person,* 537 A 2nd 1227, 109 N.J. 396. Available online. URL: http://biotech.law.lsu.edu/cases/cloning/baby_m.htm. Accessed April 26, 2009.

5

International Documents

This chapter draws together international primary source documents organized into sections, including international documents and case studies of the various countries covered in this text. The documents are arranged in chronological order within each section. Documents that have been excerpted are identified as such; all others are reproduced in full.

INTERNATIONAL DOCUMENTS

Hague Convention of 29 May 1993 on Protection of Children and Co-operation in Respect of Intercountry Adoption (1993)

The early 1990s saw a rapid increase in international adoption that coincided with the collapse of the Soviet Union and the sudden availability of thousands of children for adoption from former Soviet bloc countries. With little government oversight, particularly among sending countries, and a quickly expanding profit-driven adoption market, many child advocacy groups began to express concerns about child-trafficking, coercion, abduction, and bribery.

The Hague Convention concluded the treaty on intercountry adoption in 1993 in an effort to stem the rising tide of abuses within the international adoption industry. The primary goal of the convention was the protection of children by ensuring that all cases of international adoption were decided and arranged in the child's best interests. To execute this goal, the convention devised a system of requirements to be met by party countries, which included the establishment of a central authority as the main source of information and oversight of adoption cases, the accreditation of adoption agencies, and the assurance that all efforts to find an adoptive family for a child within his or her country of origin have been exhausted.

The Hague Convention is significant in its applicability to a range of different cultural systems, values, and governments. As an international adoption must meet the requirements of both the sending and receiving country, the

ADOPTION AND SURROGATE PREGNANCY

Hague Convention provided a set of basic international regulations that would facilitate intercountry exchange, ensure that an adoption is in a child's best interests, and protect both birth parents and adoptive parents. As of 2009, there were 78 contracting states to the Hague Convention.

The States signatory to the present Convention,

Recognizing that the child, for the full and harmonious development of his or her personality, should grow up in a family environment, in an atmosphere of happiness, love and understanding,

Recalling that each State should take, as a matter of priority, appropriate measures to enable the child to remain in the care of his or her family of origin,

Recognizing that intercountry adoption may offer the advantage of a permanent family to a child for whom a suitable family cannot be found in his or her State of origin,

Convinced of the necessity to take measures to ensure that intercountry adoptions are made in the best interests of the child and with respect for his or her fundamental rights, and to prevent the abduction, the sale of, or traffic in children,

Desiring to establish common provisions to this effect, taking into account the principles set forth in international instruments, in particular the United Nations Convention on the Rights of the Child, of 20 November 1989, and the United Nations Declaration on Social and Legal Principles relating to the Protection and Welfare of Children, with Special Reference to Foster Placement and Adoption Nationally and Internationally (General Assembly Resolution 41/85, of 3 December 1986),

Have agreed upon the following provisions—

CHAPTER I—SCOPE OF THE CONVENTION

Article 1
The objects of the present Convention are—

a) to establish safeguards to ensure that intercountry adoptions take place in the best interests of the child and with respect for his or her fundamental rights as recognized in international law;

b) to establish a system of co-operation amongst Contracting States to ensure that those safeguards are respected and thereby prevent the abduction, the sale of, or traffic in children;

c) to secure the recognition in Contracting States of adoptions made in accordance with the Convention.

Article 2

(1) The Convention shall apply where a child habitually resident in one Contracting State ("the State of origin") has been, is being, or is to be moved to another Contracting State ("the receiving State") either after his or her adoption in the State of origin by spouses or a person habitually resident in the receiving State, or for the purposes of such an adoption in the receiving State or in the State of origin.

(2) The Convention covers only adoptions which create a permanent parent-child relationship.

Article 3

The Convention ceases to apply if the agreements mentioned in Article 17, sub-paragraph *c,* have not been given before the child attains the age of eighteen years.

CHAPTER II—REQUIREMENTS FOR INTERCOUNTRY ADOPTIONS

Article 4

An adoption within the scope of the Convention shall take place only if the competent authorities of the State of origin—

a) have established that the child is adoptable;

b) have determined, after possibilities for placement of the child within the State of origin have been given due consideration, that an intercountry adoption is in the child's best interests;

c) have ensured that

(1) the persons, institutions and authorities whose consent is necessary for adoption, have been counselled as may be necessary and duly informed of the effects of their consent, in particular whether or not an adoption will

result in the termination of the legal relationship between the child and his or her family of origin,

(2) such persons, institutions and authorities have given their consent freely, in the required legal form, and expressed or evidenced in writing,

(3) the consents have not been induced by payment or compensation of any kind and have not been withdrawn, and

(4) the consent of the mother, where required, has been given only after the birth of the child; and

d) have ensured, having regard to the age and degree of maturity of the child, that

(1) he or she has been counselled and duly informed of the effects of the adoption and of his or her consent to the adoption, where such consent is required,

(2) consideration has been given to the child's wishes and opinions,

(3) the child's consent to the adoption, where such consent is required, has been given freely, in the required legal form, and expressed or evidenced in writing, and

(4) such consent has not been induced by payment or compensation of any kind.

Article 5
An adoption within the scope of the Convention shall take place only if the competent authorities of the receiving State—

a) have determined that the prospective adoptive parents are eligible and suited to adopt;

b) have ensured that the prospective adoptive parents have been counselled as may be necessary; and

c) have determined that the child is or will be authorized to enter and reside permanently in that State.

CHAPTER III—CENTRAL AUTHORITIES
AND ACCREDITED BODIES

Article 6

(1) A Contracting State shall designate a Central Authority to discharge the duties which are imposed by the Convention upon such authorities.

(2) Federal States, States with more than one system of law or States having autonomous territorial units shall be free to appoint more than one Central Authority and to specify the territorial or personal extent of their functions. Where a State has appointed more than one Central Authority, it shall designate the Central Authority to which any communication may be addressed for transmission to the appropriate Central Authority within that State.

Article 7

(1) Central Authorities shall co-operate with each other and promote co-operation amongst the competent authorities in their States to protect children and to achieve the other objects of the Convention.

(2) They shall take directly all appropriate measures to—

a) provide information as to the laws of their States concerning adoption and other general information, such as statistics and standard forms;

b) keep one another informed about the operation of the Convention and, as far as possible, eliminate any obstacles to its application.

Article 8

Central Authorities shall take, directly or through public authorities, all appropriate measures to prevent improper financial or other gain in connection with an adoption and to deter all practices contrary to the objects of the Convention.

Article 9

Central Authorities shall take, directly or through public authorities or other bodies duly accredited in their State, all appropriate measures, in particular to—

a) collect, preserve and exchange information about the situation of the child and the prospective adoptive parents, so far as is necessary to complete the adoption;

121

b) facilitate, follow and expedite proceedings with a view to obtaining the adoption;

c) promote the development of adoption counselling and post-adoption services in their States;

d) provide each other with general evaluation reports about experience with intercountry adoption;

e) reply, in so far as is permitted by the law of their State, to justified requests from other Central Authorities or public authorities for information about a particular adoption situation.

Article 10
Accreditation shall only be granted to and maintained by bodies demonstrating their competence to carry out properly the tasks with which they may be entrusted.

Article 11
An accredited body shall—

a) pursue only non-profit objectives according to such conditions and within such limits as may be established by the competent authorities of the State of accreditation;

b) be directed and staffed by persons qualified by their ethical standards and by training or experience to work in the field of intercountry adoption; and

c) be subject to supervision by competent authorities of that State as to its composition, operation and financial situation.

Article 12
A body accredited in one Contracting State may act in another Contracting State only if the competent authorities of both States have authorized it to do so.

Article 13
The designation of the Central Authorities and, where appropriate, the extent of their functions, as well as the names and addresses of the accredited bodies shall be communicated by each Contracting State to the Permanent Bureau of the Hague Conference on Private International Law.

CHAPTER IV—PROCEDURAL REQUIREMENTS
IN INTERCOUNTRY ADOPTION

Article 14

Persons habitually resident in a Contracting State, who wish to adopt a child habitually resident in another Contracting State, shall apply to the Central Authority in the State of their habitual residence.

Article 15

(1) If the Central Authority of the receiving State is satisfied that the applicants are eligible and suited to adopt, it shall prepare a report including information about their identity, eligibility and suitability to adopt, background, family and medical history, social environment, reasons for adoption, ability to undertake an intercountry adoption, as well as the characteristics of the children for whom they would be qualified to care.

(2) It shall transmit the report to the Central Authority of the State of origin.

Article 16

(1) If the Central Authority of the State of origin is satisfied that the child is adoptable, it shall—

a) prepare a report including information about his or her identity, adoptability, background, social environment, family history, medical history including that of the child's family, and any special needs of the child;

b) give due consideration to the child's upbringing and to his or her ethnic, religious and cultural background;

c) ensure that consents have been obtained in accordance with Article 4; and

d) determine, on the basis in particular of the reports relating to the child and the prospective adoptive parents, whether the envisaged placement is in the best interests of the child.

(2) It shall transmit to the Central Authority of the receiving State its report on the child, proof that the necessary consents have been obtained and the reasons for its determination on the placement, taking care not to reveal the identity of the mother and the father if, in the State of origin, these identities may not be disclosed.

Article 17

Any decision in the State of origin that a child should be entrusted to prospective adoptive parents may only be made if—

a) the Central Authority of that State has ensured that the prospective adoptive parents agree;

b) the Central Authority of the receiving State has approved such decision, where such approval is required by the law of that State or by the Central Authority of the State of origin;

c) the Central Authorities of both States have agreed that the adoption may proceed; and

d) it has been determined, in accordance with Article 5, that the prospective adoptive parents are eligible and suited to adopt and that the child is or will be authorized to enter and reside permanently in the receiving State.

Article 18

The Central Authorities of both States shall take all necessary steps to obtain permission for the child to leave the State of origin and to enter and reside permanently in the receiving State.

Article 19

(1) The transfer of the child to the receiving State may only be carried out if the requirements of Article 17 have been satisfied.

(2) The Central Authorities of both States shall ensure that this transfer takes place in secure and appropriate circumstances and, if possible, in the company of the adoptive or prospective adoptive parents.

(3) If the transfer of the child does not take place, the reports referred to in Articles 15 and 16 are to be sent back to the authorities who forwarded them.

Article 20

The Central Authorities shall keep each other informed about the adoption process and the measures taken to complete it, as well as about the progress of the placement if a probationary period is required.

Article 21

(1) Where the adoption is to take place after the transfer of the child to the receiving State and it appears to the Central Authority of that State that the continued placement of the child with the prospective adoptive parents is not in the child's best interests, such Central Authority shall take the measures necessary to protect the child, in particular—

a) to cause the child to be withdrawn from the prospective adoptive parents and to arrange temporary care;

b) in consultation with the Central Authority of the State of origin, to arrange without delay a new placement of the child with a view to adoption or, if this is not appropriate, to arrange alternative long-term care; an adoption shall not take place until the Central Authority of the State of origin has been duly informed concerning the new prospective adoptive parents;

c) as a last resort, to arrange the return of the child, if his or her interests so require.

(2) Having regard in particular to the age and degree of maturity of the child, he or she shall be consulted and, where appropriate, his or her consent obtained in relation to measures to be taken under this Article.

Article 22

(1) The functions of a Central Authority under this Chapter may be performed by public authorities or by bodies accredited under Chapter III, to the extent permitted by the law of its State.

(2) Any Contracting State may declare to the depositary of the Convention that the functions of the Central Authority under Articles 15 to 21 may be performed in that State, to the extent permitted by the law and subject to the supervision of the competent authorities of that State, also by bodies or persons who—

a) meet the requirements of integrity, professional competence, experience and accountability of that State; and

b) are qualified by their ethical standards and by training or experience to work in the field of intercountry adoption.

(3) A Contracting State which makes the declaration provided for in paragraph 2 shall keep the Permanent Bureau of the Hague Conference on Private International Law informed of the names and addresses of these bodies and persons.

(4) Any Contracting State may declare to the depositary of the Convention that adoptions of children habitually resident in its territory may only take place if the functions of the Central Authorities are performed in accordance with paragraph 1.

(5) Notwithstanding any declaration made under paragraph 2, the reports provided for in Articles 15 and 16 shall, in every case, be prepared under the responsibility of the Central Authority or other authorities or bodies in accordance with paragraph 1.

CHAPTER V—RECOGNITION AND EFFECTS OF THE ADOPTION

Article 23
(1) An adoption certified by the competent authority of the State of the adoption as having been made in accordance with the Convention shall be recognized by operation of law in the other Contracting States. The certificate shall specify when and by whom the agreements under Article 17, sub-paragraph c), were given.

(2) Each Contracting State shall, at the time of signature, ratification, acceptance, approval or accession, notify the depositary of the Convention of the identity and the functions of the authority or the authorities which, in that State, are competent to make the certification. It shall also notify the depositary of any modification in the designation of these authorities.

Article 24
The recognition of an adoption may be refused in a Contracting State only if the adoption is manifestly contrary to its public policy, taking into account the best interests of the child.

Article 25
Any Contracting State may declare to the depositary of the Convention that it will not be bound under this Convention to recognize adoptions made in accordance with an agreement concluded by application of Article 39, paragraph 2.

Article 26

(1) The recognition of an adoption includes recognition of

a) the legal parent-child relationship between the child and his or her adoptive parents;

b) parental responsibility of the adoptive parents for the child;

c) the termination of a pre-existing legal relationship between the child and his or her mother and father, if the adoption has this effect in the Contracting State where it was made.

(2) In the case of an adoption having the effect of terminating a pre-existing legal parent-child relationship, the child shall enjoy in the receiving State, and in any other Contracting State where the adoption is recognized, rights equivalent to those resulting from adoptions having this effect in each such State.

(3) The preceding paragraphs shall not prejudice the application of any provision more favourable for the child, in force in the Contracting State which recognizes the adoption.

Article 27

(1) Where an adoption granted in the State of origin does not have the effect of terminating a pre-existing legal parent-child relationship, it may, in the receiving State which recognizes the adoption under the Convention, be converted into an adoption having such an effect—

a) if the law of the receiving State so permits; and

b) if the consents referred to in Article 4, sub-paragraphs *c* and *d,* have been or are given for the purpose of such an adoption.

(2) Article 23 applies to the decision converting the adoption.

CHAPTER VI—GENERAL PROVISIONS

Article 28

The Convention does not affect any law of a State of origin which requires that the adoption of a child habitually resident within that State take place in that State or which prohibits the child's placement in, or transfer to, the receiving State prior to adoption.

Article 29
There shall be no contact between the prospective adoptive parents and the child's parents or any other person who has care of the child until the requirements of Article 4, sub-paragraphs *a)* to *c)*, and Article 5, sub-paragraph *a)*, have been met, unless the adoption takes place within a family or unless the contact is in compliance with the conditions established by the competent authority of the State of origin.

Article 30
(1) The competent authorities of a Contracting State shall ensure that information held by them concerning the child's origin, in particular information concerning the identity of his or her parents, as well as the medical history, is preserved.

(2) They shall ensure that the child or his or her representative has access to such information, under appropriate guidance, in so far as is permitted by the law of that State.

Article 31
Without prejudice to Article 30, personal data gathered or transmitted under the Convention, especially data referred to in Articles 15 and 16, shall be used only for the purposes for which they were gathered or transmitted.

Article 32
(1) No one shall derive improper financial or other gain from an activity related to an intercountry adoption.

(2) Only costs and expenses, including reasonable professional fees of persons involved in the adoption, may be charged or paid.

(3) The directors, administrators and employees of bodies involved in an adoption shall not receive remuneration which is unreasonably high in relation to services rendered.

Article 33
A competent authority which finds that any provision of the Convention has not been respected or that there is a serious risk that it may not be

respected, shall immediately inform the Central Authority of its State. This Central Authority shall be responsible for ensuring that appropriate measures are taken.

Article 34
If the competent authority of the State of destination of a document so requests, a translation certified as being in conformity with the original must be furnished. Unless otherwise provided, the costs of such translation are to be borne by the prospective adoptive parents.

Article 35
The competent authorities of the Contracting States shall act expeditiously in the process of adoption.

Article 36
In relation to a State which has two or more systems of law with regard to adoption applicable in different territorial units—

a) any reference to habitual residence in that State shall be construed as referring to habitual residence in a territorial unit of that State;

b) any reference to the law of that State shall be construed as referring to the law in force in the relevant territorial unit;

c) any reference to the competent authorities or to the public authorities of that State shall be construed as referring to those authorized to act in the relevant territorial unit;

d) any reference to the accredited bodies of that State shall be construed as referring to bodies accredited in the relevant territorial unit.

Article 37
In relation to a State which with regard to adoption has two or more systems of law applicable to different categories of persons, any reference to the law of that State shall be construed as referring to the legal system specified by the law of that State.

Article 38
A State within which different territorial units have their own rules of law in respect of adoption shall not be bound to apply the Convention where a State with a unified system of law would not be bound to do so.

Article 39

(1) The Convention does not affect any international instrument to which Contracting States are Parties and which contains provisions on matters governed by the Convention, unless a contrary declaration is made by the States Parties to such instrument.

(2) Any Contracting State may enter into agreements with one or more other Contracting States, with a view to improving the application of the Convention in their mutual relations. These agreements may derogate only from the provisions of Articles 14 to 16 and 18 to 21. The States which have concluded such an agreement shall transmit a copy to the depositary of the Convention.

Article 40

No reservation to the Convention shall be permitted.

Article 41

The Convention shall apply in every case where an application pursuant to Article 14 has been received after the Convention has entered into force in the receiving State and the State of origin.

Article 42

The Secretary General of the Hague Conference on Private International Law shall at regular intervals convene a Special Commission in order to review the practical operation of the Convention.

CHAPTER VII—FINAL CLAUSES

Article 43

(1) The Convention shall be open for signature by the States which were Members of the Hague Conference on Private International Law at the time of its Seventeenth Session and by the other States which participated in that Session.

(2) It shall be ratified, accepted or approved and the instruments of ratification, acceptance or approval shall be deposited with the Ministry of Foreign Affairs of the Kingdom of the Netherlands, depositary of the Convention.

Article 44

(1) Any other State may accede to the Convention after it has entered into force in accordance with Article 46, paragraph 1.

(2) The instrument of accession shall be deposited with the depositary.

(3) Such accession shall have effect only as regards the relations between the acceding State and those Contracting States which have not raised an objection to its accession in the six months after the receipt of the notification referred to in sub-paragraph *b)* of Article 48. Such an objection may also be raised by States at the time when they ratify, accept or approve the Convention after an accession. Any such objection shall be notified to the depositary.

Article 45
(1) If a State has two or more territorial units in which different systems of law are applicable in relation to matters dealt with in the Convention, it may at the time of signature, ratification, acceptance, approval or accession declare that this Convention shall extend to all its territorial units or only to one or more of them and may modify this declaration by submitting another declaration at any time.

(2) Any such declaration shall be notified to the depositary and shall state expressly the territorial units to which the Convention applies.

(3) If a State makes no declaration under this Article, the Convention is to extend to all territorial units of that State.

Article 46
(1) The Convention shall enter into force on the first day of the month following the expiration of three months after the deposit of the third instrument of ratification, acceptance or approval referred to in Article 43.

(2) Thereafter the Convention shall enter into force –

a) for each State ratifying, accepting or approving it subsequently, or acceding to it, on the first day of the month following the expiration of three months after the deposit of its instrument of ratification, acceptance, approval or accession;

b) for a territorial unit to which the Convention has been extended in conformity with Article 45, on the first day of the month following the expiration of three months after the notification referred to in that Article.

ADOPTION AND SURROGATE PREGNANCY

Article 47

(1) A State Party to the Convention may denounce it by a notification in writing addressed to the depositary.

(2) The denunciation takes effect on the first day of the month following the expiration of twelve months after the notification is received by the depositary. Where a longer period for the denunciation to take effect is specified in the notification, the denunciation takes effect upon the expiration of such longer period after the notification is received by the depositary.

Article 48

The depositary shall notify the States Members of the Hague Conference on Private International Law, the other States which participated in the Seventeenth Session and the States which have acceded in accordance with Article 44, of the following—

a) the signatures, ratifications, acceptances and approvals referred to in Article 43;

b) the accessions and objections raised to accessions referred to in Article 44;

c) the date on which the Convention enters into force in accordance with Article 46;

d) the declarations and designations referred to in Articles 22, 23, 25 and 45;

e) the agreements referred to in Article 39;

f) the denunciations referred to in Article 47.

In witness whereof the undersigned, being duly authorized thereto, have signed this Convention.

Done at The Hague, on the 29th day of May 1993, in the English and French languages, both texts being equally authentic, in a single copy which shall be deposited in the archives of the Government of the Kingdom of the Netherlands, and of which a certified copy shall be sent, through diplomatic

132

channels, to each of the States Members of the Hague Conference on Private International Law at the date of its Seventeenth Session and to each of the other States which participated in that Session.

Source: Hague Conference on Private International Law. "Convention on Protection of Children and Co-operation in Respect of Intercountry Adoption" (1993). Available online. URL: http://www.hcch.net/index_en.php?act=conventions.text&cid=69. Accessed May 3, 2009.

UNICEF's Position on Intercountry Adoption (2007)

Guided by the principles of the United Nations Convention on the Rights of the Child (1989), the United Nations Children's Fund (UNICEF) is a child advocacy organization that promotes children's rights by working to alleviate childhood poverty, violence, hunger, and illness in 198 countries around the world. UNICEF maintains that the right to grow and develop in a peaceful, nurturing environment is a fundamental human right and thus advocates childhood immunization, education for all (but particularly for girls), and the prevention of HIV/AIDS.

Among UNICEF's goals is the prevention of abuse and exploitation of children. In 2007, UNICEF released a statement on its position on inter-country adoption, in which it outlined the Convention on the Rights of the Child and the right of every child to be raised by his or her own parents, when possible. Notably, UNICEF emphasizes the importance of providing support for families so that international adoption remains a last resort, to be utilized only when it is expressly in a child's best interests. UNICEF's position on international adoption mirrors the mission of the Hague Convention, which insists that all attempts must be made to preserve individual families. Barring that, all attempts must be made to keep a child within his or her own community by arranging an adoption within his or her country of origin. Nevertheless, UNICEF believes that there are cases in which inter-country adoption may be the most appropriate way of meeting a child's need for a loving family.

UNICEF has received many enquiries from families hoping to adopt children from countries other than their own. UNICEF believes that all decisions relating to children, including adoptions, should be made with the best interests of the child as the primary consideration. The Hague Convention on International Adoptions is an important development, for both adopting families and adopted children, because it promotes ethical and transparent processes, undertaken in the best interests of the child. UNICEF urges

133

national authorities to ensure that, during the transition to full implementation of the Hague Convention, the best interests of each individual child are protected.

The Convention on the Rights of the Child, which guides UNICEF's work, clearly states that every child has the right to know and be cared for by his or her own parents, whenever possible. Recognising this, and the value and importance of families in children's lives, UNICEF believes that families needing support to care for their children should receive it, and that alternative means of caring for a child should only be considered when, despite this assistance, a child's family is unavailable, unable or unwilling to care for him or her.

For children who cannot be raised by their own families, an appropriate alternative family environment should be sought in preference to institutional care which should be used only as a last resort and as a temporary measure. Inter-country adoption is one of a range of care options which may be open to children, and for individual children who cannot be placed in a permanent family setting in their countries of origin, it may indeed be the best solution. In each case, the best interests of the individual child must be the guiding principle in making a decision regarding adoption.

Over the past 30 years, the number of families from wealthy countries wanting to adopt children from other countries has grown substantially. At the same time, lack of regulation and oversight, particularly in the countries of origin, coupled with the potential for financial gain, has spurred the growth of an industry around adoption, where profit, rather than the best interests of children, takes centre stage. Abuses include the sale and abduction of children, coercion of parents, and bribery.

Many countries around the world have recognised these risks, and have ratified the Hague Convention on Inter-Country Adoption. UNICEF strongly supports this international legislation, which is designed to put into action the principles regarding inter-country adoption which are contained in the Convention on the Rights of the Child. These include ensuring that adoption is authorised only by competent authorities, that inter-country adoption enjoys the same safeguards and standards which apply in national adoptions, and that inter-country adoption does not result in improper financial gain for those involved in it. These provisions are meant first and foremost to protect children, but also have the positive effect of providing assurance to prospective adoptive parents that their child has not been the subject of illegal and detrimental practices.

The case of children separated from their parents and communities during war or natural disasters merits special mention. It cannot be assumed that such children have neither living parents nor relatives. Even if both their parents are dead, the chances of finding living relatives, a community and home to return to after the conflict subsides exist. Thus, such children should not be considered for inter-country adoption, and family tracing should be the priority. This position is shared by UNICEF, UNHCR, the International Confederation of the Red Cross, and international NGOs such as the Save the Children Alliance.

Source: UNICEF Press Centre. "UNICEF's Position on Intercountry Adoption" (Nov. 2007). Available online. URL: http://www.unicef.org/media/media_41918.html. Accessed May 3, 2009.

International Surrogacy Partners (2007) (Excerpt)

While international adoption experienced rapid growth in the 1990s and early 2000s, it began to slow down after 2005 due to many factors, including legislative action on the part of sending countries in an effort to reduce the numbers of their children being adopted overseas, as well as mounting allegations of fraud, abuse, and child-trafficking. While the rates of intercountry adoption did decrease, intercountry surrogacy began to grow and expand as a new avenue to parenthood. As an outgrowth of what many have termed reproductive tourism, international surrogacy developed as a means of allowing individuals and couples to create families despite restrictive laws and/or costs in their home countries.

As a testament to increasing globalization, reproductive tourism developed in response to new advancements in reproductive technologies and a lack of uniform global regulations among the world's developed and developing nations. An infertile individual or couple desiring to become a parent or parents may not have access to certain reproductive procedures such as in vitro fertilization (IVF), egg or sperm donation, or surrogate pregnancy in their home country due to laws that ban such procedures or bar certain people from undergoing them. In some countries, the costs of such procedures are so high that many cannot afford them. Thus, such individuals may travel to another country where fertility regulations are less restrictive and/or the costs are lower.

ADOPTION AND SURROGATE PREGNANCY

Many reproductive tourism businesses have developed to assist individuals achieve their dreams of parenthood. International Surrogacy Partners is one such business, located in Ukraine and offering less costly surrogacy services that are friendlier to prospective parents, as their rights and needs are the top priority throughout the surrogacy process.

International Surrogacy Partners is a surrogate agency and pioneer in International Surrogacy. We firmly believe every individual and couple has the right to happiness through parenthood. As a nonprofit surrogate agency, we are committed to providing support and guidance to our intended parents throughout the duration of the surrogacy process, from conception through the birth of their child. . . .

Why International Surrogacy in Ukraine?

At this time, we have chosen to establish our Surrogacy program in Ukraine because Ukraine is one of the few countries to allow international surrogacy, with legislation making it advantageous for foreigners to pursue surrogacy there rather than in their home country.

- According to Ukrainian legislation, surrogate mothers are not able to choose to keep the child after birth.
- In Ukraine the cost of surrogacy is 50–60% less than the cost of the same program in the United States.
- The availability of young, healthy surrogate mothers is much greater than the U.S. There is currently no waiting time for our clients.
- All prospective surrogate mothers are under 30 years of age and in excellent health.
- Upon birth of the child the biological family's name is put on the birth certificate.

About International Surrogacy

International surrogacy has, until recently, been most common throughout Europe. We are the first U.S. based agency to have an established surrogacy program in Eastern Europe. We have exclusive rights to work with 2 prominent clinics that have many years of experience.

Ukraine, a beautiful country the size of France, is located between Russia and the countries of Eastern Europe. Ukraine was once part of the Soviet

Union and is now its own nation. The population is Slavic, like that of Russia, and speaks Ukrainian and Russian languages.

In 2007 one hundred and fifty foreign families successfully completed a surrogate pregnancy program in Ukraine.

International Surrogacy Partners' program works in cooperation with the best clinics and assisted reproductive centers, which are owned and operated by world renowned physicians. We also work closely with an experienced team of legal professionals who specialize in facilitating international surrogacies. We collaborate with this team of support staff from the beginning of your surrogacy process through the birth of your child in order to make your process as simple as possible.

Types of Surrogacy

There are three surrogacy options available for intended parents. The options vary only in terms of which intended parent is genetically related to the child, if at all. The surrogate mother is never related to the child.

- Gestational Surrogacy, with Egg Donor. The intended father provides sperm in vitro. After fertilization, the embryos are transferred to the surrogate's uterus to carry the child to term.
- Gestational Surrogacy, with the Intended Mother's Egg. A sperm donor is provided in vitro. After fertilization, the embryos are transferred to the surrogate's uterus to carry the child to term. This is a viable option for single women.
- Gestational Surrogacy, with the Intended Mother's Egg. The intended father provides sperm in vitro. After fertilization, the embryos are transferred to the surrogate's uterus to carry the child to term.

About the Surrogates and Egg Donors

It is of paramount importance to us that our surrogate mothers be accorded the full respect, dignity, and recognition of the valued partner that they are.

At International Surrogacy Partners each family is provided with several choices of surrogate mother. All surrogate mothers must complete an extensive health evaluation prior to being matched with a family. Health evaluations and personal histories of potential surrogates are provided to the family prior to their first trip to Ukraine. All surrogate mothers must be under 30 years of age and have at least one biological child of their own.

The intended parents will also be presented with Egg Donor information including, pictures, age, profession, height, weight and other details. Most egg donors are women between ages 25–35 who already have children.

Source: International Surrogacy Partners: A Partners for Adoption Agency Program. Available online. URL: www. surrogateagency.com/index.shtml. Accessed September 27, 2009.

CHINA

Anne F. Thurston. "In a Chinese Orphanage" (1996) (Excerpts)

International adoption as a humanitarian movement took hold in the 1950s with the Holts and reignited in the early 1990s with the revelation of the deplorable living conditions of orphanages in former Soviet bloc countries, particularly Romania. As more unsanitary and unlivable orphanages were exposed throughout former Soviet countries, a sense of urgency and necessity began to froth within the international adoption community. Overseas adoption invariably became intertwined with charity and child rescue.

In China, rising rates of infant abandonment in the 1980s and 1990s left orphanages crowded with healthy baby girls who, due to the one-child policy, could not be placed domestically. As accounts of their living conditions became known around the world, overseas families sought to adopt Chinese children, most of whom were not orphans but had been abandoned. Indeed, international adoption became essential to reducing the numbers of children in overcrowded institutions. The following article is an account of a Chinese orphanage and emphasizes the need for such intervention.

I HAD been warned, by friends and by the media, about the Chinese orphanage—the dying room for infants and the children being allowed to starve. But I was not prepared. I had expected the dying children to be crying, begging to be saved. Instead they were silent, withdrawn, immobile. They had no expectation of being comforted or saved, or even any obvious awareness of the two women passing by. They were miniature versions of the "Muselmänner" of the Nazi concentration camps, the ones who stopped struggling, gave up living, waited only for death—the ones from whom other inmates recoiled, as though the Muselmänner's resignation were contagious, the kiss of death. Now I, too, recoiled, in an involuntary lapse of compassion.

I cannot mention the real name of the woman who first took me to the orphanage, which is in southern China, in a complex that houses some 300 to 350 children and 250 disabled or elderly adults. I will call her Christine. . . .

The children who were old enough and able to walk were waiting at the windows when we arrived, broad smiles on their faces. They exclaimed over Christine's oversize bag when we walked in, knowing it would be filled with crackers. Christine had a surprise for them that day—sneakers in bright colors and psychedelic designs, which she distributed to the barefoot children according to approximate size. The children tried them on, jumping and prancing and running, their thumbs up in the universal language of delight. They were an unruly, unsocialized group. Some were handicapped. Others seemed retarded, though the foreign volunteers were convinced that what appeared as retardation was often really a failure to thrive, the result of too little love and attention.

The vast majority of the children, some 90 percent, were thought by the foreign volunteers to be girls, though this was not readily apparent. Their hair was cropped short, institutional-style, and their clothes were unisex shorts and T-shirts. Few of them were actually orphans. They had been abandoned—victims of China's one-child-per-family policy and of the traditional, economically motivated propensity to value males. Males both carry on the family line and provide for their parents in old age. Girls marry and then have obligations only to their husband's family. Rural China has no pension system. The retired depend for survival on their sons.

Recent census figures indicate how badly the Chinese want boys. In 1994 the worldwide sex ratio at birth was 101.5 boys for every 100 girls. In China there were 116 boys for every 100 girls. No one is certain what happens to the missing girls. Some may be aborted after a sonogram reveals a female fetus, though this practice was recently declared illegal. The traditional practice of female infanticide, described decades ago by Pearl S. Buck and Somerset Maugham, may still exist. Some baby girls may not be reported in the census. Rural families are often allowed to have two children. When the first is a girl, some families wait to record the birth until the second child proves to be a boy. Some baby girls are abandoned.

The orphanage I visited is on the outskirts of a city, but the little girls were presumed to have come mostly from rural backgrounds. China is in the midst of what must be the largest rural-to-urban migration in human history. In recent years perhaps 100 million of China's 900 million peasants have moved to cities in search of jobs. The baby girls are left at railway stations, in parks, and in front of police stations. The police are supposed to search for the parents, but most searches prove fruitless. The boys in the orphanage are for the most part severely handicapped, but they are often not abandoned, and may have family contact and visits.

Newly arrived infants are placed in a separate small room, which held about ten baby girls during my visits. Two or three staff members—untrained, minimally paid women from nearby villages who were struggling to support their own families—were on hand for the infants. The babies were cuddly, cute, and alert.

Adoption is not unusual in Chinese tradition. I have known several infertile urban couples who adopted a child from one of their married siblings. In rural areas, despite the economic value placed on boys, families without female children have sometimes adopted little girls. The current one-child-per-family policy makes domestic adoptions more difficult, however. A couple must be childless and at least thirty-five years old before regulations permit them to adopt. But the pediatrician in charge of the orphanage told me that "normal" infants do find new homes. Some forty babies had been adopted the previous year, more than twenty of them by foreigners and the rest, presumably, by Chinese. I watched one day as Susan Lee, a single Chinese-American woman who works for the Federal Aviation Administration, in Washington, D.C., met her new daughter, Rachel, then eight months old. The baby had been in the orphanage since only a few days after she was born. When I had dinner with the new family a few days later, Rachel, who had been alert and curious when I first saw her but had been unable to hold up her head, was already discernibly stronger.

Babies who are not adopted are eventually moved out of the infant room into what the foreign women call the toddlers' room, a much larger space with six rows of eight cribs each. Staffing is minimal there—three or four women for forty-eight children. The quality of care precipitously declines. It is almost impossible for the volunteers to guess the ages of the children. Many suffer such serious developmental delays that they appear and act much younger than they are. Children who have just been moved are generally placed in the middle two rows. They are given bottles but scant assistance in feeding, and the schedule is rigid. Some of the children grab their bottles and eat lustily, and some—often the same ones—demand attention, crying, spreading their arms to be held. Their eyes beg for human warmth and affection. Others are already passive and withdrawn. Their bottles lie untouched, as though they are too weak, too indifferent, or still too young to make the effort. When feeding time is over, even the unfinished bottles are collected.

For the most part those who struggle and survive are eventually moved to the first two rows, although there are no hard and fast rules. When passive children become weak, they are moved to the last two rows—by whose decision or according to what criteria, we never learned. In the months that I visited the orphanage, from October to December of 1994, I never saw the children in these cribs being fed. Christine, who has been visiting for more than two and a half years, has sometimes seen the children fed, but has never seen any of them recover. Rather, she has watched them disappear, to be replaced by new arrivals.

What Westerners call the dying room is tucked away outside, adjacent to the place where sick children are tended. Different babies were there each time I visited, so stiff and quiet, their breathing so faint, that the end could not have been far. A couple had uncorrected cleft palates. They were not being tended, nor was there any obvious sign of medical treatment.

Christine has come to accept the deaths. She has to in order to work there. She visits the dying children each week, taking a mental count, but she never touches or holds them. She feels that such human contact would be cruel to children who have never known warmth or affection or holding, and would perhaps prolong their dying. Instead she gives all her energy and unconditional love to the little ones who respond to it energetically. She and other volunteers cuddle and feed and heap copious praise on the children, who light up in their presence. A Christian-based group also visits weekly, and so do Chinese students from nearby universities. When I visited, a team of doctors from Hawaii had recently assisted Chinese physicians in performing surgery on some of the children, and the pediatrician in charge of the orphanage was soon to receive several months' training in Hong Kong, where orphanages are exceptionally well run. The situation in the orphanage, most of the foreigners seem to agree, is already several times better than when they began volunteering. . . .

My own search for an explanation has taken months. After my initial recoil from the dying children, I determined to give something to every child on subsequent visits to the orphanage—to hold and touch each one, and to feed the ones who could be fed. I stroked the hands and faces of the children who were dying and prayed that they be taken quickly, without pain, and that China would find a way to end this needless sacrifice of life. Only one of the dying children showed any sign of response. "China has too many children," a staff member said to me bitterly as I stood by the cribs.

I called upon Chinese friends for explanations, wondering whether the deaths were rooted somewhere in Chinese culture, perhaps in a different conception of what it means to be fully human. I have never known a Chinese to have moral qualms about abortion. In the Chinese view, fetuses are not yet human. Families do not traditionally celebrate a new birth until the baby is a month old. Historically, infant mortality was high in China, and the child was particularly at risk during the first month of life. Only when a child was past the maximum danger point was its arrival noted ceremonially. Too, the family is all-important in China; identity is embedded there. Perhaps children without families are denied the right to full humanity. . . .

My discussions with Chinese friends made clear both the absence of a concept of equality in Chinese culture and the fact that the handicapped are even lower in the social hierarchy than girls. But the tragedy of China's orphanages cannot be fully explained by Chinese culture. My friends assumed that only the handicapped were being allowed to die, but many of the dying children had no apparent handicaps, whereas most of the older children did. The children's handicaps were not the full explanation for why some were being allowed to die.

At an elegant dinner party in Washington a few weeks after my return I was seated next to a child psychiatrist. I told him what I had seen. "In a holocaust or war," he said, "you do not put the best surgeon in the operating room. You put him at the entrance. His job must be to decide who can be saved and who cannot. The behavior of the children you describe was so profoundly autistic that even if by some miracle they were suddenly to receive twenty-four-hour loving, mothering care, they could not have been saved." The orphanage was practicing triage. My attempt to offer comfort to the dying had been more for my benefit than for the children's, he said. They were too withdrawn to understand.

What is happening in China has parallels in the United States and elsewhere in the West. The first orphanage in the United States was founded in 1729 by an Ursuline convent in New Orleans, after an Indian attack left many children without parents. But the history of our orphanages, and of our treatment of homeless and indigent children, has not always been commendable. Early in this century, when systematic research on foundling homes began, investigators discovered alarmingly high death rates in the first year of the institutionalized children's lives—71 percent in one of Germany's great foundling homes, 90 percent in Baltimore, probably 100 percent at the Randall's Island Hospital, in New York City. Many of the children who lived suffered devastating physical and psychological damage.

René A. Spitz, in the mid-1940s, was one of the first to describe what happened to very young children who spent prolonged periods in institutions where they had no contact with their mothers. Previously happy and outgoing children from six to eleven months old became first weepy and then withdrawn, refusing to take an interest in their surroundings. After three months, Spitz wrote,

> A sort of frozen rigidity of expression appeared instead. These children would lie or sit with wide-open, expressionless eyes, frozen immobile face, and a faraway expression as if in a daze, apparently not perceiving what went on in their environment.... Contact with children who arrived at this stage became increasingly difficult and finally impossible.

Many were unable, or refused, to eat. Spitz described the syndrome not as autism, which experts now believe to have physiological causes unrelated to maternal care, but as anaclitic depression. In one institution nineteen of 123 children studied suffered severe anaclitic depression, and another twenty-six exhibited the syndrome in a milder form.

In even the best-equipped facilities and under the most hygienic conditions children with anaclitic depression are highly susceptible to infection and illness. Thirty-four of ninety-one children whom Spitz, in one study, observed in a foundling home over a two-year period died of diseases ranging from intestinal infections to measles. . . .

Western experts were discovering what Spitz described as the "evil effect" of childhood institutionalization in the mid-1940s, just as the Communists were coming to power in China. Child psychiatry had not yet developed there, and the entire psychiatric profession was ultimately discredited under Mao's regime, which often treated mental illness as a failure of ideological education. During the Cultural Revolution, when most intellectuals were persecuted and physicians were sent to the countryside, the fledgling psychiatric profession was devastated. Only in recent years has it begun to revive. Only in recent months have I seen references in the Chinese press to a childhood illness resembling Spitz's anaclitic depression or the autism described by Bruno Bettelheim and others. The Chinese term means "the syndrome of isolation and loneliness."

What if ignorance and poverty are primarily responsible for the deaths of Chinese babies? What if we accept as truth (because it is the truth) the statement by China's Ministry of Civil Affairs, which is responsible for the administration of orphanages nationwide, that "China is a developing country which has 70 million people who still do not have enough to eat or wear, and it faces many difficulties in raising and educating handicapped children and orphans"? What if neither the pediatrician in charge of the orphanage nor her staff have been introduced to the literature on the psychological effects of institutionalization on infants?

If we accept that the deplorable conditions in China's orphanages result from both poverty and the past harassment of the psychiatric profession, then perhaps we can find ways to share with China what we have learned from our own history of failure to nurture abandoned and orphaned children. Many in China, including some officials at the Ministry of Civil Affairs, continue to welcome our cooperation. Chan Kit-ying, a social worker from Hong Kong, has helped local Ministry of Civil Affairs officials in Nanning, Guanxi; a Nanning orphanage; and the Hong Kong orphanage Mother's Choice to introduce foster care, train orphanage staff, and connect the Nanning orphanage with international adoption agencies. The benefits to the children have been stunning.

For foreigners to have a lasting effect on the situation in China's orphanages, more trained people like Chan Kit-ying will have to be willing to work on the ground, in China, cooperating with Chinese officials and orphanage staff. But the learning process will be a lengthy one. Chinese orphanages will not improve overnight. In the meantime, both China and the United States have regularized the procedures for adoptions. Michael Chang, of the American consulate in Guangzhou, where immigration permits are issued, reports that adoptions of Chinese children by U.S. citizens have approximately doubled in the past year, to about 250 a month, and he expects the number to keep growing.

Within a generation Chinese men will be suffering from a shortage of women to marry, and little girls will be highly valued. Perhaps by then China will have had its own movement against the institutionalization of children.

Source: Anne Thurston. "In a Chinese Orphanage." The Atlantic Online (April 1990). Available online. URL: www. theatlanticmonthly.com/issues/96Apr6/orphan/orphan.htm. Accessed September 27, 2009.

China Center for Adoption Affairs. "Measures for Registration for the Adoption of Children by Chinese Citizens" (2005)

Since the implementation of China's one-child policy in 1978, infant abandonment has been on the rise, resulting in state-run orphanages that are overcrowded and understaffed. While there exists an overwhelming cultural preference for boys and the vast majority of children in China's orphanages are girls, many orphans are nevertheless adopted domestically by Chinese parents. Many contemporary Chinese parents have expressed to researchers their desire for a daughter, as well as the widespread sentiment (reflected among parents in most other countries) that a family is complete with both a boy and a girl.

The Chinese government's strict family planning laws, however, place the same restrictions on adoptive parents as birth parents. Not only must adoptive parents be childless, but they must show proof of infertility, thereby guaranteeing that they will not give birth to future children in addition to their adopted child.

Equally strict rules are applied to birth parents who formally relinquish their children for adoption. Not only are they required to provide documentation

145

that attests to their reasons for relinquishing their child, but they are required to agree not to give birth to any more children, because this would violate the one-child policy.

While such regulations may act as deterrents to adopting or formally terminating one's parental rights, the Chinese government's ultimate aim is to redesign the traditional family unit so that it includes only one child, thereby reducing the country's population. Despite discouraging policies, Chinese parents nevertheless continue to adopt.

(The Measures were approved by the State Council on May 2, 1999, and promulgated by Order No. 15 of the Ministry of Civil Affairs on May 25, 1999. The Measures take effect at promulgation.)

. . .

Article 5

The adopters shall present at the registration office with a petition and the following verifying documents:

1. Registration Card for Residence and Identity Card for Residence of the adopters;

2. Documents from employers, or country/city neighborhood committees verifying marriage status, status of children, able to demonstrate the ability to rear and educate the adoptee; and

3. Documents from the county level (or up) verifying no medical condition that hinders the adoption;

To adopt abandoned infants/children who are living in the institutes, the adopters need to also submit information regarding the status of their fertility, provided by the family planning committee where the adopters reside regularly. If the adopted children are not living in the social welfare institutes and they are either infants/children whose parents can not be ascertained or found, or orphans bereaved of parents, the adopters will need to provide the following in addition to above:

1. Childless Proof, issued by the family committee where the adopters regularly reside; and

2. Finding information regarding the abandoned infants/children provided by the police.

...

If a social welfare institute places a child, the institute shall provide an original record stating when the abandoned infant/child entered the institute, a certificate from the public security office, verifying finding of the child, finding report, or the death certificate or announcement of orphans whose parent died.

If the guardians place children for adoption, the guardians need to submit verification of actual conduct that demonstrates a history conducive of their attempts to fulfill the responsibilities as guardians; death certificate or announcement of the biological parents; or proof that the adoptees' parents are legally incompetent or may severely harm the adoptees.

If the biological parents place their children for adoption, the parents shall submit the agreements between the parents and the local family planning committees, agreeing to not violate the national family planning regulations. If the reason for placing their children for adoption is unusual difficulties rearing the children, the parents shall provide documents verifying the difficulties from their employers, or country/city neighborhood committees. Among those, if the reason is one of the parents passing away or missing, the spouses need to provide documents verifying that the other parent is deceased or missing. If children are adopted by relatives of the adopters by blood of the same generation and up to the third degree of kinship, the biological parents shall also provide documents verifying the kinship from the public security offices or notary offices.

If the adopted children have special needs, documents verifying the specific special needs from a county level (or up) shall be submitted.

Article 7
The registration offices shall process the registrations within 30 days, beginning the day after they receive an application and all supporting documentation. The registration offices then shall issue adoption decrees, providing the applicants satisfy the requirements of the Adoption Law. The registration offices will notify applicants should their application be denied. The relationship of adoption is established on the day of registration.

The registration offices shall post public announcements in an attempt to locate the biological parents, if the biological parents cannot be ascertained or found, prior to the registration. If the biological parents or guardians fail to come forth within 60 days to claim the children, the children will be deemed abandoned. The dates of posting will not be calculated toward the dates of the registration process.

. . .

Article 10

The registration offices shall process terminations of adoptions within 30 days, beginning the day after they receive the request/application and all required supporting documentation. The offices will then terminate the relationship, retrace the adoption decrees, and issue certificates for determination of adoption, providing the termination requests satisfy the regulations of the Adoption Law.

Article 11

Organizations that provide verifying documents shall provide the documents truthfully. If false documents are provide by the organizations, the documents shall be confiscated. The registration offices can, therefore, suggest that the organizations and/or those involved receive administrative or disciplinary punishments.

Article 12

If the parties to the adoption relationship intentionally forge their documents so as to obtain the adoption decree, the adoption shall be invalid. The adoption registration offices shall null the adoption registration and confiscate the adoption decree.

Article 13

The templates of the adoption decree and certificate of termination of adoption will be designed by the Ministry of Civil Affairs of the State Council.

Source: China Center for Adoption Affairs. "Measures for Registration for the Adoption of Children by Chinese Citizens" (Dec. 2005). Available online. URL: http://www.china-ccaa.org/site%5Cinfocontent%5CGNSY_20051018011109187_en.htm. Accessed May 7, 2009.

China.org.cn. "China Grapples with Legality of Surrogate Motherhood" (2006)

With complex family planning laws, the legal status of surrogate pregnancy is debatable in China. The business of surrogacy in China is similar to its practice in the United States. In a traditional surrogate pregnancy, the surrogate mother is evaluated based on her appearance, education level, and overall demeanor, as she is not merely providing a service but her own genetic material. The notable difference between Chinese surrogacy and surrogacy elsewhere lies in the categorization of surrogate mothers and the hierarchy of price ranges depending on her qualities. While surrogacy centers in the United States and other developed nations typically offer flat rate fees for all surrogates while allowing contracting couples to select their preferred surrogate, some Chinese surrogacy centers offer a range of different prices, with higher fees for more attractive and better educated surrogates. Presently, gestational surrogacy is illegal in China due to foreseeable legal problems in determining parentage.

Intermediary agencies that facilitate surrogate pregnancies have emerged in eastern China's Jiangsu and Zhejiang provinces.

A *Shanghai Morning Post* reporter went undercover to find out more about these agencies that typically only have virtual offices on the Web. The reporter contacted two agencies posing as a potential customer and surrogate mother.

The report was published on May 22 and the following are the key findings of the investigation.

Women who apply to be surrogate mothers are classified into nine groups according to their appearance, educational background and other aspects, and paid accordingly, usually between 40,000 and 100,000 yuan. They reportedly sign a payment agreement with the agencies. But legal experts say that agreements signed between the agencies and surrogate mothers have no legal effect, making it difficult to protect surrogate mothers' rights and interests should anything go awry.

Ms Lai, a surrogacy agent in Shanghai, said that a surrogate mother with a junior college certificate can expect to be paid 100,000 yuan (US$12,077) in fees, which is what those in the business call "compensation for the heart of God". Payment is made in cash and excludes living expenses, accommodation, medical examinations, delivery fees and other related expenses. Lai said that one surrogate mother was recently paid 120,000 yuan (US$14,500). She was a university graduate, and apparently young and beautiful.

ADOPTION AND SURROGATE PREGNANCY

According to Lai, the procedure to become a surrogate mother is fairly straightforward. The potential surrogate mother fills in a form, giving personal information including name, age, height, weight, educational level and marital status.

After a gynecological check-up, the agent arranges a meeting between the surrogate mother and customer, usually within a day or two.

For customers seeking surrogate mothers, the waiting period for a suitable candidate can take as long as two months. They have to pay agents 1,000 yuan (US$121) before they can look at photographs of candidates.

All in all, a customer would spend between 130,000 and 140,000 yuan (US $15,700-16,908) for the deal; 100,000 yuan in fees to the surrogate mother, 14,000 yuan to the agency, and the rest to cover the surrogate's medical and living expenses.

Lai said that her company doesn't have an office address because all communications are by telephone and meetings can take place anywhere.

There is a fair amount of information to be found on such agencies' websites. They describe two methods of effecting a surrogate pregnancy; either artificially inseminating the surrogate with both the sperm and ovum of the customer couple, or with only the sperm. Mr Liu, owner of the second agency, said that the artificial insemination procedure is done in "regular hospitals and is absolutely safe."

Asked if impregnation through sexual intercourse was a possibility, Liu said it isn't because none of the parties would agree to it.

The two agencies investigated claimed that they do not accept sex workers or those who work in establishments that offer sexual services as potential surrogates. They also stressed that potential applicants do so voluntarily.

One of the agencies had 113 names on their surrogates list, the oldest being 34 and the youngest 19. More than half of those registered have a college or junior college education, two thirds are unmarried, and half of the remaining one third are divorced. Most of the applicants are from outside Shanghai.

Lai and Liu had similar stories to tell when asked what inspired them to start such an agency. They both said that they had a friend who was deserted by her husband because she couldn't have children, and her miserable experiences made them want to help women in similar predicaments.

Further, they stressed that the practice is not illegal, adding that it's "a loving care activity."

Liu said that his company has successfully handled over 20 cases so far, while Lai reckons her agency signs an agreement every three or four days.

Both also said that business in Shanghai is good where demand is high.

Ge Shannan, a lawyer and expert in the field of women's and children's rights with Shenhui Lawyer's Office, said that there are no relevant laws or regulations that cover surrogate pregnancies. This is because legislation typically always lags behind real life. "That means such activities are not under the umbrella of legal protection," Ge said. She added that since the surrogate agreement does not have legal effect, any suits brought in the event of breach will not be handled by the courts.

Xia Hua, another lawyer with Zhengyi Huaxia Lawyer's Office, stressed that "not all the things in demand are reasonable and legal."

Regulations Concerning Human-Assisted Reproduction Technology issued by the Ministry of Health in 2001 stipulate that any medical establishment that performs operations for the purposes of effecting a surrogate pregnancy should be punished.

On the Internet forums, the topic is also hotly debated with more users voting against surrogacy. Many call it "renting a belly," while others have condemned it as being no different from taking a concubine if sexual intercourse is involved. In a recent online survey, 51 percent of respondents said the practice is an abominable one, and relevant laws should be drafted to prohibit it.

Source: China.org.cn. "China Grapples with Legality of Surrogate Motherhood" (June 2006). Available online. URL: http://www.china.org.cn/english/2006/Jun/170442.htm. Accessed May 8, 2009.

INDIA

Aditya Bharadwaj. "Why Adoption Is Not an Option in India: The Visibility of Infertility, the Secrecy of Donor Insemination, and Other Cultural Complexities" (2003) (Excerpts)

The family unit in India is complex and highly ritualized. In a culture in which caste, class, and kinship ultimately establish identity, marriage and childbirth are addressed with the utmost care and concern through elaborate ceremonies and rituals. Public marriage celebrations and ceremonial child baths announce the family identity to the rest of the community.

Genetics and relatedness play a critical role in the establishment of kinship relationships, which is why infertility can be devastating. For newlywed couples, a diagnosis of infertility can be perceived with shame, and many do not tell their families, but rather seek help in secrecy. The following article addresses the public stigma of infertility and the desire among infertile couples to conceive a child with the help of donor gametes, if necessary, in order to maintain an appearance of reproductive health. To adopt is to announce one's inability to conceive naturally, and adopted children are traditionally seen as outsiders. This article examines the irony of refusing to consider adopting an "outsider" into the family, while secretly utilizing an "outsider's" genetic material.

Cultural importance of children

In the Hindu normative order, the birth of a child—a son, in particular—marks the important shift in the man/woman; celibacy/marriage; father/mother axis. The cog in this structure, narrowly defined as *the son,* and at its broadest as *offspring,* connects the physical with the meta-physical. It is the task of making these physical and meta-physical connections that makes the son a very important requirement according to the ancient legal codes and scriptures. The assigned importance of a son over a daughter, however, must be understood in the context of the gendered norms permeating the Hindu patriarchal order where the male principle is sustained through the agency of male offspring. According to most ancient texts—codes of law and the Upanisads alike—the son is the perpetuation of the self. The man, through the agency of his son, recreates himself; and in this sense is reborn as and in his son.

. . .

Infertility and secrecy: some cultural complexities

In India, infertility—like fertility—is socially visible and hence an object of social control and management. Fertility not only makes conception and reproduction visual entities, but also makes human sexuality visibly public. Absence of offspring in a marriage therefore becomes more visible then their presence. Any measures to restore the "visuality" of fertility must traverse socially defined and approved routes bound by the sacrament of marriage. As in many cultures across the world, the Hindu cosmology conceptualizes an intimate connection between the body and the progeny. This corporeal connection between married body and its offspring is at once biological and social. It inextricably binds mother (womb), father (semen) and child (foetus) in an immutable triad. A "double conceptual bind" unites the biological and social aspects of reproduction by transmuting symbiosis between the socially visible aspects of reproduction such as kinship relations and the invisible biological aspects of sexual reproduction into a "taken-for-granted fact." The cultural "imaginings" of visible social triad of mother/father/child as underscored by an invisible biological triangle of womb, semen and foetus are intimately linked to such cultural conceptions.

Infertility becomes a stigmatized condition when these superimposed triads are destabilized by a married partnership. Married couples who turn to assisted conception do so in the hope of restoring the (visible) "social triad" and to create an illusion of culturally "unproblematic visuality" of fertility.

. . .

Through the course of participant observation at an IVF clinic in a private Delhi Hospital, a number of instances were encountered where the couples enlisted clinicians' help in crafting "official kinship" (mother/father/ child) from more "practical kinship" truths (donor/egg/sperm/embryo) for the consumption of their families and the community. Referring to a patient whom I had briefly met on the morning of this interview, Dr. Neeta said:

The man this morning, he was really under stress. He cried a lot on the day he came to know that he doesn't have sperms, he really cried a lot and the girl also (referring to the wife) cried a lot and then they again came back to me. Next day they were feeling a little better and they said 'we are ready for the treatment (IVF) with donation,' sperm donated conception. I said I am not ready today, you need some more time to talk to each other, go home and then they took two months and after two months they are back and now they are happy, but this man is still going to tell in society that it is "my sperm. Dr. Neeta has taken it out with a small needle and it has been injected in my wife" and they are going to keep the secret throughout their life. The wider family doesn't know and they have told me if they (family members) phone "please don't say anything about our treatment and if somebody phones from our house (*sic*) just say that I have taken out the sperm with a small needle . . ."

The couple appears to be partially concealing their treatment at home. On account of not having clear-cut information on the treatment procedure the couple fears that the family members might call the doctor for more information. The clinician is drawn into the lie that the couple is destined to live for the rest of their lives. Similarly, the following entry in the field notes journal—9 June 1998—on a new patient consultation is revealing:

A young couple walks in.

Woman: Dr. Neeta we called yesterday. We have slight problem can you take a look at these reports and tell us what is happening.

Man: We are married for two and half years and I am in the construction business.

Dr. Neeta is silently reading the reports the couple brought with them.

Woman: (anxious) Do you think something can be done?

Dr. Neeta: (still looking down at the reports) There is no way you can produce sperms (interrupted)

Woman: (high pitched voice) Why this has happened? Why?

Dr. Neeta: Y chromosome genetic test (interrupted)

Man: Is there any way we can correct this?

Dr. Neeta: Donor insemination . . .

Woman: Go for sperm donation! We are not prepared for that, what do we tell the family?

Dr. Neeta: Don't tell the family (interrupted)

Woman: That's one mistake we have made! They all know about the fact that he is not producing. I am not satisfied! I want to know everything there is to know (referring to azoospermia).

Dr. Neeta: We have handsome, well-educated, good-looking boys coming to us for sperm donation and we match the patients and the donor, blood group, etc.

Woman: (thoughtfully) We can also tell them (i.e., the family) that now it is possible to inseminate (using her husband's sperm) or some such excuse!

Dr. Neeta: I had a couple come to me who was anxious about the same thing. The man would ask me to contact him only on the cell (to fix appointments, consult on donor profiles etc.) and if I had to call him at home because they lived in a joint family I had to pretend to be his wife's friend, they even gave me a pseudonym and I (or the assistant) had no choice but to pretend and play along this little game and give the impression that I was his wife's close friend. They went for donor insemination and passed it off as their own.

The need to conceive quickly and reticently is often crucial to the survival of a marriage overburdened by familial pressure. For the couple above, for example, the practical arrangements to conceive were becoming too difficult to manage given that the entire family knew that "he is not producing."

. . .

Keeping it in the family: the taboo on speech

The preference for "keeping it in the family" is quite commonplace amongst some men and their family members. These men, according to clinicians, come to the clinics either on the pretext of consulting with the doctor on the appointment of an appropriate donor or with a straightforward request to include a family donor. Dr. Shanta, when asked to comment on what people look for in a "good donor," revealed that:

People bring family, the father of the (infertile) man, the brother of the man. I don't know how it affects their personal life!

Dr. Kamraj also explained how in her years of practising in Madras, she has had to contend with demands from some individuals wishing to keep the source of sperm and egg donations within the family:

. . . sometimes a man comes and says "I'll get my brother's sperm, my father's sperm." I said, "no way you do that, I will not treat over here." I tell the lady, "a man is unpredictable, Y chromosome is very bad (*sic*) (and) then they will make advances on you and claim your (sexual) rights, are you mentally prepared for that?" So I tell them, "I will not do it here, you can go wherever. Unidentified egg and sperm donor is best" and I say, "the best comes to you, I will match the (blood) group, I'll match even caste, community, I try and match everything" and therefore I don't agree with all of this but I have sister donors, that I allow (but) sperms, no! Only unidentified, but eggs from own sister is fine . . .

. . .

Couples/men who pursue clinical conception in relative anonymity and in insulation from their families approach the issue of alien input in the process of conception differently. In such cases the concern is centred more on the outcome of pregnancy than its actual source. To cite Dr. Shanta again:

Our society is still not so liberated that they accept adoption. They (couples) accept taking donor oocyte, they accept artificial insemination by donor semen anything but they want to deliver the baby so the whole world can see that she has delivered a baby. So many men have got very near normal sperm but out of sheer frustration they say 'oh use any sperm you want I want a baby,' they just don't care! They just want to prove their fertility that is all . . . a woman at some stage in the family wants to prove it . . . the man just wants to prove to the world that his wife has produced a child, that he is capable of fathering a child . . .

There is some truth in Dr. Shanta's assertion. Barring a handful of couples, a great majority, when asked to share their views on donated gamete conception, felt it was acceptable as long as it was kept quiet.

. . .

A publicly visible child incorporated into the family without any corporeal connectedness with the family unit makes the child/couple vulnerable to social ridicule and stigma that is perceived to be worse than being called infertile. Rekha and Sudhir had not given any thought to the idea of adoption, as Sudhir had uncritically prejudged the possibility as unacceptable because of the callous social attitude:

AB: Would you consider adoption?

Sudhir: No!

Rekha: I have considered.

AB: What is your objection to adoption?

Sudhir: There is no objection to it as such, immediately on the face of it I have said no. I have not even given a thought to it. Basic instinctive reaction! Maybe over a period of time I will change, I don't know, maybe, I'm not yet! The biggest problem in adoption over here in India, and it's going to stay till people mature in their thinking, is (that an) adopted child is a bastard child! It's the future of the child (interrupted)

Rekha: How much can they protect themselves (interrupted)

Sudhir: That is the problem with adoption—the stigma attached to the child. Parents can understand because they are of particular age, they are mature enough to think, they have taken their decision for adoption, but what about the kid?

Rekha: Why should you make a child suffer? Why should we make another human being suffer for us?

Sudhir and Rekha were voicing a widespread fear. The idea of a "bastard child" is seen as contaminating family formation in the eyes of the community, so that couples fear that, by adopting, they would condemn the child to live a life full of jibes and ridicule.

Source: Aditya Bharadwaj. "Why Adoption Is Not an Option in India: The Visibility of Infertility, the Secrecy of Donor Insemination, and Other Cultural Complexities." *Social Science & Medicine* 56 (May 2003): 1,867–1,880.

Amelia Gentleman. "India Nurtures Business of Surrogate Motherhood" (2008) (Excerpts)

Since its legalization in 2002, commercial surrogacy has become a thriving industry in India. While couples pay significantly lower fees and costs in India than they would in many other countries, such as the United States, the minimal fee paid to a surrogate is often more than she would otherwise have made over several years. Further, a lack of regulation of the fertility industry presents opportunities to couples and individuals who have been barred from certain procedures in their home countries. While surrogacy is legal in Israel, gay men are barred from commissioning a surrogate pregnancy. In several European countries, older women and single individuals are excluded from many fertility procedures. India's fertility trade and surrogacy programs present an inviting chance for such individuals to create families of their own.

Critics have expressed concern over the disparity of wealth and education between commissioning couples and Indian surrogate mothers, leading some to question the ethics of reproductive tourism.

An enterprise known as reproductive outsourcing is a new but rapidly expanding business in India. Clinics that provide surrogate mothers for foreigners say they have recently been inundated with requests from the United States and Europe, as word spreads of India's mix of skilled medical professionals, relatively liberal laws and low prices.

Commercial surrogacy, which is banned in some states and some European countries, was legalized in India in 2002. The cost comes to about $25,000, roughly a third of the typical price in the United States. That includes the medical procedures; payment to the surrogate mother, which is often, but not always, done through the clinic; plus air tickets and hotels for two trips to India (one for the fertilization and a second to collect the baby).

"People are increasingly exposed to the idea of surrogacy in India; Oprah Winfrey talked about it on her show," said Dr. Kaushal Kadam at the Rotunda clinic in Mumbai. Just an hour earlier she had created an embryo for Mr. Gher and his partner with sperm from one of them (they would not say which) and an egg removed from a donor just minutes before in another part of the clinic.

The clinic, known more formally as Rotunda—The Center for Human Reproduction, does not permit contact between egg donor, surrogate mother or future parents. The donor and surrogate are always different women; doctors say surrogates are less likely to bond with the babies if there is no genetic connection.

There are no firm statistics on how many surrogacies are being arranged in India for foreigners, but anecdotal evidence suggests a sharp increase.

Rudy Rupak, co-founder and president of PlanetHospital, a medical tourism agency with headquarters in California, said he expected to send at least 100 couples to India this year for surrogacy, up from 25 in 2007, the first year he offered the service.

"Every time there is a success story, hundreds of inquiries follow," he said.

. . .

Under guidelines issued by the Indian Council of Medical Research, surrogate mothers sign away their rights to any children. A surrogate's name is not even on the birth certificate.

This eases the process of taking the baby out of the country. But for many, like Lisa Switzer, 40, a medical technician from San Antonio whose twins are being carried by a surrogate mother from the Rotunda clinic, the overwhelming attraction is the price. "Doctors, lawyers, accountants, they can afford it, but the rest of us—the teachers, the nurses, the secretaries—we can't," she said. "Unless we go to India."

Surrogacy is an area fraught with ethical and legal uncertainties. Critics argue that the ease with which relatively rich foreigners are able to "rent" the wombs of poor Indians creates the potential for exploitation. Although the government is actively promoting India as a medical tourism destination, what some see as an exchange of money for babies has made many here uncomfortable.

The Ministry of Women and Child Development said in February that it was weighing recommending legislation to govern surrogacy, but it is not imminent.

An article published in The Times of India in February questioned how such a law would be enforced: "In a country crippled by abject poverty," it asked, "how will the government body guarantee that women will not agree to surrogacy just to be able to eat two square meals a day?"

Even some of those involved in the business of organizing surrogates want greater regulation. "There must be protection for the surrogates," Mr. Rupak said. "Inevitably, people are going to smell the money, and unscrupulous operators will get into the game. I don't trust the industry to police itself."

Yonatan Gher, an Israeli, made his first trip to Mumbai with his partner in January to visit a fertility clinic.

He said that the few doctors offering the service now were ethical and took good care of the surrogates but that he was concerned this might change as the business expanded.

Mr. Gher and his partner, who asked not to be named to preserve his privacy, have worked through their doubts and are certain they are doing a good thing.

"People can believe me when I say that if I could bear the baby myself I would," he said. "But this is a mutually beneficial answer. The surrogate gets a fair amount of money for being part of the process."

They are paying about $30,000, of which the surrogate gets about $7,500.

"Surrogates do it to give their children a better education, to buy a home, to start up a small business, a shop," Dr. Kadam said. "This is as much money as they could earn in maybe three years. I really don't think that this is exploiting the women. I feel it is two people who are helping out each other."

Mr. Gher agreed. "You cannot ignore the discrepancies between Indian poverty and Western wealth," he said. "We try our best not to abuse this power. Part of our choice to come here was the idea that there was an opportunity to help someone in India."

In the Mumbai clinic, it is clear that an exchange between rich and poor is under way. On some contracts, the thumbprint of an illiterate surrogate stands out against the clients' signatures.

Although some Indian clinics allow surrogates and clients to meet, Mr. Gher said he preferred anonymity. When his surrogate gives birth later this year, he and his partner will be in the hospital, but not in the ward where she is in labor, and will be handed the baby by a nurse.

The surrogate mother does not know that she is working for foreigners, Dr. Kadam said, and has not been told that the future parents are both men. Gay sex is illegal in India.

Israel legalized adoption by same-sex couples in February, but such couples are not permitted to hire surrogates in Israel to become parents. A fertility doctor recommended Rotunda, which made news in November when its doctors delivered twins for another gay Israeli couple.

Rotunda did not allow interviews with its surrogate mothers, but a 32-year-old woman at a fertility clinic in Delhi explained why she is planning on her second surrogacy in two years.

Separated from her husband, she found that her monthly wages of 2,800 rupees, about $69, as a midwife were not enough to raise her 9-year-old son. With the money she earned from the first surrogacy, more than $13,600, she bought a house. She expects to pay for her son's education with what she earns for the second, about $8,600. (Fees are typically fixed by the doctor and can vary.) "I will save the money for my child's future," she said.

The process requires a degree of subterfuge in this socially conservative country. She has told her mother, who lives with her, but not her son or their neighbors. She has told the few who have asked her outright that she is bearing a child for a relative.

So far, for the Israeli couple, the experience of having a baby has been strangely virtual. They perused profiles of egg donors that were sent by e-mail ("We picked the one with the highest level of education," Mr. Gher said). From information that followed, they rejected a factory worker in favor of a housewife, who they thought would have a less stressful lifestyle.

Mr. Gher posts updates about the process on Facebook. And soon the clinic will start sending ultrasound images of their developing child by e-mail. Highly pixelated, blown-up passport photos of the egg donor and surrogate mother adorn a wall of their apartment in Israel.

"We've been trying to half close our eyes and look at it in a more holistic way to imagine what she would actually look like," Mr. Gher said of the donor's blurred image. "These are women we don't know, will never know, who will become in a way part of our lives."

Source: Amelia Gentleman. "India Nurtures Business of Surrogate Motherhood." *New York Times* (3/10/08). Available online. URL: www.nytimes.com/2008/03/10/world/Asia/10surrogate.html. Accessed September 27, 2009.

GREAT BRITAIN

Kim Cotton and Denise Winn.
For Love and Money (1985) (Excerpts)

In 1985, Kim Cotton became the first surrogate mother in Britain to go public with her pregnancy. Having been artificially inseminated with the sperm of the contracting father, Cotton conceived and later gave birth to a baby girl. She had never met the couple for whom she would become a surrogate in exchange for £6,500, and she later sold her story for an additional £15,000. Kim Cotton's pregnancy became the subject of fierce debate in the United Kingdom over the ethics of conception for money. As money was so heavily involved in Cotton's case, many accused her of selling her child, and immediately after the baby was born she was taken into custody by social services and made a ward of the court. Neither Kim Cotton nor the contracting parents were allowed to take her home. However, as Cotton expressed her explicit desire not to take custody of the child, the High Court had no choice but to grant custody to the contracting couple, who were deemed to be caring and compassionate people who would provide a loving home for the child.

Kim Cotton went on to establish COTS (Childlessness Overcome Through Surrogacy), a nonprofit program that matched surrogates with contracting couples, but she resigned from her position as chairperson in 1999 due to increasing controversy and tighter governmental crackdowns on commercial surrogacy.

Talking to the agency

Geoff listened as Kim eagerly tried to express all the thoughts that had been whirling round in her head for days, the possibilities, the fears and the reservations. He was used to Kim's impulsive enthusiasms, and he felt, just as Kim had, that the possibility of any of this actually happening was remote. But he was quite sincere when he said, 'It's up to you. I can't say yes or no. But if you decided to do it, I'll support you,' and agreed that although it seemed an unnatural act it was justifiable if it fulfilled some desperate couple's deep desire for a child.

. . .

For Kim the conversation was a relief. Voicing this apparently wild fantasy that had taken possession of her had been the first hurdle, and it was now behind her. Once the idea was out in the open, at least to some extent, she started to sound out other members of her own family for their views. First she told her mother, who, remembering her own desire for children in the face of initial opposition, decided it was a marvelous idea if Kim could really bring herself to do it. For herself, she knew she couldn't give a child away. She also felt she would rather Kim did it for nothing. 'But I guess I'm not the perfect angel type.' Kim wrote in her diary later, 'because I want to improve the circumstances of my own family too.'

Next she mentioned the surrogacy idea to her sister-in-law Lyn as they were both taking their daughters to their Thursday afternoon ballet class. To her distress Lyn was appalled and disgusted, and when they arrived back at Kim's brother's house with the children, Neal was equally scathing. 'That's just the same as being a prostitute. Why don't you do that instead?' he demanded.

'Oh, come on, Neal,' retorted Kim. 'You know it isn't the same at all.' But although they parted amicably he wouldn't be budged. Kim's father, mindful of money as always, only commented that anyone who could do it deserved £60,000 not a mere £6,500 while Jill said it didn't feel right, a view shared by Iain who, although a practising Catholic, was still generous enough to say to Kim, 'It's your life and your choice.' They both felt, however, that the emotional stress might be too much and that she wouldn't be able to give away the baby.

Martyn and his wife had similar views. 'If it is what you want to do, then I suppose you'll do it,' said Ann. 'But if it was me, I know I would feel bereaved after.'

But as the days passed the idea became more and more firmly rooted in Kim's mind, support and opposition both serving to spur her on. One day, when she and Geoff were in the car taking Jaime to the swimming pool, she turned to him and asked him what he thought about her having a baby for someone else. She told him that some couples couldn't have babies by themselves and that she was thinking of helping them. 'It wouldn't be a brother or a sister for you,' she said. 'But Mummy would be paid and then we would be able to buy you the pool table you want.' Jaime was already a proficient pool player and longed for his own table. But even his delight at such a glorious prospect didn't prevent him from saying, 'Could you do it for just a little money, so that the couple have plenty left to look after the baby?'

· · ·

Kim

Do you feel that you considered all the possible pitfalls before going ahead with a pregnancy as a surrogate?

Looking back on it, no. I was just so enchanted by the idea of doing something so novel and exciting and, at the same time, so marvellous for the couple and so helpful for me. I din't want to be put off and I'm always an optimist anyway. I thought hard about whether I could carry another baby that wasn't my husband's and then give it up and, though obviously I couldn't be sure, I felt extremely strongly that I could.

I think I must have blotted out any deep fears and feelings about carrying another man's child while living with Geoff. I saw it as something we were both entering into for a common end and that I would feel no more involved with the child than he was. I knew I never wanted to meet the father and I wouldn't have considered surrogacy at all if insemination had to be by sex. That would have made it all too tangible. Whereas, this way, it all seemed so remote from reality that I didn't even think I could consider the child my own. The way I looked at it, any child that wasn't Geoff's and therefore wasn't born from love (I think of Jamie and Anouska as love-children), wouldn't be mine either.

I saw myself as the vehicle for the baby to enter the world. It's just a sad reality that sometimes it takes three to make a baby instead of two. I was going to be the carrier, a postman delivering a very special parcel.

. . .

What made you so confident that you could give up the baby at birth?
I never took it for granted that it would be easy. I knew that, whatever I might think, my hormones might take over and my body might fight my mind. I thought, for instance, about how instantly I had fallen in love with Anouska after that wonderful birth. But I couldn't believe it would be the same, under the circumstances, and I also knew it just wouldn't be in me to devastate those desperate parents in that way. After all, it would be the husband's natural child. His right to it was as great as, if not greater than, mine, as he had no other chances. I felt that the thought of bringing such joy to those people who must, till now, have given up all hope, would give me the courage to let the baby go. And anyway, how could I even have considered keeping the baby, when it wasn't Geoff's child?

On the practical side, it made it easier knowing, from my own two children, just what hard work babies are. All those sleepless nights and feeds and nappy-changing. It was a plus to know that this time after the birth the responsibility wouldn't be mine and I could go home and sleep for a week if I wanted.

. . .

Source: Kim Cotton and Denise Winn. *Baby Cotton: For Love and Money.* London: Darling Kindersten, 1985, pp. 29–30, 35–37.

Amelia Hill. "Adoption Agencies Shun U.K.: Developing Countries Brand British Safeguards as 'Unsuitable' for Children Who Need a Family" (2006)

Due to lax policies and weak central government oversight of international adoption in the United Kingdom, sending countries have expressed a general reluctance to allow their children to be adopted by British couples. Much of the problem stems from fluctuating opinions of overseas adoption by social workers. While some approve of the practice, others are strongly opposed and refuse to participate in foreign adoptions, which has led many couples to circumvent the law and adopt illegally, without home studies or thorough investigations into their suitability. Other cases of international adoption in Britain have been disrupted when it was determined that adoption officials were not properly certified.

The United Kingdom has the lowest intercountry adoption rate of all developed nations, and a recent report released by UNICEF ranks it as having one of the lowest rates of child well-being among developed countries.

BRITONS ADOPT fewer children from abroad than any other nationality because an increasing number of developing countries believe Britain is an unsuitable home, research reveals.

The study, which shows that many countries are automatically rejecting applications from British families, comes in the wake of attempts by Madonna and her husband, Guy Ritchie, to adopt a 14-month-old boy from Malawi.

A few days ago, an African court granted an interim order allowing David Banda to leave the impoverished African state. But the couple returned to London at the weekend without the child after human rights groups in Malawi revealed that they were to seek a court injunction tomorrow to stop the adoption. The couple may also have to go through rigorous local authority checks in this country before they are allowed to bring in the child from abroad, under the 're-adoption' laws that were introduced in 1993 to prevent illegal trafficking of children.

It emerged last night that the boy's uncle has demanded to see David's prospective new home. The African uncle, Pofera Banda, said: 'If this child is taken, as we've been told, when will our child be visiting us? When will we visit him? How much contact will there be between us and him?'

The difficulties faced by other Britons trying to adopt from abroad is causing people to turn to countries whose approach to the process is less rigorous, such as Guatemala and Bulgaria, raising questions about whether the children are being freely given up by their parents.

'Most other countries seeking children from overseas have individual agreements with the foreign governments, detailing the post-adoption care the children will receive,' said Dr Peter Selman, chairman of the Network for Intercountry Adoption, who presented his research in Barcelona last week.

Overseas adoption in Britain remained largely unorganised and unregulated until the Adoption Act in 1999. Experts say Britain still fails to take overseas adoptions seriously. 'The list of countries who now refuse to even consider applications from Britain is growing. If nothing changes, there is a real danger that the number of foreign children available to British families will dry up completely,' said Gill Haworth, director of the Intercountry Adoption Centre. In Norway, the rate of foreign adoptions is 15 for every 100,000 inhabitants and in Spain it is 13. In Britain it is 0.55.

Selman says: 'The demand to adopt foreign children is so high that states looking to place children with overseas families can take their pick from countries across the world,' he said.

'The attitude these countries hold is correct—our procedures are embarrassingly underdeveloped. If I was a government wondering where to send my children, I would not touch a country that makes as little effort as Britain.'

Source: Amelia Hill. "Adoption Agencies Shun U.K.: Developing Countries Brand British Safeguards as 'Unsuitable' for Children Who Need a Family." *Observed* (10/15/06). Available online. URL: www.guardian.co.uk/society/2006/oct/15/adoptionandfostering.childrenservices. Accessed September 27, 2009.

Helen Weathers. "Now I Realise How Hopelessly Naïve I Was to Become Britain's First Surrogate Mother, Admits Kim Cotton" (2008) (Excerpts)

Twenty-three years after her involvement in the much publicized "Baby Cotton" scandal, Kim Cotton recounts her story in the following interview and admits that while she does not regret her actions, she does regret the general circumstances in which they occurred. Now a grandmother, she still supports surrogate pregnancy, but maintains that it is in need of greater regulation.

Shortly after the Baby Cotton scandal of the 1980s, the British government passed legislation banning commercial surrogacy, allowing payment only for necessary expenses. The definition of necessary expenses is open to interpretation, however, which has allowed surrogacy centers to continue to operate. A number of surrogacy controversies have developed since the birth of Baby Cotton, and Kim Cotton's name inevitably surfaces in the discussion.

Shortly after the birth of her first grandchild three years ago, Kim Cotton had the following conversation with her daughter Anouska.

ADOPTION AND SURROGATE PREGNANCY

Besotted with her newborn baby, Anouska told her mother: "I could never, ever do what you did."

What Kim Cotton did 23 years ago has haunted her ever since.

. . .

So how does Kim, 51, feel about it all now? Does she agree with her 28-year-old daughter?

Does she regret giving away Baby Cotton, who, having been conceived with her egg and the sperm of the father, was biologically half hers?

Kim thinks carefully before she speaks.

"No, I don't regret it," she says.

"How can you regret creating a life and helping an infertile couple to become parents?

"How can you regret giving them that joy? What I do regret is the way in which it was done."

Kim, married to Geoff and the mother of two young children when she agreed to become a surrogate, never met the Swedish couple she helped.

For 23 years they have remained anonymous, and Kim has received not one single letter or photograph of the daughter she conceived for them.

This she now believes was wrong and blames her own youthful naivety for believing she could walk away emotionally unscathed.

Indeed, shortly after Baby Cotton was born she said: "You can cut off all maternal feeling if you try hard enough."

. . .

Over the years, however, she has learned to her cost that you can't cut off all feeling—maternal or not.

"In my 20s I was a timid little mouse—I wouldn't say boo to a goose.

"I thought I was a nobody, but through surrogacy I thought I could become a somebody," she says, admitting that she was also partly motivated by money.

"I had two young children. I'd had two trouble-free pregnancies and I thought this was the one thing I was really good at.

"When you are helping someone else have a baby, you feel so good about yourself, and with the money I received I could improve the quality of my children's lives.

"I don't know how I knew I'd be able to give up the baby, but somehow I knew that I could.

"But I now feel it was wrong to do it for a couple I'd never met and with whom I've had no contact since.

"I've had contact over the years with a friend who was involved in the surrogacy, so I know a little bit about them, but I don't know if her parents have told Baby Cotton about me."

In 1991, Kim also carried twins for an infertile friend who did not pay her.

"My second experience of surrogacy was completely different.

"It was fantastic. We became very close and are still friends to this day.

"I see her children all the time and it worked out very well.

"And that's how I think it should be. If a couple are desperate to be parents, they should be there throughout the pregnancy.

"They should be there for every scan and ante-natal appointment.

"A surrogate needs a positive relationship with the people she is helping.

"I believe it is important for the surrogate's emotional health."

Then she adds: "You know, I'm not hard to find, so if Baby Cotton knows about me and really wanted to get in contact, I think she would have done by now."

One gains the impression that this would be entirely welcome.

"I've talked to my own daughter about it and she understands why I did it—but now that she's a mother herself, she knows that she could never do it herself, and I respect that.

"She has never criticised me for it; it's just something she would find impossible."

These days, Kim, married for 33 years, mother to Anouska, 28, and Jamie, 31, and grandmother of two, likes to distance herself from the whole thorny issue of surrogacy.

In 1988 she founded the charity COTS (Childlessness Overcome Through Surrogacy), an introduction agency for surrogates and potential parents, but quit in 1999 after a series of scandals, for which she felt personally and unfairly blamed, and a damning exposé on television's *Panorama*.

There were tales of surrogates refusing to hand over the babies once they were born, of secret abortions and health scares, of some surrogate mums becoming physically attracted to the sperm donors and of adoptive mums changing their minds at the 11th hour, leaving the surrogate holding the baby.

Such cases prompted legislation making it illegal for surrogates to be paid, allowing them "expenses" instead, but still there are people who believe Kim—albeit it with the best intentions—opened an ethical and moral can of worms.

· · ·

"For years, whenever surrogacy went wrong, I'd get the blame—and it drove me to the brink of a nervous breakdown.

"I became a very defensive and hard person, but now that I have distanced myself I am much happier and softer.

"Surrogacy changed me as a person—but it wasn't all for the bad.

"I learned to stand up for myself and what I believe in.

"I don't think I'd be running a company now if I hadn't been through that experience."

Kim still believes that surrogacy can be a force of good and should not be outlawed.

More than 500 surrogate babies have been born since COTS was set up and, she says, despite popular belief, the vast majority have been successful.

"It's only the disasters you ever hear about," says Kim, "not the success stories.

"There are hundreds of children—happy children—and their parents who wouldn't exist today if it hadn't been for surrogacy."

Source: Helen Weathers. "Now I Realise How Hopelessly Naïve I Was to Become Britain's First Surrogate Mother, Admits Kim Cotton." *Daily Mail* (February 2008). Available online. URL: http://www.dailymail.co.uk/femail/article-514230/Now-I-realise-hopelessly-naive-I-Britains-surrogate-mother-admits-Kim-Cotton.html. Accessed May 9, 2009.

GUATEMALA

Juan Carlos Llorca. "Guatemala Adoption Fraud: Couple Pursues Baby's Identity/California Pair Wanted Girl but Decided to Expose 'Horrifying' System" (2008)

Despite numerous efforts to curtail fraud and baby-buying in the Guatemalan adoption industry, the lucrative business persisted through various other means. Accounts of faked DNA samples, mothers coerced into relinquishing their children, and falsified birth certificates eventually led to a governmental crackdown that left thousands of intercountry adoptions in a state of limbo. Many adoptive parents in the United States pushed for speedy processing of the adoptions, but the delicate and complex web of falsified documents, bribery, and possible kidnapping has forced both the U.S. and Guatemalan governments to hold all adoption cases until each has been carefully investigated.

171

ADOPTION AND SURROGATE PREGNANCY

The following article describes one family's suspicion that their adopted daughter's DNA sample was faked. For years, the U.S. and Guatemalan governments have relied on DNA sampling as the primary means of stanching fraud and eliminating the practice of hiring women to pose as birth mothers. In recent months, however, cases have surfaced in which children's DNA samples have been switched and signed off by a doctor. Investigations into several adoption cases have led to criminal charges.

GUATEMALA CITY—Jennifer and Todd Hemsley had to give up their child to save her.

Like thousands of other would-be parents, the California couple made a $15,500 down payment to a U.S. agency that guaranteed quick, hassle-free adoptions of Guatemalan babies. And like the others, they were caught in a bureaucratic limbo after Guatemala began cracking down on systemic fraud last year.

Many Americans with pending adoptions lobbied hard for quick approval of their cases, trying to bypass a new system designed to prevent identity fraud and the sale or even theft of children to feed Guatemala's $100 million adoption business.

But Jennifer Hemsley did what Guatemala's new National Adoptions Council says no other American has done this year: She refused to look the other way when she suspected her would-be daughter's identity and DNA samples were faked.

She halted the adoption of Maria Eugenia Cua Yax, whom the couple named Hazel. She stayed in Guatemala for months, spending thousands of dollars, until she could deliver the girl into state custody.

Her decision could mean the Hemsleys—Jennifer is a freelance designer and Todd creates visual effects in the film industry—may never be able to adopt the little girl they nicknamed la boca, or "mouth" in Spanish, in honor of her outsized spirit.

"It's so crazy. None of this makes any sense," Hemsley said.

But she says it was the only thing she could have done.

"It wasn't even a choice. We did what I hope any parent would do: put their child first."

The Hemsleys say they had many reasons for suspicion. But the final straw was a doctor's statement that said DNA samples were taken from the baby and birth mother on a date when Hazel was with Jennifer Hemsley. She said her Guatemalan attorney told her: "Don't worry about it. You want the adoption to go through, don't you?"

If all it takes is a doctor's signature to hide a switch in DNA, it would challenge the bedrock evidence on which the U.S. Embassy has depended to guarantee the legitimacy of thousands of Guatemalan adoptions over the past 10 years.

Neither country has the appetite for challenging already-approved adoptions. But Hemsley says anyone who has doubts about an adopted baby's identity should know that the Guatemalan DNA evidence might be worthless.

Guatemala's quick adoptions made the nation of 13 million the world's second-largest source of babies to the U.S. after China. But last year the industry was closed down, starting with an August 2007 raid on what had been considered one of the country's most reputable adoption agencies.

Voluminous fraud has been exposed since then—false paperwork, fake birth certificates, women coerced into giving up their children and even baby theft. At least 25 cases resulted in criminal charges against doctors, lawyers, mothers and civil registrars.

Thousands of adoptions, including that of the Hemsleys, were put on hold until this year, when the newly formed National Adoptions Council began requiring birth mothers to personally verify they still wanted to give up their children. Of 3,032 pending cases, nearly 1,000 were dismissed because no birth mother showed up.

Prosecutors suspect many of the babies in these cases never existed—that Guatemalan baby brokers registered false identities with the council in hopes of matching them later to babies obtained through fraud.

Understaffed and with few resources, the adoptions council ruled out new DNA tests as too costly and time-consuming. All but a few hundred cases have been pushed through in the months since.

"The ramifications are immense," Hemsley said. "How many children adopted by U.S. families may have had DNA falsifications such as this, and the U.S. adopting family is unknowing of the fraud?"

Prompted by the Hemsleys, Guatemalan investigators are trying to determine Hazel's true identity and have opened a criminal investigation into the people who vouched for her paperwork—from the U.S. adoption agency to Guatemalan notaries, foster parents, a doctor and the laboratory that said it collected the girl's DNA.

Jaime Tecu, a former prosecutor who now leads investigations for the adoptions council, praised Jennifer Hemsley.

"This makes me believe that there are people who still hold ethical values," Tecu said.

In an earlier case of switched DNA, Esther Sulamita, a girl stolen at gunpoint and given a false identity, was recognized and recovered by her birth mother in July just before an Indiana couple could adopt her.

Dr. Aida Gutierrez handled the DNA for both Hazel and Esther Sulamita. Now under investigation for allegedly forging birth documents, she told prosecutors she followed established procedures.

The problem could be solved by improving the chain of custody over DNA evidence—for example, by requiring new mother-and-child saliva samples taken under the supervision of a government authority that would send it directly to U.S. labs for testing.

But the embassy still says it must depend on the ethics of the Guatemalan doctors involved. The adoptions council president, Elizabeth de Larios, says more DNA tests would mean more costs and "more and more months of being away from loving families" for the babies.

Guatemala's old, fraud-plagued adoption industry was still going full speed in June 2007 when the Hemsleys first held the 4-month-old girl.

"It was magical and a gift, and a feeling beyond description," Jennifer Hemsley said.

But even before their case was turned over to the adoptions council, the Hemsleys were suspicious. The supposed birth mother disappeared after a brief meeting where she "had no visible reaction at all to the child," Jennifer Hemsley said.

174

Medical reports seemed obvious forgeries, without letterhead or doctor's signature. And during a critical hearing, Jennifer Hemsley said, her Guatemalan advisers tried to pay a stranger to pose as Hazel's foster mother.

"Todd and I felt a lot like, 'Gee, is this really happening? Maybe we should just look the other way and keep plodding along,' because every time I tried to tell someone, nobody cared," Jennifer Hemsley said. "I couldn't look the other way. I just couldn't turn my head."

Ricardo Ordonez, the Hemsleys' adoption attorney, denied any fraud and vowed to clear his name by producing the birth mother for new DNA tests. Another court hearing is pending.

If the Hemsleys had walked away, as hundreds of other Americans did after problems surfaced, Hazel would likely have been abandoned or reoffered for adoption under another false identity, Tecu said. Instead, Jennifer Hemsley stayed with Hazel for months, draining more than $70,000 from a second mortgage on their home and paying for a trusted nanny.

"She was a real take-charge little girl," Jennifer Hemsley said. "We had a little walker for her, and she's just a real daredevil. She always let you know what she wanted."

Finally, as a colleague of Ordonez threatened to take the girl away, she asked the adoptions council for a "rescue."

The new rules require authorities to consider Guatemalan citizens before Americans, and several dozen Guatemalan couples are in line ahead of the Hemsleys. But they aren't giving up yet.

Jennifer Hemsley returned this month to Guatemala City, where she briefly held Hazel—now more than 19 months old—at a crowded orphanage. She emerged devastated.

Crying and shaking, she said Hazel had open sores on her face and a cut on her head. Within hours, she managed to persuade authorities to transfer the girl to a better nursery while the case is resolved.

"I think about her every day," Jennifer Hemsley said. "It's horrifying on many levels. It's horrifying for Guatemalan women who may have missing children.

It's horrifying for adoptive families in the U.S. My parents are devastated over this. This affects our whole entire family, our friends, our neighbors."

Source: Juan Carlos Llorca. "Guatemala Adoption Fraud: Couple Pursues Baby's Identity/California Pair Wanted Girl but Decided to Expose 'Horrifying' System." *Houston Chronicle* (Nov. 2008).

Embassy of the United States, Guatemala. "Warden Information: Rumors of Child Stealing" (2007) (Excerpt)

The lack of government oversight of adoption, in addition to much-publicized cases of kidnapping and coercion, has led many Guatemalan families to fear for their children's safety. In some villages, this has led to the formation of vigilante groups, who fear that foreigners (Americans, in particular) are kidnapping infants and toddlers to be adopted, or rather sold, to U.S. families. Intermingled with such fears is the suspicion that Guatemalan baby brokers and wealthy American couples are arranging adoptions for the purposes of organ harvesting. While such concerns have not been substantiated, they speak to a general lack of information as well as a population-wide distrust of the international adoption trade. Such fears are justified when a pregnant Guatemalan woman is offered money in exchange for her baby, having no knowledge of the buyer's intentions or motives. In a culture in which the family is central to community life, the lack of regulation within the Guatemalan adoption industry and the secrecy surrounding its means of procuring children has bred fear and suspicion.

Rumors of child theft for organ harvesting is a more literal projection of a nationwide resentment of exploitation. While it is unlikely that children who are kidnapped for the adoption trade are stolen for the purpose of organ harvesting, such rumors speak to the perceived reality that Guatemalans are being exploited as a source of babies for wealthy foreigners. Until firm regulations are implemented and information regarding the intercountry adoption industry is widely disseminated, such fears and resentment will likely persist.

Particularly virulent rumors of child stealing and of murder for organ harvesting have recently surfaced in two separate areas of Guatemala frequented by American tourists. On June 15, 2007, a Guatemalan child from Camotan, Chiquimula (near the border with Honduras, on the main road leading from Guatemala to the Copan Mayan ruins) was found dead and mutilated. Three local women who allegedly acted as go-betweens for foreign adoptions were accused by a mob of kidnapping and killing the girl. One of these women was killed by the mob and the other two were severely injured. Locals burned a police car in nearby Jocotan, and forced the police out of Jocotan and Camotan.

Since late May 2007, rumors have been circulating in the El Golfete area of the Rio Dulce near Livingston, Izabal, of babies being stolen from neighboring villages by armed men. Local authorities did respond to villagers' reports, but were not able to confirm any such cases. Despite that response, residents of small villages in the area remain mobilized and suspicious of all outsiders, including foreigners.

Another incident in Cunen, Quiche, resulted in a local riot with travel on the road from Cunen to Santa Maria Nebaj temporarily interrupted while the PNC re-establishes control. Americans are advised to exercise caution in these areas.

Rumors of child stealing have resulted in the lynching deaths of several Guatemalan citizens this year. Although no foreigners have been reported to be the victim of such attacks recently, Americans are reminded to avoid gatherings of agitated people. Avoid close contact with children, including taking photographs, especially in rural areas. Such contact can be viewed with deep alarm and may provoke panic and violence.

Source: U.S. Embassy, Guatemala. "Warden Information: Rumors of Child Stealing" (July 2007). Available online. URL: http://guatemala.usembassy.gov/wardene20070703.html. Accessed May 11, 2009.

Human Rights Watch. "Letter to the Guatemalan Congress Regarding Marriage and Family Law" (2007)

In 2007, the Guatemalan government introduced the Integral Protection for Marriage and Family Act, which proposed a new, legal definition of family as that which consists of two heterosexual parents and their naturally conceived offspring. Such legislation would exclude nearly 40 percent of Guatemalan families from the legal definition of family, which could result in potential human rights violations if the new definition of family finds no legal relationship between a child and his or her parents or siblings. While the Act specifically targets single and homosexual parents, the new definition would also exclude children who have been conceived via assisted reproductive technology. Of even more concern to human rights groups is the Act's call for mandatory support from all political representatives, under threat of punishment if any politician calls for a different definition of family.

ADOPTION AND SURROGATE PREGNANCY

The Lesbian, Gay, Bisexual, and Transgender Rights Program within the international organization Human Rights Watch issued a public letter to the Guatemalan congress urging officials to vote against the Act. As of 2009, the Guatemalan congress has not voted on it.

On behalf of Human Rights Watch, I urge you to vote against the approval of the "Integral Protection for Marriage and Family Act." This legislative initiative would write discriminatory treatment of families into law.

- Exclude almost 40% of Guatemala's families and children from the protection given to other families (the bill would eliminate single-parent or other non-nuclear families from the definition of "family," and bar same-sex couples and their families from any form of legal recognition);
- Exclude children who were conceived thanks to artificial insemination and other treatments, potentially barring them from the definition of "family";
- Commit Guatemala to endorse this restrictive definition of the family at all international as well as national gatherings, and punish Guatemalan government representatives who publicly support a different definition.

The United Nations Development Programme has reported that 39.86% of families in Guatemala are non-nuclear ones. This bill attacks the rights and legal status not only of these diverse forms of the family, but of the children reared in them. Guatemala should stand on the side of children and their families—not deprive them arbitrarily of recognition and rights.

The act would establish that "family essentially originates, exclusively, from the conjugal union between a man and a woman, and its legal foundation, in harmony with its essence, its purity, its nature, its reason of being, its values and original meaning, through marriage, as well as through a legally declared de facto union and other social forms, such as a religious ceremony or ritual, custom or cultural practice, among others." (article 1 (a))

In addition to its definition of marriage, the act would restrict civil unions (uniones de hecho) to the partnership of a man and a woman with the capacity to marry, thereby eliminating any possibility for the legal recognition of same-sex relationships. It would declare that the family extends only to "procreation in the natural form," and includes only "children procreated as a result of the natural union between both partners," with a sole exception for adoption—thus vaguely but sweepingly bringing the status of children born through assisted reproductive technologies into question.

And it would enforce upon all representatives of the Guatemalan state the obligation to support this definition, in international as well as national settings, making it a crime to do otherwise.

Article 1 of the Guatemalan Constitution states that the Guatemalan State is founded, among other goals, to protect the family. Article 47, commits the state to protecting families "on the legal basis of marriage, the equality of rights for spouses, responsible parenting, and the right to family planning." However, the Constitution does not define either a family or marriage in terms of the union of a man and a woman or suggest that protection will only be given to a family composed of a man and a woman. Rather, the Constitution affirms equality in a manner inconsistent with this bill—declaring that "[i]n Guatemala, all human beings are free and equal in dignity and rights."

By contrast, the proposed law shows a clear intent to codify discrimination against certain family structures. Vice President of the Congress, Oliverio García Rodas has indicated that its principal aim is discriminatory: to restrict any state recognition of the families formed by same-sex couples. García Rodas has stated that "Congressmen are worried by a news report related to the celebration of same-sex marriages." Yet the bill would also adversely affect single-parent families, divorced parents, and many unmarried heterosexual couples, as well as many indigenous family structures. It could potentially affect the legal status of children born with the assistance of reproductive technologies.

The Law of Social Development, passed in 2001, has already expanded the concept of nuclear family to include single mothers and fathers as well as indigenous family structures, opening reproductive health services and other forms of family care to them.

This law would potentially endanger such vital service provision. The bill's proposed definition would encode not only indifference but prejudice toward the multiple forms of family in society.

The American Convention on Human Rights, to which Guatemala is a party, establishes the rights pertaining to family in Article 17(1). It states that as "the natural and fundamental group unit of society," the family "is entitled to protection by society and the state." The Convention does not restrict the concept of family but leaves room to include different structures. The Inter-American Court recognized this in its judgment in *Aloeboetoe et al. v. Surinam,* explaining "that it is necessary to take into account the family structure" of a particular indigenous group in allocating compensation to

179

survivors, regardless of whether that structure is recognized by the state in the form of marriage.

Other international bodies recognize the need for respect towards different forms of families. The UN Committee on the Rights of the Child, which interprets the Convention on the Rights of the Child, has stated that with regard to the "family environment," the Convention reflects "different family structures arising from various cultural patterns and emerging family relationships" and "refers to various forms of families, such as the extended family, and is applicable in a variety of families such as the nuclear family, re-constructed family, joint family, single-parent family, common-law family and adoptive family." The UN High Commissioner for Refugees has gone further and specifically recommended that the right to family unification include same-sex partners. In its view, States should adopt "a pragmatic interpretation of the family. . . . Families should be understood to include spouses; those in customary marriage; long-term cohabitants, including same-sex couples; and minor children until at least age eighteen."

The discriminatory aim of the law also contravenes international human rights protections for equality. The UN Committee on the Elimination of Discrimination against Women (charged with interpreting and monitoring compliance with the UN Convention on the Elimination of all Forms of Discrimination against Women, or CEDAW, to which Guatemala is a party since August 1982) has stressed that women's enjoyment of rights and access to services should not depend on their marital status.

The International Covenant on Civil and Political Rights (ICCPR), to which Guatemala acceded without reservations in 1992, affirms the equality of all people in its articles 2 and 26. In the 1994 case of *Nicholas Toonen v. Australia*, the United Nations Human Rights Committee, the international body of experts that monitors compliance with the ICCPR, found that both these provisions should be understood to include sexual orientation as a status protected against discrimination. Specifically it held, that "reference to 'sex' in articles 2, para. 1 and article 26 is to be taken as including sexual orientation." The UN Human Rights Committee has held that same-sex relationships must be recognized for the purposes of pensions and other benefits in the cases of *Young v. Australia* and, most recently, in *X v. Colombia*.

Similarly, the Inter-American Commission on Human Rights also has concluded that gender-based distinctions in rights in relation to the family cannot be justified. In *Maria Eugenia Morales v. Guatemala*, the Commission found a violation to the rights of family life in reference to Article 16(1) of CEDAW. It found Guatemala in breach of its international obligations and determined that "specific steps . . . must be taken to ensure substantive equality in family law and family relations."

The Yogyakarta Principles on the application of international human rights law in relation to sexual orientation and gender identity, released in 2007, draw together these international protections for family and for non discrimination. The Principles hold that "[e]veryone has the right to found a family, regardless of sexual orientation or gender identity. Families exist in diverse forms. No family may be subjected to discrimination on the basis of the sexual orientation or gender identity of any of its members."

The Principles urge states to "[e]nsure that laws and policies recognise the diversity of family forms, including those not defined by descent or marriage, and take all necessary legislative, administrative and other measures to ensure that no family may be subjected to discrimination on the basis of the sexual orientation or gender identity of any of its members, including with regard to family-related social welfare and other public benefits, employment, and immigration."

They also urge that "in all actions or decisions concerning children . . . the best interests of the child shall be a primary consideration, and that the sexual orientation or gender identity of the child or of any family member or other person may not be considered incompatible with such best interests."

Neither children nor adults should have to face the state's discrimination or rejection of their families. By voting down this bill, the Guatemalan Congress will protect all families and their members.

Sincerely,
Scott Long
Director
Lesbian, Gay, Bisexual and Transgender Rights Program

C.C.
Office of the High Commissioner for Human Rights
Inter-American Commission on Human Rights

Source: Human Rights Watch. "Letter to the Guatemalan Congress Regarding Marriage and Family Law." (Sept. 2007). Available online. URL: http://www.hrw.org/en/news/2007/09/30/letter-guatemalan-congress-regarding-marriage-and-family-law. Accessed May 11, 2009.

PART III

Research Tools

6

How to Research
Adoption and Surrogacy

By now it is likely clear that the issues of adoption and surrogate pregnancy are multifaceted and intricately intertwined with a range of other issues that would not, at first glance, appear to have anything to do with family formation. While many societies think of the family as private and detached from the competitive world of business, politics, and commerce, this may only be the case for a few privileged individuals. Family and kinship is a central (and often sacrosanct) element of virtually every individual life; every individual has origins in some human community, whether those bonds were biologically or socially forged. To maintain a belief in the detachment and seclusion of family life from public life is to overlook the fact that many families involve—and indeed, require—outside intervention in the process of their formation, be it through a doctor, a lawyer, an agency, legislation, a surrogate mother, or a birth family.

The manifold angles and perspectives from which to look at the issues of adoption and surrogate pregnancy can be confusing and a little disorienting. So much has been recorded and documented, dating back to prehistory, that simply trying to sort through the myriad first-person accounts, news reports, legal documents, medical documents, and articles and the like can be overwhelming. The first step in the process is developing an understanding of the issue.

BECOMING FAMILIAR WITH THE TOPIC

Before you begin your research, it is important to understand the use of language as a framing device when discussing adoption and surrogate pregnancy. Issues relating to family are often controversial, and adoption and surrogate pregnancy have certainly seen their fair share of debate. While serious journalists often endeavor to adopt a neutral tone when discussing such issues, no one who truly takes an interest in the issues of adoption and surrogate pregnancy ever comes to the debate without an opinion. This is not to suggest that there are no objective resources on adoption and surrogate pregnancy, but rather that the best approach to the topic is one of awareness of bias and leanings.

Language serves as a particularly tricky means of reframing the issue in a positive or negative slant. A simple manipulation of language can forever muddle the meaning of a term and redesign the framework of debate. Several terms used to define adoption and surrogate pregnancy have invited much scrutiny and controversy over the years due to their lack of clarity or sensitivity. One such term is *surrogate mother.*

Surrogate Mother

In the late 1970s, U.S. attorney Noel Keane began contracting women to undergo artificial insemination with the intention of becoming pregnant and relinquishing the resulting child for adoption to the biological father and his wife or partner. As he took his new idea to the media—namely daytime TV and radio talk shows—journalists and news reporters began referring to these women as *surrogate mothers.* The term implied that the women were stand-ins, or carriers, not the real mothers. In essence, however, the term was a misnomer as the women involved in surrogate pregnancy in its early days of development were genetically related to the children they had conceived and thus were the natal mothers of those children. Even today, the majority of surrogate pregnancies are traditional, meaning they involve artificial insemination of the surrogate mother, which means that the surrogate is, in fact, the genetic mother.

What does the term *surrogate mother* mean, then? We can interpret the development of this term as public sympathy for and identification with contracting parents. The emotional devastation caused by infertility is not difficult to comprehend. Many people know someone who suffers from infertility, and the reality of one's inability to have children can be heartbreaking.

The implications of this subtle misnomer became most apparent during the Baby M trial in the 1980s. As Mary Beth Whitehead fought the Sterns for custody of the baby she had conceived using her own egg and Richard Stern's sperm, media accounts of the situation referred to her as the surrogate mother, while Richard Stern was never referred to as anything other than the father, which already framed the debate in his favor. Language is a powerful tool in setting the stage for an argument, and one has to wonder how the outcome of the custody battle may have differed if Mary Beth Whitehead had been referred to as the mother of Baby M.

Today, almost half of all surrogates are gestational surrogates, meaning they are not genetically related to the child, and in this case the term *surrogate* is appropriate; the surrogate is, literally, a stand-in or carrier. Of course, the argument can be made that motherhood is not defined by genetics at all but rather by the intent to love, which is why adoptive mothers are no less maternal than biological mothers. In a strictly biological sense, however, the term *surrogate* is correctly applied to gestational surrogates, while inappropriately applied to traditional surrogates.

Birth Mother

Adoption language can be just as tricky as surrogacy language. In the 1960s, the development of positive adoption language was explicitly intended to positively reframe adoption and validate the position of adoptive parents. Little debate arose over the new terms, which included such changes as referring to the adoptive parents as simply the parents, and adoptable children as waiting children. In reference to the biological mother, however, debate has arisen over the term *birth mother*, as it was changed from real or natural mother. Advocates for birth parents' rights prefer the term *first mother*, as many feel that birth mother insensitively implies a purely gestational relationship. Some have argued that the term suggests that birth mothers are little more than incubators, with no emotional relationships with their children.

Unlike surrogate, birth mother is not a misnomer, but rather a loaded word. In this case, we must distinguish the difference between denotation and connotation. Denotation refers to the literal meaning of a word, while connotation refers to the suggestiveness of a word or term. In this situation, the term *birth mother* is technically correct but is considered by birth parents' advocacy groups to have negative connotations.

Just as we must consider the framework of surrogacy arguments, we must consider the way in which discussions of adoption might be different if different terms were used. If mother is used in place of birth mother, while the technical term *adoptive mother* is maintained, the framework for the discussion suddenly changes. If there exists any antagonistic relationship between the birth parents and the adoptive parents, the argument can easily be reframed in favor of one or the other, simply by referring to one by its technical term and the other by a more emotive term.

Reproductive Tourism

Much discussion has arisen in recent years regarding the term *reproductive tourism* and its implications for the infertile. The very use of the word *tourism* implies leisure, vacation, and recreation. The term suggests a sense of frivolity that may not accurately reflect the feelings of most infertile individuals who travel abroad in search of reproductive procedures that are not available to them or that they cannot afford in their home countries. Such individuals report feeling forced to seek help outside of their home countries due to legislation that has specifically barred them from receiving certain fertility treatments and/or exorbitant costs. In many countries, it is illegal for gay men and single women to receive fertility treatments or contract a surrogate pregnancy. In Israel, where altruistic surrogacy is legal, gay men are directly excluded from being able to enter into a surrogacy contract. In Italy, recent legislation has made it illegal for single women or women over a certain age to undergo in vitro fertilization (IVF). In many countries, particularly Latin American and largely Catholic nations, cryopreservation and destruction of embryos is illegal, which leaves clients with the options of creating only one or two embryos at a time (which can be extremely costly), or donating unused embryos to other infertile couples.

Reproductive tourism, at best, suggests that infertile individuals from wealthy countries are traveling to poverty-stricken countries to obtain a "deal" while enjoying a leisurely vacation. At worst, the term suggests the deliberate, imperialistic exploitation of impoverished communities by individuals from wealthy countries in their desire to obtain a baby.

To really understand the issue, it is important to take into consideration the many factors involved in reproductive tourism, including the fact that many impoverished, third world nations see opportunities for economic growth in the reproductive industry. One must also consider the fact that the majority of individuals traveling abroad in search of reproductive help are doing so out of a sense of necessity. Some researchers have advocated for the application of such terms as *transnational reproduction* or *intercountry reproduction.*

Media Accounts

Media portrayals of the above-mentioned situations are numerous, and the language used to describe such scenarios can be subtly loaded. One article in a recent issue of *Marie Claire* on commercial surrogacy in India is cleverly titled "Womb for Rent" and refers to the practice as "outsourcing wombs."[1] The byline of the story reads: "Customer service, tech support . . . these days we outsource everything to India. So why not pregnancy? Here is a report on the growing number of Indian women willing to carry an American child."

In this article, international commercial surrogacy is unambiguously framed as the exploitation of impoverished Indian women by wealthy Westerners. The author emphasizes her perception of the callous intrusion of commerce on family formation in her reference to "renting" out one's womb, as well as the commodification of babies and human bodies in her reference to "outsourcing" pregnancy. At the same time, the author appears to be plac-ing equal blame for the commercialization of family on the Indian women who are "willing to carry an American child," suggesting that such women are intentionally choosing money over ethics. In this article, the author appears to make little to no effort to assume a neutral voice.

A 1987 article in *Time* magazine, on the other hand, does endeavor to adopt a neutral voice, but makes similar accusations regarding the Baby M case and the surrogacy industry. The author writes:

> *Picture Whitehead at the outset of the bargain. She has a body to sell or to rent, a mobile incubator, and she could use the money . . . What she does not take into account is that sudden surge of delight in the middle of the night that every pregnant woman knows when the baby swivels, or the depression brought on by the puffiness in her face, or any of the tempera-mental swings that arc throughout the pregnancy. She does not take her dreams or reveries into account, her imagining what the baby will look like or grow up to be. Most acutely, she fails to anticipate that onrush of inexpressible satisfaction when the baby is laid across her breast in the delivery room.[2]*

In this passage, the argument against surrogacy is framed within a sentimen-tal portrait of motherhood as contrasted against unfeeling nature of com-merce ("a mobile incubator"). Mary Beth Whitehead is essentially described as a woman who "does not take into account" the maternal emotions that she will be helpless against. Interestingly, while Mary Beth Whitehead is por-trayed as a woman unable to surmount her maternal emotions to rationally enter into a contract, she is never actually referred to as the baby's mother. Rather, the author refers to Whitehead's agreement to "bear [Stern's] baby" and to "volunteer her pregnancy."

Both articles frame their discussions of surrogacy as an exploitation of women, without sufficiently addressing the surrogates' agency in the arrange-ments. While the author of the article in *Marie Claire* openly condemns international commercial surrogacy as directly exploitative, the *Time* author assumes a more sympathetic voice that belies its portrayal of women as being incapable of overcoming their emotions to enter into contracts regarding children and pregnancy and therefore not full participants in the arrange-ments. The framework for the *Time* author's discussion of surrogacy takes the axiomatic position that all women are natural mothers and inherently nurtur-ing, which does not correspond to current research that shows that the vast majority of surrogate mothers do not form attachments to the children they carry. Even more noteworthy is the author's ultimate conclusion that regardless of Mary Beth Whitehead's inability to overcome her maternal "instincts," the baby is not hers; it is William Stern's.

Such media portrayals must be closely scrutinized to develop a full understanding of the issue *as it is perceived by the writer,* which is why it is important to be able to critically examine language and its use as a framing tool.

PERSPECTIVES AND ANGLES

Adoption and surrogate pregnancy, like many other controversial topics, are not stand-alone issues; they overlap with a plethora of other social, political, scientific, and religious issues. One of the reasons adoption and surrogate pregnancy are so controversial is because they cannot be isolated from such debates but rather invite discussion of exploitation, bioethics, legislative action, and economics. To effectively gauge the topics and their modern relevance, you would do well to familiarize yourself with some of the other issues involved in discussions of adoption and surrogate pregnancy and map out a list of questions to ask when conducting your research. These questions will help guide you as you search through sources to develop your own position on the topic.

Gender Issues/Women's Rights

A number of discussions about adoption and surrogate pregnancy argue woman's position in family formation as well as the process of entering into contracts. When considering this angle of adoption and surrogate pregnancy, there are many elements to take into account, such as sexual equality, birth mothers' rights, and women's agency. When looking at adoption, we must examine our most inherent beliefs, such as the social stigma of unplanned pregnancy. Is an unintended pregnancy something to be ashamed of? Should we encourage sealed records and anonymity, or should we foster a more open approach to adoption? What risk do we run in doing either?

Equally important to consider are the rights of birth mothers. At what point is the birth mother no longer entitled to claim authority over her child? How long should the birth mother have to change her mind after relinquishing her child for adoption? Should she have the right to reclaim the child at all, or is the belief in a pregnant woman's inability to see past her emotions to think rationally when relinquishing her child a remnant of patriarchy? When considering other, more openly patriarchal cultures, one must ask how much autonomy pregnant women have at all. How much real authority do they have in the decision-making process?

Similar questions can be asked regarding surrogate pregnancy and the rights of surrogate mothers, but a new dimension of women's rights envelops this area. Is surrogacy exploitative of women, or do women have the right to utilize their bodies as they choose? More important, can women enter into such contracts when their own genetic material, emotions, and even their own children are the subjects of such a transaction? Or do many societies have an overly sentimental picture of maternity and are simply uncomfortable with the notion that women may not form inherent, biological attachments to the children they carry?

The questions about women's rights are plentiful, and many more can be asked in order to sufficiently understand this area of adoption and surrogacy.

Race

Another controversial area of adoption and surrogate pregnancy is the issue of race, particularly as it pertains to globalization and international programs. Like the issue of women's rights, much of the discussion of race and racism in adoption and surrogate pregnancy centers on exploitation. Are ethnic minorities being exploited and abused so that wealthy couples can have the children they desire?

When considering this question as it relates to adoption, many other questions arise. Are ethnic minority communities subject to racist rules regarding child welfare, resulting in the removal of their children? Is it fair to apply the same rules to two widely differing cultures or are theories of child welfare universal? Does a child have the right to grow up in his or her ethnic community?

As the question of exploitation relates to international adoption, one must consider the ethics of adopting infants from overseas. Is it a humanitarian effort, or is it a means of acquiring a hard-to-find baby? Is it ethically responsible to take children from one country and bring them to another at all, or is it a form of neocolonialism? What will be the global effect of removing so many children from impoverished and/or developing nations and placing them in wealthy developed nations? What effect will this have particularly on the major sending countries, such as China and Guatemala?

As the question of race pertains to surrogate pregnancy, similar questions with slight variations can be asked. In regards to international surrogacy, are impoverished nations being exploited for the benefit of couples from wealthy countries? In the United States and other developed nations, are ethnic minority women being used to gestate babies for wealthy couples? Will surrogacy become a menial labor job to be delegated to immigrants and the poor?

ADOPTION AND SURROGATE PREGNANCY

Politics

Both adoption and surrogate pregnancy are politically divisive issues that overlap with other major political issues, such as abortion, gay rights, and children's rights. Virtually every country has two major political parties: one conservative and one liberal, and each side tends to take a different stance on issues such as adoption and surrogate pregnancy. In the United States, the Republican Party rejects abortion and gay rights, which typically means that they also reject a gay couple's right to adopt as well as a surrogate mother's right to conceive and abort a child if she so chooses. Some conservative organizations foster a direct link between abortion and adoption as they encourage young and/or single women to choose not to abort but rather relinquish their babies for adoption.

At times, however, a particular topic, such as surrogate pregnancy, is not divided along party lines. Both conservatives and liberals may share the view that surrogate pregnancy is exploitative and a commodification of women and children, or both may share the view that surrogacy is a viable solution for infertile couples and should be federally regulated.

When considering the issue of adoption as a political talking point, you must investigate other political ideals of the country in which you are studying the topic. What laws exist to regulate adoption? Are gay couples and single people allowed to adopt? Does the country allow adoption of only a limited number of children? Does the government support the right to anonymity by maintaining sealed records?

In the case of surrogacy, does the country you are researching maintain any laws at all to regulate surrogate pregnancy? Does legislation allow for both altruistic and commercial surrogacy? Because this is also an issue of women's rights, you should find out if abortion is legal, as that contextualizes the issue within the frame of a woman's right to use her body as she chooses. Are gay couples allowed to contract a surrogate mother? What laws exist to protect the surrogate mother and contracting parents in the event that a dispute arises? Does legislation define the child as that of the surrogate mother until she terminates her parental rights, or does the law require that the contracting parents' names go on the child's birth certificate once it is born?

The laws that a government implements, as well as the positions that rival political parties take, reveal a nation's approach to emerging issues of technology, human rights, and globalization, so this is an important area to study, particularly if you are researching the topics of adoption and surrogacy as they exist in just one country.

SOURCES

There exists a wide range of sources on adoption and surrogate pregnancy, from first-person accounts to commentary and analysis. Knowing how to use and interpret sources appropriately can be just as difficult as finding them in the first place, so it is important to understand what types of sources are available to you and how to use them to support your research. Equally important is an understanding of where your sources come from. Are you reading the publication of an established, credible organization or an extremist group? Does the statistical information you are citing come from a university study or was it drafted by a for-profit business that has a personal stake in the debate? Such questions will help you determine whether your sources are reliable and appropriate to your research.

Primary and Secondary Sources

When researching adoption and surrogate pregnancy, you will run into a slew of personal accounts, studies, psychological assessments, memoirs, news reports, journal articles, graphs, and statistics. How do you tell the difference between primary and secondary sources?

PRIMARY SOURCES

Primary sources are first-person accounts or sources that directly relate to the issue. Such sources include interviews, memoirs, letters, speeches, diaries, propaganda, corporate advertisements, legal documents, and artwork. Numerical data can also be a primary source, such as birth registrations, marriage licenses, death records, and federal censuses.

Primary sources are used in other documents for analysis. Thus, when you use a primary source in your own research, you assume the responsibility of critically examining that source. This might mean studying the nuances and connotations of a political speech or interpreting the meaning of statistical information.

First-person accounts can be particularly useful when providing a detailed, personal glimpse into the experiences of adoption and surrogate pregnancy. They will not only enhance your research, but make the topic more emotionally and personally accessible. Gaining an understanding of what it would feel like to give a child up for adoption or be a child who was placed for adoption may provide you with new vantage points from which to observe the issue and allow you to formulate a more informed opinion.

While first-person accounts are very useful to your research, they do not provide all of the information you will need, and sometimes they are simply not reliable. First-person accounts are, by definition, one individual's experiences and are thus not comprehensive and cannot flesh out the entirety of a topic. A surrogate mother's description of a court-ordered removal of her child will give you a personalized glimpse into the complexities of surrogacy but cannot accurately portray the feelings or experiences of the contracting parents. Further, her account—as any first-person account—is biased and may omit or alter information.

Read first-person narratives to acquire a better grasp of an issue but make sure you do so in a balanced way. If you read a first-person account of an issue, make sure you read an opposing viewpoint. Additionally, be sure to use first-person narratives that are reliable, such as published memoirs and letters. Avoid overly emotional blogs or Internet message boards, which are not only one-sided by nature, but may not be reliable.

SECONDARY SOURCES

Secondary sources consist of documents and other media that analyze and comment on primary sources. Secondary sources come in the form of biographies, essays, journal articles, news reports, and research studies. The main difference between primary and secondary sources is the way in which they can be used in your research. Primary sources require analysis to formulate and bolster your argument or thesis, while secondary sources are used to add credibility to your argument once it is formed. For example, if you are researching international adoption in Guatemala, you would use first-person accounts and numerical data to establish your position on the matter and then bring in the voice of an authority who may have studied the issue extensively to back up your argument.

Secondary sources can be highly beneficial to your research for a number of reasons. First, they provide a more comprehensive look at the matter. A university study of adopted children and how they adapt to their new families depending on age will provide you with a much more balanced and thorough overview of the issue than a first-person account from an adoptee or an adoptive parent. Further, scholars who have studied the matter comprehensively will likely have a better understanding of the various nuances and complexities of the issue, such as causal relationships, psychological states, environmental factors, and historical data. If you think you may be interested in pursuing further research in this area of study in college or graduate school, developing a strong familiarity with the top scholars and researchers in this field will be important to your future academic goals.

While researching secondary sources, you will have to be aware of bias and credibility. As any secondary source is another individual or group's evaluation of the topic, you should be conscious of fairness in coverage of the issue, as well as whether your source is credible. When citing a study of adopted children, find out who funded the study. Was the study commissioned by a for-profit entity that was, in turn, validated by the study? If so, you may want to find a second opinion.

Web Resources

Thanks to the advent of the Internet, a large portion of your research can be done at home. Web sites, databases, newspaper archives, and encyclopedias can all be accessed from your computer. Internet research naturally comes with a warning to be cautious of who and what your sources really are, as virtually anything can be published on the Web; nevertheless, there are responsible ways to conduct online research.

ENCYCLOPEDIAS

Online encyclopedias house a wealth of information that will help you become more closely acquainted with the topic of adoption and surrogate pregnancy. From dates and time lines to medical definitions and explanations, online encyclopedias can provide a skeleton for your research.

Most online encyclopedias can be accessed with a paid subscription, like the online Encyclopedia Britannica, which can provide fact-checked and verified information on adoption and surrogate pregnancy as well as interrelated topics. However, the most popular and well-known free online encyclopedia is likely Wikipedia, which acts as a sort of search engine into which you can enter almost any term and find an encyclopedia entry. Wikipedia is useful in its comprehensive range of subjects, from popular issues to vague and highly specialized topics. Research with caution, however, as the authors of such entries are not always scholars or authorities on an issue, and occasionally information can be skewed and even inaccurate.

JOURNAL DATABASES

A peer-reviewed journal refers to a journal in which every article is vetted by a group of scholars to ensure accuracy and academic integrity. The articles are often written for a specialized readership for the same reason other articles and pieces of literature are published: to provide a new and unique perspective on a general issue. Most peer-reviewed journals publish their articles online but most require a subscription fee to access those articles. If you attend a college or university, you will likely have free access to a variety of different journal databases that focus on different areas of study, including arts and humanities, social sciences, physical sciences, and mathematics.

Many databases are even more specific, focusing on literature, psychology, biology, geology, and more. Each database carries a number of journals so that, if you are not a college student, you need only subscribe to the database itself to access the journals.

Knowing how to search through databases is critical to finding the right article. Most online databases have been designed to support Boolean searches. Named after 19th-century mathematician, George Boole, a Boolean search uses specific operators to broaden or narrow search results. Search operators include:

- AND: Combining terms with the word AND will ensure that your results contain both search terms. For example, entering "surrogate AND pregnancy" will ensure that you receive results on surrogate pregnancy, as opposed to results on other forms of the word "surrogate" or individual results on pregnancy.

- OR: Using the operator OR will broaden your search to include synonyms and similar terms. For example, international adoption is also referred to as intercountry and overseas adoption. To broaden your search, you would enter the terms "international OR intercountry OR overseas AND adoption."

- NOT: Entering a search term that includes NOT will specify results that exclude certain terms, thereby narrowing your search. If you want to run a search on adoption that does not include foster care, you might enter the terms "adoption NOT foster."

NEWSPAPER ARCHIVES

Many newspapers publish their archives online, and searches can be performed on the publication's Web site. Due to the decline in print newspapers and the rising number of online-only newspapers, many newspaper Web sites require subscriptions to generate revenue. Many colleges and high schools maintain subscriptions to newspaper Web sites, and you may be able to use an Internet database provided by your school library to search a variety of newspaper archives at once. If you cannot access a school newspaper database, you may consider entering your search terms into a regular search engine, which will also provide a limited array of past newspaper articles. Your search will generate more results if it involves high-profile cases, such as the Baby M case. When using a general search engine, consider entering a specific case in order to yield more newspaper articles.

AGENCY/BUSINESS WEB SITES

Researching agency and business Web sites is a useful way of gaining a better understanding of business practices, nonprofit versus for-profit organizations, campaigns, specialized terms, and the community that exists around adoption and surrogate pregnancy. Visiting an adoption agency Web site will expose you to the marketing and advertising practices that seek to match children with families. Some Web sites post pictures and profiles of waiting children—namely those in foster care—and ask prospective parents to become a child's "forever family." Web sites devoted to surrogacy and infant adoption often post pictures of babies and happy families as well as artwork that is meant to evoke feelings of love, affection, and parent-child closeness. Both adoption and surrogacy Web sites often feature sections that detail laws and regulations for the areas in which they are located, which will provide you with a more detailed perspective on state and local laws.

Visiting such Web sites will also familiarize you with local and national communities devoted to promoting adoption and/or surrogate pregnancy and changing or creating legislation. Following links to campaign Web sites will give you a greater understanding of movements that are taking place within the world of adoption and surrogate pregnancy right now.

An obvious and unavoidable downside to using agency and business Web sites for your research is the problem of bias. Because for-profit agencies and businesses have their own interests at heart, much of the information provided on their Web sites will not be suitable for actual citation in your work. Rather, such Web sites should be used as conduits to other, more objective sources of information.

Print Resources

Print resources generally come in the form of books, journals, magazines, and newspapers, many of which you can find at your local library. Books will provide the most comprehensive and specialized information for your research, as they typically address a topic from a number of different angles while thoroughly analyzing various elements of an issue itself. When trying to decide which books are most relevant to your research, first check the publication date. Was the book written recently? If so, the information provided will be more up to date and pertinent to your research. Next, scan the table of contents, as there may be a chapter specifically devoted to the area of adoption and surrogate pregnancy that you are researching. If not, check the index for specific terms.

If you live near a university, consider paying for a library card so that you can access the multitude of volumes the university library is likely to house. A university library will more than likely offer a much wider array of print and online resources than your local community library.

Personal Accounts

Many people have been personally affected by adoption and surrogate pregnancy, and you may want to consider asking friends and family members to share their personal experiences with you. Be aware that some people may be hesitant to talk about deeply personal matters, such as infertility and abuse, but if they are comfortable talking with you, set up a time to meet in a calm and private place. While you will not likely be able to use the information you receive for purposes of citation, you will build a more personal relationship with the topic that will enable you to empathize with people who have experienced adoption and surrogate pregnancy.

---

[1] Abigail Haworth. "Womb for Rent: Surrogate Mothers in India." *Marie Claire* (May 2009). Available online. URL: http://www.webmd.com/infertility-and-reproduction/features/ womb-rent-surrogate-mothers-india. Accessed May 17, 2009.

[2] Roger Rosenblatt. "Baby M." *Time* (April 1987). Available online. URL: http://www.time. com/time/magazine/article/0,9171,963927-1,00.html. Accessed May 17, 2009.

7

Facts and Figures

1. International Adoptions to the United States, 1998–2009

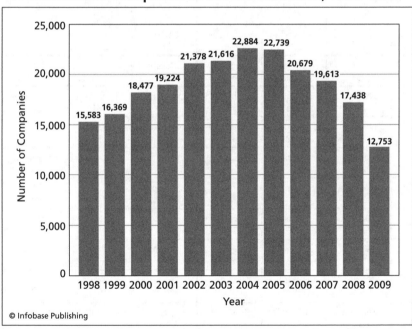

© Infobase Publishing

This graph shows the total number of children adopted internationally to the United States between 1998 and 2009.

Source: United States Department of State. "Total Adoptions to the United States." Available online. URL: http://adoption.state.gov/news/total_chart.html. Accessed April 15, 2010.

2. International Adoptions to the United States by Sending Country, 2004–2009

	FY 2009	FY 2008	FY 2007	FY 2006	FY 2005	FY 2004
1	China 3,001	Guatemala 4,123	China 5,453	China 6,493	China 7,906	China 7,044
2	Ethiopia 2,277	China 3,909	Guatemala 4,728	Guatemala 4,135	Russia 4,639	Russia 5,865
3	Russia 1,586	Russia 1,861	Russia 2,310	Russia 3,706	Guatemala 3,783	Guatemala 3,264
4	South Korea 1,080	Ethiopia 1,725	Ethiopia 1,255	South Korea 1,376	South Korea 1,630	South Korea 1,716
5	Guatemala 756	South Korea 1,065	South Korea 939	Ethiopia 732	Ukraine 821	Kazakhstan 826
6	Ukraine 610	Vietnam 751	Vietnam 828	Kazakhstan 587	Kazakhstan 755	Ukraine 723
7	Vietnam 481	Ukraine 457	Ukraine 606	Ukraine 460	Ethiopia 441	India 406
8	Haiti 330	Kazakhstan 380	Kazakhstan 540	Liberia 353	India 323	Haiti 356
9	India 297	India 307	India 416	Colombia 344	Colombia 291	Ethiopia 289
10	Kazakhstan 295	Colombia 306	Liberia 314	India 320	Philippines 271	Colombia 287
11	Philippines 281	Haiti 302	Colombia 310	Haiti 309	Haiti 234	Belarus 202
12	Taiwan 253	Philippines 291	Philippines 265	Philippines 245	Liberia 183	Philippines 196
13	Colombia 238	Taiwan 267	Haiti 190	Taiwan 187	Taiwan 141	Bulgaria 110
14	Nigeria 110	Liberia 249	Taiwan 184	Vietnam 163	Mexico 88	Poland 102
15	Ghana 103	Nigeria 148	Mexico 89	Mexico 70	Poland 73	Mexico 89
16	Mexico 72	Mexico 103	Poland 84	Poland 67	Thailand 72	Liberia 86
17	Uganda 69	Ghana 101	Thailand 67	Brazil 66	Brazil 66	Nepal 73
18	Thailand 56	Kyrgyzstan 78	Kyrgyzstan 61	Nepal 66	Nigeria 65	Nigeria 71
19	Jamaica 54	Poland 77	Brazil 55	Nigeria 62	Jamaica 63	Brazil 69
20	Poland 50	Thailand 59	Uganda 54	Thailand 56	Nepal 62	Thailand 69

This table shows the total number of children adopted internationally to the United States between 2004 and 2009, by sending country.

Source: United States Department of State. "Total Adoptions to the United States." Available online. URL: http://adoption.state.gov/news/total_chart.html. Accessed April 15, 2010.

3. International Adoptions to the United States and Europe, 1995–2006

COUNTRY	1995	1999	2003	2004	2006
United States	8,987	16,363	21,616	22,884	20,679
France	3,034	3,597	3,995	4,079	3,977
Italy	2,161	2,177	2,772	3,402	3,188
Spain	815	2,006	3,951	5,541	4.472
Sweden	895	1,019	1,046	1,109	879
Netherlands	661	993	1,154	1,307	816
Germany	537	977	674	650	583
Denmark	548	697	523	528	450
Norway	488	589	714	706	448
Belgium	430	450	430	470	383
UK	154	312	301	334	364
Ireland	52	191	358	398	313
Total to Europe	10,429	13,716	16,922	19,501	16,561
Total to all Countries [1]	22,161 (19)[2]	32,912 (22)	41,529 (23)	45,287 (23)	39,736[2] (22)
% to Europe	47%	42%	41%	43%	42%
% to USA	41%	49%	52%	51%	52%
Other states[3]	12%	9%	7%	6%	6%

[1] The other countries included in the overall totals are Australia, Canada, Finland, Iceland, Luxembourg, New Zealand, and Switzerland — with addition of Cyprus, Israel, and Malta from 1999 and Andorra from 2001.

[2] Figures in brackets indicate number of countries for which data were available each year.

[3] Australia, Canada, New Zealand, and Israel

This table shows the number of children adopted internationally to the United States and selected European countries between 1995 and 2006, by receiving country.

Source: Peter Selman. "Intercountry Adoption in Europe 1995–2006: Patterns, Trends, and Issues." Annual Conference of the Social Policy Association, Edinburgh (June 2008). Available online. URL: http://www.icasn.org/resources/research/Intercountry%20Adoption%20in%20Europe%201998%20to%202006%20-%20patterns,%20trends,%20and%20issues.pdf. Accessed July 8, 2009.

4. International Adoptions to the United States by Sex and Age, 2002

Female	64%
Male	36%
Under 1 year old	46%
1–4 years old	43%
5–9 years old	8%
Over 9 years old	3%

These tables show the percentages of children adopted internationally to the United States by sex and age.

Source: Evan B. Donaldson Adoption Institute. "International Adoption Facts" (2002). Available online. URL: http://www.adoptioninstitute.org/FactOverview/international.html. Accessed July 6, 2009.

5. U.S. Adoptions in 1992 and 2001

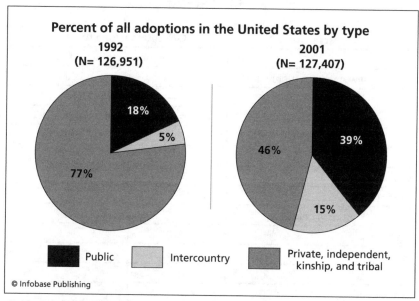

Percent of all adoptions in the United States by type

This table shows a comparison of total adoptions by type (public, intercountry, and private/independent/kinship/tribal) in 1992 and 2001.

Source: Child Welfare Information Gateway. "How Many Children Were Adopted in 2000 and 2001?" (2004). Available online. URL: http://www.childwelfare.gov/pubs/s_adoptedhighlights.cfm. Accessed July 7, 2009.

6. Preferences for Adopted Children in the United States, 2002

Characteristic	Currently seeking to adopt	
	Number in thousands	
Number of women in denominator[1]	600	600
	Percent who ...	
	Prefer	Prefer or would accept[2]
Sex of child		
Boy	28.9	95.0
Girl	34.6	97.2
Indifferent	36.5	N/A
Race of child		
Black	10.0	86.9
White	20.1	91.4
Other race	16.9	94.9
Indifferent	52.2	N/A
Race of woman and child		
Not Hispanic or Latina women:		
White, single race		
Black child	—	83.6
White child	35.2	100.0
Child of another race	17.5	94.6
Indifferent	45.5	N/A
Black or African American, single race		
Black child	32.9	87.5
White child	—	75.0
Child of another race	*	92.7
Indifferent	50.5	N/A
Age of child		
Younger than 2 years old	49.2	94.1
2–5 years old	22.3	78.7
6–12 years old	16.1	58.6
13 years old or older	*	30.9
Indifferent	7.6	N/A

Characteristic	Currently seeking to adopt	
	Number in thousands	
Number of women in denominator[1]	600	600
	Percent who . . .	
	Prefer	Prefer or would accept[2]
Disability status		
No disability	55.1	100.0
With a mild disability	21.6	89.0
With a severe disability	*	30.3
Indifferent	22.8	...
Number of children		
Single child	56.3	100.0
Two or more siblings at once	27.3	74.6
Indifferent	16.5	...

–Quantity zero.

*Figure does not meet standards of reliability or precision.

[1] Current adoption seekers were asked about preferences if they were not seeking to adopt a child they already knew.

[2] Only women who did not indicate a specific attribute were asked if they would accept a child of a different attribute. For example, only women who indicated they wanted a boy were asked if they would accept a girl.

NOTE: This table replicates Chandra et al., 2005, Table 84.

This table shows the number of women in the United States in 2002 who were 18–44 years of age and seeking to adopt a child not already known to them and the percentage who preferred or would have accepted a child with the selected characteristic.

Source: U.S. Department of Health and Human Services, Centers for Disease Control and Prevention, National Center for Health Statistics. "Adoption Experiences of Women and Men and Demand for Children to Adopt by Women 18–44 Years of Age in the United States, 2002." Vital and Health Statistics (Aug. 2008). Available online. URL: http://www.cdc.gov/nchs/data/series/sr_23/sr23_027.pdf. Accessed July 8, 2009.

7. Adoption Demand in the United States, 2002

Characteristic	All ever-married women			Ever-married women who have ever considered adoption			Ever-married women who have ever taken steps to adopt		
	Number in thousands	Percent who ever considered adoption[1]	Standard error	Number in thousands[2]	Percent who took steps to adopt	(Standard error)	Number in thousands[3]	Percent who ever adopted a child	Standard error
Total[4]	35,845	35.8	1.06	12,823	16.8	1.27	2,150	23.6	3.85
Age									
18–29 years	8,487	34.4	1.66	2,918	7.4	1.36	216	*	*
30–34 years	7,971	36.5	1.94	2,910	16.2	2.21	471	15.1	6.77
35–39 years	9,041	37.7	1.89	3,409	19.1	2.65	651	18.5	4.91
40–44 years	10,345	34.7	2.47	3,587	22.6	2.87	812	37.1	7.19
Marital or cohabiting status									
Currently married	28,323	35.2	1.16	9,962	18.1	1.56	1,801	25.5	4.34
First marriage	23,078	34.3	1.04	7,915	16.1	1.40	1,272	22.8	4.06
Second or later marriage	5,245	39.0	3.57	2,047	25.8	3.92	529	31.9	10.11
Formerly married	7,522	38.0	2.20	2,862	12.2	1.63	349	13.8	6.85
Parity									
0 births	6,347	49.3	1.81	3,130	17.8	2.44	558	36.7	8.61
1 or more births	29,498	32.9	1.11	9,693	16.4	1.40	1,591	19.0	4.10
Ever used infertility services									
Yes	6,563	57.2	2.03	3,757	28.4	2.84	1,069	31.8	6.10
No	29,282	31.0	1.13	9,066	11.9	1.37	1,081	15.4	4.24
Fecundity status									
Surgically sterile	12,933	33.5	1.56	4,334	21.8	2.66	945	23.9	5.78
Impaired fecundity	5,269	53.6	2.72	2,823	28.0	2.93	791	26.3	7.13
Fecund	17,642	32.1	1.45	5,667	7.3	1.24	414	17.6	6.55

Education[5]								
No high school diploma or GED	3,816	24.7	2.31	942	15.4	3.81	145	*	*
High school diploma or GED	10,691	33.6	2.12	3,587	20.3	2.94	729	31.6	8.16
Some college, no bachelor's degree	10,728	38.9	1.56	4,177	16.2	2.24	675	17.3	5.88
Bachelor's degree or higher	9,728	39.0	1.64	3,795	15.8	2.05	599	25.3	6.72
Percent of poverty level[6]								
0–149 percent	8,719	31.4	1.69	2,738	15.6	2.59	428	4.8	2.89
150–299 percent	10,356	34.4	2.22	3,566	16.1	2.86	573	40.7	9.39
300 percent or higher	16,537	38.8	1.34	6,420	17.9	1.89	1,149	22.1	4.75
Hispanic origin and race								
Hispanic or Latina	5,265	33.8	2.25	1,780	15.0	2.34	267	*	*
Not Hispanic or Latina: White, single race	24,817	35.8	1.35	8,888	16.2	1.49	1,443	27.1	5.39
Black or African American, single race	3,242	41.3	2.81	1,339	22.8	3.90	305	22.0	7.92

* Figure does not meet standards of reliability or precision.

[1]Includes women who have adopted children in the past, women who have ever considered adoption, and women who are currently seeking to adopt.

[2]Due to rounding of percentages and numbers, multiplying the number of women by the percentage who have ever considered adoption may not yield the numbers presented in this column. The numbers presented here were produced using actual (unrounded) figures.

[3]Due to rounding of percentages and numbers, multiplying the number of women who have ever considered adoption by the percentage who have ever taken steps to adopt may not yield the numbers presented in this column. The numbers presented here were produced using actual (unrounded) figures.

[4]Includes women of other or multiple race and origin groups, not shown separately.

[5]Limited to women 22–44 years of age at time of interview. GED is General Educational Development diploma.

[6]Limited to women 20–44 years of age at time of interview.

This table shows the adoption demand among ever-married women in the United States in 2002 who were 18–44 years of age, by selected characteristics.

Source: U.S. Department of Health and Human Services, Centers for Disease Control and Prevention, National Center for Health Statistics. "Adoption Experiences of Women and Men and Demand for Children to Adopt by Women 18–44 Years of Age in the United States, 2002." *Vital and Health Statistics* (Aug. 2008). Available online. URL: http://www.cdc.gov/nchs/data/series/sr_23/sr23_027.pdf. Accessed July 22, 2009.

8. Children Born to Single Mothers Relinquished for Adoption in the United States, 1973–2002

RACE	YEAR OF CHILD'S BIRTH				
	BEFORE 1973[1]	1973– 1981[1]	1982– 1988[1]	1989–1995 (standard error)[1]	1996–2002 (standard error)[2]
All Women[3]	8.7	4.1	2.0	0.9 (0.03)	1.0 (0.33)
Black or African American women[4]	1.5	0.2	1.1	—	—
White women[4]	19.3	7.5	3.2	1.7 (0.55)	1.3 (0.54)

−Quantity zero.

*Figure does not meet standards of reliability or precision.

[1] Infants relinquished at birth only (figures replicated from Chandra et al., 1999, Table 5).

[2] Infants reliquished at birth or within the first month of life.

[3] Includes women of other races, not shown separately.

[4] Includes women of Hispanic origin and women of multiple races who chose this as the single race that best describes them.

This table shows the percentage of children among those born in the United States between 1973 and 2002 to never-married women under 45 years of age who were relinquished for adoption, by race and according to the year of the child's birth.

Source: U.S. Department of Health and Human Services, Centers for Disease Control and Prevention, National Center for Health Statistics. "Adoption Experiences of Women and Men and Demand for Children to Adopt by Women 18–44 Years of Age in the United States, 2002." Vital and Health Statistics (Aug. 2008). Available online. URL: http://www.cdc.gov/nchs/data/series/sr_23/sr23_027.pdf. Accessed July 8, 2009.

9. Perceptions of Adoptive Parents in the United States, 2002

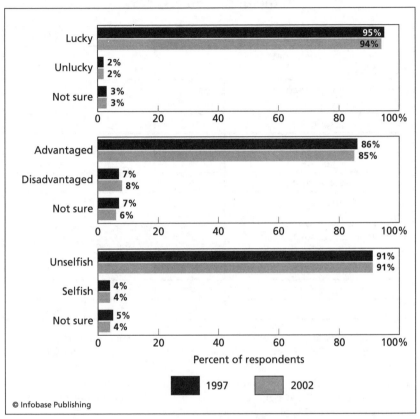

This table shows a comparison of survey respondents' positive and negative perceptions of adoptive parents in 1997 and 2002. Interviewees responded to the question: "In your opinion, when parents adopt a child, are the parents . . . ?" The number of people interviewed were 1,416 in 2002 and 1,554 in 1997.

Source: Dave Thomas Foundation for Adoption. "National Adoption Attitudes Survey" (June 2002). Available online. URL: http://www.adoptioninstitute.org/survey/Adoption_Attitudes_Survey.pdf. Accessed July 22, 2009.

10. Racial Differences in Views of Birth Parents in the United States, 1997

Birth Mothers	Total	Black	White
Generally disapprove of birth mothers' decision	23%	52	20
By putting child up for adoption mothers are being . . .			
Irresponsible	16%	38	12
Uncaring	13%	35	10
Selfish	14%	31	11
Birth Fathers			
Generally disapprove of birth fathers' decision	29%	56	25
By putting child up for adoption fathers are being . . .			
Irresponsible	26%	54	21
Uncaring	24%	50	20
Selfish	23%	45	20

This table shows differences between black and white racial demographics regarding their views of birth mothers and fathers and their decision to relinquish a child for adoption.

Source: Evan B. Donaldson Adoption Institute. "Benchmark Adoption Survey: Report on the Findings" (Oct. 1997). Available online. URL: http://www.adoptioninstitute.org/survey/Benchmark_Survey_1997.pdf. Accessed July 8, 2009.

11. Total World Fertility Rates, 1998

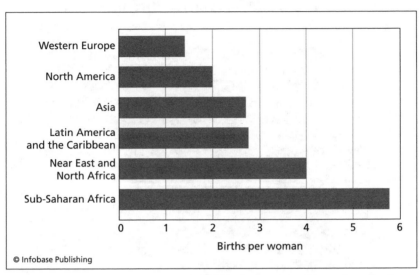

This table shows fertility rates among selected continents in 1998 by number of births per woman.

Source: U.S. Department of Commerce, Economics and Statistics Administration, Bureau of the Census. "International Brief: World Population at a Glance: 1998 and Beyond" (Jan. 1999). Available online. URL: http://www.census.gov/ipc/prod/wp98/ib98-4.pdf. Accessed July 7, 2009.

12. Percentage of Women in Developing Countries Who Have No Say in Their Own Health Care Needs

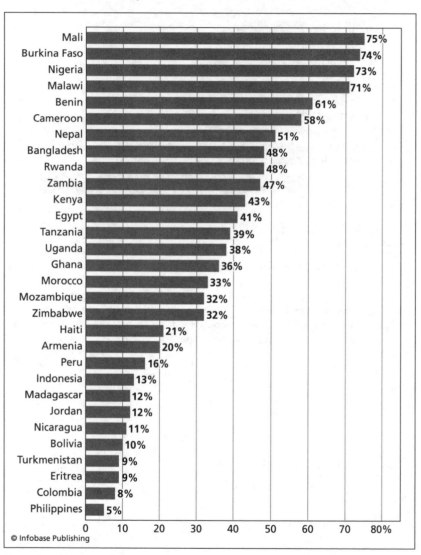

© Infobase Publishing

This table shows the percentage of women in selected developing countries whose husbands exclusively make the decisions regarding their health care.

Source: UNICEF. "The State of the World's Children 2009: Maternal and Newborn Health" (2009). Available online. URL: http://www.unicef.org/sowc09/docs/SOWC09-Figure-2.8-EN.pdf. Accessed July 22, 2009.

13. Millennium Development Goals on Maternal and Child Health, 2005

Millennium Development Goal 4: Reduce child mortality	
Targets	Indicators
4.A: Reduce by two thirds, between 1990 and 2015, the under-five mortality rate	4.1 Under-five mortality rate 4.2 Infant mortality rate 4.3 Proportion of 1-year-old children immunized against measles
Millennium Development Goal 5: Improve maternal health	
Targets	Indicators
5.A: Reduce by three quarters, between 1990 and 2015, the maternal mortality ratio	5.1 Maternal mortality ratio 5.2 Proportion of births attended by skilled health personnel
5.B: Achieve, by 2015, universal access to reproductive health	5.3 Contraceptive prevalence rate 5.4 Adolescent birth rate 5.5 Antenatal care coverage (at least one visit and at least four visits) 5.6 Unmet need for family planning

This table shows the development goals set by the UN General Assembly to reduce infant mortality and improve maternal healthcare by 2015.

Source: United Nations General Assembly, 2005 World Summit. "Millennium Development Goals on Maternal and Child Health." Available online. URL: http://www.unicef.org/sowc09/docs/SOWC09-Figure-1.1-EN.pdf. Accessed July 8, 2009.

14. U.S. State Laws on Surrogacy, 2005

	Bans Contracts	Bans Payment to Surrogate	Bans Payment but Allows for Services	Prohibits Payment to Third Parties	Permits Payment for Lawyer Services	Voids Paid Contracts	Voids Unpaid Contracts	Intended Parents Are Legal Parents	Intended Parents Are Legal Parents, but Time to Change Mind	Surrogate and Husband Are Legal Parents	Regulates Unpaid Surrogacy	Regulates Paid Surrogacy
Arizona	x					x	x			x***		
Arkansas								x				
District of Columbia	x											
Florida*			x*	x*	x*	x*		x*				
Florida**			x**	x**	x**	x**			x**			
Illinois*					x*			x*				
Indiana						x	x					
Kentucky		x		x		x						
Louisiana						x**						
Michigan		x		x		x	x					
Nebraska						x						
Nevada			x					x				
New Hampshire			x	x	x	x	x		x		x	
New York			x	x		x	x					
North Dakota						x	x			x		
Texas*								x*				
Utah		x		x		x	x		x	x***		
Virginia		x		x	x	x			x			x
Washington		x		x	x	x						

* Laws apply specifically to gestational surrogacy.

** Laws apply specifically to traditional surrogacy.

**** Law declared unconstitutional in court.

This table shows U.S. state laws on surrogate pregnancy by legality of the contract, type of surrogacy, payment to third parties, status of intended parents, and regulation.

Sources: National Conference of State Legislatures, "Surrogacy Statutes," March 4, 2005, in author's files; Brandel (1995); "Table IV: State Laws on Surrogacy," www. kentlaw.edu/isit/TABLEIV.htm (accessed May 12, 2004); American Surrogacy Center, "Legal Overview of Surrogacy Laws by State," 2002, www.surrogacy.com/legals/map.html (accessed January 24, 2005).

15. International Laws on Surrogacy, 2004

	Bans Contracts	Bans Payment to Surrogate	Prohibits Payment to Third Parties	Intended Parents Are Legal Parents	Surrogate and Husband Are Legal Parents	Regulates Unpaid Surrogacy
Australia		x	x		x	
Austria	x					
Canada		x				
Denmark		x				
Egypt	x					
France	x					
Germany	x					
Hong Kong		x	x	x		x
Israel				x		
Italy	x					
Japan	x					
Netherlands	x					
Norway	x					
Russia				x		
Spain	x					
Sweden	x					
Switzerland	x					
UK		x				

This table shows various surrogacy laws concerning validity of the contract, payment to third parties, status of the intended and surrogate parents, and regulation by country.

Sources: Kepler and Bokelmann (2000); East Coast Assisted Parenting (2000); Surrogacy UK, "Registering the Birth of a Surrogate Child and the Law," www.surrogacyuk.org/legalities.htm, and "Surrogacy Arrangements Act 1895," www.surrogacyuk.org/surrogacyact1895.pdf (both accessed October 3, 2006); Taylor (2003); Ruppe (2003); Government of South Australia, "Reproductive Technology: Legislation around Australia," 2006, www.dh.sa.gov.au/reproductive-technology/other.asp (accessed October 2, 2006); T. Smith (2004); Hong Kong Department of Justice, "Prohibition against Surrogacy Arrangements on Commercial Basis, Etc.," Bilingual Laws Information System, www.legislation.gov.hk/blis_ind.nsf/0/6497234f26732f184825696200330659?OpenDocument (accessed October 3, 2006); Center for Genetics and Society (2004); Teman (2003a, 2003b); Kahn (2000).

8

Key Players A to Z

ABRAHAM AND SARAH (2000–1500? B.C.E.) Biblical couple who arrange a surrogate pregnancy. The Genesis version of the story relates that Sarah is unable to conceive. In Hebrew tribal culture, a woman's identity and future were defined by motherhood, and Sarah is said to remedy the situation by giving her Egyptian slave, Hagar, to her husband, Abraham. In ancient Mesopotamia, this practice was acceptable and even common. Abraham impregnates Hagar, who later bears a son named Ishmael. However, when Hagar becomes proud and behaves arrogantly toward her barren mistress, Sarah drives her out of the tribe. Hagar flees to Egypt but is visited by an angel who announces that her child will be a great leader of the Hebrews, and Hagar returns to the tribe. In the Qur'an, the story is much the same, except that instead of fleeing to Egypt of her own accord, Abraham remedies the acrimony between Hagar and Sarah by resettling Hagar and Ishmael in the land of Paran.

ARISTOTLE (384–322 B.C.E.) Greek philosopher who tutored world leaders and is credited as a pivotal developer of Western philosophy. The son of the physician to the Macedonian king Amyntas II, Aristotle was born into political influence. Orphaned at the age of 10, he went to live with his uncle Proxenus of Atarneus, who taught him poetry and rhetoric. At the age of 18, Aristotle became a student under Plato. In 343 B.C.E., King Philip II of Macedon invited Aristotle to tutor his son, Alexander, who would later become Alexander the Great. Aristotle also tutored the future kings Ptolemy and Cassander before opening his own school. Aristotle's theories on morality, aesthetics, government, and science have profoundly influenced contemporary Western thought.

THOMAS BARNARDO (1845–1905) British doctor and child advocate responsible for boarding out more children overseas than any other individual of his time. Upon observing the many children sleeping in gutters and on rooftops in London's East End, Barnardo was inspired to dedicate himself to protecting poor and orphaned children. In 1868, he opened a home for destitute children, and so many children arrived that overcrowding prompted him to open more homes. He also quickly began boarding children out to homes in the country and not long after began placing out children overseas in Canada, the United States, and Australia. He was partly responsible for a change in British law that prioritized the rights of children over those of parents. By the time of his death, he had sent 18,000 children overseas.

OSCAR BERGER (1946–)   Former president of Guatemala. Born into a wealthy Belgian/Guatemalan family with vast sugar and coffee holdings, Berger was president of Guatemala from 2004 to 2008. In 2006, UNICEF presented a donation of $28 million to the Guatemalan Division of Social Welfare, which was run by Berger's wife, Wendy de Berger. The donation came with the condition that all international adoptions be halted and processed according to the standards set down in the Hague Convention. In late 2007, President Berger announced the Ortega Law, which suspended all adoptions as of January 1, 2008, for individual processing. The law made no provisions for care of the children awaiting adoption and proposed no plan for future children entering the adoption system. As of 2009, several thousand adoptions are still suspended, and Guatemala is still in the process of becoming Hague compliant.

VIOLA BERNARD (1907–1998)   Social psychiatrist. Born in New York to wealthy German-Jewish parents, Bernard had access to educational opportunities that were closed to most young girls, which likely affected the development of her social awareness. Bernard believed in a socially holistic approach to psychiatry, specifically one that included an acknowledgement of the relationships between mental health, civil rights, urban poverty, interactions between individuals, and public institutions. As the chief psychiatric consultant of Louise Wise Services, one of the nation's first specialized adoption agencies, Bernard continuously worked for reforms within the agency to ensure equal protection for all children. Her insistence on racial integration of the staff as well as the establishment of interracial adoption made Louise Wise Services one of the adoption agencies to embrace ethnic diversity.

CHARLES LORING BRACE (1826–1890)   Reverend, child advocate, and founder of the orphan trains. Having studied divinity and theology at Yale and the Union Theological Seminary, Brace moved to New York and devoted himself to working in the streets rather than in a church. After witnessing the squalid conditions of life on the streets for the city's orphans and destitute children, he made the connection between the poverty, over-crowding, and abuse with which the children grew up and the crime and violence that they would inevitably go on to embrace. Distrustful of orphan-ages, where he believed homeless children were raised to be dependent on charity, Brace founded the orphan trains, a large-scale child-emigration endeavor that sought to relocate thousands of children from the slums of New York to western and midwestern farming communities. After his death in 1890, the Brace Memorial Farm was founded to teach farm skills, social skills, and manners to impoverished urban children.

LOUISE BROWN (1978–) World's first test-tube baby. John and Lesley Brown of Oldham, England, had been unable to conceive for nine years due to Lesley's blocked fallopian tubes. In 1977, the Browns agreed to undergo in vitro fertilization, understanding that the procedure was experimental, but not knowing that no live baby had yet resulted from it. The procedure was a success, and Louise Brown was born on July 25, 1978, through a planned cesarean section, weighing five pounds, 12 ounces. The birth of Louise Brown created an explosion of demand among other infertile couples. Four years later, the Browns conceived another daughter through in vitro, and she became the 40th test-tube baby.

PEARL S. BUCK (1892–1973) Novelist, humanitarian, and advocate for special needs, transracial, and international adoptions. As the child of Prot-estant missionaries, Buck grew up in China and later moved to the United States. After giving birth to a sickly and mentally disabled daughter, she underwent a hysterectomy. She went on to adopt seven mixed-race children and in 1949 established her own adoption agency after failing to find an agency that would place a dark-skinned infant of mixed racial heritage. Buck believed firmly in civil rights and intercultural education, and she was openly critical of social workers who refused to place children of color despite the numbers of people who wanted to adopt them.

MARK AND CRISPINA CALVERT Contracting couple from Califor-nia who were awarded parental rights in a custody battle with a surrogate mother. Mark and Crispina Calvert were unable to conceive children as Crispina had had a hysterectomy, so in 1990 they chose to enlist the help of a surrogate mother Anna Johnson. Because Crispina still had her ovaries, her own egg was fertilized with Mark's sperm, and the resulting embryo was implanted in Anna's uterus with the agreement that she would receive $10,000. Shortly thereafter, Anna demanded immediate payment in full, or she would refuse to relinquish the baby. The Calverts filed a lawsuit, and Anna argued that although she was not genetically related to the baby, she had developed an emotional bond with him. The trial court found in favor of the Calverts, determining that the true mother in such surrogacy disputes was the woman who intended to raise the baby.

HENRY DWIGHT CHAPIN (1857–1942) Pediatrician who pushed for mental health considerations for adopted children but also urged for the assessment of genetic fitness of waiting children. Eugenics was gaining popularity in the late 19th century, and many people placed the blame for crime, violence, and vagrancy on genetic unfitness. Henry Chapin believed that genetically fit individuals were more likely to suffer from infertility, and society was thus in need of "better" adoptable babies. The only way to ensure genetic quality among future generations, he argued, was to prevent physically and genetically defective people from reproducing. Such people, he insisted, need to be quarantined to prevent social contamination. His wife, Alice Chapin, founded the Alice Chapin Nursery, which today survives as the Spence-Chapin Adoption Services.

STEPHEN CONROY (1963–) Australian Labor Party member of the senate representing the state of Victoria. Born in England and raised in Australia, Stephen Conroy became a member of the senate in 1996. In 2006, unable to conceive on their own, he and his wife, Paula Benson, opted to have a child through the use of an egg donor and a surrogate mother. In all Australian states, the surrogate mother is the legal mother of the child, and most states consider commercial surrogacy a criminal offence. Unusual for any surrogacy arrangement in Australia, Conroy's name was immediately placed on the child's birth certificate as the father. Shortly after the announcement of the arrangement, the state of Victoria announced an overhaul of anti-surrogacy legislation that would legalize altruistic surrogacy. Commercial surrogacy remains illegal.

KIM COTTON (1957–) England's first commercial surrogate mother. On January 4, 1985, Kim Cotton, housewife and mother of two, gave birth to a baby girl through England's first commercial surrogacy contract, with the agreement that she would receive £6,500. Several months before giving birth, news of the arrangement leaked to the press, and Kim Cotton sold her story for an additional £15,000. On giving birth, the British courts intervened and deemed the arrangement akin to baby-selling. A week later, the contracting parents were granted full custody and were allowed to leave the country with the baby, with whom Cotton has never had contact. Shortly after the court case made headlines, England passed the Surrogacy Arrangements Act to prohibit surrogacy for profit.

DENG XIAOPING (1904–1997) Leader of the Communist Party of China from 1978 to 1989. An adherent of Mao Zedong's communist policies, Deng was appointed to the position of general secretary of the Communist Party of China. After the Cultural Revolution left China socially and economically debilitated, Deng implemented new economic reforms that partially opened China to the global market, and he is credited with making China one of the fastest-growing economies in the world. One of his reforms was the One-Child Policy, which restricted urban Chinese families to one child only. Realizing the economic destabilization that Mao's insistence on population increase had wrought, Deng understood that the only way for China to compete in the global market was if the nation's population was limited, thereby reducing the demand on its natural resources and increasing the individual savings rate. Despite controversies regarding human rights violations, a 2007 study by University of California, Irvine, found the policy to be highly effective.

HELEN AND CARL DOSS   The Dosses adopted 12 mixed-race children in the 1940s and 1950s. Known as the United Nations family, the Dosses were unique in their defiance of race-matching. They adopted 12 children of Filipino, Hawaiian, Balinese, Indian, Mexican, Malayan, and Native American ancestry. When they attempted to adopt a mixed-race girl of African-American descent, they ran into fierce resistance from family and friends. They were featured in *Reader's Digest* and *Life* in the late 1940s, and in 1954 Helen wrote a book detailing their family life, *The Family Nobody Wanted*, in which she addressed racism and race-matching. The book was serialized, adapted to film, and translated into seven languages.

ROBERT EDWARDS (1925–)   British medical researcher who helped develop in vitro fertilization, resulting in the birth of Louise Brown. As a professor at Cambridge University, Robert Edwards was the first scientist to fertilize a human egg in vitro by determining the length of time the egg needed to mature, the conditions the sperm and the egg needed to conceive, and the point at which the developing blastocyst could be reintroduced into the uterus. To retrieve more eggs and further his research, Edwards partnered with gynecologist Patrick Steptoe. They spent several years perfecting the procedure, with numerous failures, until 1978, when they met John and Lesley Brown. Lesley Brown became pregnant via IVF and successfully carried to term, giving birth in 1979 to Louise Brown, the world's first test-tube baby.

DEREK FORREST   Family solicitor in a British law firm who helped alter surrogacy legislation. Derek Forrest wrote to the *Times* to publicize a unique challenge facing his clients, a married couple who could not conceive on their own because the wife had no uterus. They contracted with a surrogate

220

mother who carried a child conceived with their own genetic material. After the surrogate gave birth, the couple took the child home but were told by local authorities that they had to follow normal adoption proceedings. Even though they were the genetic parents of the child, they were forced to register first as foster parents in order to legally adopt their own child. After the case went public, an amendment to the Human Fertilization and Embryology Act of 1990 passed parliament, and the couple became the first contracting couple to acquire parental rights under the Act.

ANNA FREUD (1895–1982) Psychoanalyst who specialized in child development and developed theories on the importance of human contact and attachment. The youngest child of Sigmund Freud, Anna Freud moved to London during World War II where she studied young children who had been separated from their parents during the Blitz. With her friend Dorothy Burlingham, she observed children who sucked their thumbs and rocked obsessively, banged their heads against walls, and displayed a number of other unusual behaviors. In their book *Infants Without Families*, Freud and Burlingham theorized that such behaviors were the direct result of separation and lack of human affection, and that institutionalization was therefore detrimental to children as it could never replicate true family connection.

SIGMUND FREUD (1856–1939) Father of psychoanalysis. Sigmund Freud pioneered the study of unconscious drives and desires and how they manifest as neuroses and psychoses in individuals. Particularly well known are his theories of child development, including the Oedipus complex, the family romance, and the childhood stages of sexual development, such as the oral, anal, and genital phases. Applications of psychoanalytic theory to adopted children, birth mothers, and adoptive parents brought attention to notions of identity, attachment, and child mental health that were not previously considered in the adoption process. Psychoanalysis was also used as a means of ascribing negative characteristics and neuroses to both birth mothers and infertile women.

ARNOLD GESELL (1880–1961) Psychologist and adoption advocate. In the first half of the 20th century, Arnold Gesell openly called for professional regulation of adoption and minimum standards for the adoption process. As the head of Yale's Clinic of Child Development, he ran a series of mental and behavioral tests on local children between the 1910s and the 1930s. He insisted on the validity of a universal pattern of development for all children that aided in matching children with parents. He addressed such topics as pre-placement testing, appropriate placement age, and adoption supervision and openly supported sealed records. Though he did not subscribe to the popular belief in eugenics that so many other psychologists and adoption scholars were embracing, Gesell did believe in testing children to match them with an appropriate set of parents.

HENRY HERBERT GODDARD (1866–1957)   Psychologist and proponent of intelligence testing. Just prior to World War II, many psychologists around the world were embracing eugenics, and Henry Herbert Goddard was a singular authority in the eugenics movement in the early 1910s. As the director of the Training School for Backward and Feeble-Minded Children in Vineland, New Jersey, Goddard translated the French Binet-Simon intelligence scales and distributed them widely as means of testing children for mental defects. He firmly believed in institutionalization for mentally retarded children and openly opposed adoption of such children. He documented the feebleminded Kallikak family and, like other eugenicists, insisted that the feebleminded should be quarantined so as not to pollute the human gene pool. He is also credited with introducing the word *moron* into the English lexicon. His book, *The Kallikak Family*, was reprinted in Germany in 1933 as the Nazis were coming to power.

BERTHA AND HARRY HOLT (1904–2000, ?–1964)   After learning about the pitiful living conditions of Korean War orphans, Bertha and Harry Holt were moved to act. Through a special act of congress in 1955, the Holts were allowed to travel to Korea to adopt eight orphans, making them a family of 14. They began helping others adopt from overseas and, though they were not licensed social workers and often overlooked minimum standards, they set their own standards, which usually required adoptive parents to be "saved." The Holts viewed their work as an act of Christian charity rather than social work, which unsettled many adoption professionals who feared that the Holts were undermining hard-won standards and regulations that had been put into place to protect children. In the 1960s, the Holts began to follow standard professional procedures.

ANNA JOHNSON (1961–   )   Surrogate mother who refused to relinquish the baby and consequently altered surrogacy legislation in California. A nurse and an African-American single mother, Anna Johnson agreed to carry the Calverts' baby as a gestational surrogate in exchange for $10,000. When she demanded payment in full under threat of refusing to hand over the baby, the Calverts filed a lawsuit. The case is significant for a number of reasons: 1) Johnson was black and the Calverts were white and Filipino, which called race into question; and 2) the case effectively changed the legal definition of motherhood in California. When Anna Johnson petitioned for visitation rights, she was denied based on the judge's ruling that she had no claim to the child. The legal mother, the judge ruled, is the woman who *intended* to create and raise the child.

EMPEROR JUSTINIAN I (483–565 C.E.) Byzantine emperor who revised and compiled all of Roman law into a collection known as Corpus Juris Civilis. In 529 C.E., Emperor Justinian I embarked on a project to revise all of Roman law, a feat that had never before been done. *Corpus Juris Civilis* (Body of civil law) consisted of four parts: the Codex Justinianus, Digesta (or Pandectae), Institutiones, and Novellae. Book I of Institutiones includes mandates on adoption practices and specifies who may adopt and who may be adopted. According to Book I, adoption does not dissolve the natural father's rights; women, however, have no rights to their own children. Further, adoption must imitate nature, thus the adopter must be a full 18 years older than the adoptee.

DEBORAH KALLIKAK (1889–1978) The primary subject of Henry Herbert Goddard's book, *The Kallikak Family: A Study in Heredity of Feeble-Mindedness.* Deborah came to the Vineland Training School at the age of eight, and Goddard used her and her family as validation of his argument for the isolation of the feebleminded. Goddard traced Deborah's family tree and found that her great-great-great grandfather had produced two family lines: one intelligent and morally upstanding and the other—the result of a dalliance with an unnamed barmaid—feebleminded and morally corrupt. Though Goddard was unable to convince Deborah's teachers that she was feebleminded, he remained convinced of her mental defectiveness. He went to the extent of including pictures of Deborah's family in his book and altering the faces to make them appear more sinister and deformed.

NOEL KEANE (1938–1997) First lawyer in the United States to draft a formal surrogacy contract. After receiving his law degree from the University of Detroit, Keane entered a general law practice in Dearborn, Michigan. In 1976, he was approached by a married couple seeking a surrogate, and he drafted the first formal surrogacy contract between a couple and an unpaid surrogate. He is infamously known as the lawyer responsible for the 1986 Baby M case, in which the surrogate mother, Mary Beth Whitehead, refused to relinquish her baby. The year before the Baby M case went to trial, his surrogacy practice had grossed $600,000. By the time of his death, he had opened surrogacy centers in California, New York, Nevada, Michigan, and Indiana.

RICHARD LEVIN, M.D. One of the first surrogacy practitioners and the head of Surrogate Parenting Associates, Inc. In 1979, Dr. Richard Levin was approached by an infertile couple desperate to have a baby. He suggested a donor woman or surrogate mother and subsequently helped the couple arrange a surrogate pregnancy. The attorney general of the State of Kentucky challenged the legality of Surrogate Parenting Associates, Inc., but the Kentucky supreme court found in favor of Surrogate Parenting Associates. Though he specializes in tubal ligation reversals, he maintains a surrogacy practice as well as a Web site: www.babies-by-levin.com.

BARBARA MANNING   Surrogacy center director who arranged the Baby Cotton surrogacy case. When Kim Cotton decided to become a surrogate mother, she contacted the Surrogate Parenting Centre of Great Britain, which was then headed by Barbara Manning. Manning acted as the intermediary between Cotton and the anonymous contracting couple and would collect fresh semen from the contracting father at one location and bring it to Cotton at her home, where she would inseminate herself. After several months, Cotton became pregnant and Manning took the story to the press. Cotton sold her story for £15,000 and became the subject of an international flurry over the ethics and legality of surrogacy.

MAO ZEDONG (1893–1976)   Leader of the Communist Party of China and the People's Republic of China. Chairman Mao led the Communist Party in the overthrow of the Kuomintang and became the leader of the People's Republic of China in 1949. In his endeavors to implement heavy industry and collective farms, he encouraged Chinese citizens to produce many children, as he saw a large population as the key to economic and social growth. During Chairman Mao's reign, the average Chinese woman had five children. This number dropped dramatically when Deng Xiaoping succeeded Mao and instituted the one-child-only policy to cap off the population spike.

SIR WALTER MONCKTON (1891–1965)   Lawyer and political adviser whose report on a case of child abuse resulted in a nationwide movement to revise boarding-out practices. In 1945, a 12-year-old boy named Dennis O'Neill died in state care due to malnourishment and abuse. The Home Secretary chose Sir Walter Monckton to investigate the circumstances that led to the boy's death, and his report detailed the fact that Dennis and his brother had been taken from their parents and placed with a man of ill repute. There was no governmental oversight of the placement, and there was no state inquiry into the boys' well-being after placement. The report riled the British people, who demanded child welfare reform, and the British government instituted a massive restructuring of child care services.

MOSES (1391–1271 B.C.E.)   Biblical prophet who is adopted and raised by the pharaoh's daughter. In Exodus of the Bible, Moses is born at a time of war when, fearing that the Hebrews will betray Egypt, the pharaoh commands the death of all Hebrew boys. Moses's mother, Jochebed, sets him adrift in a basket of bulrushes on the Nile River to spare him from death. The pharaoh's daughter, Thermuthis, finds the baby and adopts him into the royal family. The version of the story in the Qur'an recounts Moses's abandonment as a command from God to Jochebed to set him adrift on an ark on the Nile, thereby trusting him completely to God's will. In the Qur'an, Moses is not discovered by the pharaoh's daughter, but by his wife, who convinces the pharaoh to adopt him as they are unable to have children of their own.

MUHAMMAD (570–632)   Founder of Islam. Born in the Arabic city of Mecca, Muhammad was orphaned as an infant and was sent to live with Bedouin foster parents. He moved between several sets of parents before going to live with his uncle, who taught him the business of trade. He married at age 25 and at age 40, he is said to have received his first revelation from God. He subsequently established the religion of Islam, which translates to "surrender." He is believed to have had 13 wives and/or concubines, and he is also known to have adopted a son. In Islamic tradition, an adopted child is not considered the legal child of the adoptive parents but rather maintains his or her natal family's line. Thus, an adopted son cannot take the name of his adoptive father.

L. K. PANDEY   Child advocate responsible for changing adoption legislation in India. In 1982, a young Indian child died while being transported to an adoptive home overseas. The child's death caused an uproar, as until that point, there was no governmental oversight or supervision of adoption practice. In 1984, child advocate L. K. Pandey complained to the Supreme Court that adoption agencies and social groups that placed Indian children in intercountry adoptions were engaging in malpractice. He alleged that children were being mistreated and even sold overseas. The case of *L. K. Pandey v. Union of India* resulted in the creation of the Central Adoption Resource Agency (CARA) and a governmental overhaul of previous adoption practices.

NAYNA PATEL (1962?–)   India's first and most successful surrogacy director. The commercial surrogacy industry in India took hold in Anand in the western state of Gujarat. At the Anand-based Akanksha clinic, run by Dr. Patel, more than 100 couples are serviced each year. Patel has been widely featured in the media, defending commercial surrogacy and her clinic, which pays local, impoverished women to act as surrogates. At any one time, she may have 15 to 20 surrogates pregnant with the children of couples from around the world. All of her surrogates are housed and cared for in a local hostel until delivery.

JUSTINE WISE POLIER (1903–1987) Judge and child advocate who championed adoption as a matter of social justice. Justine Wise Polier was the daughter of Louise Waterman Wise, who established one of the country's first specialized adoption agencies, the Free Synagogue Child Adoption Agency. Polier was passionate about children's rights and saw adoption as a means of creating responsible, law-abiding citizens. She was an early opponent of racial and religious matching, and when she became the president of the board of directors of her mother's adoption agency, which she renamed Louise Wise Services, Polier restructured the program to include African-American and transracial adoptions.

JOHN ROCK, M.D. (1890–1984) American scientist who specialized in bypassing blocked fallopian tubes. John Rock, a practicing Catholic and father of five, believed in the importance of children and family and dedicated his practice to helping other couples create their own families. Realizing the problem of infertility and blocked fallopian tubes, Rock pioneered tubal reconstructions, although the success rate was only 7 percent. In 1937, he heard about experiments in in vitro fertilization in animals and applied himself to the task of researching it in humans. In 1944, Rock and his lab technician performed the first fertilization of a human egg outside of the human body. It would be decades before researchers would find a way to successfully transfer in vitro fertilized embryos back into the womb.

MARIETTA SPENCER American social worker who helped pioneer positive adoption language in the mid-1970s. Positive adoption language is designed to emphasize the adopted child's complete removal from the natal family and assimilation into the adoptive family, as well as the empowerment of birth parents who make the choice to relinquish their child for adoption. Before Spencer helped establish positive adoption language, certain terms were often inflammatory and perpetuated the notion that adoptive families were artificial. Spencer sought to replace the term *real* or *natural mother* with birth mother, and the term *surrendering* a baby for adoption to placing a baby for adoption.

PATRICK STEPTOE (1913–1988) British gynecologist and medical researcher who helped develop the process of in vitro fertilization. In 1951, Patrick Steptoe began working at Oldham General and District Hospital in Northeast England, where he developed a method of retrieving human eggs using a laparoscope. In 1966, he teamed up with the Cambridge physiologist Robert Edwards to perfect the technique of IVF. It took years for the duo to develop a way to successfully transfer a fertilized egg back into the uterus, and most women who were impregnated were unable to carry for a full trimester.

In 1977, Steptoe and Edwards produced the first successful IVF pregnancy, and the following year, the world's first test-tube baby was born.

WILLIAM AND ELIZABETH STERN (1944– , 1944–) Contracting couple at the heart of the infamous Baby M case. In 1985, William Stern, a biochemist and the only child of Holocaust survivors, and Elizabeth Stern, a pediatrician, hired 26-year-old Mary Beth Whitehead to be artificially inseminated with William's sperm, carry a child for them, and then terminate her parental rights upon delivery. When Whitehead refused to give up her baby, the Sterns took her to court. Elizabeth Stern argued that because of her self-diagnosed multiple sclerosis, pregnancy could pose a risk to her health. William Stern argued that as the only child of parents who had survived the Holocaust, he desired a genetic child of his own. The Sterns were later awarded custody of the baby.

JESSIE TAFT (1882–1960) Advocate for adoption professionalization. Jessie Taft entered the field of social work in the early 1910s, when it was still considered nonprofessional charitable sector. She joined the University of Pennsylvania School of Social Work in 1934, as well as the Children's Aid Society of Pennsylvania, and championed adoption reform by way of minimum standards, supervision, field research, and outcome studies. Taft believed in the therapeutic effects of adoption and argued against such theories as feeblemindedness and moral defectiveness. Rather, she argued, adoption is a forum for providing help to children, birth parents, and adoptive parents. She and her partner, Virginia Robinson, adopted two children of their own.

SOPHIE VAN SENDEN THEIS (1885–1957) America's first adoption professional and the first person to publish a large-scale outcome study on adopted children. Sophie van Senden Theis entered the field of social work in 1907 and was a firm proponent of minimum standards, empirical research, and specialized training for adoption professionals. In 1921, she published one of the first training manuals for child placement, and in 1924 she released *How Foster Children Turn Out,* an outcome study on 910 children placed by the New York State Charities Association between 1898 and 1922. She personally facilitated the adoption of two children by fellow social worker Jessie Taft and her partner, Virginia Robinson.

EMPEROR TRAJAN (52–117) Adopted Roman emperor who brought Rome to its height. Born in Italica, Spain, Trajan was the first non-Italian emperor of Rome. His father had been a military commander and politician under Vespasian, and Trajan, too, entered the military when he was of age and quickly rose to prominence. Emperor Nerva appointed Trajan governor of Upper Germany in 96 C.E., and the following year Trajan received a handwritten note from Nerva informing him of the emperor's decision to adopt him. Under Trajan, the Roman Empire reached its greatest expanse, encompassing modern-day Iraq and Romania.

DAME MARY WARNOCK (1924–) British philosopher and writer who chaired an inquiry into assisted reproductive technology that resulted in the Warnock Report. An existentialist who wrote widely on morality and the mind, Dame Mary Warnock chaired a number of inquiries, including one into special education, and advised a committee on animal experiments. In the early 1980s, she chaired the Committee of Inquiry into Human Fertilisation and Embryology, which produced the Warnock Report. The report recommended that legislation be introduced to ban all types of surrogacy arrangements and criminalize those who arranged them. The report was released at the same time as Kim Cotton became Britain's first commercial surrogate mother.

MARY BETH WHITEHEAD (1959–) American surrogate mother at the center of the Baby M custody dispute. Mary Beth Whitehead was 26 years old when she was selected by a wealthy couple in their 40s, William and Elizabeth Stern, to be their surrogate. Whitehead signed a contract agreeing to be artificially inseminated and receive $10,000 upon termination of her parental rights. When Whitehead changed her mind, the Sterns took her to court. The trial judge upheld the contract and awarded full custody to the Sterns without visitation rights for Whitehead. The Supreme Court of New Jersey later reversed the ruling and awarded joint custody to the Sterns and Whitehead, naming Whitehead the baby's legal mother. The ruling further determined that surrogacy contracts are not legal or enforceable.

LOUISE WATERMAN WISE (1874–1947) Child advocate and founder of one of the United States' first specialized adoption agencies. The daughter of wealthy German-Jewish parents, Louise Waterman Wise received a thorough education and went on to marry Rabbi Stephen Samuel Wise, one of the founders of the National Association for the Advancement of Colored People. Louise was committed to charity work and when she learned that Jewish orphans were routinely institutionalized as no mainstream adoption agencies would take them, she established the Free Synagogue Child Adoption Agency. After her death, her daughter, Justine Wise Polier, took over the agency and renamed it Louise Wise Services.

9

Organizations and Agencies

AARP Grandparent Information Center
URL: http://www.aarp.org/life/grandparents
601 E Street NW
Washington, DC 20049
Phone: (202) 434-2296

The American Association of Retired Persons Grandparent Information Center provides informational resources for grandparents, including step-grandparents and grandparents raising grandchildren. The information center also helps individuals navigate specific issues, such as visitation rights for grandparents, caring for grandchildren, raising grandchildren full time, and how grandparents can play a positive role in their grandchildren's lives. The information center also hosts online communities of grandparents, as well as information for health care professionals, advocates and policy makers, teachers and school administrators, and corporate professionals.

Action Alliance for Children
URL: http://www.4children.org
1201 Martin Luther King Jr. Way
Oakland, CA 94612
Phone: (510) 444-7136

Action Alliance for Children is a children's advocacy group that promotes education for childcare providers, educators, child-welfare professionals, and other children's services providers in California. AAC produces an award-winning bimonthly magazine, *Children's Advocate*, which was established in 1973 and covers trends, public policy, and activism campaigns. The magazine also discusses a wide range of issues, including childcare, health, poverty, elderly care, child development, advocacy, and school-age children. The magazine is printed in both English and Spanish.

Adult Survivors of Child Abuse
URL: http://www.ascasupport.org
The Morris Center
PO Box 14477
San Francisco, CA 94114

Adult Survivors of Child Abuse (ASCA) is a nonprofit organization devoted to helping adult survivors of abuse find help in overcoming their childhood abuse. The program's intention is to help survivors change their self-identities from victims to survivors to thrivers. The psychological model used for healing survivors uses a three-stage framework specifically designed for victims of child abuse. The healing framework includes remembering, which involves addressing one's abuse and committing to recovery; mourning, which involves identifying problem areas in one's adult life and grieving for one's lost childhood; and healing, which involves coming to terms with one's abuse and making the resolution to strengthen oneself despite it.

American Fertility Association
URL: http://www.theafa.org
305 Madison Avenue, Suite 449
New York, NY 10165
Phone: (888) 917-3777

The American Fertility Association (AFA) is a national nonprofit organization committed to preventing infertility and providing information and resources for reproductive health, infertility prevention, and family building. The AFA provides a number of services and materials free of charge, including an online library, monthly online "webinars," a toll-free support number, and daily fertility news. The organization also hosts an online community and guidance for finding support groups, in addition to an e-newsletter and an online educational module. Visitors can also use the network to find a physician or therapist.

American Foster Care Resources, Inc.
URL: http://www.afcr.com
PO Box 271
King George, VA 22485
Phone: (540) 775-7410

Founded in 1983, American Foster Care Resources (AFCR) is a nonprofit organization that provides informational resources for and about foster care. The organization is also a publisher that provides resources to foster care providers, children and families, and placing agencies. AFCR publishes the quarterly *Fos-*

ter Care Journal. Publications are available online, and AFCR's Web site also provides downloadable materials on independent living, in-service resources, recruitment, and other resources.

American Society for Reproductive Medicine
URL: http://www.asrm.org
1209 Montgomery Highway
Birmingham, AL 35216-2809
Phone: (205) 978-5000

The American Society for Reproductive Medicine (ASRM) is a nonprofit organization committed to educating the public and professionals about reproductive medicine, including infertility, menopause, contraception, and sexuality. The organization was founded in Chicago in 1944 by a group of fertility specialists. Many past members of ASRM became the first physicians to perform today's standard fertility treatment procedures, such as donor insemination and in vitro fertilization. Today, the society is instrumental in the creation and support of national contraceptive and infertility research centers, as well as helping to shape and promote legislation.

The American Surrogacy Center
URL: http://www.surrogacy.com
3050 Matlock Drive
Kennesaw, GA 30144
Phone: (770) 426-1107

The American Surrogacy Center (TASC) was founded in 1997 by a contracting mother whose son was the first child born of a surrogate arrangement in the state of Georgia. The president of TASC created the Web site as a forum where surrogate mothers and contracting parents can independently locate and contact one another to arrange a surrogate pregnancy. In addition to a comprehensive classified matching service, the Web site offers information on surrogacy law, news updates, and online support groups.

The Annie E. Casey Foundation
URL: http://www.aecf.org
701 St. Paul Street
Baltimore, MD 21202
Phone: (410) 547-6600

The Annie E. Casey Foundation was established in 1948 to promote public policy, human services, and community efforts that support vulnerable and disadvantaged families. The foundation, created by former UPS CEO Jim Casey, distributes grants to states, cities, and communities that are endeavoring to meet the needs of children and families. The foundation's major initiatives include family economic success, leadership development, juvenile detention alternatives, family to family (a family preservation initiative), and KIDS COUNT (a child-welfare tracking initiative).

Bastard Nation
URL: http://www.bastards.org
PO Box 1469
Edmond, OK 73083-1469
Phone: (415) 704-3166

Bastard Nation is an organization that advocates for the rights of adult and child adoptees, particularly in regard to access to sealed records. Bastard Nation opposes sealed records, supports legislation that would allow adult adoptees to have access to identifying information, and promotes the worldwide renunciation of sealed records. The Bastard Nation Web site provides frequent updates on state and federal legislation regarding adoptee rights, as well as ways to get involved in local, state, and nationwide campaigns. The Web site also provides comprehensive information regarding adoption law, adoptees' rights, and state and federal laws.

British Association for Adoption and Fostering
URL: http://www.baaf.org.uk
Saffron House
6–10 Kirby Street,
London, EC1N 8TS
United Kingdom
Phone: (011–44–20) 7421-2600

The British Association for Adoption and Fostering (BAAF) is a nonprofit organization dedicated to providing support for adoptive and foster parents, as well as protection for children separated from their birth families. BAAF believes that every child deserves a safe and stable home environment, secure attachments to his or her care providers, and an adoption or foster care arrangement that meets his or her specific needs. BAAF also believes that, when possible, every effort should be made to preserve families.

Casa Guatemala
URL: http://www.casa-guatemala.org
14 calle 10-63 Zona 1

Guatemala City
Guatemala
Phone: (011–502–2) 331-9408

Casa Guatemala is a shelter that provides food, housing, health care, and education to more than 250 children who are there due to abandonment, abuse, and poverty. Casa Guatemala is a nongovernmental organization and relies on donations, volunteers, and revenue from the related Hotel Backpackers. The shelter is divided up into three separate sites: the infant home and medical center, which houses infants and toddlers in addition to providing free medical care to local children and adults; the teenagers' home and administration office; and the children's village, which houses children between the ages of five and 16. The Casa Guatemala Web site provides information for travelers and backpackers who would like to volunteer onsite.

Central Adoption Resource Authority
URL: http://www.adoptionindia.nic.in
Ministry of Women & Child Development
West Block 8, Wing 2, 2nd Floor
R.K. Puram, New Delhi-110066
India
Phone: (011–91–11) 2618-0194

Established in 1990, the Central Adoption Resource Authority (CARA) is committed to placing India's orphaned, abandoned, and destitute children with loving families. Following the *Pandey v. Union* trial, in which a child advocate alleged mistreatment and malpractice within the international adoption industry in India, CARA was initially established for the implementation of Hague standards. Today it oversees both domestic and intercountry adoptions, although its primary goal is to find homes for parentless Indian children within India.

Childlessness Overcome Through Surrogacy
URL: http://www.surrogacy.org.uk
Moss Bank
Manse Road
Lairg
IV27 4EL
England
Phone: (011–44–15) 4940-2777

Founded in 1988 and formerly headed by England's first commercial surrogate mother, Kim Cotton, Childlessness Overcome Through Surrogacy

(COTS) is a nonprofit organization that matches surrogate mothers with contracting couples. In 2007, the organization celebrated its 600th surrogate birth. Because commercial surrogacy is illegal, COTS maintains that its surrogates are only reimbursed for reasonable expenses. While it is also illegal to advertise for a surrogate mother, surrogates and couples can discuss surrogacy and their experiences on the Web site message board.

Children Now
URL: http://www.childrennow.org
1212 Broadway, 5th Floor
Oakland, CA 94612
Phone: (510) 763-2444

Children Now is a national organization that seeks to reassign more public resources to children. Through a combination of research and advocacy, Children Now emphasizes strategic, bipartisan efforts to address a number of issues, such as creating a more child-friendly media, ensuring that every child has access to health and oral care, implementing improvements in K–12 education and making early education accessible to all children, disseminating thorough and quantifiable research on children's services, and encouraging parents to talk to their children about drugs and sex.

Children's Defense Fund
URL: http://www.childrensdefense.org
25 E Street, N.W.
Washington, DC 20001
Phone: (800) CDF-1200

The Children's Defense Fund (CDF) was created in 1973 to influence and shape policies that affect childhood poverty, child abuse and neglect, child health care, and education. Their priorities include ending child poverty, providing children and pregnant women with comprehensive health and mental health coverage, protecting children from abuse and neglect and ensuring children's right to live in a safe, permanent family, ensuring that every child can read at grade level by the fourth grade, and ending the criminalization of children by implementing prevention and intervention programs.

The Children's Partnership
URL: http://www.childrenspartnership.org
1351 Third Street Promenade, Suite 206

Santa Monica, CA 90401
Phone: (310) 260-1220

The Children's Partnership is a national nonprofit organization committed to serving disadvantaged children. The organization performs research and analysis to advocate for underserved children in public policy debates, particularly as they pertain to health care coverage. The organization's major priorities include health care coverage for every child, providing resources to parents to help them ensure that their children grow up in a safe and healthy environment, and equipping children with opportunities to develop the technological skills necessary to compete in the global economy.

Child Rights Information Network
URL: http://www.crin.org
East Studio
2, Pontypool Place
London, SE1 8QF
United Kingdom
Phone: (011–44–20) 7401-2257

The Child Rights Information Network (CRIN) is a global network that coordinates action and disseminates information on children's rights around the world. The network has more than 2,000 member organizations and supports rights, rather than charity, for children. The goals of the network include providing support for the implementation of the UN Convention on the Rights of the Child, educating others on emerging issues in child welfare, and providing support for advocacy initiatives. CRIN believes that education and information are the keys to realizing and protecting children's rights around the world.

Child Welfare League of America
URL: http://www.cwla.org
2345 Crystal Drive, Suite 250
Arlington, VA 22202
Phone: (703) 412-2400

Established in 1920, the Child Welfare League of America (CWLA) is the nation's oldest and largest membership-based child welfare organization. CWLA carries a membership of 800 child service agencies and promotes national programs regarding adoption, foster care, teenage pregnancy prevention, teenage parenting, group residential care, kinship care, homelessness, substance abuse prevention, and mental health. The organization also strongly supports research and empirical data through its Research and Evaluation

Unit, which organizes data and resources and provides evidence-based information regarding the efficacy of certain children's services.

Concerned United Birthparents
URL: http://www.cubirthparents.org
PO Box 503475
San Diego, CA 92150-3475
Phone: (800) 822-2777

Concerned United Birthparents (CUB) is a nationwide organization that advocates for the rights of birth parents. Established in 1976, CUB began as a support system for birth parents who had relinquished their children for adoption. Today, CUB members include birth parents, adoptive parents, and adoptees, and the organization provides support for all individuals who have been affected by adoption. The organization also supports efforts toward adoption reform, preventing unnecessary family separations, assisting relatives who have been separated through adoption in locating one another, and educating the public on adoption-related issues.

Evan B. Donaldson Adoption Institute
URL: http://www.adoptioninstitute.org
120 East 38th Street
New York, NY 10016
Phone: (212) 925-4089

The Evan B. Donaldson Adoption Institute was founded in 1995 to help improve adoption policy and practice. The Adoption Institute supports adoption research, education, and advocacy and provides information for lawmakers and the media in an effort to help structure improvements in adoption law. The institute also encourages employer support for adoption, supports adoptees' rights to access birth records, advocates the development of a legal framework to address parenthood through assisted reproductive technology, and promotes ethical standards for adoption professionals.

Families USA Foundation
URL: http://www.familiesusa.org
1201 New York Avenue NW, Suite 1100
Washington, DC 20005
Phone: (202) 628-3030

Families USA is a national nonprofit organization dedicated to providing high-quality, accessible health care to all Americans. As an advocate for health care consumers, the organization acts as a watchdog over government decisions and policies that affect health care, coordinates public education campaigns regarding the importance of health care, produces health care policy reports, and provides support to state and community-based organizations. The organization also manages the Health Action Network, which includes organizations and individuals advocating for health care consumers.

Families with Children from China
URL: http://www.fwcc.org
255 West 90th Street, 11C
New York, NY 10024
Email: Caugh@aol.com

Families with Children from China (FCC) is an international network of parent support groups for families who have adopted children from China. The organizations goals are to support families with Chinese adopted children by providing post-adoption and Chinese culture programs, encourage adoption from China and support waiting families, and advocate for children waiting in Chinese orphanages. The organization supports a number of chapters throughout the United States, Canada, and the United Kingdom.

Family Equality Council
URL: http://www.familyequality.org
41 Winter Street, 4th Floor
Boston, MA 02108
Phone: (617) 502-8701

In 1979, a group of gay fathers formed an organization with the goal of providing support for other gay dads. Originally called the Gay Fathers Coalition, the group soon expanded to include lesbian mothers and eventually came to be known as the Family Equality Council, devoted to working for equality for lesbian, gay, bisexual, and transgender parents nationwide. The group's mission is to achieve equality for all families by actively promoting public awareness, public education, storytelling, and progressive legislation.

Ferre Institute
URL: http://www.ferre.org
124 Front Street
Binghamton, NY 13905
Phone: (607) 724-4308

The Ferre Institute was established in 1974 with a mission to promote infertility services, genetics services, and family building services, such as adoption.

The Ferre Institute offers a unique community genetics program that provides genetic counseling for medical decisions based on detailed medical histories and test results. The Institute also offers a family building program that assists ethnic minorities and gay and lesbian individuals in the creation of their families. In addition to such programs, the Ferre Institute also provides a free phone counseling service called the Pregnancy Risk Network, which counsels women and medical professionals on substances and illnesses that can have negative effects on fetal development.

Growing Generations
URL: http://www.growinggenerations.com
5757 Wilshire Boulevard, Suite 601
Los Angeles, CA 90036
Phone: (323) 965-7500

Growing Generations was created in 1996 as the first surrogacy agency to provide services exclusively to the gay and lesbian community. Since its establishment, Growing Generations has expanded to include all family types, including heterosexual couples, married couples, single individuals, GLBT individuals and couples, and HIV-positive individuals and couples. The agency provides a surrogacy program, egg donor program, and sperm donor program. The company's mission is to help build families of choice throughout the world.

Guatemala Adoptive Families Network
URL: http://www.guatefam.org
PO Box 176
Watertown, MA 02471
Email: info@guatefam.org

Guatemala Adoptive Families Network was established by families with children adopted from Guatemala in an effort to support Guatemalan families and children. The organization promotes projects that raise the standard of living for families in Guatemala, improve living conditions in Guatemalan orphanages, and ensures the ethical adoption of children who were legally and voluntarily relinquished. They also encourage adoptive parents to make an informed decision to adopt from Guatemala and maintain a lasting relationship with Guatemala and the Guatemalan people.

Guttmacher Institute
URL: http://www.guttmacher.org
125 Maiden Lane, 7th floor

New York, NY 10038
Phone: (212) 248-1951

The Guttmacher Institute, named after family planning physician Alan F. Gutt-macher, was established in 1968 as the Center for Family Planning Program Development, a semiautonomous division of Planned Parenthood Federation of America. Today the Institute is an autonomous nonprofit institution devoted to advancing sexual and reproductive health through research, policy analysis, and public education. The goals of the Institute include protecting and ensuring that all individuals worldwide have access to family planning and sexual health resources, thereby reducing the number of unwanted pregnancies, preventing and treating sexually transmitted diseases, and encouraging the formation of planned families.

Hague Conference on Private International Law
URL: http://www.hcch.net/index_en.php
Scheveningseweg 6
2517 KT The Hague
Netherlands
Phone: (011–31–70) 360-4867

Founded in 1893, the Hague Conference on Private International Law (HCCH) is a global intergovernmental organization, with 70 member countries from every continent. As a meeting point of several legal traditions, HCCH develops legal frameworks in response to global issues. As many personal, family, and commercial situations now involve more than one country (such as intercountry adoption), the goal of HCCH is to unify nations' laws to establish legal standards and protect individual rights.

Hague Evaluation
URL: http://www.hagueevaluation.com
Email: consultant@hagueevaluation.com

Hague Evaluation is an organization that provides comprehensive adoption consultation services, as well as a unique training service for adoption personnel wishing to become more involved in intercountry adoption. The organization also provides information regarding the Hague Convention on Intercountry Adoption, Hague standards, and accreditation. The Hague Evaluation Web site provides frequent updates on new laws emerging in relation to international adoption, as well as in-depth analysis of adoption standards and practices by country.

Hands of Help
URL: http://www.handsofhelp.org
PO Box 1703
Crows Nest NSW 1585
Australia
Email: info@handsofhelp.org

Hands of Help was founded in 2005 by Phoebe Williams, a medical student at the University of Sydney in Australia. Hands of Help, a nonreligious charity, was created in response to poverty and the suffering of children and families in East Africa, namely Uganda. It has since, however, branched into a more inclusive organization that works to combat poverty, hunger, disease, and ignorance in all developing countries, as well as disadvantaged communities within developed countries. The organization relies on donations and volunteers, and the Web site offers information on how to get involved.

Holt International
URL: http://www.holtinternational.org
PO Box 2880
1195 City View
Eugene, OR 97402
Phone: (541) 687-2202

Holt International is a nonprofit, Christian organization that specializes in locating adoptive families in the United States for abandoned, orphaned, and destitute children in poverty-stricken and war-torn countries. The agency was founded in the mid-1950s by Bertha and Harry Holt in response to reports of Amerasian children languishing in Korean orphanages. The Holts became the first couple to adopt children from overseas, and the Holt agency became the first international adoption service. While it began as a charitable organization, Holt International soon developed and expanded to become the United States' largest adoption agency, uniting roughly 40,000 children with families in the United States since its inception.

Human Rights Watch
URL: http://www.hrw.org
350 Fifth Avenue, 34th Floor
New York, NY 10118-3299
Phone: (212) 290-4700

Human Rights Watch was established in 1978 with the creation of Helsinki Watch, an organization created to monitor government compliance with the Helsinki Accords throughout the Soviet bloc. Helsinki Watch developed a methodology of publicizing and shaming human rights violators, which served to draw international attention to human rights abuses throughout the Soviet bloc. This methodology expanded and was applied to other countries and continents. Human Rights Watch is dedicated to protecting and preserving human rights through research methodology and strategic advocacy efforts that work to promote social, cultural, and economic rights.

HumanTrafficking.org
URL: http://humantrafficking.org
Academy for Educational Development
1825 Connecticut Ave. N.W.
Washington, DC 20009-5721
Phone: (202) 884-8916

Humantrafficking.org is a Web site that was developed by the Center for Gender Equity at the Academy of Educational Development. The Center for Gender Equity is dedicated to advancing the rights of girls and women to education, health, and economic participation. Humantrafficking.org was created to facilitate communication between governmental programs and nongovernment organizations (NGOs) working to combat human trafficking. The Web site provides country-specific information regarding trafficking laws and statistics, as well as academic, governmental, and NGO resources and publications to help fight human trafficking.

Immigrant Legal Resource Center
URL: http://www.ilrc.org
1663 Mission Street, Suite 602
San Francisco, CA 94103
Phone: (415) 255-9499

The Immigrant Legal Resource Center (ILRC) was founded in 1979 by Bill Hing, an immigrant rights attorney who sought to create an organization that would provide expert technical assistance in immigration law and policy. ILRC is a national nonprofit resource center that works to educate immigrants, legal professionals, and other organizations about immigrant rights through legal trainings, educational resources, and advocacy efforts. ILRC also provides Know Your Rights presentations in cooperation with other immigrant rights organizations to educate immigrants about their rights and how to protect those rights.

Indian Council of Medical Research
URL: http://icmr.nic.in
V. Ramalingaswami Bhawan

Ansari Nagar, New Delhi – 110029
India
Phone: (011–91–11) 2658-8895

The Indian Council of Medical Research (ICMR), the oldest medical research body in the world, is the central organization responsible for the formulation, coordination, and promotion of biomedical research in India. Among the council's research subjects are the prevention and management of diseases, birth control, maternal and child health, health care delivery, mental health, and cancer. In accordance with the legalization of commercial surrogacy in India, the ICMR released guidelines to help govern assisted reproductive technology and surrogacy.

The International Committee Monitoring Assisted Reproductive Technologies
URL: http://www.icmartivf.org
540 University Avenue, Suite 200
Palo Alto, CA 94301
Phone: (408) 647-9809

The International Committee Monitoring Assisted Reproductive Technologies (ICMART) is an international nonprofit organization that seeks to research, analyze, and disseminate information on assisted reproductive technology to educate individuals and professionals and ensure the standardization of assisted reproductive technology definitions and registries. ICMART was developed in response to the global flourishing of assisted reproductive technologies despite little to no standard global regulations or definitions. The organization specializes in independent research, publication of data, and providing information on safety, efficacy, and availability of assisted reproductive technologies.

International Society for the Prevention of Child Abuse and Neglect
URL: http://www.ispcan.org
245 W. Roosevelt Road Building 6, Suite 39
West Chicago, IL 60185
Phone: (630) 876-6913

The International Society for the Prevention of Child Abuse and Neglect (ISPCAN) was developed in 1977 to provide a forum for child-welfare professionals around the world to unite in combating child cruelty. ISPCAN provides training and resources to prevent physical abuse, sexual abuse, neglect, child homelessness, child prostitution, emotional abuse, child labor, and child victims of war. The organization aims to increase awareness of worldwide child abuse, advance international efforts to end it, and educate the public and professionals through up-to-date research and academic data.

The Latin American Network for Reproductive Medicine
URL: http://www.redlara.com
Phone: (011–52–477) 714-9809
Email: direjecutiva@redlara.com

The Latin American Network for Reproductive Medicine (Red Latinoamericana de Reproducción Asistida, or REDLARA) is a network of 141 centers that provide assisted reproductive technologies throughout Latin America. REDLARA monitors 90 percent of accredited fertility centers in Latin America and the Latin American Registry of Assisted Reproduction, which is housed within REDLARA, catalogues and reports on each individual institution within the network. The organization holds annual conferences and offers an online continuing education program to provide information and specialization for medical professionals.

Latin America Parents Association
URL: http://www.lapa.com
PO Box 339–340
Brooklyn, NY 11234
Phone: (718) 236-8689

Latin America Parents Association (LAPA) is a nonprofit organization comprised of a community of families who have adopted children from Latin America and wish to help others do the same. LAPA provides members with an adoption source kit with frequent updates regarding conditions in Latin America, a network of families involved in the adoption process, invitations to cultural and educational events, and the opportunity to participate in international relief efforts throughout Latin America. Eighty percent of the money received through membership fees and adoption source kits is donated to child-care institutions in Latin America.

Louise Wise Services
URL: http://louisewise.org
PO Box 999
Tenafly, NJ 07670
Phone: (201) 567-2065

Founded in 1916 by Louise Wise, Louise Wise Services (LWS) works to provide adoption, foster care, and general child welfare services to families. One of the first specialized adoption agencies in the country, Louise Wise Services was originally the Free Synagogue Child Adoption Committee and specialized in locating families for parentless Jewish children. In the 1950s and 1960s, the agency grew to include African-American adoptions and transracial adoptions. Today, the LWS's mission is to protect and promote child well-being within their families and communities.

Medical Tourism Corporation
URL: http://www.medicaltourismco.com
7000 Occidental Road
Plano, TX 75025
Phone: (800) 661-2126

Medical Tourism Corporation is a company that specializes in locating overseas doctors and hospitals to provide clients with low-cost, high-quality medical, dental, and cosmetic procedures. The company works with clients to plan a health care trip, which includes accommodation and recuperation time. The overseas medical procedures offered through Medical Tourism Corporation include fertility procedures, assisted reproductive procedures, and surrogate pregnancy services.

The Mother's Bridge of Love
URL: http://www.motherbridge.org
9 Orme Court
London W2 4RL
United Kingdom
Phone: (011–44–20) 7034-0686

The Mother's Bridge of Love (MBL) was founded in 2004 with the mission of facilitating communication and information-sharing between China and the Western world regarding adopted Chinese children. MBL works to promote education for and about Chinese children living abroad as well as those adopted in China, and the organization's main projects include Support Chinese Children, which provides support for disabled Chinese children, the Children's Journal Project, and the Art Exhibitions Project, which promotes the artistic talents of young Chinese.

The National Black Child Development Institute
URL: http://www.nbcdi.org
1313 L Street, NW, Suite 110
Washington, DC 20005-4110
Phone: (202) 833-2220

The National Black Child Development Institute (NBCDI) is a nonprofit organization dedicated to improving the quality of life for African-American children and families throughout the nation. The organization promotes such programs as Love to Read, which encourages parents and caregivers to help improve African-American children's academic performance, African American Parents' Project, Center for the Social and Emotional Foundations for Early Learning, and Entering the College Zone, which engages students and parents in a college-preparatory program.

The National Children's Advocacy Center
URL: http://www.nationalcac.org
210 Pratt Avenue
Huntsville, AL 35801
Phone: (256) 533-KIDS

The National Children's Advocacy Center (NCAC) is a nonprofit organization that offers training, prevention, intervention, and treatment services to combat child abuse and neglect in the United States. NCAC provides several educational, training, and professional services to enable professionals to fight child abuse in their own regions and establish community programs to educate the public. The organization's prevention and intervention programs highlight the need to address and remedy the roots of child abuse and neglect and get involved when abuse is suspected. NCAC's therapy programs work to help survivors and their families come to terms with their abuse.

National Family Preservation Network
URL: http://www.nfpn.org
3971 North 1400 East
Buhl, ID 83316
Phone: (888) 498-9047

The National Family Preservation Network (NFPN) works to provide support and resources for families through initiatives that focus on family preservation, family reunification, and fatherhood. NFPN is a nonprofit organization that was founded in 1992 to work with child welfare professionals to prevent unnecessary family separation, promote services to safely reunite families, encourage fathers to be involved in their children's lives, and promote improvements within child welfare organizations and agencies. While NFPN does not work directly with families, it works to develop family assessment tools for the child welfare system and training materials for father involvement.

North American Council on Adoptable Children
URL: http://www.nacac.org
970 Raymond Avenue, Suite 106
St. Paul, MN 55114
Phone: (651) 644-3036

North American Council on Adoptable Children (NACAC) is an organization dedicated to finding permanent homes for children in the United States and Canada who have lived in public care, especially special needs children, including school-age, drug-exposed, physically and/or mentally disabled, and ethnic minority children. NACAC was founded in 1974 by adoptive parents and operates through advocacy efforts, public policy, education, adoption support, and parent leadership development.

The Organization of Parents Through Surrogacy
URL: http://www.opts.com
PO Box 611
Gurnee, IL 60031
Phone: (847) 782-0224

The Organization of Parents Through Surrogacy (OPTS) is a nationwide non-profit organization that provides educational resources, networking opportunities, and referral services for surrogate mothers and contracting parents who wish to arrange a surrogate pregnancy. OPTS is not an agency but provides a classifieds listing, a message board, news articles, media analysis, and legislative updates. OPTS consists of volunteers, including contracting parents, surrogate mothers, and reproductive specialists, and the organization's primary mission is to provide support and resources to those considering surrogacy.

Parents for Ethical Adoption Reform
URL: http://www.pear-now.org
526 N. President Avenue
Lancaster, PA 17603
Email: reform@PEAR-now.org

Parents for Ethical Adoption Reform (PEAR) is a nonprofit organization devoted to reforming the adoption system to reflect the needs of adopted children, adoptive parents, and birth parents. PEAR works to ensure that families are able to make informed, educated decisions during the adoption process, that the adoption system is transparent, ethical, and respects the rights of each individual within the adoption triad, and that all families have access to support services. In addition to these priorities, PEAR's goals include the creation of a code of ethics for adoption professionals, as well as the creation of a consumer reporting board.

RESOLVE: The National Infertility Association
URL: http://www.resolve.org
1760 Old Meadow Rd., Suite 500
McLean, VA 22102
Phone: (703) 556-7172

Resolve is a nonprofit organization with the only established nationwide network that works to promote reproductive health and ensure equal access to family building solutions for individuals suffering from infertility. Through advocacy and public education, Resolve seeks to provide support and information for those experiencing infertility. Resolve offers resources for individuals and professionals in the form of publications, support groups, educational programs, and online communities. In addition to these resources, the organization offers weekly teleseminars and opportunities for volunteering.

Save the Children
URL: http://www.savethechildren.org.uk
1 St John's Lane
London EC1M 4AR
United Kingdom
Phone: (011–44–20) 7012-6400

Save the Children began in 1919 in response to a British blockade that left children in the cities of Berlin and Vienna starving and suffering from tuberculosis and rickets. Today, Save the Children works to prevent child exploitation, neglect, and abuse, and to ensure that every child receives proper health care, nutrition, and education. Operating in more than 50 countries, the organization focuses on issues of health, education, protection, and hunger and offers aid to regions that have been devastated by natural disasters, war, and other emergencies.

Surrogacy in Canada Online
URL: http://www.surrogacy.ca
RR2 Mitchell, Ontario
N0K 1N0
Canada
Phone: (519) 393-8205

Surrogacy in Canada Online is an information and referral service for surrogate mothers and contracting parents. Founded by gestational surrogate Sally

Rhoads, the Web site began as a journal that documented the various stages of her pregnancy for the intended parents of the twins she carried. The Web site then branched into an informational resource for all individuals considering surrogacy. The organization is not an agency and does not arrange surrogate pregnancies, but rather provides resources, information, referrals, and a support network for those who wish to arrange a surrogate pregnancy.

Surrogate Mothers Online, LLC
URL: http://www.surromomsonline.com
Email: info@surromomsonline.com

Surrogate Mothers Online was created in 1997 by a gestational surrogate whose goal was to create an educational resource for surrogate mothers and contracting parents. The Web site is entirely run by surrogate mothers and former surrogate mothers and provides publications, news articles, a question-and-answer section, sample contracts, and a section of classifieds. The Web site is intended to provide information and support to individuals who are considering surrogacy or an egg/sperm donor arrangement.

United Nations Children's Fund
URL: http://www.unicef.org
125 Maiden Lane, 11th Floor
New York, NY 10038
Phone: (212) 686-5522

Operating in 190 countries, the United Nations Children's Fund (UNICEF) works to uphold the UN Convention on the Rights of the Child. Through advocacy, public policy, and research and analysis, UNICEF aims to ensure child survival and development, free compulsory education for boys and girls, prevention and treatment of HIV and AIDS, and the protection of all children from abuse and exploitation. UNICEF specifically addresses such topics as health and disease prevention, childhood immunization, nutrition and nutrient deficiencies, water sanitation and hygiene, and health-promoting life skills.

U.S. Children's Bureau
URL: http://www.acf.hhs.gov/programs/cb
Administration on Children, Youth and Families
1250 Maryland Avenue, SW, Eighth Floor
Washington, DC 20024

Established by President Taft in 1912 to investigate infant mortality, birthrates, and juvenile courts, the Children's Bureau is one of two bureaus within the

Administration on Children, Youth, and Families, Administration for Children and Families, of the Department of Health and Human Services. The mission of the Children's Bureau is to develop programs that prevent child abuse and find permanent homes for children who cannot return to their families. The Children's Bureau manages such areas of child welfare as child abuse and neglect, child protective services, family preservation and support, adoption, foster care, and independent living.

World Health Organization
URL: http://www.who.int/en
Avenue Appia 20
1211 Geneva 27
Switzerland
Phone: (011–41–22) 791-2111

The World Health Organization (WHO) is the authority on health within the United Nations and is responsible for addressing global health issues, advising public policy, monitoring global health statistics, and articulating norms and standards. WHO's 6-point agenda includes promoting health development, particularly among disadvantaged groups, fostering health security, strengthening health care systems, monitoring research and new information, enhancing partnerships with other organizations, agencies, donors, and individuals, and improving performance and efficiency. In recent years, fertility treatments have become increasingly advanced and accessible, which has prompted WHO to launch investigations into the use of fertility procedures worldwide.

10

Annotated Bibliography

The following resources on adoption and surrogate pregnancy are arranged into eight categories:

Adoption and the Issues
Surrogate Pregnancy and the Issues
Adoption and Surrogate Pregnancy Worldwide
Adoption and Surrogate Pregnancy in the United States
Adoption and Surrogate Pregnancy in China
Adoption and Surrogate Pregnancy in India
Adoption and Surrogate Pregnancy in England
Adoption and Surrogate Pregnancy in Guatemala

Within each category, the resources are grouped into "Books," "Articles and Studies," "Web Documents," and "Other Media." "Other Media" may consist of documentaries, films, and television programs.

Some of the resources listed in this chapter are aimed specifically at individuals and couples who wish to pursue adoption or surrogate pregnancy in the creation of their family. Such resources, while not adhering to an academic or professional standard, can be very helpful in researching the topic of adoption and surrogate pregnancy as they often outline federal, state, and international laws, the processes involved, terminology and key individuals, and typical outcomes. Resources marked with an asterisk (*) are those meant for individuals considering adoption or surrogate pregnancy.

ADOPTION AND THE ISSUES
Books

*Beauvais-Godwin, Laura, and Raymond Godwin. *The Complete Adoption Book: Everything You Need to Know to Adopt a Child.* Cincinnati, Ohio: Adams Media, 2005.

Annotated Bibliography

Resource for those considering adoption. Topics addressed include finding a birth mother, meeting the birth mother, birth fathers' rights, the home study, infant adoption, agency adoption, open adoption, independent adoption, international adoption, and more. The authors also address concerns related to drug and alcohol abuse during pregnancy, transracial adoption, and children with special needs.

Brodzinsky, David, and Jesus Palacios (eds). *Psychological Issues in Adoption: Research and Practice*. Westport, Conn.: Praeger Publishers, 2005. Examines the psychological impact of adoption as the practice of adoption continues to change and evolve. Contributing authors analyze attachment, trauma, and bonding within the contexts of international adoption, transracial adoption, foster care, drug and alcohol exposure, abuse, single-parent adoption, and homosexual adoptive parents.

*Gray, Deborah. *Attaching in Adoption: Practical Tools for Today's Parents*. Indianapolis, Ind.: Perspectives Press, 2002. Defines "attachment" and the role of attachment in successful adoptions. Gray discusses such topics as self-esteem, childhood grief, developmental delays, children who have been abused or neglected, and children who have experienced multiple foster care placements. She also discusses successful attachment situations and how to create a strong, loving family.

*Keck, Gregory, Ph.D., and Regina Kupecky, L.S.W. *Adopting the Hurt Child: Hope for Families with Special-Needs Kids*. Colorado Springs, Colo.: Pinon Press, 1995. Examines the process of adopting a child who has suffered abuse and neglect and how to prepare oneself and one's family for such a child. The authors describe the challenges that come with adopting an abused child, particularly the psychological and emotional coping mechanisms that children develop, the trauma of neglect and loss, and problems within the child welfare system. The authors also discuss intercountry adoption of abused children.

*———. *Parenting the Hurt Child: Helping Adoptive Families Heal and Grow*. Colorado Springs, Colo.: Pinon Press, 2002. A sequel to *Adopting the Hurt Child*, this book details the challenges of parenting an adopted child who has suffered abuse and neglect, as well as the disruption that an adopted special needs child can bring to a family. The authors probe such issues as attachment disorders, control issues, and successful parenting techniques. They also provide resources on family, finances, and cultural differences.

Rosenthal, James, and Victor Groze. *Special-Needs Adoption: A Study of Intact Families*. Westport, Conn.: Praeger Publishers, 1992. Reports the results of a study of families who adopted special needs children, including older children, sibling groups, ethnic minority children, and children with disabilities. The authors assess the outcomes of different types of adoption, including transracial adoptions, adoptions by minority families, adoptions of children of different ages, single-parent adoptions, and adoptions by less educated or lower-income families.

Rothman, Barbara Katz. *Weaving a Family: Untangling Race and Adoption*. Boston: Beacon Press, 2005. Offers a blended sociological and personal perspective on transracial adoption and the various sociohistorical considerations that work together to create the transracial family. The author discusses commercialism and

251

consumerism in the process of family building, race in the United States, whiteness studies, genetics, Jewish-black relations, and understanding slavery and the African diaspora.

Simon, Rita J., and Rhonda M. Roorda. *In Their Siblings Voices: White Non-Adopted Siblings Talk about Their Experiences Being Raised with Black and Biracial Brothers and Sisters*. New York: Columbia University Press, 2009. Presents the stories of 20 children from the same families depicted in *In Their Own Voices: Transracial Adoptees Tell Their Stories*, to examine their experiences with multiracial adoption in the 1960s and 1970s.

———. *In Their Own Voices: Transracial Adoptees Tell Their Stories*. New York: Columbia University Press, 2000. Discusses the social, historical, and psychological significance of transracial adoption, particularly the arrangement whereby an African-American or mulato child is placed with white parents. The authors also offer a unique overview of the rhetoric surrounding the debate on transracial adoption, including arguments for and against the practice, as well as the relationship between transracial and international adoption.

Trenka, Jane Jeong, Julia Chinyere Oparah, and Sun Yung Shin. *Outsiders Within: Writing on Transracial Adoption*. Cambridge, Mass.: South End Press, 2006. A collection of personal essays, poems, and studies that examine unequal power distribution among the white privileged adopters and birth parents of color, the sense of identity loss and uncertainty among transracial adoptees, and the sociological links between domestic and international transracial adoption. The editors and authors urge for adoption reforms to ensure family preservation among domestic and international communities of color.

Verrier, Nancy. *The Primal Wound: Understanding the Adopted Child*. Self-published, 1993. Discusses adoption from a psychoanalytical perspective. The primal wound refers to a child's sense of emotional separation from his or her parents, and Verrier addresses such topics as abandonment, fetal development and attachment, infant awareness, and the experience of adoption. Also discussed are attachment and bonding, interrupted bonding, and birth mother fantasies.

Articles and Studies

Bonds-Raake, Jennifer M. "College Students' Attitudes Towards Adoption." *College Student Journal* 43 (March 2009): 132–135. Reports the results of an experiment in which college students were presented with a fictitious scenario whereby a family decides to adopt a second child. Students reported their level of approval, as well as their thoughts on adoption, and results reveal that they respond more positively to a couple's decision to have a biological child than an adopted child. Attitudes also varied depending on how many children a couple already had and how financially stable a couple was.

Brown, Jason D., and Susan Roger. "Children with Disabilities: Problems Faced by Foster Parents." *Children and Youth Services Review* 31 (Jan. 2009): 40–46. Assesses the results of a questionnaire in which licensed foster parents in Canada were asked to

Annotated Bibliography

name the biggest problems they had encountered in fostering a child with disabilities. Eighty-five responses reported problems with obtaining specialized professional services, the costs of raising a child with a disability, dealing with the health care system, and dealing with a child's individual behavioral problems.

Erich, Stephen, Heather Kanenberg, Kim Case, et al. "An Empirical Analysis of Factors Affecting Adolescent Attachment in Adoptive Families with Homosexual and Straight Parents." *Children and Youth Services Review* 31 (March 2009): 398–404. Examines 154 adoptive families with gay/lesbian and straight adoptive parents and the factors affecting adolescent attachment. The results of the study reveal no correlation between parent sexual orientation and adolescent attachment, but they do reveal a relationship between age at placement, number of placements prior to adoption, and adolescent attachment.

Goldberg, Abbie E. "Lesbian and Heterosexual Preadoptive Couples' Openness to Transracial Adoption." *American Journal of Orthopsychiatry* 79 (Jan. 2009): 103–117. Uses data from 147 white preadoptive lesbian and heterosexual couples to assess adopters' attitudes toward transracial adoption. The author determines that level of openness is affected by the adopters' perceptions of ethnic diversity in their communities, family support/non-support, and attitudes about race.

Passmore, Nola L., and Heather M. Chipuer. "Female Adoptees' Perspectives of Contact with Their Birth Fathers: Satisfaction and Dissatisfaction with the Process." *American Journal of Orthopsychiatry* 79 (Jan. 2009): 93–102. Discusses the results of a study in which 17 women who had been adopted before the age of two met their birth fathers and reported their feelings of satisfaction with the meeting. Four factors were identified as affecting satisfaction, including birth fathers' attributes and behavior, adoptees' expectations, behavior of the birth mother or adoptive family, and circumstances surrounding the adoption.

Smolin, David. "Child Laundering: How the International Adoption System Legitimizes and Incentivizes the Practices of Buying, Trafficking, Kidnapping, and Stealing Children." *Bepress Legal Series* (August 2005). Available online. URL: http://law.bepress.com/expresso/eps/749/. Accessed October 20, 2009. Define and analyzes incidences of "child laundering," wherein children are stolen or kidnapped from their families and home countries and "laundered" through the intercountry adoption system to become adoptable orphans. The article then proposes reforms to the intercountry adoption system to reduce the numbers of children taken from their families.

Van der Vegt, Esther J. M., Jan van der Ende, Robert F. Ferdinand, et al. "Early Childhood Adversities and Trajectories of Psychiatric Problems in Adoptees: Evidence for Long Lasting Effects." *Journal of Abnormal Child Psychology* 37 (Sept. 2008: 239–249. Study of a sample of 1,984 adoptees who were adopted at the mean age of 29 months to determine if early childhood adversity negatively affected psychological development. Parents provided information on abuse, maltreatment, and number of placements, and the researchers determined that early childhood adversity prior to adoption significantly increased the likelihood of developing psychiatric problems later in life.

Web Documents

Adoption.com. "Single Parent Adoptions: Why Not?" Available online. URL: http://library.adoption.com/articles/single-parent-adoptions-why-not.html. Accessed June 18, 2009. Argues for the right of single people to adopt based on evidence that single adoptive parents are just as capable of raising children as married adoptive couples. This article cites studies and reports that reveal no negative impacts suffered by children raised by single adoptive parents versus married adoptive parents. The article also distinguishes between children who suffer negative impacts due to divorce and household disruption and children who are adopted into single-parent homes.

Axness, Marcy. "When Does Adoption Begin?" Available online. URL: http://www.birthpsychology.com/birthscene/adoption14.html. Accessed June 19, 2009. Examines theories of fetal psychology and whether a birth mother's stress levels and detachment negatively affect fetal development. Axness analyzes both scientific sources and a personal account from a birth mother who believes that her feelings of emotional isolation and detachment traumatized her developing fetus.

———. "In Defense of the 'Primal Wound.'" Available online. URL: http://www.adopting.org/primal.html. Accessed June 19, 2009. Analyzes early infant/fetal psychology and the theory that at birth the infant experiences profound emotional trauma that results from being separated from his or her mother. The author discusses her own experience as an adoptee and argues that individuals are shaped not only by their early childhood experiences, but by their experiences in the womb. From this perspective, she urges adoptive parents to understand and empathize with their child's primal wound.

Cahn, Naomi. "Old Lessons for a New World: Applying Adoption Research and Experience to Assisted Reproductive Technology." Available online. URL: http://www.adoptioninstitute.org/publications/2009_02_OldLessons.pdf. Accessed June 18, 2009. Discusses the possibility of using adoption policies and research to improve policies and practices within the field of assisted reproduction, such as sperm and egg donation. The author specifically addresses the areas of secrecy and telling a child about his or her origins, market forces, and nontraditional families.

Howard, Jeanne. "Expanding Resources for Children: Is Adoption by Gays and Lesbians Part of the Answer for Boys and Girls Who Need Homes?" Available online. URL: http://www.adoptioninstitute.org/publications/2006_Expanding_Resources_for_Children%20_ March_.pdf. Accessed June 18, 2009. Reports the findings of an extensive review of research and policy over the last several decades to determine how children fare when raised by homosexual parents as opposed to heterosexual parents, and whether homosexual parents can be used as a resource for children who need permanent homes. The findings report no differences between children raised by gay and lesbian parents versus heterosexual parents, and laws that prohibit or preclude homosexual parents from adopting are putting parentless children at a distinct disadvantage.

Johnson, Patricia Irwin. "Speaking Positively: Using Respectful Adoption Language." Available online. URL: http://www.perspectivespress.com/pjpal.html. Accessed

June 18, 2009. Argues for the use of positive adoption language in describing the adoption process as a method of eliminating misconceptions of the adoptive family as artificial, tentative, or not the real thing. Johnson examines the way in which adoption language frames the global perception of adoption and reassigns authority and responsibility.

Leftwich, Gail. "Transracial Adoption: A Community Conversation." Available online. URL: http://www.abanet.org/publiced/focus/f96adop.html. Accessed June 18, 2009. Discusses the challenges that face families with transracially and transculturally adopted children. The parents surveyed expressed concerns related to external racism and bigotry, as well as the potential for their adopted child to experience a sense of cultural or ethnic loss. The parents in this survey reported their efforts to expose their adopted children to their cultures of origin, including Native American tribes, African-American churches, and trips abroad to visit birth countries.

Turski, Diane. "'Respectful' Adoption Language: Rebuttal." Available online. URL: http://www.exiledmothers.com/speaking_out/respectful_adoption_language. html. Accessed June 18, 2009. Counters Patricia Irwin Johnson's article "Speaking Positively: Using Respectful Adoption Language." Turski argues that positive adoption language reaffirms the parental role of adoptive parents at the expense of birth parents. Turski speaks from her experience of being forced to relinquish her child for adoption in the 1960s, a time when single mothers, especially pregnant teenagers, had few choices.

SURROGATE PREGNANCY AND THE ISSUES
Books

Ehrensaft, Diane. *Mommies, Daddies, Donors, Surrogates: Answering Tough Questions and Building Strong Families.* New York: The Guilford Press, 2005. Addresses the difficult and complex issues that arise within "biosocial" families, including shared genes and social parenthood, telling children of their genetic or birth origins, and feelings of jealousy between intended mothers and surrogates. Ehrensaft is a therapist who counsels such nontraditional families, so the book is written from a psychological and therapeutic perspective.

*Erickson, Theresa Marie. *Assisted Reproduction: The Complete Guide to Having a Baby with the Help of a Third Party.* Lincoln, Nebr.: iUniverse, 2005. A guide for intended parents who are considering surrogacy. The author discusses how to cope with infertility, choosing an alternative family-building option, and when to consider surrogacy. Erickson also discusses how to calculate the costs of surrogacy, selecting and screening surrogates, and telling friends and family about one's decision to pursue surrogacy. In addition to her discussion of surrogacy, Erickson provides an overview of egg/sperm/embryo donation and the ethical debates on assisted reproduction.

Fletcher, Joseph F. *The Ethics of Genetic Control: Ending Reproductive Roulette: Artificial Insemination, Surrogate Pregnancy, Nonsexual Reproduction, Genetic*

Control. Buffalo, N.Y.: Prometheus Books, 1988. Discusses the ethics of reproductive technology, including artificial insemination, in vitro fertilization, surrogate pregnancy, abortion, contraception, and genetically inherited diseases. Fletcher also discusses the philosophical contexts of reproductive technology, including the evolutionary process and religion.

*Griswold, Zara. *Surrogacy Was the Way: Twenty Intended Mothers Tell Their Stories.* Gurnee, Ill.: Nightengale Press, 2005. Documents the experiences of 20 women who arranged surrogate pregnancies in their quests for children. The book outlines their reasons for choosing surrogacy, including unexplained infertility, cancer, and diseases, as well as the unique challenges each woman faced in selecting a surrogate and undertaking the process of surrogacy. This book is written specifically from the perspective of intended parents and is meant to be a resource for other intended parents considering surrogacy.

Kohl, Beth. *Embryo Culture: Making Babies in the Twenty-First Century.* New York: Sarah Crichton Books, 2007. Offers a thorough examination of the ethics and processes of assisted reproductive technology. A personal narrative, Kohl describes her own experiences with in vitro fertilization and discusses major social questions about assisted reproduction, such as commerce and the fertility industry, multiple pregnancy, frozen embryos, preterm labor, and the health problems associated with low birth weight. She also addresses questions about assisted reproduction and religion.

Martin, Emily. *The Woman Inside the Body: A Cultural Analysis of Reproduction.* Boston: Beacon Press, 1987. Discusses the results of the author's study of 165 women and their experiences of menstruation, childbirth, and menopause. Martin discusses not only the class differences she observed in individual women's views of female bodily functions but also the social and medical fragmentation of the female self and the female body. The author addresses such issues as physicians' mechanical treatment of childbirth as production and the pervasive Western belief in menstruation and menopause as negative events of disruption and discord.

Mundy, Liza. *Everything Conceivable: How the Science of Assisted Reproduction is Changing Our World.* New York: First Anchor Books, 2007. Provides a detailed examination of changing human relationships, family structures, and kinship ties through assisted reproductive technologies. Mundy offers case studies that prompt speculation about the definition of parenthood, siblinghood, and family, particularly as she analyzes the relationships between surrogate mothers, egg donors, sperm donors, contracting parents, and the medical community. Each case study reveals the powerful desire to construct a family and the ends to which many people will go to have a child.

Rapley, Sandra Watson. *Intended Parents: Miracles Do Happen: A True-Life Success Story of Having Children Through Surrogacy.* Lincoln, Nebr.: iUniverse, 2005. Recounts the author's experiences in learning of her infertility, exhausting all infertility procedure options, and finally choosing to enlist the help of a surrogate. In the author's case, a female relative volunteered to carry the couple's child and later delivered twin boys.

Annotated Bibliography

Ryan, Maura. *Ethics and Economics of Assisted Reproduction: The Cost of Longing.* Washington D.C.: Georgetown University Press, 2001. Offers detailed observations on the fertility industry and the ethics of commercialism in assisted reproduction. Ryan addresses infertility and the medical community, the medical construction of infertility, procreative liberty, social equity and access to health care, and assisted reproduction in the context of religion and faith.

Shanley, Mary L. *Making Babies, Making Families: What Matters Most in an Age of Reproductive Technologies, Surrogacy, Adoption, and Same-Sex and Unwed Parents' Rights.* Boston: Beacon Press, 2001. Addresses pluralistic family values and their ethical footholds in an age of evolving reproductive technologies and individual rights. The topics discussed include transracial and open adoption, the market for eggs and sperm, surrogate pregnancy, and the rights of unwed fathers. The book specifically addresses the debate over family values and normative family structures.

Spar, Deborah L. *The Baby Business: How Money, Science, and Politics Drive the Commerce of Conception.* Boston: Harvard Business School Publishing, 2006. Discusses the market for infants and the questionable ethics of such practices as egg and sperm donation, surrogate pregnancy, designer babies, and adoption. Spar examines the high prices paid for eggs and sperm from genetically in-demand donors, the exploitation of surrogate mothers for wealthy (white) Western couples, adoption practices that border on baby-selling, and the new legal definition of parenthood as those who make a contractual claim on an infant.

*Ziegler, Stacy. *Pathways to Parenthood: The Ultimate Guide to Surrogacy.* Boca Raton, Fla.: BrownWalker Press, 2005. A how-to guide for intended parents who are considering surrogacy. The author discusses her own decision to pursue a surrogate pregnancy arrangement, as well as different types of arrangements and how to get started. Ziegler outlines how to find and contact a surrogate, making the decision to use an agency or arrange a surrogate pregnancy independently, as well as how to choose whether to pursue traditional or gestational surrogacy.

Articles and Studies

Van den Akker, Olga B. A. "A Longitudinal Pre-Pregnancy to Post-Delivery Comparison of Genetic and Gestational Surrogate and Intended Mothers: Confidence and Genealogy." *Journal of Psychosomatic Obstetrics and Gynecology* 25 (Dec. 2005): 277–284. Explores the decision-making process for women who choose to become mothers via surrogacy and how they make the decision to have a genetically related or unrelated child, as well as women who become surrogates and how they make the decision to gestate and relinquish a genetically related or unrelated child. The study reexamines the participants six months after delivery of the baby to explore their thoughts and confidence in their decisions.

Chervenak, F. A., and L. B. McCullough. "How Should the Obstetrician Respond to Surrogate Pregnancy?" *Ultrasound in Obstetrics and Gynecology* 33 (Jan. 2009): 131–132. Discusses the ethical dilemmas faced by obstetricians when dealing with a surrogate pregnancy arrangement. The authors discuss the general complexities of a surrogate pregnancy arrangement from the perspective of a physician who has obligations to the pregnant surrogate, the fetus, and the contracting parents. They also discuss physicians' individual ethics and consciences in dealing with requests for help in arranging a surrogate pregnancy.

Golombok, Susan, Clare Murray, Emma Lycett et al. "Surrogacy Families: Parental Functioning, Parent-Child Relationships, and Children's Psychological Development at Age 2." *The Journal of Child Psychology and Psychiatry* 47 (Feb. 2006): 213–222. Compares 37 surrogacy families with 48 egg donation families and 68 natural conception families at the time of the children's second birthdays to determine if there are any major differences in family functioning and parent-child relationships. The study finds more positive parent-child relationships among the surrogacy families and no significant difference in socioemotional or cognitive development between surrogacy children and naturally conceived children.

Hovatta, Outi. "Ethical Aspects of Oocyte-Donation, In Vitro Fertilization Surrogacy, and Reproductive Cloning." *Acta Obstet Gynecol Scand* 79 (2000): 921–924. Analyzes the ethics of egg donation, gestational surrogacy, and cloning as a treatment for infertility. The author probes such topics as the sale of eggs versus egg sharing (the process whereby a woman undergoes egg retrieval for her own IVF procedure and opts to donate some of her eggs in exchange for a reduced price), conflicts between surrogates and intended parents, and the fear of identity loss in cloning procedures.

Jorgensen, Henrik Kjeldgaard. "Paternalism, Surrogacy, and Exploitation." *Kennedy Institute of Ethics Journal* 10 (March 2000): 39–58. Examines the potential for exploitation in an altruistic surrogacy arrangement and whether paternalistic interference is justified. The author argues that altruistic surrogacy can be exploitative but the only socially acceptable form of interference commonly comes from someone within the surrogate's social circle. Jorgensen questions whether the state or a particular group or individual should be responsible for interfering in such an arrangement.

Mitchard, Jacquelyn. "Why the Bias Against 'Created' Children?" *Houston Chronicle* (Feb. 1998): 6. Discusses the controversy surrounding a case in which a young woman died from leukemia and her parents enlisted a surrogate mother to carry an embryo conceived using their daughter's egg. Mitchard addresses several viewpoints and argues from her own perspective as an adoptive mother that no ethical boundaries are crossed in the creation of a "wanted" child.

New York Times. "It's Baby-Selling, and It's Wrong." (June 1988). Available online. An editorial that accuses the language of surrogacy of being deliberately misleading. The author argues that a couple that hires a surrogate mother is not paying for the pregnancy but paying for the baby. To recognize the legality of a surrogacy contract, the author posits, is to recognize the legal right of one person to purchase another.

Tong, Rosemarie. "Feminist Bioethics: Towards Developing a 'Feminist' Answer to the Surrogate Motherhood Question." *Kennedy Institute of Ethics Journal* 6 (March 1996): 37–52. Discusses the problematic lack of uniformity among feminist discourse in addressing the issue of surrogate pregnancy. While some feminist bioethicists argue that surrogate pregnancy enhances woman's reproductive autonomy, others contend that surrogacy is degrading and exploitative. Tong proposes coming to a consensus on biomedical principles, practices, and policies.

Van Zyl, Liezl, and Anton van Niekerk. "Interpretations, Perspectives, and Intentions in Surrogate Motherhood." *Journal of Medical Ethics* 26 (2000): 404–409. Examines ethical theories of surrogate pregnancy and arguments for and against the practice. The authors address concerns over the potential for exploitation, traditional beliefs regarding family, childbearing, and maternal bonding, and a woman's legal right to enter a contract. The authors examine three interpretations of surrogate pregnancy as put forth by ethicists, surrogacy agencies, and surrogate mothers.

Web Documents

Allis, Trevor. "The Moral Implications of Motherhood by Hire." Available online. URL: http://www.issuesinmedicalethics.org/051mi021.html. Accessed June 19, 2009. Examines the controversies and major discussion points of surrogacy, including the socioeconomic statuses of surrogates versus commissioning couples, commodification of women and children, defining motherhood, and the use of surrogacy when the contracting couple is not infertile.

Athar, Shahid, M.D. "Islamic Medicine: Islamic Perspective in Medical Ethics." Available online. URL: http://www.islam-usa.com/im18.html. Accessed September 10, 2009. Examines common questions regarding present-day social issues within an Islamic context. Issues include assisted suicide and the right to die, abortion, organ transplants, surrogate pregnancy, and AIDS. In the case of surrogate pregnancy, the author concludes that surrogacy is not permitted within Islam due to the sacredness of the womb.

Christian Apologetics and Research Ministry. "Is Surrogate Pregnancy Okay?" Available online. URL: http://www.carm.org/questions/about-sexuality/surrogate-pregnancy-okay. Accessed June 18, 2009. Discusses the morality of surrogate pregnancy within a specifically Christian context. The author acknowledges such biblical tales of surrogacy as that of Abraham, Sarah, and Hagar, and arrives at the conclusion that surrogate pregnancy is morally acceptable as long as no extramarital sexual intercourse is involved and other embryos are not destroyed, as is often the case in IVF.

Congregation for the Doctrine of Faith. "Instruction on Respect for Human Life in its Origin and on the Dignity of Procreation: Replies to Certain Questions of the Day." Available online. URL: http://www.catholic.com/library/respect_human_life_cdf1.asp. Accessed June 19, 2009. A theological outline issued by the Catholic Church on the ethics and morality of biomedical technology. The document discusses the philosophical nature of human dignity and its pertinence to the human embryo and its identity. The document also analyzes the church's standing on biomedical intervention in procreation.

*The Fertility Institutes. "Becoming a Surrogate." Available online. URL: http://www.
fertility-docs.com/surrogates_becoming.phtml. Accessed June 18, 2009. Provides
step-by-step instructions on how to become a surrogate mother, including making initial contact with the Fertility Institutes and providing information on past
pregnancies and current health, undergoing a physical and psychological evaluation, evaluating prospective contracting couples, meeting prospective contracting couples, and entering into a contract with a couple. This guide also outlines
eligibility requirements.

Jadva, Vasanti, Clare Murray, Emma Lycett et al. "Surrogacy: The Experiences of Surrogate Mothers." Available online. URL: http://humrep.oxfordjournals.org/cgi/
content/abstract/18/10/2196. Accessed June 19, 2009. Assesses the experiences of
34 women who have given birth to a surrogate child, including their reasons for
choosing to become a surrogate, views of their relationships with the contracting
couples, experiences in relinquishing the children, and the responses from friends
and family. The study reveals no emotional or psychological complications among
surrogates during or following their pregnancies.

*Jenn Z./Surrogate Mothers Online, LLC. "Is Surrogacy for You?" Available online.
URL: http://www.surromomsonline.com/articles/you.htm. Accessed June 18,
2009. Offers a list of checkpoints for women who are considering becoming surrogate mothers. Points to consider include physical health and past pregnancies,
support system and how loved ones will respond, emotional issues and knowing if
one will be able to relinquish a baby after delivery, medical issues, including daily
injections and potential for multiples, and knowing whether one can terminate a
pregnancy or selectively reduce excess fetuses.

Peterson, Iver. "The Vatican on Birth Science; Hospitals Acted Ahead of the Vatican."
Available online. URL: http://www.nytimes.com/1987/03/11/world/the-vatican-
on-birth-science-hospitals-acted-ahead-of-the-vatican.html. Accessed June 19,
2009. Reports the Vatican's ruling on surrogacy as immoral and unethical shortly
after the Baby M trial. Many Catholic hospitals were already discouraging surrogacy by asking surrogates not to give birth at their hospitals.

ScienceDaily. "Surrogacy Still Stigmatized, Though Attitudes Changing Among
Younger Women." Available online. URL: http://www.sciencedaily.com/releases/
2008/07/080706194247.htm. Accessed June 19, 2009. Reports the results of a
study conducted by Professor Olga van den Akker in which 187 women were selected from the general population and surveyed on their willingness to become
surrogates. Individuals who reported a willingness to become a surrogate mother
also placed a higher importance on family and children than those who would not
become a surrogate mother.

*Turner, Merritt Morrison. "What You Should Expect an Agency to Provide." Avail-
able online. URL: http://www.surrogacy.com/Articles/news_view.asp?ID=37. Accessed June 19, 2009. Reviews standard practices within surrogacy and what
intended parents should expect from the agencies they contact, such as a free initial consultation, medical and psychological reports from the surrogates' screening process, psychological counseling, a careful matching process that takes into

account each party's view on selective reduction and abortion, should there be something wrong with the fetus. The agency should also be willing to facilitate and monitor all future contact between the couple and the surrogate, if that is what the couple prefers.

*Vlietstra, Jeanne. "The Importance of Professional Guidance in Third Party Reproduction." Available online. URL: http://www.surrogacy.com/Articles/news_view. asp?ID=34. Accessed June 19, 2009. Discusses the surrogacy process and when couples should consider enlisting the help of a professional with experience in managing surrogacy arrangements. The author emphasizes the importance of finding a professional who can facilitate communication and understanding between the parties while also managing the business element of the arrangement.

Zouves, Christo, M.D. "Multiple Pregnancy: The Dilemma." Available online. URL: http://www.opts.com/multipreg.htm. Accessed June 19, 2009. Outlines the statistical leap in multiple pregnancies since 1980 and the challenges that directly result from it, including low birth weight, birth defects, pre-term labor, and risks to the mother's health, such as high blood pressure and diabetes. The author suggests ways to prevent a multiple pregnancy, including reducing the number of embryos transferred to the uterus but acknowledges that this will disenfranchise some patients who cannot afford multiple cycles.

ADOPTION AND SURROGATE PREGNANCY WORLDWIDE

Books

Blyth, Eric, and Ruth Landau. *Third Party Assisted Conception Across Cultures: Social, Legal, and Ethical Perspectives.* London: Jessica Kingsley Publishers, 2004. A collection of essays detailing various cultural approaches to conception in 13 countries from North and South America, Africa, Europe, Australia, and Asia. The issues addressed include the role of government in family formation, potential commodification of the body, regulation, and cultural concepts of family.

Botros, Rizk, Juan Garcia-Velasco, Hassan Sallam, and Antonis Makrigiannakis. *Infertility and Assisted Reproduction.* New York: Cambridge University Press, 2008. A collection of essays from biomedical professionals around the world on infertility and assisted reproductive technology. Divided into four parts, the essays address the physiology of reproduction, infertility evaluation and treatment, assisted reproduction, and ethical considerations in assisted reproduction. Many of the essays are written for a specialized audience of other medical professionals, but others, particularly in the section on ethical considerations, cover more general topics, such as stem cell research and providing ART procedures for perimenopausal women.

*Chasnoff, Ira, M.D., Linda Schwartz, Ph.D., Cheryl Pratt, Ph.D., Gwendolyn Neuberger, M.D. *Risk and Promise: A Handbook for Parents Adopting a Child from Overseas.* Chicago: NTI Upstream, 2006. Discusses the challenges and complexities of intercountry adoption within the context of medicine and developmental psychology. The authors advise prospective adoptive parents on how to face the unique situation of overseas adoption and what to expect.

*Davenport, Dawn. *The Complete Book of International Adoption: A Step-By-Step Guide to Finding Your Child*. New York: Broadway Books, 2006. Offers accessible and digestible advice for parents considering international adoption. Davenport thoroughly outlines the international adoption process and discusses such topics as choosing between domestic and international adoption, choosing the region from which the child will come, determining costs, and understanding legal issues. She also discusses such issues as knowing when it is time to adopt, telling other children, friends, and family about one's decision to adopt, and dealing with anxieties about the process.

Doss, Helen. *The Family Nobody Wanted*. Holliston, Mass.: Northeastern Publishing, 2001. Originally written in 1954, this book chronicles the Doss family and their 12 internationally and transracially adopted children. As the Dosses were adopting at a time of rampant racial prejudice and cultural ignorance, they faced a number of challenges in creating their family and experienced the ugliness of racism. The family, nevertheless, became a model for international and transracial adoption, which began to flower years later, in the 1960s and 1970s.

Howell, Signe. *The Kinning of Foreigners: Transnational Adoption in a Global Perspective*. New York: Berghahn Books, 2007. Approaches intercountry adoption from a socio-anthropological perspective to analyze cultural forces that produce abandoned children in sending countries, sending countries' perspectives on international adoption, methodologies to solve the problem of unwanted children among sending countries, and cultural identity among adoptees and adoptive families.

Jacobson, Heather. *Culture Keeping: White Mothers, International Adoption, and the Negotiation of Family Difference*. Nashville, Tenn.: Vanderbilt University Press, 2008. Examines international adoption with a focus on Chinese and Russian programs, as the two countries together provide the largest number of children adopted internationally into the United States. Jacobson analyzes the relatively new practice among American adoptive parents of incorporating their children's birth culture into their daily lives through naming, providing ethnic food and toys, traveling to countries of origin, and participating in cultural events.

Miller, Laurie, C. M.D. *The Handbook of International Adoption Medicine: A Guide for Physicians, Parents, and Providers*. New York: Oxford University Press, 2005. Offers insight into unique health issues that arise in the process of an international adoption, including the effects of institutionalization on children; regional consideration; prenatal exposure to smoking, alcohol, and drugs; malnutrition; infectious diseases; the effects of abuse and stress; and developmental delays. The book also offers facts and statistics on international adoption.

Pretorius, Diederika. *Surrogate Motherhood: A Worldwide View of the Issues*. Springfield, Mass.: Charles C. Thomas Publishers, 1994. Offers a global perspective on the issues surrounding surrogate pregnancy, including the laws, policies, and practices of a number of other nations. Pretorius provides a more focused overview of surrogacy as it is practiced in South Africa and the events that prompted the implementation of surrogacy legislation.

Register, Cheri. *Beyond Good Intentions: A Mother Reflects on Raising Internationally Adopted Children.* Saint Paul: Yeong & Yeong Book Company, 2005. A collection of 11 personal essays that address the challenges and struggles of raising internationally adopted children. The author discusses race, multiculturalism, and the inherent problems of color-blindness from the perspective of a white adoptive parent of Korean children.

————. *Are Those Kids Yours?: American Families with Children Adopted from Other Countries.* New York: The Free Press, 1991. Examines the issues involved in parenting internationally adopted children. As the adoptive mother of two Korean daughters, Register addresses such issues as facilitating adaptation to a multicultural American society, the ethics of removing children from their ethnic and cultural origins, the politics of sending versus receiving countries, the rights of birth parents, and racism in the United States. The book also discusses what it means to be a global family.

Reid, Theresa. *Two Little Girls: A Memoir of Adoption.* New York: Berkeley Publishing Group, 2006. Details the author's personal experience with international adoption. As a memoir, the book provides an unflinching account of the author's decision to adopt from Eastern Europe and the complexities and obstacles that she faced along the way, including political bureaucracy, last-minute holdups, and the possibility of an adoption shutdown in the sending country. Reid also describes her and her husband's decision to be self-reflective and honest with one another about their adoption fears, hopes, and desires.

Sclater, Shelley Day, Rachel Cook, and Felicity Kaganas. *Surrogate Motherhood: International Perspectives.* Portland, Ore.: Hart Publishing, 2003. A collection of essays from professionals representing a number of disciplines on international approaches to surrogate pregnancy. The authors address the legal, ethical, cultural, and psychological implications of surrogacy in Britain, Israel, the United States, and New Zealand. The issues addressed include altruism and the body, religious perspectives, ethics and technology, market forces, counseling, relationships, and regulation.

Tokar, Brian. *Redesigning Life? The Worldwide Challenge to Genetic Engineering.* New York: Palgrave, 2001. A collection of essays from various authors that addresses the biomedical manipulation of plant, animal, and human life. The authors discuss genetically engineered crops, market forces in genetic science, national policies around the world that are resisting genetic engineering, and genetic science and human rights. Essays address such topics as designer babies, cloning, and eugenics.

Volkman, Toby Alice, Kay Johnson, Barbara Yngvesson, and Laurel Kendall. *Cultures of Transnational Adoption.* Durham, N.C.: Duke University Press, 2005. A collection of essays that discuss various aspects of international adoption from major sending countries, including China, Korea, and Latin America. The authors explore the concepts of cultural roots and ethnicity, kinship and biology, the politics of sending and receiving countries, adoptions within sending countries, and the culturally transformative power of intercountry adoption.

Articles and Studies

Behreandt, Denise L. "Adoption Options Dwindle." *The New American* 24 (2008): 28–29. Discusses the United States' implementation of the Hague Convention on Intercountry Adoption and the impact that it will have on international adoptions. Behreandt focuses on Guatemala and the thousands of Guatemalan children who are adopted internationally each year, the Guatemalan notaries that arrange such adoptions, and the international adoption agencies.

Brakman, Sarah-Vaughan, and Sally Scholz. "Adoption, ART, and a Re-Conception of the Maternal Body: Toward Embodied Maternity." *Hypatia* 21 (2006). Criticizes the pervasive social view of maternity as genetic or biological, which tends to exclude mothers through adoption and assisted reproductive technology. Rather, the authors posit a feminist embodied maternity that emphasizes the experience of motherhood over genetic or biological connection.

Cilleruelo, M. J., F. de Ory, J. Ruiz-Contreras et al. *Vaccine* 26 (Oct. 2008): 5,784–5,790. Reports the findings of a study of the immunization statuses of 637 internationally adopted children. Vaccination statuses of the international adoptees reflected poor global vaccine protection, and correlations were found between children's vaccination status and their country of origin. In descending order, the least immunizations were found among children from Eastern Europe, India, Latin America, China, and Africa.

Dalen, Monica, Anders Hjern, Frank Lindblad et al. "Educational Attainment and Cognitive in Adopted Men—a Study of International and National Adoptees, Siblings, and a General Swedish Population." *Children and Youth Services Review* 30 (Oct. 2008): 1,211–1,219. Evaluates reports that internationally and nationally adopted young men had lower average scores on intelligence tests at military conscription than nonadopted men. Korean adoptees were found to have higher educational attainment than non-Korean adoptees, and both international and national adoptees were found to have lower educational attainment if they were adopted when they were older.

Dickens, Bernard. "Legal Developments in Assisted Reproduction." *International Journal of Gynecology and Obstetrics* 101 (May 2008): 211–215. Provides an overview of changing laws and policies around the world regarding assisted and third-party reproduction. The author addresses the topics of vetoing embryo transfer when a relationship ends following the creation of embryos for in vitro fertilization, surrogate mothers who sue for custody, and preimplantation genetic diagnosis. Dickens analyzes case studies and compares the different approaches that two or more countries take to the same situation.

Inhorn, Marcia C., and Pasquale Patrizio. "Rethinking Reproductive 'Tourism' as Reproductive 'Exile.'" *Fertility and Sterility* (Feb. 2009): 1–3. Argues that the term *reproductive tourism* is insensitive and erroneous as it implies a sense of leisure,

264

recreation, and frivolity. The authors counter that individuals who make the decision to travel abroad to seek fertility services do so because they cannot receive such services in their home countries, and thus reproductive tourism should be renamed reproductive exile.

Juffer, Femmie, and Marinus H. van Ijzendoorn. "Adoptees Do Not Lack Self-Esteem: A MetaAnalysis of Studies on Self-Esteem of Transracial, International, and Domestic Adoptees." *Psychological Bulletin* 133 (Nov. 2007): 1,067–1,083. Provides a detailed analysis of 88 studies to determine if adoptees exhibit lower self-esteem than their nonadopted peers. The authors take into consideration possible consequences of abuse, neglect, and malnutrition prior to adoption, self-consciousness due to a lack of resemblance with adoptive parents, and feelings of cultural or ethnic isolation. They found no difference in self-esteem between adoptees and nonadopted individuals.

Pennings, G. "Reproductive Tourism as Moral Pluralism in Motion." *Journal of Medical Ethics* 28 (2002): 337–341. Discusses the phenomenon of reproductive tourism and the widespread call for a solution to stop individuals from crossing borders to receive services that are not available to them in their home countries. Pennings examines three possible solutions: internal moral pluralism, coerced conformity, and international harmonization. Pennings defends the practice of reproductive tourism, which he claims is a form of tolerance that maintains peace among cultures of differing values.

Selman, Peter. "Trends in Intercountry Adoption: Analysis of Data from 20 Receiving Countries, 1998–2004." *Journal of Population Research* 23 (Sept. 2006): 183–204. Discusses the sudden surge in international adoptions between 1998 and 2004 and the implications of rising rates of intercountry adoption worldwide. Between 1998 and 2004, international adoption increased by 42 percent, with the United States constituting the largest portion of international adoptions. Selman discusses trends and problems in data collection, as well as the potential for developing a standardized means of comparison between countries.

Senecky, Yehuda, Hanoch Agassi, Dov Inbar et al. "Post-Adoption Depression among Adoptive Mothers." *Journal of Affective Disorders* 115 (May 2009): 62–68. Discusses the results of a study of the psychological and emotional health of 39 women following each one's international adoption. Due to the sudden changes that a child brings to the life of any first-time parent, 15.4 percent of the adoptive mothers studied exhibited symptoms of depression, similar to the rate of postpartum depression in the general population. Notably, women who exhibited symptoms of depression after adopting had also exhibited symptoms of depression prior to adopting.

Teman, Elly. "The Social Construction of Surrogacy Research: An Anthropological Critique of the Psychosocial Scholarship on Surrogate Motherhood." *Social Science & Medicine* 67 (Oct. 2008): 1,104–1,112. Discusses and critiques the psychosocial empirical research that has been performed on surrogate mothers and their motivations for participating in surrogate pregnancy arrangements. Teman argues that researchers around the world have conducted surrogacy studies with the preconceived belief that surrogate mothers are psychologically abnormal and/or the victims of trauma. Teman provides evidence to the contrary and suggests that such researchers are merely expressing their own cultural anxieties and prejudices.

Tieman, Wendy, Jan van der Ende, and Frank C. Verhulst. "Young Adult International Adoptees' Search for Birth Parents." *Journal of Family Psychology* 22 (Oct. 2008): 678–687. Examines 1,417 international adoptees in the Netherlands between the ages of 24 and 30 and their individual decision-making processes about whether or not to search for their birth parents. The participants were divided into four groups: uninterested non-searchers, interested non-searchers, searchers, and reunited searchers. The study found that an international adoptee's decision to search was often precipitated by external forces, such as the divorce of adoptive parents, combined with natural curiosity.

Wilson, Samantha L., Terri L. Weaver, Mary Michaeleen Cradock, and Janet E. Kuebli. "A Preliminary Study of the Cognitive and Motor Skills Acquisition of Young International Adoptees." *Children and Youth Services Review* 30 (May 2008): 585–596. Reports the results of a study of the developmental trajectory of young children following their adoptions abroad. The first developmental assessment was conducted within two months of the international adoption and the second six months later. The authors found that children who had spent their early years in an institution exhibited mild to severe developmental delays at the first developmental assessment. The second assessment, however, revealed that approximately half of those children had improved significantly.

Web Documents

Australasian Bioethics Information. "Reproductive Tourism Flourishing." Available online. URL: http://www.australasianbioethics.org/Newsletters/063-2003-02-14.html. Accessed June 23, 2009. A brief article that discusses the recent phenomenon of reproductive tourism. Physicians comment on the practice of referring patients to foreign clinics, where certain fertility services may be legal or simply less expensive. Within the European Union, laws and policies fluctuate so much between countries that patients can shop around for affordable or offered procedures.

Biel, Lindsey. "Sensory Integration Problems in International Adoption." Available online. URL: http://www.comeunity.com/adoption/health/sensory-integration-adoption.html. Accessed June 23, 2009. Discusses the signs of a sensory integration problem, what causes such a problem, and how to treat it. Children adopted from overseas, especially those who spent their early months/years in an orphanage, are at particular risk for developing a sensory integration problem, which includes an aversion to many touch sensations, noises, and movements. Malnourishment, low birth weight, and a lack of sensory stimulation in infancy often lead to sensory integration issues.

The Evan B. Donaldson Adoption Institute. "International Adoption Facts." Available online. URL: http://www.adoptioninstitute.org/FactOverview/international.html. Accessed June 22, 2009. Provides an overview of international adoption facts and statistics, including top sending countries, rates of international adoptions between 1991 and 2001, age and sex of internationally adopted children, and changing circumstances of sending countries that affect international adoption rates.

Graff, E. J. "The Lie We Love." Available online. URL: http://www.foreignpolicy.com/story/cms.php?story_id=4508. Accessed June 23, 2009. Discusses the problem of supply and demand within the international adoption industry. Graff notes the fact that international adoption began as a charitable effort but has since become an industry that continues to operate on the general assumption that babies born in developing countries need adoptive parents from developed countries. Graff outlines the reality that overseas children who need families are typically over the age of five and tend to have mental or physical disabilities.

Jenista, Jerri Ann, M.D. "Infectious Disease and the Internationally Adopted Child." Available online. URL: http://www.comeunity.com/adoption/health/infectious-disease.html#Hepatitis%20B. Accessed June 22, 2009. Discusses the phenomenon of international adoption and the need for a standardized protocol to screen internationally adopted children for diseases. The author suggests performing a review of immunizations; a blood count and urinalysis; and screening tests for hepatitis B, HIV, tuberculosis, syphilis, and intestinal parasites. The author notes the fact that the circumstances of sending countries leading to the availability of children for adoption often include war, poverty, and abandonment, thereby necessitating careful screening for disease.

Kahn, Michael. "Experts Say Reproductive Tourism a Growing Worry." Available online. URL: http://uk.reuters.com/article/idUKL2492408820080724. Accessed June 23, 2009. Discusses reproductive tourism and the complications that can result from cross-border care, including clinics that provide inadequate care, erroneous or lack of information on egg and sperm donors, and the risk of multiple pregnancy. The article expresses the need for awareness campaigns and standardization.

Rice, Mary. "Increasing Reproductive Tourism in Europe Is a 'Safety Valve' That Promotes Peaceful Coexistence." Available online. URL: http://news.bio-medicine.org/biology-news-3/Increasing-reproductive-tourism-in-Europe-is-a-safety-valve-that-promotes-peaceful-coexistence-11269-1/. Accessed June 23, 2009. Takes a unique approach to the often controversial discussion of reproductive tourism by suggesting that the widely varying laws on assisted reproduction in the European Union should not be standardized to establish a uniform code on assisted reproduction ethics, but rather should be viewed as a facilitator to the peaceful coexistence of individuals with widely varying religious and ethical views.

Snyder, Steven. "Our Surrogacy Program Is Unique." Available online. URL: http://www.fertilityhelp.com/index.php/Our-Surrogacy-Program-Is-Unique.html. Accessed June 23, 2009. Provides a description of the surrogacy program directed by the International Assisted Reproduction Center (IARC). Snyder, the executive director of the program, details the processes of selecting and screening surrogates and defines the role that IARC assumes during the selection, negotiation, and IVF/insemination processes.

Traver, Amy E. "Gender and International Adoption." Available online. URL: http://www.socwomen.org/fall08_fact_sheet.pdf. Accessed June 22, 2009. Examines the variety of gendered forces that influence international adoption. Among sending countries, Traver discusses preference for sons in Korea and the one-child policy in China. Among receiving countries, Traver focuses primarily on the United States as the dominant receiving country within the international adoption community and American adoptive parents' preference for girls.

United Nations Children's Fund. "The State of the World's Children 2009." Available online. URL: http://www.unicef.org/sowc09/docs/SOWC09-FullReport-EN.pdf. Accessed June 23, 2009. Examines trends, challenges, and issues in maternal and newborn health around the world. Outlining policies and programs in maternal and newborn health, with a focus on Africa and Asia, the report emphasizes the need to develop a continuum of care for maternal, newborn, and child health.

Other Media

*Adoption Learning Partners. "Medical Issues in International Adoption Course." Available online. URL: http://www.adoptionlearningpartners.org/medical_issues. cfm. Accessed June 23, 2009. A downloadable 2.5 credit course that guides pre-adoptive parents through the medical needs, health risks, and conditions that many internationally adopted children face. Topics in this online course include medical issues as a result of institutional care and medical issues that are specific to a child's country of origin. Meets Hague training requirements.

*———. "Conspicuous Families: Race, Culture, and Adoption Course." Available online. URL: http://www.adoptionlearningpartners.org/conspicuous_families.cfm. Accessed June 23, 2009. A downloadable 1.5 credit course that provides helpful insights for pre-adoptive parents considering adopting a child of a different race, ethnicity, or cultural origin from their own. Course topics include diversity, collective experiences of transracial families, and developing skills for responding to insensitive comments. Meets Hague training requirements.

American Public Health Association. "Reproductive Tourism: Ethical and Health Concerns." Available online. URL: http://apha.confex.com/apha/136am/webprogram/Session23361.html. Accessed June 23, 2009. A set of downloadable audio recordings form a panel session at the 136th Annual APHA Meeting in 2008. Presentation titles include "Reproductive Tourism, Reproductive Rights, and Human Health," "Public Health and Reproductive Tourism: The Impact of Buying and Selling Fertility Services in a Global Market," "Reproductive Tourism: An Overview of International Regulation," and "Reproductive Tourism: Exploitation, Agency, and Public Health."

Gardner, Janet. *Precious Cargo: Vietnamese Adoptees Discover Their Past.* Directed and co-produced by Janet Gardner and co-produced by Pham Quoc Thai. 56 min. DVD. San Francisco, Calif., 2001. Documents a group of adult Vietnamese adoptees who were brought to the United States during Operation Babylift as they travel back to Vietnam to confront the poverty, beauty, and complexity of their birth country, as well as their own feelings of loss and identity.

ADOPTION AND SURROGATE PREGNANCY IN THE UNITED STATES

Books

Dorow, Sara. *Transnational Adoption: A Cultural Economy of Race, Gender, and Kinship.* New York: New York University Press, 2006. Charts the development and current practice of intercountry adoption between China and the United States. Dorow documents the adoption process from Chinese institutions and bureaucracies to U.S. agencies, including interviews with both Chinese and American adoption professionals, advocacy groups, government officials, and adoptive families.

Duxbury, Micky. *Making Room in Our Hearts: Keeping Family Ties Through Open Adoption.* New York: Routledge, 2007. Discusses open adoption as a positive family-building experience for every member of the adoption triad based on over 100 interviews with adoption professionals, adoptive parents, birth parents, and adoptees. While closed adoption may promote uncertainty, a sense of loss, and a crisis of identity among adoptees, open adoption allows adoptees to understand their history and birth circumstances.

Fessler, Ann. *The Girls Who Went Away: The Hidden History of Women Who Surrendered Children for Adoption in the Decades before* Roe v. Wade. New York: Penguin, 2007. Details the author's interviews with several women who were sent to homes for unwed mothers between 1945 and 1973, where they were forced to relinquish their children for adoption. Fessler includes information on American history in the decades between 1940 and 1980.

Herman, Ellen. *Kinship by Design: A History of Adoption in the Modern United States.* Chicago: The University of Chicago Press, 2008. Provides a rich, well-researched account of the history of adoption practice and policy in the United States. Beginning in 1900, Herman charts the course of adoption from matching children with parents who they physically and intellectually resembled, to the emergence of transracial and intercountry adoption in the latter half of the century.

John, Jaiya. *Black Baby White Hands: A View from the Crib.* Silver Spring, Md.: Soul Water Rising, 2005. Depicts the author's childhood as the transracially adopted African-American child of white parents. Though his adoptive parents were well intentioned, John struggled to understand his own identity as an African American living in a white community and eventually reunited with his birth family in adulthood.

Mallon, Gerald P. *Lesbian and Gay Foster and Adoptive Parents: Recruiting, Assessing, and Supporting an Untapped Resource for Children and Youth.* Washington D.C.: Child Welfare League of America, 2006. Provides information and resources for adoption professionals and gay and lesbian families seeking to adopt. Mallon discusses gay and lesbian identity, U.S. laws and policies on gay adoption, challenges in gay adoptive parenting, and recruiting and assessing gay adoptive parents. Mallon also provides case vignettes and affirming policies from national organizations.

Markens, Susan. *Surrogate Motherhood and the Politics of Reproduction*. Berkeley: University of California Press, 2007. Outlines the history of surrogacy in the United States, including laws, proposed legislation, case studies, media portrayals, and the language of surrogacy. Markens places particular emphasis on framing devices in the public debate over surrogacy as she compares infamous surrogacy disputes, media and newspaper reports, and state laws. The result is a unique portrayal of surrogacy as it has been created and received within American culture.

Menichiello, Michael. *A Gay Couple's Journey Through Surrogacy: Intended Fathers*. Binghampton, N.Y.: The Haworth Press, 2006. Describes one gay couple's decision to have a child through traditional surrogacy and the process by which they achieved this. This memoir, which is interspersed with actual journal entries, follows Menichiello and his partner as they research their options, select a surrogate, and experience the challenges associated with pregnancy and childbirth.

Pavao, Joyce Maguire. *The Family of Adoption*. Boston: Beacon Press, 1998. Emphasizes the importance of openness in adoption and the need for communication within all types of adoption, from domestic and infant adoptions to transracial, international, and foster care adoptions. Pavao discusses the psychological and social complexity of the adoptive family and unique situations that face adopted children, such as more challenging adolescence and the tendency to daydream, particularly in closed adoption situations.

Pertman, Adam. *Adoption Nation: How the Adoption Revolution Is Transforming America*. New York: Basic Books, 2000. Examines the power of adoption to transform American culture by promoting the creation of non-traditional families. Emphasis on finding parents for children has created more gay, transracial, and single-parent families. Pertman also addresses the movement toward open adoption and the way in which openness dispels negative adoption stereotypes.

Quiroz, Pamela Anne. *Adoption in a Color-Blind Society*. Lanham, Md.: Rowman & Littlefield Publishers, 2007. Explores the concept of color-blindness and how it relates to family formation and adoption, particularly when infant adoption fees often directly correspond with a child's race. Quiroz provides ethnographic evidence to support her argument that color-blindness is not in practice in the field of adoption.

Ragoné, Helena. *Surrogate Motherhood: Conception in the Heart*. Boulder, Colo.: Westview Press, 1994. One of the first ethnographic studies of surrogacy in the United States. Ragoné interviewed surrogate mothers, contracting parents, and surrogacy center directors to clinically analyze the rising incidence of surrogacy, and along the way she found patterns in rhetoric, motives of surrogates and contracting parents, coping strategies, and business practices. Nevertheless, she sensitively emphasizes the hurt, longing, and need that participants in surrogacy arrangements experience.

Riben, Mirah. *The Stork Market: America's Multi-Billion Dollar Unregulated Adoption Industry.* Dayton, Ohio: Advocate Publications, 2007. Critically examines commerce within the adoption industry and how money has created a supply-and-demand enterprise that commodifies infants and children. Riben focuses on abuses within the American adoption industry and questions whether money can ever be removed from the adoption process, or put toward child welfare programs.

Wolf, Joanne Small. *The Adoption Mystique: A Hard-Hitting Exposé of the Powerful Negative Social Stigma That Permeates Child Adoption in the United States.* Bloomington, Mich.: Authorhouse, 2007. Examines the current state of adoption policy and practice in the United States and how the adoption culture of secrecy and shame has generated negative myths and stereotypes about adoption, adoptees, adoptive parents, and birth parents. Wolf argues for adoption reform to reframe adoption in a positive light.

Wright, Marguerite. *I'm Chocolate, You're Vanilla: Raising Healthy Black and Biracial Children in a Race-Conscious World.* New York: Jossey-Bass Inc., 1998. Examines the way in which young children perceive race and skin color and how they come to understand the social construction of race through a series of phases. Based on Wright's clinical research, she discusses how young children perceive race, how adults can avoid projecting their own negative perceptions of race on to their children, and how parents can help their children overcome racism.

Articles and Studies

Burleigh, Nina. "A Dad's Adoption Nightmare." *People* 71 (Jun 2009): 92–96. Details the struggles of one Utah family who realized that the 4-year-old girl they had adopted from Samoa had actually been kidnapped from her Samoan parents. The Utah-based adoption agency Focus on Children was later charged with adoption fraud related to cases involving 60 Samoan children who were taken from their families.

Damelio, Jennifer, and Kelly Sorensen. "Enhancing Autonomy in Paid Surrogacy." *Bioethics* 22 (June 2008): 269–277. Explores various arguments and debates over the exploitative potential of surrogacy and how exploitation can be avoided. The authors propose a soft law that requires surrogate mothers to undergo a period of training and education prior to agreeing to become surrogates, rather than total permission or an outright ban on the practice.

Dwyer, James G. "A Constitutional Birthright: The State, Parentage, and the Rights of Newborn Persons." *UCLA Law Review* 56 (April 2009): 755–835. Questions the ethics of automatically granting parental rights to birth parents, especially if the birth parents are unfit. Dwyer examines state parentage laws that assign immediate parental rights to birth parents even though they may have criminal records, a history of child maltreatment, and/or history of substance abuse, and probes the question of whether this may be a violation of a newborn person's constitutional rights.

Kahan, Michelle. "'Put Up' on Platforms: A History of Twentieth-Century Adoption Policy in the United States." *Journal of Sociology & Social Welfare* 33 (Sept. 2006): 51–72. Examines the history of adoption in the United States as it relates to social issues such as race, class, welfare, poverty, and gender. Kahan reviews the period of the orphan trains up through the 1990s, when contraception and abortion reduced the number of children available for adoption.

Kessler, Bree. "Recruiting Wombs: Surrogates as the New Security Moms." *Women's Studies Quarterly* 37 (2009): 167–182. Discusses an article in *Newsweek* describing the recent rise in military wives choosing to act as gestational surrogates. Kessler examines the social, cultural, and nationalistic forces that have shaped military wives' views of surrogacy as a form of national service.

Podolny, Erin V. "Are You My Mother?: Removing a Gestational Surrogate's Name From the Birth Certificate in the Name of Equal Protection." *University of Maryland Law Journal of Race, Religion, Gender, & Class* 8 (2008): 351–376. Examines the case of an unmarried man who contracted with a gestational surrogate to bear a child conceived using his sperm and a donor egg. The gestational surrogate gave birth to twins, and her name was put on the birth certificate according to hospital policy. She and the contracting father went to court to have her name removed, and the court concluded in favor of the removal.

Roes, Jennifer. "Adopting Broader Horizon Helps Foster Kids; Mass. Places Children in Puerto Rico." *Boston Herald* (June 2009). Details the recent decision by the Massachusetts Adoption Resource Exchange to place foster children with permanent families in Puerto Rico, which is a U.S. territory and thus qualifies as an option for domestic adoption.

Ryan, Scott, Nina Nelson, and Carl Siebert. "Examining the Facilitators and Barriers Faced by Adoptive Professionals Delivering Post-Placement Services." *Children & Youth Services Review* 31 (May 2009): 584–593. Reports the results of a study in which adoption professionals were asked to describe barriers that prevent families from receiving post-adoption services and how these barriers can be overcome. The results revealed macro-level barriers within the field of adoption, itself.

Schwartz, Lita Linzer. "Aspects of Adoption and Foster Care." *Journal of Psychiatry & Law* 36 (2008): 153–169. Provides an overview of adoption history in the United States as a background for examining aspects of adoption and foster care today. Schwartz discusses the perspectives of the adoptee, the adoptive parents, and the adoption professionals to determine the potential for conflicts due to differing interpretations of facts. She also discusses children who experience multiple placements within the foster care system and the potential for stress and trauma.

Webley, Kayla. "Behind the Drop in Chinese Adoptions." *Time* 173 (June 2009). Available online. URL: www.time.com/time/world/article/0,8599,1894333,00.html. Accessed September 29, 2009. Discusses the 51 percent drop in adoptions of Chinese children by U.S. parents between 2005 and 2008. Webley outlines the Chinese government's new guidelines for overseas adoption, which exclude parents who are obese, have taken antidepressants in the past two years, or who have a facial disfigurement.

Annotated Bibliography

Web Documents

Ali, Lorraine, and Raina Kelley. "The Curious Lives of Surrogates." *Newsweek* (April 2008). Available online. URL: http://www.newsweek.com/id/129594. Accessed June 24, 2009. Describes surrogacy in the United States with a focus on military wives who are choosing to act as gestational surrogates at record rates.

Dailard, Cynthia. "Out of Compliance?: Implementing the Infant Adoption Awareness Act." *Guttmacher Report on Public Policy* 7 (Aug. 2004). Available online. URL: http://www.guttmacher.org/pubs/tgr/07/3/gr070310.html. Accessed June 24, 2009. Criticizes the Infant Adoption Awareness Act, which mandates that family-planning counselors present information on adoption as an option to women coping with an unintended pregnancy, and reports on the effects of the Act on both family-planning and adoption practices.

Macomber, Jennifer Ehrle, Rob Green, and Regan Main. "Kinship Foster Care: Custody, Hardships, and Services." The Urban Institute. *Snapshots of America's Families III* (Nov. 2003). Available online. URL: http://www.urban.org/publications/310893. html. Accessed June 24, 2009. Outlines kinship care in the United States and provides statistical information on how many families have a kinship care structure, how many children are in kinship care arrangements, and the family demographics of kinship care.

Mohler, Albert. "Wombs for Rent? *Newsweek* Looks at Surrogate Mothers." (April 2008). Available online. URL: http://www.albertmohler.com/blog_read.php?id=1125. Accessed June 24, 2009. Takes a conservative Christian approach to the debate over surrogacy and its social, cultural, and moral implications. Mohler is a Christian radio talk-show host and his article is a response to an article in *Newsweek.*

Schabner, Dean. "Why It Costs More to Adopt a White Baby." ABC News (March 2008). Available online. URL: http://abcnews.go.com/US/story?id=91834&page=1. Accessed June 24, 2009. Examines the discrepancy in fees to adopt a white baby ($35,000–$50,000) versus a black baby ($4,000). Schabner interviews Rev. Ken Hutcherson, who likens the practice to baby-selling and accuses the adoption industry of discrimination.

U.S. Census Bureau, U.S. Department of Commerce, Economics and Statistics Administration. "Adopted Children and Step-Children: 2000." *Census 2000 Special Reports* (Oct. 2003). Available online. URL: http://www.census.gov/prod/2003pubs/censr-6.pdf. Accessed June 24, 2009. Provides statistical information on the number of households that include biological children, step-children, and adopted children. This is the first census in U.S. history to include "adopted son/daughter" as a category of relationship separate from "natural born son/daughter."

U.S. Department of Health and Human Services, Centers for Disease Control and Prevention, National Center for Health Statistics. "Adoption Experiences of Women and Men and Demand for Children to Adopt by Women 18–44 Years of Age in the United States, 2002." *Vital and Health Statistics* (Aug. 2008). Available online. URL: http://www.cdc.gov/nchs/data/series/sr_23/sr23_027.pdf. Accessed June 24, 2009. Provides a thorough overview of adoption statistics in the United States, including how many individuals consider adopting, how many take the first steps to adopt, and how many complete the process.

*U.S. Department of State, Office of Children's Issues. "Intercountry Adoption from A–Z." Available online. URL: http://adoption.state.gov/pdf/Intercountry%20Adoption%20From%20A-Z.pdf. Accessed June 24, 2009. A complete step-by-step guide to adopting internationally. Though the document is arranged in alphabetical order, it actually provides information from the beginning to the completion of the adoption process, including choosing an agency and deciding where to adopt, to support groups and post-adoption services.

*———. "The Hague Convention on Intercountry Adoption: A Guide for Prospective Adoptive Parents." Available online. URL: http://adoption.state.gov/pdf/PAP_Guide-1.pdf. Accessed June 24, 2009. Provides a general guide to the Hague Convention on Intercountry Adoption and the Intercountry Adoption Act of 2000 for parents seeking to adopt internationally.

Wallace, Kelly. "Surrogates: Redefining Motherhood." CBS News (Jan. 2009). Available online. URL: http://www.cbsnews.com/stories/2009/01/25/sunday/main4751784.shtml. Accessed June 24, 2009. Discusses surrogacy in the United States and the process of arranging a surrogate pregnancy. Topics discussed include screening surrogates, matching surrogates with parents, motives of contracting parents and surrogates, the Baby M case, and the risk of custody disputes.

Other Media

Child Welfare Information Gateway. (June 2009). Available online. URL: http://www.childwelfare.gov. Accessed June 24, 2009. A Web site produced by the Children's Bureau of the U.S. Department of Health and Human Services that provides information on child abuse, family permanency, adoption, statistics, and other resources for research on adoption in the United States.

Ganz, Sheila. *Unlocking the Heart of Adoption*. Produced and directed by Sheila Ganz. 56 min. Pandora's Box Productions, 2002. DVD. Chronicles the lifelong process of adoption and the issues that birth parents, adoptive parents, and adoptees grapple with, including the concepts of identity and loss. The filmmaker is, herself, a birth mother and she interviews several other individuals in the adoption triad to weave together a history of adoption in the United States spanning the last 70 years.

Herman, Ellen. "The Adoption History Project." Department of History, University of Oregon (July 2007). Available online. URL: http://darkwing.uoregon.edu/~adoption/. Accessed June 24, 2009. A Web site that offers a complete history of adoption in the United States, including a time line, a list of topics, relevant individuals and organizations, adoption studies and science, and a document archive.

Kirilenko, Andrei. *Technostorks*. Produced and directed by Andrei Kirilenko. 51 min. Technostorks, LLC, 2006. DVD. Follows three U.S. couples in their quest to conceive after learning of their infertility. Focused primarily on in-vitro fertilization, the film documents the couples' operating room visits to undergo egg retrievals and embryo transfers and probes the couples' perspectives on infertility, parenthood, and assisted reproduction.

Liem, Deann Borshay. *First Person Plural*. Produced and directed by Deann Borshay Liem. 56 min. POV, American Documentary, Inc., 2000. DVD. Chronicles the childhood of filmmaker Deann Borshay Liem who was adopted from Korea by an American family in 1966. She retained memories of her birth family, however, and as an adult she learned that her biological mother was still alive in Korea.

ADOPTION AND SURROGATE PREGNANCY IN CHINA

Books

Davis, Deborah, and Stevan Harrell. *Chinese Families in the Post-Mao Era*. Berkeley: University of California Press, 1993. A collection of essays written by 11 anthropologists and sociologists that discuss urban and rural family structures and the ways in which they deal with marriage, the one-child policy, and decollectivization following the death of Mao Zedong.

Evans, Karin. *The Lost Daughters of China: Adopted Girls, Their Journey to America, and the Search for a Missing Past*. New York: Tarcher/Putnam, 2000. Depicts the author's struggle to adopt her Chinese daughter, during which she is exposed to the reality of the thousands of Chinese girls who are abandoned every year and subsequently adopted overseas. Evans takes a personal approach to the sociopolitical complexities of infant abandonment and adoption in China.

Gilmartin, Christina, Gail Hershatter, Lisa Rofel, and Tyrene White. *Engendering China: Women, Culture, and the State*. Cambridge: President and Fellows of Harvard College, 1994. An interdisciplinary collection of essays from scholars in China and the United States that discuss historical female figures in China, sexuality and reproduction, prostitution, women's writing, the gendering of work, portrayals of women in contemporary Chinese fiction, and more.

Johnson, Kay Ann. *Wanting a Daughter, Needing a Son: Abandonment, Adoption, and Orphanage Care in China*. St. Paul, Minn.: Yeong & Yeong Book Company, 2004. Sheds light on the complex cultural, social, and political forces that have led to the high rates of female infant abandonment in China, as well as the overcrowding of Chinese orphanages and China's emergence as the leading sending country in international adoptions. Johnson writes from the dual perspective of China scholar and adoptive parent of a Chinese child.

Milwertz, Cecilia. *Accepting Population Control: Urban Chinese Women and the One-Child Family Policy*. Richmond, Surrey, UK: Curzon Press, 1997. Examines the social and cultural implications of the one-child policy and addresses both critics, who accuse the Chinese government of inflicting human rights abuses in the name of the policy, and advocates, who want to implement the policy elsewhere. Milwertz's data concludes that women in China comply with the policy without coercion, and because of Chinese culture's Confucian traditions, the policy would not be effective elsewhere.

Articles and Studies

Jacobs, Andrew. "In China, a Preference for Sons Fuels a Grim Trade; Authorities Are Reluctant to Investigate, Despairing Parents Say." *International Herald Tribune* (April 2009). Reports on kidnappings and child trafficking in China, where boys are sold overseas or domestically to rural families desperate for a male heir, while girls are sold to orphanages for international adoption. Parents of missing children accuse the Chinese government of turning a blind eye to the practice of child trafficking.

Johnson, Kay, Huang Banghan, and Wang Liyao. "Infant Abandonment and Adoption in China." *Population & Development Review* 24 (Sept. 1998): 469–510. Reports the results of research conducted between 1993 and 1996 on infant abandonment and adoption and the close interconnectedness of the two practices in China. The authors researched the combination of birth-planning policies and cultural preferences for sons that have led to a high incidence of infant abandonment and, consequently, the unofficial adoption of foundlings by many urban families.

Luo, Nih, and Kathleen Ja Sook Bergquist. "Born in China: Birth Country Perspectives on International Adoption." *Adoption Quarterly* 8 (2004): 21–39. Explores Chinese perspectives on international adoption, including the views of government officials, orphanage administrators, and a sample of the general population. The researchers found an overall positive response to international adoption.

Naftali, Orna. "Empowering the Child: Children's Rights, Citizenship, and the State in Contemporary China." *China Journal* (Jan. 2009): 79–103. Reports on children's rights and citizenship status in China, as well as Chinese views on children and autonomy, education, and adoption. The author asserts that Chinese children are encouraged to be more independent and self-governing than children in other countries.

Po-Wah, Julia Tao Lai. "Right-Making and Wrong-Making in Surrogate Motherhood: A Confucian Feminist Perspective." *Linking Visions: Feminist Bioethics, Human Rights, and the Developing World.* Lanham, Md.: Rowman & Littlefield, 2004: 157–180. Examines the implications of surrogacy on women's roles in Confucian China. Po-Wah argues that separating childbearing from motherhood disenfranchises Chinese mothers and reduces their authority within the family structure.

Zhang, Hong. "China's New Rural Daughters Coming of Age: Downsizing the Family and Firing Up Cash-Earning Power in the New Economy." *Signs: Journal of Women in Culture & Society* 32 (2007): 671–698. Takes a positive approach to the one-child policy, which the author argues has allowed daughters to claim more of their parents' attention, receive an education, and go on to take white-collar jobs and provide for their families, none of which would have been possible prior to the policy's implementation.

Zhu, Wei Xing, Li Lu, and Therese Hesketh. "China's Excess Males, Sex-Selective Abortion, and One Child Policy: Analysis of Data from 2005 National Intercensus

Annotated Bibliography

Survey." *British Medical Journal* 338 (April 2009): 920–923. Examines data from 2005 on the ratio of males to females under the age of 20 in China. The authors found an excess of 32 million Chinese men to Chinese women, with the highest disparity in second-order births and children under four.

Web Documents

China Internet Information Center. "Gestational Surrogacy Banned in China." (June 2001). Available online. URL: http://www.china.org.cn/english/2001/Jun/15215. htm. Accessed June 25, 2009. Reports on the Chinese Ministry of Health's decision to issue a regulation that bans gestational surrogacy, citing the potential for problems that the government cannot yet address, such as what type of action should be taken if a surrogate refuses to relinquish the child, and who is responsible for the child if he or she is born with birth defects.

Kane, Penny, and Ching Y. Choi. "China's One Child Family Policy." *British Medical Journal* 319 (Oct. 1999): 992–994. Available online. URL: http://www.pubmed central.nih.gov/articlerender.fcgi?artid=1116810. Accessed June 25, 2009. Provides a general overview of China's one-child policy based on the authors' field visits to China over the course of 25 years. The article discusses the political and social climate that prompted the policy's implementation, regions where the policy has been most successful, and discrimination against female children.

The Schuster Institute for Investigative Journalism. "Adoption: China." Brandeis University (2008–09). Available online. URL: http://www.brandeis.edu/investigate/ gender/adoption/china.html. Accessed June 25, 2009. Provides an overview of adoption issues in China, including statistics, history, and regulation. The article also addresses controversies such as baby-buying, infant abandonment, and western demand for healthy infants.

Shapiro, Dorit Opher. "Our Journey to China." *Adoptive Families* (2009). Available online. URL: http://www.adoptivefamilies.com/articles.php?aid=1329. Accessed June 25, 2009. A personal narrative detailing one family's journey to China to adopt their new daughter. The article describes the family's decision to adopt, the process of adopting, and their first meeting with the baby whom they would adopt.

Thurston, Anne F. "In a Chinese Orphanage." *Atlantic Monthly* (April 1996). Available online. URL: http://www.theatlantic.com/issues/96apr/orphan/orphan.htm. Accessed June 25, 2009. Publicizes the journalist's undercover infiltration of a Chinese orphanage and the appalling living conditions of the children. Many infants suffered from a failure to thrive, at which point they were moved to a dying room.

Tingting, Zhang. "China Grapples with Legality of Surrogate Motherhood." China.org. cn (June 2006). Available online. URL: http://www.china.org.cn/english/2006/ Jun/170442.htm. Accessed June 25, 2009. Reports on one Chinese journalist who contacted Chinese surrogacy centers, posing as a potential surrogate. The report details the surrogacy system in China, which categorizes women based on age, education level, and appearance.

Other Media

National Geographic. China's Lost Girls. 43 min. National Geographic video (2004). DVD. Examines the effects of China's one-child policy, which has resulted in the abortion, abandonment, and murder of millions of Chinese girls. Host Lisa Ling follows American families as they travel to China to adopt and explores the visible gender gap and its possible implications.

Neumann, Jezza. *China's Stolen Children.* Produced by Kate Blewett and Brian Woods. Directed by Jezza Neumann. 88 min. True Vision (2008). Explores the child-trafficking crisis facing China as a result of the one-child policy. Because the Chinese government refused to cooperate with filmmakers, the documentary was filmed entirely undercover, with the film crew posing as tourists to gather information on the alarming stolen-child black market.

Stanek, Carolyn. *Found in China.* Produced and directed by Carolyn Stanek. 82 min. Tai-Kai Productions (2007). DVD. Follows six Midwestern families with adopted Chinese daughters as they travel to China to observe the culture and traditions. The documentary focuses on the nine to 13-year-old girls as they attempt to weave together their own stories and make sense of their birth circumstances.

ADOPTION AND SURROGATE PREGNANCY IN INDIA

Books

Bhargava, Vinita. *Adoption in India: Policies and Experiences.* Thousand Oaks, Calif.: Sage, 2005. Examines adoption practices and policies in India, focusing primarily on domestic adoption while including cultural and governmental perspectives on international adoption. Bhargava analyzes both macro-level issues of adoption in India, such as policy and cultural trends, as well as micro-level issues within families and communities.

Hajratwala, Minal. *Leaving India: My Family's Journey from Five Villages to Five Continents.* New York: Houghton Mifflin Harcourt Publishing Group, 2009. A personal memoir that illustrates the Indian diaspora, otherwise known as the Indian brain drain. Hajratwala researches her family history to its mythical origins, through her great-grandfather's decision to leave their village for Fiji in the midst of a famine. Some relatives join him there, while others relocate to South Africa and the United States.

Miró, Asha. *Daughter of the Ganges: The Story of One Girl's Adoption and Her Return Journey to India.* New York: Atria Books, 2006. A memoir that details Miró's return to India since being adopted by a couple in Spain in 1974, at the age of six. In India, Miró hears conflicting accounts of her story. The woman who claims to be her birth mother is later discovered to be a fraud, and the story of being abandoned by her father is not entirely true. The memoir follows her struggles to put her own story together.

Annotated Bibliography

Seymour, Susan C. *Women, Family, and Childcare in India: A World in Transition.* New York: Cambridge University Press, 1999. Presents data from the author's longitudinal study of 24 Hindu families of different castes and classes to research the lives of women and children, the socialization and education of girls, and the perspectives of fathers and husbands on women's roles in the home and community. The author chronicles the lives of 132 children over the course of three decades.

Umrigar, Thrity. *First Darling of the Morning: Selected Memories of an Indian Childhood.* New York: HarperPerennial, 2004. Chronicles the middle-class Parsi childhood of journalist Thrity Umrigar in the 1960s and 1970s, who reminisces on her affection for her father and her mother's sometimes violent strictness. As Umrigar matures into a bright young woman, she becomes aware of class differences and those living in poverty in India.

Articles and Studies

Bharadwaj, Aditya. "Why Adoption Is Not an Option in India: The Visibility of Infertility, the Secrecy of Donor Insemination, and Other Cultural Complexities." *Social Science and Medicine* 56 (May 2003): 1,876–1,880. Outlines the complex cultural traditions and perspectives on family that discourage adoption and prompt many infertile couples to secretly pursue gamete donation and in vitro fertilization.

Chang, Mina. "Womb for Rent." *Harvard International Review* 31 (2009): 11–12. Reports on commercial surrogacy in India and India's new role as the global destination for surrogate mothers. The article discusses the attraction of surrogacy among poor Indian women, the rationale of contracting couples seeking surrogates abroad, and the bioethical issues that the state must untangle.

Dey, Indira, and Ramendra Narayan Chaudhuri. "Gender Preference and Its Implications on Reproductive Behavior of Mothers in a Rural Area of West Bengal." *Indian Journal of Community Medicine* 34 (Jan. 2009): 65–67. Reports the disruption of the natural course of reproduction due to son preference in India and sex-selective abortion. The study presents statistical information for women who prefer a particular sex ratio among their children, as well as women using contraceptives.

Garg, S., and A. Nath. "Female Feticide in India: Issues and Concerns." *Journal of Postgraduate Medicine* 54 (2008): 276–279. Analyzes the practice of female feticide in India, the declining sex ratio, and the cultural practices that devalue women's position in society, such as the dowry system, family name, and the need for a son as the family provider and caretaker for aging parents.

Rani, N. Indira. "Child Care by Poor Single Mothers: Study of Mother-Headed Families in India." *Journal of Comparative Family Studies* 37 (2006): 75–91. Investigates the challenges faced by poor, mother-headed families in India, such as a lack of financial resources that prevents marrying off daughters and finding employment for sons, and the lower rate of education completion among children of mother-headed families than other children.

279

ADOPTION AND SURROGATE PREGNANCY

Web Documents

Chopra, Anuj. "Childless Couples Look to India for Surrogate Mothers." *Christian Science Monitor* (April 2006). Available online. URL: http://www.csmonitor.com/2006/0403/p01s04-wosc.html. Accessed June 25, 2009. Provides an overview of commercial surrogacy in India, as well as a more focused look at individual families and community responses to surrogacy.

Gentleman, Amelia. "India Nurtures Business of Surrogate Motherhood." *New York Times* (March 2008). Available online. URL: http://www.nytimes.com/2008/03/10/world/asia/10surrogate.html. Accessed June 25, 2009. Reports the unique circumstances of commercial surrogacy in India, the plight of poor surrogate mothers, and the couples who travel to India due to the high costs and lack of availability in their home countries.

Nelson, Dean. "India Pleads: Adopt Our Orphan Girls." *Sunday Times* (April 2007). Available online. URL: http://www.timesonline.co.uk/tol/news/world/asia/article1627008.ece. Accessed June 25, 2009. Explores the problem of infant abandonment in India and the difficulty of placing parentless children with families domestically. The article details the Indian government's decision to allow for a broader intercountry adoption policy to address the nation's rising number of abandoned children.

Office of Children's Issues, United States Department of State. "Country Specific Information for India." Available online. URL: http://adoption.state.gov/country/india.html. Accessed June 25, 2009. Provides information on adopting from India for U.S. adoptive parents who are considering international adoption. The page details who may adopt and the process for adopting, and provides a list of contacts in India who can offer more information and guidance.

Ramachandran, Sudha. "India's New Outsourcing Business: Wombs." *Asia Times Online* (June 2006). Available online. URL: http://www.atimes.com/atimes/south_asia/hf16df03.html. Accessed June 25, 2009. Examines commercial surrogacy in India and its emergence as a leader in reproductive tourism. The author questions the autonomy of commercial surrogates, who may be facing pressure from their families to bring in money.

Other Media

Briski, Zana, and Ross Kauffman. *Born into Brothels.* Produced and directed by Zana Briski and Ross Kauffman. 83 min. Velocity Home Entertainment (2005). DVD. Follows Zana Briski as she teaches photography to children who live in the red light district of Calcutta. As the sons and daughters of prostitutes, many of the children face the likelihood of becoming prostitutes themselves until Briski teaches them photography and works to find them homes outside of the brothels.

Ray, Rick. *The Soul of India.* Produced and directed by Rick Ray. 90 min. Rick Ray Films (2001). DVD. Documents the various landscapes, cultures, architectural feats, and religions of India. Director Rick Ray explores the jungles, deserts, cities, mountains, and beaches of India, as well as Hinduism, Buddhism, Christianity,

Islam, the Jain faith, and the Sikh faith. Through his travels, which also explore cultural ideas of marriage, family, caste, and death, Rick Ray weaves a brilliant tapestry of life in India.

Wood, Michael. *Story of India.* Produced and directed by Jeremy Jeff. 360 min. PBS (March 2009). DVD. Presents a general overview of India since the nation obtained independence from Britain. British historian Michael Wood examines the country's diverse population, expanding economy, and its role as the world's largest democracy.

ADOPTION AND SURROGATE PREGNANCY IN GREAT BRITAIN

Books

Cocker, Christine, and Lucille Allain. *Social Work with Looked After Children.* Exeter, Devon, UK: Learning Matters, 2008. Provides information on children in state care for those interested in engaging in social work. The book examines the needs of Looked After Children (LAC) and the social worker's role in their lives. Other topics include legislation and residential and foster care, as well as the needs of children in state care.

Keating, Jenny. *A Child for Keeps: The History of Adoption in England, 1918–45.* New York: Palgrave Macmillan, 2009. Examines modern adoption law in England as it took formation between 1918 and 1945. Keating discusses changing families and attitudes toward children's and parents' rights, the development of child protection legislation, the perceived need for secrecy, and the first sanctioned adoptions.

Langer, Alvin, and Godwin I. Meniru. *Cambridge Guide to Infertility Management and Assisted Reproduction.* Cambridge: Cambridge University Press, 2001. Discusses infertility diagnosis and treatment, such as in vitro fertilization and other procedures. The book serves as a medical guide and includes descriptions of techniques, practices, and medical interventions.

*Lord, Jenifer. *Adopting a Child: A Guide for People Interested in Adoption.* London: British Association for Adoption and Fostering, 2008. Provides an overview of the U.K. adoption system and the process for adopting in the United Kingdom.

*Morris, Ann. *The Adoption Experience: Families Who Give Children a Second Chance.* London: Jessica Kingsley Publishers, 1999. Presents an informative guide to several different types of adoption and children. The book includes information on infant, special needs, and transracial adoption, as well as adopting children who have been abused, and adoption by gay and single parents.

Smith, Fergus, Roy Stewart, and Deborah Cullen. *Adoption Now: Law, Regulation, Guidance, and Standards.* London: British Association for Adoption and Fostering, 2006. Written primarily for adoption professionals, the book provides information on adoption laws and regulations, including the National Minimum Standards.

Articles and Studies

Community Care. "Haringey Disciplines Staff over Child Protection Cases." (April 2009): 6. Reviews a recent case in England in which a 17-month-old boy died after suffering over 50 injuries, many of which he received while he was seen by social services. The Haringey Council responded by suspending two staff members and dismissing an agency practitioner for their mishandling of the case.

Forrester, Donald, Keith Goodman, Christine Cocker et al. "What Is the Impact of Public Care on Children's Welfare? A Review of Research Findings from England and Wales and Their Policy Implications." *Journal of Social Policy* 38 (July 2009): 439–456. Examines the causes of poor outcomes for children in public care and attempts to reduce the number of children in public care. The authors argue that such attempts are misguided, and that Britain should adopt a Scandinavian approach to public care, which acts as family support.

Hayes, Peter. "Deterrents to Intercountry Adoption in Britain." *Family Relations* 49 (Oct. 2000): 465–471. Reviews problems within the British adoption practice and policy that prevents couples from adopting internationally. Hayes addresses the issues of varying opinions on intercountry adoption by adoption professionals, weak central government control, and unauthorized adoptions.

Jadva, Vasanti, Clare Murray, Emma Lycett et al. "Surrogacy: The Experiences of Surrogate Mothers." *Human Reproduction* 8 (2003): 2,196–2,204. Provides statistical information on British surrogate mothers, including their backgrounds, motivations, and experiences with surrogacy. The study finds that surrogate mothers generally have positive experiences with surrogacy.

Mcintosh, Jennifer. "Four Young People Speak about Children's Involvement in Family Court Matters." *Journal of Family Studies* 15 (May 2009): 98–103. Presents speeches by four young people, delivered to an audience of judges, lawyers, and mental health practitioners in England. The event was the launch of the new CAFCASS (Children and Family Court Advisory Support Service) initiative, Children First.

Purewal, S., and O. B. A. van den Akker. "British Women's Attitudes Towards Oocyte Donation: Differences and Altruism." *Patient Education and Counseling* 64 (Nov. 2005): 43–49. Presents data from a study of British women and their attitudes toward egg donation, which found that Asian women, women who practiced a religion, and those who anticipated disapproval from their families over egg donation had a less favorable attitude toward donation.

Taylor, Amy. "Sealed Off from Scrutiny." *Community Care* (April 2009): 18–19. Evaluates child welfare in Britain and the government's review of the child protection system. The report also includes a reference to a report by a domestic violence charity that avers that accountability among family court professionals must be ensured.

Annotated Bibliography

Web Documents

BBC News. "UK Accused of Failing Children" (Feb. 2007). Available online. URL: http://news.bbc.co.uk/2/hi/uk_news/6359363.stm. Accessed June 26, 2009. Discusses a report released by UNICEF that placed the United Kingdom at the bottom of a table of child well-being among industrialized nations. The report revealed that child poverty in the United Kingdom has doubled since 1979.

British Association for Adoption and Fostering. "Fostering and Adoption Statistics (England)" (2008). Available online. URL: http://www.baaf.org.uk/info/stats/england.shtml. Accessed June 26, 2009. Provides statistical information on adoption and foster care in England, including the number of children adopted from foster care and the ages of those adopted.

Dyer, Clare. "Judge Warns Agencies after Surrogate Mother Dupes Couples to Keep Babies." *Guardian* (Oct. 2007). Available online. URL: http://www.guardian.co.uk/uk/2007/oct/31/law.world. Accessed June 26, 2009. Reports on a case in England in which a surrogate mother conceived two successive children via artificial insemination and told the contracting parents that she had miscarried in order to keep the children. She retained custody of her 4-year-old daughter, but her 18-month-old son was removed from her care.

Hutchinson, Martin. "Surrogate Mothers Happy in Their Role," BBC News (July 2003). Available online. URL: http://news.bbc.co.uk/2/hi/health/3037912.stm. Accessed June 26, 2009. Responds to a study led by Vasanti Jadva on the psychological effects experienced by surrogate mothers, in which the researchers found that the majority of surrogate mothers enjoyed their experiences with surrogacy.

Taylor, Amy. "Gay Couples Overlooked in Adopters Shortage," *Community Care* (Nov. 2008). Available online. URL: http://www.communitycare.co.uk/Articles/2008/11/05/109856/gay-couples-overlooked-in-adopters-shortage.html. Accessed June 26, 2009. Discusses adoption among gay and lesbian couples and argues that the slow rate of adoption among gay couples is due to the personal beliefs and prejudices of social workers when making child placement decisions.

Other Media

History Channel. *A History of Britain: The Complete Collection.* 900 min. A&E Home Video (July 2008). DVD set. Originated as a History Channel TV series, this DVD set provides a thorough historical outline of British history, including Roman Britain, the Norman Conquest, Elizabeth I, the Scottish rebellions, and more. The documentary also touches on language, architecture, ceremonies, and religion.

Leveugle, Lucy. *Addicted to Surrogacy.* Produced and directed by Lucy Leveugle, co-produced by Jess Fowle. True North Productions (2009). TV program. Follows four "serial" surrogate mothers through their pregnancies, including Britain's most prolific surrogate mother, the world-record holder of surrogate pregnancies, a first-time surrogate mother, and a surrogate carrying twins that will be her sixth and 7th surrogate children. The documentary investigates the intense drives and motivations of women who become "addicted" to surrogacy.

ADOPTION AND SURROGATE PREGNANCY IN GUATEMALA

Books

Archdiocese of Guatemala. *Guatemala: Never Again!* New York: Orbis Books, 1999. In 1998, Bishop Juan Gerardi released a historic study of human rights abuses in Guatemala between 1970 and 1990. Two days later, he was assassinated. This book is the Recovery of Historical Memory report, which features eyewitness accounts and discussions about the nature and origins of the violence that Guatemala experienced.

Erichsen, Jean. *Butterflies in the Wind: The Truth About Latin American Adoptions.* Lincoln, Nebr.: Authors Choice Press, 1992. Details the story of a white, American family that adopts twin girls and later a son from Colombia and the cultural and ethnic challenges they face along the way. Erichsen discusses the complexity of being a transracial family, as she, her husband, and their three biological sons are of white German/Scandinavian origin, while their adopted children are darker-skinned Colombians.

Hollingsworth, Jerry. *Children of the Sun: An Ethnographic Study of the Street Children of Latin America.* Newcastle-upon-Tyne, UK: Cambridge Scholars Publishing, 2008. Researches and reports on the subculture of street children in Latin America. Hollingsworth discusses socialization, illegal drug use, criminal behaviors, and lack of education among street children, as well as their expectations for the future.

Jonas, Susanne. *The Battle for Guatemala: Rebels, Death Squads, and U.S. Power.* Boulder, Colo.: Westview Press, 1991. Presents a history of Guatemala's civil war, the longest war in the history of the Western Hemisphere. Jonas examines the social forces, economic factors, and critical events that set the stage for the war, as well as the involvement of the indigenous peoples, women, and U.S. forces.

Luna, Florencia. *Bioethics and Vulnerability: A Latin American View.* New York: Rodopi, 2006. Examines the challenges facing bioethics in Latin America, particularly among vulnerable and disadvantaged populations, such as women and the illiterate. Luna explores AIDS and reproductive rights, assisted reproduction and the experiences of women in Latin America, and abuses in biomedical research.

Menchu, Rigoberta. *I, Rigoberta Menchu: An Indian Woman in Guatemala.* Brooklyn, N.Y.: Verso Books, 1982. Chronicles the childhood and upbringing of Rigoberta Menchu, a member of the Quiche mestizo group in Guatemala, as she witnesses two of her brothers die in infancy due to malnutrition and later sees her mother, father, and brother murdered by the Guatemalan military. Though details of Menchu's story have been questioned by historians, the book nevertheless presents the struggles of the Mayans in Guatemala and political and cultural conflicts that persist in Guatemalan society today.

Annotated Bibliography

Articles and Studies

Carroll, Rory. "Child-Trafficking Fears as Guatemalan Police Rescue 46 from House: Mothers Pressured to Put Babies up for Adoption, Illegal Agencies Target Sales to Western Parents." *Guardian* (Aug. 2007). Available online. URL: www.guardian.co.uk/world/2007/aug/14/internationalcrime. Accessed September 29, 2009. Reports on an event in which 46 children lacking documentation were found in a house in Antigua and were believed to have been obtained by an illegal adoption agency.

Daly, Laura Beth. "To Regulate or Not to Regulate: The Need for Compliance with International Norms by Guatemala and Cooperation by the United States in Order to Maintain Intercountry Adoptions." *Family Court Review* 45 (Oct. 2007): 620–637. Discusses the potential consequences of ceasing all adoptions between Guatemala and the United States. Daly uses case studies from such countries as Romania and Cambodia, which also experienced a suspension of adoptions.

Gibbons, Judith L., Samantha L. Wilson, and Christine A. Rufener. "Gender Attitudes Mediate Gender Differences in Attitudes Towards Adoption in Guatemala." *Sex Roles* 54 (Jan. 2006): 139–145. Studied the correlation between attitudes toward adoption and attitudes toward traditional gender roles. The researchers found that women viewed adoption more favorably while men, specifically men who demonstrated traditional attitudes of machismo, viewed adoption less favorably.

Luna, Florencia. "Assisted Reproduction in Latin America: Some Ethical and Sociocultural Issues." *Infertility and Assisted Reproductive Technologies from a Regional Perspective.* World Health Organization (July 2006): 31–40. Discusses the unique challenges facing assisted reproduction in Latin American culture, where human embryos are afforded rights and personhood and abortion is illegal.

Marquez, Claudia Lima. "Assisted Reproductive Technology (ART) in South America and the Effect on Adoption." *Texas International Law Journal* 35 (2000): 65–91. Explores law and regulation of the fertility industry in Latin America, where assisted reproduction is both unregulated and highly restrictive. Marquez discusses illegal embryo destruction, as well as the prohibition of providing ART services to gay couples and single women.

Web Documents

Guettler, Ellen. "Finding the Birth Mother." American RadioWorks, American Public Radio (2009). Available online. URL: http://americanradioworks.publicradio. org/features/adoption/g1.html. Accessed June 26, 2009. An interview with Susi, a Guatemalan woman who works with American adoptive parents to find their children's birth mothers and provide them with information and photographs of their children. Because birth mothers often receive little to no information about their children after relinquishment, many are grateful for Susi's service.

Long, Scott. "Letter to the Guatemalan Congress Regarding Marriage and Family Law." Human Rights Watch (Sept. 2007). Available online. URL: http://www.hrw. org/en/news/2007/09/30/letter-guatemalan-congress-regarding-marriage-and-fa mily-law. Accessed June 26, 2009. A letter to the Guatemalan congress regarding

285

their consideration of a law that would implement a new legal definition of the family as consisting of a married, heterosexual couple and their naturally conceived offspring.

The Schuster Institute for Investigative Journalism. "Adoption: Guatemala." Brandeis University (2008–2009). Available online. URL: http://www.brandeis.edu/investigate/gender/adoption/guatemala.html. Accessed June 26, 2009. Investigates adoption practices in Guatemala, including statistical information as well as fraud, baby-buying, coercion, and kidnapping.

Singh, Susheela, Elena Prada, and Edgar Kessler. "Induced Abortion and Unintended Pregnancy in Guatemala." *Family Planning Perspectives* 32 (Sept. 2006). Available online. URL: http://www.guttmacher.org/pubs/journals/3213606.html. Accessed June 26, 2009. Reports the statistics of unintended pregnancy, the number of women who seek induced abortions, and the number of women who are hospitalized annually due to complications from an induced abortion.

Other Media

PBS—NOW. *Child Brides: Stolen Lives.* Produced by Amy Bucher. (Oct. 2007). TV Program. Available online. URL: http://www.pbs.org/now/shows/341/index.html. Accessed June 26, 2009. Investigates the practice of underage marriage among girls in the countries of Guatemala, India, Nigeria, and the United States, and the way in which it negatively affects their health, education, and development.

Sigel, Newton Thomas, and Pamela Yates. *When the Mountains Tremble.* Produced by Peter Kinoy and directed by Newton Thomas Sigel and Pamela Yates. 83 min. New Video Group (2004). DVD. Originally released in 1983, *When the Mountains Tremble* documents the life of Rigoberta Menchu and the Guatemalan government's persecution of the indigenous Mayans. The documentary addresses the government's cruelty and violence against the Mayans, as well as the American government's involvement in the struggle.

Specogna, Heidi. *The Short Life of José Antonio Guttierez.* Produced and directed by Heidi Specogna. 89 min. Atopia, Sep 2007. DVD. Documents the life of José Antonio Guttierez, whose family is destroyed by the Guatemalan civil war, and who ends up in an orphanage. Guttierez's life serves as a backdrop for a general discussion of corruption in Guatemala, the civil war, and the American government's involvement in foreign affairs.

Chronology

1780 B.C.E.

• King Hammurabi of Babylon commissions a code of laws, which are neatly arranged into groups that address everything from trade and property to family life and religious worship. The code contains the first recorded adoption law, which specifies that an adopted child becomes a full heir, with all the rights of a biological child. If a man adopts a son and then goes on to marry and have biological children of his own, the adopted son is entitled to one-third of a child's share in goods.

2000–1500 B.C.E.

• According to Genesis, the nomadic Hebrew couple Sarah and Abraham were unable to conceive, so Sarah offered her Egyptian slave Hagar to Abraham to act as a surrogate, a practice common in Mesopotamia at the time. Hagar is impregnated, but begins to behave impudently toward Sarah, who drives her from the camp. Hagar flees to Egypt but is visited by an angel, who informs her that her son Ishmael will be a great leader of the Hebrews, and Hagar returns to Abraham and Sarah. In the Qur'an, the story relates that Abraham resettles Hagar and Ishmael in the land of Paran to settle the jealousy between the two women.

1391 B.C.E.

• In a time of national crisis in Egypt, the pharaoh orders all Hebrew boys to be killed. Jochebed, Moses's mother, sets him adrift on the Nile in a basket made of bulrushes. He is later found and adopted by the pharaoh's daughter, Thermuthis. In the Qur'an, Jochebed is instructed to trust God's will and set her son adrift on the Nile as an act of faith, at which point Moses is found and adopted by the pharaoh's wife, who is unable to conceive.

ADOPTION AND SURROGATE PREGNANCY

384–322 B.C.E.

• In Greece, Aristotle is born into the aristocracy but orphaned at age 10. He goes to live with his uncle Proxenus of Atarneus who becomes his teacher. At 18, Aristotle becomes a student of Plato, and in 343 B.C.E., he is invited to tutor Alexander, the son of King Philip II of Macedon.

145 B.C.E.

• In China, one of the earliest recorded adoptions recounts the part-mythological, part-historical story of a woman who becomes pregnant by a god and abandons her son, whose illegitimacy she fears will bring her bad luck. The baby is found by another woman and named "Ji," which translates as "abandonment."

52–117

• In Rome, Trajan rises to prominence when he joins the military, catching the attention of Emperor Nerva, who appoints him governor of Upper Germany in 96 C.E. The following year, Trajan receives a note informing him of his adoption by Emperor Nerva. Trajan later becomes emperor, and under his rule Rome reaches its greatest expanse, encompassing modern-day Iraq and Romania.

490

• The Roman Council of Vaisons condemns the practice of exposure, in which an infant is abandoned in an open space to die or be claimed by a passing stranger. The council promulgates a decree whereby a child that cannot be raised by its mother will be placed with another family.

500–600

• As Christianity begins to take hold as a major cult, the Christian condemnation of child exposure results in many infants being abandoned on church doorsteps. Forced to find a way to ensure the protection of the abandoned children who come under their care, the clergy develops the practice of oblation, whereby a child is raised in a monastery and dedicated to monastic life. This marks the first move toward institutional care for abandoned or orphaned children. "Binding out" also becomes common. Older children are apprenticed out to local households, where they can learn a useful trade, though there is little distinction between apprenticeship and indentured servitude.

529

• Emperor Justinian I embarks on a project to revise and document all of Roman law, a feat that has never before been broached. The resulting collection, *Cor-*

pus Juris Civilis, consists of four parts: Codex Justinianus, Digesta (or Pandectae), Institutiones, and Novellae. Book I of Institutiones includes regulations on adoption practice. Adoption does not dissolve the natural father's rights; women, however, have no rights to their own children. Further, adoption must imitate nature, thus the adopter must be a full 18 years older than the adoptee.

570–632

• The Muslim prophet, Muhammad, is born in the city of Mecca and orphaned as an infant. He moves between several sets of foster parents as a young child and eventually comes under the care of his uncle, who teaches him the business of trade. Muhammad receives his first revelation at the age of 40 and goes on to establish the religion of Islam, which translates as "surrender." Though Muhammad adopts a son that he names after himself, he later reports that this practice is to be discontinued according to Allah's wishes. Thus, while Muslims are allowed to care for and raise nonbiological children, Islamic law prohibits legal adoption of nonbiological children.

787

• The first foundling hospital is established by the archpriest of Milan, Italy.

937

• Textual evidence suggests that Chinese foot-binding arises during the South Tang dynasty, which is renowned for its dancing girls, with their tiny feet. Foot-binding becomes a standard practice among elite families. The bones of a young girl's feet are broken and reshaped to resemble a crescent. Bound feet are believed to be intensely erotic and also display a family's wealth as they render women virtually immobile.

1250?

• The Italian jurist Odofredus asserts that a child born outside of wedlock is a product of "criminal intercourse" and thus not only lacks the right to receive support from his or her father, but is not really the child of his or her father at all.

1285

• In medieval England, the Statute of Westminster II, *De Donis*, mandates that entailed land must remain within the family and may not be willed away to anyone other than natural heirs or descendants. This does not, however, include adopted children, as family law specifies that only biological and legitimate children may inherit. The law also does not permit legitimization of children born to a couple prior to marriage.

1487

- The *Malleus Maleficarum* (Hammer of the witches) is published by two Catholic inquisitors and states that childlessness and infertility as experienced by married couples is the direct result of witchcraft.

1502

- India's colonial era begins when Portuguese explorers establish the first trading post at Kollam, Kerala.

1523

- The Spanish explorer Pedro de Alvarado conquers the Mayan people and names Guatemala a Spanish colony.

1600–1700

- In England, an unmarried mother who is found to have concealed the death of her baby is presumed guilty of infanticide unless she can prove her innocence, such as preparing for the baby's birth by buying bedding and other supplies.

1601

- The passage of the Elizabethan Poor Law establishes a system whereby orphaned children may be boarded out to families that will receive compensation in the form of a monthly payment by their local parishes. The Poor Law also provides a number of apprenticeships for older children. In Ireland, the Poor Law eclipses the Brehon Laws on the rights of fostered children, birth parents, and foster parents, which derive from Gaelic tradition.

1684

- *Aristotle's Master Piece* is published anonymously. It theorizes that conception occurs through the mingling of male and female "semence," which, for the first time, suggests that a woman also contributes a "seed" that is vital to conception.

1710

- The Society for the Promotion of Christian Knowledge in England promotes the idea of parochial workhouses as a means of making the poor work for their food and shelter. In a further attempt to discourage individuals from falling into and maintaining a life of poverty, the conditions of many of the subsequent workhouses that develop in England throughout the 18th and 19th centuries are appalling, and the majority of those living and laboring in them are young children, the ill and disabled, and the elderly.

Chronology

1732–1744

- British law requires that a woman who is unmarried and pregnant must publicly declare that she is carrying a bastard and name the father. The father is thus required to support his illegitimate child and the mother, and any failure to do so can result in jail time. The mother is to be publicly whipped.

1739

- The first foundling hospital is established in London as a home for the education and upbringing of abandoned and destitute children. Infants are sent to wet nurses in the countryside, and teenagers are apprenticed out.

1779

- James Graham becomes famous for supposedly curing the Duchess of Devonshire's infertility. Graham specializes in curing infertility through electrotherapy. Men sit on chairs that emit light electric shocks while women sit on magnetic thrones. For 500 guineas a night, couples can rent the Celestial Bed, which vibrates.

1795

- The Speenhamland System in England is devised as an amendment to the Poor Law and a means of combating poverty due to a spike in grain prices. Families are paid extra to keep wages at a set level, but the system ultimately contributes to greater levels of poverty because employers pay below subsistence levels and low wages remain unchanged.

1797

- The British philosopher Thomas Spence publishes *The Rights of Infants*, in which he calls for the abolition of the aristocracy, common ownership of land, and equal distribution of revenue.

1798–1826

- The British scholar the Reverend Thomas Robert Malthus condemns foundling hospitals in his treatise *An Essay on the Principle of Population*, arguing that such hospitals discourage marriage and contribute to overpopulation.

1802

- The British Parliament passes a series of acts known as the Factory Acts, which set a limit on the number of hours that can be worked by women and children. The Health and Morals of Apprentices Act establishes a regulatory framework for factory conditions, particularly for child workers.

ADOPTION AND SURROGATE PREGNANCY

1804

• The Napoleonic Code in France actively discourages adoption by mandating that adopters be at least 50 years old, infertile, older than the adoptee by 15 years, and foster the adoptee for a minimum of six years.

1821

• Guatemala obtains its independence from Spain and becomes part of the Mexican empire.

1834

• Dissatisfaction with the Elizabethan Poor Law system leads many social reformers to demand harsher penalties for those who request relief from poverty. Social ills, reformers like Jeremy Bentham and Thomas Robert Malthus argue, are best remedied with discipline and punishment. The Poor Law Amendment Act is passed under the belief that only a fear of poverty can induce people to work and earn wages. In an effort to make workhouses even less inviting, they are designed to mirror prison life. Families who enter workhouses are routinely separated, inmates are forced to wear prison-style uniforms, and little food is provided to make the diet less than what inmates would receive outside the workhouse. The conditions are worse in Ireland, where a lack of funding and too few workhouses exacerbate the Potato Famine.

1837–1901

• Throughout her reign, Queen Victoria establishes several orphanages that are distinct from workhouses and provide safer and healthier living conditions.

1832

• The New England Association of Farmers, Mechanics, and Other Working-men in the United States officially condemns child labor.

1836

• Massachusetts creates the first U.S. child labor law, which mandates that children under 15 who work in factories must attend school for at least three months of the year.

1838

• Charles Dickens publishes *Oliver Twist*, which calls attention to the conditions of workhouses, the lives and suffering of street children, child labor, and child criminality in England.

Chronology

1839

- The Custody of Infants Act in England assigns custody of all children under the age of seven to their mothers.

1840

- Day nurseries open in Boston to provide child care for low-income working mothers and widows who need to earn an income, and to prevent children from wandering the streets.

1851

- Massachusetts passes the first adoption law in the United States, which recognizes the adopted child's welfare as being the primary responsibility in any adoption procedure. Prior to the passage of the law, adoption arrangements in the United States were informal and often based on the needs and wishes of the parents rather than the child's best interests.

1853

- Charles Loring Brace establishes the Children's Aid Society in New York to provide services and protection to homeless, orphaned, and destitute children and ensure their healthy growth and development into responsible adults.

1854

- Charles Loring Brace develops and launches the orphan trains to ship children out of the urban slums of the East Coast and relocate them with Protestant farming families in the Midwest. He believes that family life, Christian values, and farm work will help steer the children away from lives of crime and immorality and help them develop into responsible, compassionate adults. It is the largest child relocation endeavor in U.S. history.

1857

- The Industrial Schools Act is established to remedy the problem of juvenile delinquency by removing poor and neglected children from their homes and sending them to industrial schools.

1868

- Dr. Thomas Barnardo takes a tour of London's East End under the guidance of a local street child and he is moved by the number of children sleeping on rooftops and in gutters. In response, he opens the first of his many homes for destitute children. He begins boarding children out to homes in the countryside, but the number of orphans and street children coming to him for help soon becomes overwhelming, and he begins placing children overseas in

Canada, Australia, and the United States. By 1905, the number of children he has sent overseas has reached 18,000.

- The Massachusetts Board of State Charities begins paying for children to board with local families, which begins the movement of placing orphaned or destitute children in the care of families rather than institutions.

1869

- In the United States, Samuel Fletcher, Jr., escapes after his parents lock him in a cellar for several days. He notifies the police and his parents are found guilty of child abuse, one of the first court rulings in the United States to recognize a child's right to protection from abuse.

1870

- In England, the National Education League is established with the objective of promoting free elementary education for all children, without any religious affiliation.
- The Elementary Education Act 1870 is implemented in England to provide compulsory elementary education for children between the ages of five and 12. It is also the first act to officially segregate church and state in the public school system.
- In China, the practice of paying to adopt a stranger's son as an heir becomes standard, and such children differ from other adopted children in that they are considered full and complete members of their adoptive family, severing all ties with their natal family.

1871

- Baby farming is a persistent problem in England, and on any given day, a young, unmarried mother can find a baby farmer who is willing to take her infant for a fee with the unspoken agreement that the child will be sold, killed, or neglected until it dies of starvation. When 11 babies are found in a state of extreme starvation in a house in Brixton, the Parliamentary Select Committee on the Protection of Infant Life is established; it enacts legislation to combat baby farming and regulate fostering.

1874

- Eight-year-old Mary Ellen Wilson is regularly abused by her adoptive parents, and police finally remove her from the home when the New York head of the Society for the Prevention of Cruelty to Animals notifies authorities. The New York Society for the Prevention of Cruelty to Children is established.

Chronology

1880

- In England, the Elementary Education Act 1880 establishes attendance officers to enforce compulsory education and fine parents who do not send their children to school because they want them to earn an income.

1881

- The American Federation of Labor proposes a total ban on employing children under 14 in all states.

1889

- Hull-House, founded by Jane Addams and Ellen Gates Starr in Chicago, Illinois, becomes one of the first organizations to provide after-school programs for children.

1891

- Michigan becomes the first state to set standards for potential adoptive parents, who must satisfy the court judge that they are of good moral character, can provide a suitable home, and are able to support and educate a child.

1898

- New York State Charities Aid Association is one of the first U.S. organizations to establish a specialized child-placement program.
- The Catholic Home Bureau is organized in New York by the St. Vincent de Paul Society and becomes the first Catholic agency to place children in homes rather than orphanages. Other U.S. cities follow suit.

1904

- In England, the Prevention of Cruelty to Children Act grants the National Society for the Prevention of Cruelty to Children the right to intervene in cases of child protection.
- In the United States, the first school of social work, the New York School of Applied Philanthropy, is established.

1905

- Borstals, a type of youth prison that focuses on rehabilitation of delinquent youths, are established in the United Kingdom to separate child offenders from adult prisoners. Borstals emphasize education, discipline, and authority, and do not allow corporal punishment. Birching, the use of a birch rod on the buttocks, is allowed only in cases of physical assault of an officer, and only on male inmates over the age of 18.

• A team of British scientists discover sex hormones in animals.

1907

• In England, the Notification of Births Act requires that parents inform their local medical officer of health immediately following the birth of a child. It is the officer's responsibility to arrange for a health visitor to attend to the new mother and instruct her on how to care for the infant.

1908

• In the United States, the eugenicist Henry Herbert Goddard, director of the Training School for Backward and Feeble-Minded Children in Vineland, New Jersey, acquires the French Binet Scale and administers the test to children in his institution to measure their intelligence.

1909

• In the United States, the first White House Conference on the Care of Dependent Children determines that poverty does not provide sufficient grounds for removing children from their families. When they must be removed for more pressing reasons, however, they must be placed in private family homes.

1911

• Dr. Arnold Gesell opens the Clinic of Child Development at Yale University, where he runs a series of behavioral and social tests on children to determine a universal pattern of development that will aid in the process of matching adoptive children with suitable parents.

1912

• Congress creates the U.S. Children's Bureau to monitor and address issues of child welfare in the United States. Julia Lathrop is appointed chief of the Children's Bureau, becoming the first woman to head a federal agency.

• Henry Herbert Goddard publishes *The Kallikak Family*, in which he traces the Kallikak family line and concludes that a genetic intermingling between fit and unfit individuals can produce several generations of feebleminded people. He not only warns of the dangers of allowing genetically unfit people to reproduce freely, but opposes the adoption of feebleminded children, who he believes should be institutionalized and quarantined from the general population.

1914

• Clara Andrew of England founds the National Children's Adoption Association (NCAA) in an effort to find families for war orphans. Her work receives support from prominent figures, such as Princess Alice, Countess of Athlone. Andrew makes it standard practice to destroy a child's records upon adoption.

1915

- The Child Welfare League of America is formed under the title of Bureau for Information Exchange Among Child-Helping Organizations.

1917

- Minnesota passes the first law mandating home studies, investigations into individual cases of adoption, and confidentiality.

1918

- In England, the National Council for the Unmarried Mother and Her Child is established to address the sudden rise in illegitimate births during World War I.

- The Maternity and Child Welfare Act is developed in England in response to the Notification of Births Act and provides free medical care to newborns and children under five. Although the work is performed largely by volunteers, it results in an astounding decline in infant and child mortality.

1919

- In response to the poverty and starvation that children in central, eastern, and southern Europe are experiencing as a result of World War I, sisters Eglantyne Jebb and Dorothy Buxton found the Save the Children Fund in London, England, with the objective of creating an international organization for the protection of children.

- The U.S. Children's Bureau sets minimum standards for adopting.

- Jessie Taft, a U.S. adoption advocate, authors "Relation of Personality Study to Child Placing."

1921

- Marie Stopes, a Scottish author, paleobotanist, and feminist, opens the first family-planning clinic, the Mothers' Clinic, in London. The clinic provides free family-planning advice to married women and collects information on scientific developments in contraception. A proponent of eugenics and rumored to be a Nazi sympathizer, Stopes argues for the forcible sterilization of those unfit to parent and for the abolition of child labor among the lower classes. The Mothers' Clinic marks a turning point in British history, in which women may take control of their fertility.

- The U.S. Children's Bureau launches the first field study to focus on illegitimacy and child welfare in Boston, Massachusetts.

- The American Association of Social Workers is formed.
- The Child Welfare League of America adopts a constitution that emphasizes minimum standards as a key priority.

1923

- Eglantyne Jebb drafts the Declaration of the Rights of the Child, which is endorsed by the League of Nations General Assembly the following year as the World Child Welfare Charter.

1924

- Sophie van Senden Theis publishes the first major outcome study, *How Foster Children Turn Out,* which studied 910 children placed by the New York State Charities Aid Association between 1898 and 1922. The study challenges assumptions of adopted children as genetically unfit or morally tainted due to their illegitimacy. Theis notes that many children who are removed from bad environments and placed in foster homes grow into capable adults.

1926

- The Adoption of Children Act is implemented, becoming the first law on adoption in England and Wales. The Act provides a legal framework for adoption to prevent child abuse and exploitation by baby farmers and other questionable individuals. There is controversy over whether or not to seal an adopted child's birth records, but many adoption societies insist that sealed records are necessary for a child's complete assimilation into a new family.

1929

- In India, the Child Marriage Restraint Act officially bans marriages involving minors under penalty of imprisonment.

1930s

- The pharmaceutical companies Schering-Kahlbaum and Parke-Davis begin mass producing commercial estrogen.

1931

- Jorge Ubico becomes president of Guatemala. His administration becomes known for its repressiveness.

1933

- The Children and Young Persons Act of the United Kingdom raises the age of criminal responsibility from seven to eight, mandates that no one under the age of 18 may be hanged for a criminal offense, enforces punishments for anyone over the age of 16 found to have neglected a child, and establishes a minimum age of 14 for full-time employment.

1935

- In the United States, the Social Security Act provides aid for dependent children, disabled children's programs, and child welfare, which leads to extensive development of the foster care system.
- The American Youth Congress releases "The Declaration of the Rights of American Youth."

1938

- Following Kristallnacht in Nazi Germany, a delegation of Jewish British leaders appeals to Prime Minister Neville Chamberlain to grant Jewish children temporary admission to the country with the promise of later reemigration, and payment of guarantees for refugee children by the Jewish community. The cabinet allows for the admission of Jewish children under the age of 17.

1939

- Germany's invasion of Poland marks the beginning of World War II, followed by declarations of war on Germany by countries in the British Commonwealth and France.

1943

- U.S. president Franklin Delano Roosevelt proposes the United Nations Relief and Rehabilitation Administration (UNRRA) to provide relief for liberated Europe. UNRRA provided billions of U.S. dollars to aid some 8 million refugees.

1944

- Harvard medical professor John Rock becomes the first person to fertilize human ova outside of the womb. His research is groundbreaking and provides hope for parents throughout the United States, but he discontinues his work.
- In Guatemala, President Ubico is overthrown and Juan José Arevalo assumes his place. Arévalo institutes a number of social reforms, including land redistribution and the establishment of a social security system.

1945

- The United Nations Charter, the treaty that establishes the purposes of the United Nations, sets criteria for membership in the United Nations, and defines the organizations and institutions within the United Nations, is signed at the United Nations Conference on International Organization.

- The United Nations Educational, Scientific and Cultural Organization (UNESCO) is founded as a specialized branch of the United Nations. As an offshoot of the League of Nations' International Commission on Intellectual Cooperation, UNESCO's mission is to foster international collaboration in the areas of science, education, and culture to promote respect for justice, the rule of law, and the human rights and freedoms proclaimed in the UN Charter. UNESCO operates five distinct programs: education, natural sciences, social sciences, culture, and communication. Julian Huxley, a prominent member of the British Eugenics Society, becomes the first director general of UNESCO.

1946

- The United Nations International Children's Emergency Fund is cofounded by Maurice Pate, an American humanitarian, and Ludwik Rajchman, a Polish bacteriologist. Created by the United Nations General Assembly, its original goal is to provide emergency food and medicine to children whose lives have been devastated by World War II. UNICEF is later renamed the United Nations Children's Fund.

1947

- India wins its independence from British colonial rule and commences a brutal and violent partition between Hindus and Muslims that results in the creation of Pakistan.

1948

- The United Nations General Assembly adopts the Universal Declaration of Human Rights, which is the first global agreement on the rights of all individuals. Authors include John Peters Humphrey of Canada, P. C. Chang of China, René Cassin of France, Charles Malik of Lebanon, and Eleanor Roosevelt of the United States.

- In the United Kingdom, the Children Act 1948 is developed in response to the more than one million children who were displaced by the war and became severely emotionally disturbed. The Children Act 1948 mandates the establishment of a Children's Committee and the appointment of a Children's Officer in every county.

- In the United States, the first recorded transracial adoption of an African-American infant by white parents takes place in Minnesota.

1949

- Following several decades of civil war and hostility, Mao Zedong officially proclaims the People's Republic of China.

Chronology

1950

- A new marriage law in China bans polygamy, foot-binding, and child marriage.

- Chairman Mao favors a pronatalistic population policy and encourages Chinese citizens to have many children.

- The Chinese Agrarian Reform Law seizes land from wealthy landowners and farmers and redistributes it to peasants.

1953

- The National Urban League Foster Care and Adoptions Project is the first national endeavor to find adoptive families for African-American children.

- Scientists perform the first successful cryopreservation of spermatozoa.

1954

- Helen Doss publishes *The Family Nobody Wanted*, a narrative about international adoption, and Jean Patton publishes *The Adopted Break Silence*, a collection of first-person narratives from adoptees.

- In a coup backed by the U.S. government, Colonel Carlos Castillo becomes president of Guatemala and halts land reforms.

1955

- A special act of congress allows the U.S. couple Bertha and Harry Holt to adopt eight Korean War orphans. The Holts are inspired by a sense of Christian charity to find American families for overseas orphans, and go on to arrange international adoptions for friends and others. Adoption professionals decry the Holts' actions as undermining decades of struggle to establish minimum standards for adoption.

- The American author, adoption advocate, and adoptive parent, Pearl S. Buck, accuses social workers of preventing the adoption of children and sustaining black market adoptions to preserve their jobs.

1956

- The Hindu Adoption and Maintenance Act (HAMA) prohibits non-Hindus from adopting Indian children. Christians, Muslims, and other non-Hindus can apply for legal guardianship of an Indian child, but they are not considered adoptive parents. The Act also restricts parents to adopting only one child of each sex.

- The Immoral Traffic (Prevention) Act in India makes the recruitment of an adult or child for the purposes of exploitation punishable by a prison term of at least one year.

ADOPTION AND SURROGATE PREGNANCY

1958

- The Indian Adoption Project is coordinated by the Child Welfare League of America through funding from the Bureau of Indian Affairs and the U.S. Children's Bureau. Over the course of several years, the project places 395 Native American children with white families throughout the United States. Though well-intentioned, cultural misinterpretations and misunderstandings lead to the unnecessary removal of some children. The project comes to an end in the late 1960s at the urging of Native American tribal leaders, who consider it a form of cultural genocide.

- In China, Chairman Mao announces his second five-year-plan, the Great Leap Forward, which seeks to intensify collectivization and promote rapid industrialization. Individual collectives are merged into massive communes, communal kitchens replace private plots, and work points replace money and wages. Mao's habit of purging dissenters leads officials within his administration to falsely report successful grain production in the communes, which results in the government's seizure of all of the communes' food, ushering in a famine that will kill 43 million people.

1959

- The United Nations General Assembly adopts the Declaration of the Rights of the Child, which defines children's rights and addresses maternal protection, healthcare, food, shelter, and education.

1960

- The psychiatrist Marshall Schechter publishes a study in which he claims that adopted children are 100 times more likely to end up in clinical populations than nonadopted children. This study contributes to the ongoing debate over the relationship between adoption and mental illness.

1961

- In the United States, the Immigration and Nationality Act incorporates provisions for international adoption.

1962

- Katherine Oettinger, chief of the U.S. Children's Bureau, leads a special conference on child abuse. It prompts proposals for legislation requiring doctors to notify law enforcement agencies when they suspect that a child is being abused.

- Between 1962 and 1972, approximately 300 million babies are born in China, constituting the country's largest population growth. The sudden population surge strains natural resources.

Chronology

1965

• The Los Angeles County Bureau of Adoptions initiates the first program to recruit single parent adopters for special needs children.

1966

• In China, Mao Zedong encourages China's youth to mobilize against the "Four Olds": Old customs, Old Habits, Old Culture, and Old Ideas. The movement to wipe out all traces of the bourgeoisie becomes known as the Cultural Revolution.

1969

• President Nixon creates the Office of Child Development to coordinate Head Start and U.S. Children's Bureau programs.

1970s

• The Indian government introduces a provision to the 1956 Hindu Adoption and Maintenance Act to allow overseas couples to apply for legal guardianship of an Indian child with the intention of adopting that child in their home countries. This allows for the first international adoptions from India.

• In Guatemala, a military program to eliminate left-wing dissenters results in the killing of 50,000 people.

1970

• Adoptions in the United States reach their statistical peak at 175,000 per year, almost 80 percent of which are arranged by agencies.

1971

• The world's first commercial sperm bank opens in New York. Within a few years, commercial sperm banks will become a highly profitable business, generating over $100,000,000 a year.

1972

• The U.S. National Association of Black Social Workers opposes transracial adoptions on the same grounds as Native American tribes who opposed the Indian Adoption Project: Placing African-American children with white parents, they argue, amounts to cultural genocide. Their campaign is unsuccessful.

• *Stanley v. Illinois* advances the rights of unwed fathers in adoption proceedings by requiring informed consent and proof of parental unfitness before termination of parental rights.

• In China, the State Council attempts to initiate a nationwide birth control campaign, with little effect.

ADOPTION AND SURROGATE PREGNANCY

1973

- In the United States, *Roe v. Wade* legalizes abortion, which, combined with new developments in contraception and access to birth control, leads to a precipitous decline in the number of infants available for adoption.

1975

- The Children Act 1975 grants adoptees in England and Wales access to their birth records.
- The Chinese government recommends a maximum family size of two children in urban areas and three to four children in rural areas.

1977

- Deng Xiaoping comes to power following the death of Chairman Mao in China.

1978

- In the United States, Congress passes the Indian Child Welfare Act, which defines Native American children as collective resources necessary for the survival of their tribes. It is one of the first laws regarding child welfare that does not consider child safety and well-being on a case-by-case basis. Without a tribal affiliation, adoption of a Native American child is made extremely difficult, if not impossible.
- In England Louise Brown, the world's first test tube baby, is born after her mother conceives through the first successful in vitro fertilization procedure.

1979

- UNESCO declares the International Year of the Child, which is signed by the United Nations secretary-general Kurt Waldheim. The proclamation is meant to call attention to the global problems that continue to affect children, including malnutrition and lack of education. A multitude of events take place around the world in celebration of the International Year of the Child to highlight children's needs.
- In China, Deng Xiaoping institutes the one-child policy, which restricts families to a maximum of one child. The national birthrate drops from 5.8 children to 2.9 children per woman.

1980

- In the United States, the Adoption Assistance and Child Welfare Act provides funding to states that support subsidy programs for special needs adoptions.

The Act also provides funding for family preservation, reunification, and abuse prevention programs.

- The Michigan attorney Noel Keane drafts the first surrogacy contract.

1981

- In Guatemala, rising guerilla activity leads to a military campaign to wipe out opponents. Military death squads systematically kill 11,000 people.

1982

- One hundred babies have been born via surrogate pregnancy in the United States.
- The Indian Supreme Court mandates that all adoption agencies must register with the government, which leads to substantially improved living conditions in orphanages.

1984

- Following the death of an Indian child en route to an overseas adoptive family, child advocate L. K. Pandey complains to the Indian Supreme Court that adoption agencies that place children with overseas families are engaging in malpractice, alleging that corruption, lack of uniform law, and weak government oversight is resulting in the abuse and sale of Indian children.

1985

- In England, the Children's Society opens the first refuge for the more than 100,000 children under 16 who run away from home every year.
- The first successful gestational surrogate pregnancy is recorded, in which one woman's ova were extracted, fertilized, and transferred to another woman's uterus.

1986

- In the United States, Mary Beth Whitehead gives birth to Baby M, but refuses to hand her over to William and Elizabeth Stern, the contracting parents. The Sterns take Whitehead to court to seek legal enforcement of the surrogacy contract, and the trial court upholds the contract, granting sole custody of Baby M to the Sterns and terminating Whitehead's parental rights. The case later goes to the New Jersey Supreme Court, which overturns the trial court's ruling and recognizes Whitehead as Baby M's mother, though primary custody remains with the Sterns.

1988

- There are 1,661 overseas adoptions of Indian children and only 398 domestic adoptions.

ADOPTION AND SURROGATE PREGNANCY

1989

- The UN Convention on the Rights of the Child, which outlines the civil, political, economic, social, and cultural rights of children, is established as international law. Countries that ratify the international convention are obligated to comply with it by international law, and compliance is monitored by the United Nations Committee on the Rights of the Child.

- In England, the Children Act of 1989 establishes a legal system for child protection regulations and addresses the concept of parental responsibility and children's rights in situations of divorce. The Act also applies to childcare providers and adoptive and foster parents. The UN monitoring committee, however, reports that the best interests of the child are not adequately reflected in this piece of legislation.

- In Guatemala, a failed attempt to overthrow the president results in a new surge in violence. The death toll since 1980 has reached 100,000, with another 40,000 men, women, and children missing.

1990s

- The Guatemalan government mandates DNA testing to ensure that a child being relinquished for adoption is, in fact, the offspring of the individual relinquishing the child.

1990

- The *Calvert v. Johnson* case in California results in a new definition of motherhood. When Anna Johnson, a gestational surrogate, refuses to relinquish the baby she is carrying for Mark and Crispina Calvert, the Calverts sue for custody and the court upholds their parental rights and defines the true mother as the woman who intends to create and raise the child.

- In India, the Central Adoption Resource Authority (CARA) is established to regulate domestic and international adoption and actively locate parents for orphaned and destitute Indian children. CARA's first priority is to locate a family domestically. If one cannot be found, a child may be considered for international adoption.

1990–1996

- Ten public inquiries are commissioned regarding concerns over children in public care in England. The reports reveal wide-ranging institutional abuse of children, which William Utting, the Chief Inspector of Social Services during the period of the highest abuse rates, blames on ignorance within the child protective system.

Chronology

1992

• China allows the adoption of Chinese children by overseas applicants for the first time, and in its first year, 206 children are adopted by American couples.

• The Adoption Law of the People's Republic of China becomes the first law to regulate domestic and international adoptions in China.

1993

• The Hague Convention on the Protection of Children and Co-operation in Respect to Intercountry Adoption establishes a framework of international regulations for intercountry adoptions. The Hague Convention mandates the creation of a central authority to oversee all intercountry adoptions as well as the assurance that every effort has been made to keep a child with his or her parents, or within his or her community of origin.

1994

• The Multiethnic Placement Act in the United States prohibits federally funded adoption agencies from denying transracial adoptions on the basis of race alone. It is the first federal law to address race in adoption.

• The worldwide sex ratio is 101.5 boys for every 100 girls. In China, this ratio is 116 boys for every 100 girls.

• Due to the skewed sex ratio in India, the Indian government proposes and later implements the Prenatal Diagnostic Technique Acts, which prohibits the disclosure of the sex of a fetus to prevent sex-selective abortion.

• A Latin American network of fertility specialists convenes in Chile to come to a consensus on the ethical and legal status of assisted reproduction.

1996

• The China Center of Adoption Affairs (CCAA) is established to regulate international adoptions by screening overseas adoption agencies, examine applications from overseas adopters, and match Chinese children with applicants.

• Newly elected president of Guatemala Alvaro Arzu conducts a purge of senior military personnel and signs peace agreements with rebels, bringing the civil war to an end.

1997

• The Adoption and Safe Families Act emphasizes permanency planning for children and the reduction of the amount of time children spend in foster care and the number of placements they experience. The Act devises a "fast track" system of adoption for children who cannot be reunited with their families.

1998

- Oregon voters pass a ballot measure that allows adult adoptees to access their birth records.

1999

- The United Kingdom is found to have the worst child poverty rate in the European Union, and Prime Minister Tony Blair announces the government's plan to eradicate child poverty within 20 years.
- A UN-backed commission reports that 93 percent of all human rights abuses during the Guatemalan civil war were committed by security forces. Officially, the Guatemalan civil war claimed 200,000 lives, with 626 Mayan villages completely wiped out.

LATE 1990S

- The approaching 2000 census and a rigid birth-planning crackdown in China leads to a surge in the number of abandoned infant girls.

2000

- One hundred and eighty-nine countries sign the United Nations' Millennium Development Declaration, which establishes new millennium goals, such as reducing poverty, reducing child mortality rates, combating AIDS and other diseases, and fostering global partnerships.
- The United Nations estimates that 200 million females around the world are demographically "missing" due to a combination of infanticide, sex-selective abortion, and female mortality. In India, 1.71 million females are missing, while 1.73 million females are missing in China.
- In India, the Juvenile Justice Act allows non-Hindus to adopt in India and removes restrictions on how many children of either sex may be adopted by a family.

2001

- The Chinese Ministry of Health issues a ban on gestational surrogacy due to the complicated process of determining the true parents, as well as how to address problems that arise from a surrogate's unwillingness to relinquish the child or the contracting parents' unwillingness to take a child born with a deformity.
- The Chinese government reduces the minimum age for adopting a child from 35 to 30 years.
- The Chinese birthrate has fallen from 2.9 children per woman in 1979 to 1.98 children per woman.

Chronology

2002

• The Care Standards Act in England revises the law on the inspection and regulation of public care institutions and creates the post of Director of Children's Rights.

• India legalizes commercial surrogacy and quickly becomes a leader in reproductive tourism as couples from developed nations flood the country in search of qualified doctors and inexpensive surrogate mothers.

• Guatemala accedes to the Hague Convention on Intercountry Adoption, but the country's failure to comply with Hague standards leads to many countries' refusal to participate in international adoption programs with Guatemala; these include Spain, Great Britain, Germany, the Netherlands, and Canada.

2003

• When eight-year-old Victoria Climbie was abused and murdered by her guardians in England in 2000, a public inquiry found that in the years leading up to her death, she had contact with social services, police, the National Health Service, local churches, and the National Society for the Prevention of Cruelty to Children, all of which noted signs of abuse but failed to take action. In 2003, Climbie's death leads to the creation of the post of Children's Commissioner and the government initiative, Every Child Matters, which aims to protect the health, safety, potential, and well-being of every child in the United Kingdom.

2004

• Sex-selective abortion in China is banned under the newly adopted Population and Family Planning Law and the Law on Maternal and Infant Health Care, though no legal punishments yet exist to enforce the ban.

• In India, CARA proposes a set of uniform guidelines for all adoption agencies operating in India; these include encouraging Indian couples to adopt homeless and orphaned children.

2005

• International adoptions in China reach an all-time high as 14,500 children are adopted by overseas families, compared with 2,500 in 1995.

2006

• In England, the Make Poverty History campaign demands trade justice, third world debt relief, and more aid. The UK Office of Communications bans the ads, claiming that they are wholly political in nature. Nevertheless, many nongovernment organizations (NGOs) launch a coalition to help ensure the government's promise to eliminate child poverty by 2020.

- In India, the Child Marriage Prohibition Act reinforces the Child Marriage Restraint Act of 1929, but includes provisions for voiding a marriage involving a minor and for creating the post of Child Marriage Prohibition Officer.

- Two hundred and seventy infants under the age of one are adopted from Guatemala every month, but only 400 children in all of the Guatemalan orphanages for the year of 2006 are under the age of 12. Charges of kidnapping and child trafficking emerge as several Guatemalan mothers claim that their children were stolen. Many kidnapped children are discovered to be en route to adoptive families in the United States.

2007

- China introduces new regulations on international adoption that severely restrict who may adopt from China. The new regulations exclude individuals under the age of 30, gay and lesbian couples, single adopters, overweight individuals, and anyone with a facial deformity.

- Some 35 percent of India's population is living below the poverty line.

- The United States ratifies the Hague Convention on Intercountry Adoption, leading to a suspension of all adoptions from non-Hague compliant countries, such as Guatemala.

- The Guatemalan Congress announces its consideration of the Integral Protection for Marriage and Family Act, which would officially redefine the family as that which consists of two married, heterosexual parents and their naturally conceived offspring. The Act would exclude single and gay parents, adopted children, and offspring conceived through assisted reproduction from the legal definition of "family." Human rights groups around the world protest.

- Fears of child abductions for organ trafficking lead a mob in Camotan, Guatemala, to kill two women suspected of killing a young local girl for her heart and kidneys.

- The U.S. Embassy in Guatemala begins mandating two DNA tests to prove a parent-child relationship when relinquishing a child for adoption.

2008

- In England, Baby P, a 17-month-old boy, is murdered by his parents while he is on the at risk register of the Haringey Social Services. The Office for Standards in Education, Children's Services, and Skills (OFSTED) investigates and confirms that between April 2007 and August 2008, 282 children died of neglect or abuse while in the public care system.

- The Chinese Family Planning Minister announces that China will maintain the one-child policy for another 10 years.

- Due to recent restrictions on who may adopt from China, the rate of U.S. adoptions from that country drops to 3,911, compared with 7,903 in 2005.
- Guatemala becomes the leading sending country for international adoptions into the United States. International adoption is the largest economic sector in Guatemala.
- In September, reports of rampant kidnappings, coercion, and adoption fraud prompts the U.S. government to officially discontinue all adoptions from Guatemala until the Guatemalan government becomes Hague compliant.

2009

- The director of Guatemala's Peace Archive announces at a press conference that children reported "missing" during the civil war, particularly in the years 1986 and 1987, were in fact kidnapped by security forces. The children of disappeared people were taken by security forces and placed in government-run orphanages and some were later sold to adoptive parents.
- The Chinese government begins to crack down on the practice of surrogacy and several surrogate mothers come forward to report forced abortions.
- In the United States, the national rate of unemployment reaches 9.8 percent in September, the highest level since 1983, and the global recession forces many adoption and surrogacy agencies to file for bankruptcy.
- Haiti is devastated by an earthquake that destroys many of its structures, leaving the deeply impoverished nation with little food, water, or shelter. Many fear for the nation's 380,000 orphans. In February, 10 Americans from an Idaho-based charity known as New Life Children's Refuge are detained on kidnapping charges for attempting to smuggle 33 Haitian children out of the country.
- China becomes the leading sending country for international adoptions into the United States, closely followed by Ethiopia, and Russia.

2010

- Russia considers suspending adoptions of its children by U.S. citizens after an American woman sends her adopted son alone on a flight back to Moscow with a note saying he was violent and had severe psychological problems.

Glossary

adoptee rights the rights of adult adoptees to access their original birth records. The term is mainly used in reference to the adoptee rights movement in the United States and elsewhere, which protests sealed records and legislation that bars adoptees from accessing their birth information.

adoption fraud forged documents and/or DNA tests to change a child's identity to that of an orphaned or abandoned child, therefore making him or her eligible for adoption. This occurs in cases of coercion or kidnapping.

adoption triad the relationship between the birth parents, the adoptive parents, and the adopted child in the arrangement of an adoption. The parties may not know one another; the triad simply refers to the parties involved in an adoption arrangement whose needs and rights must be given equal consideration.

adoptive parent an individual who is in the process of adopting a child into his or her family, thereby becoming that child's full-time parent. Positive adoption language encourages the use of the term *adoptive parent* during the arrangement, after which the adoptive parent should simply be referred to as the parent.

altruistic surrogacy a surrogate pregnancy that is arranged for a charitable purpose, usually with little or no money exchanged outside of basic medical expenses. In many countries and states, this is the only permissible surrogacy arrangement.

amniocentesis a procedure in which a needle is inserted through the abdominal wall of a pregnant woman to collect a sample of amniotic fluid, which will be tested for genetic defects. This procedure is usually done in the first trimester and may jeopardize a pregnancy.

artificial insemination a procedure in which semen is collected from the father or donor and inserted into the intended mother or surrogate's vagina with the intention of impregnation.

assisted reproduction procedures and therapies that are designed to help couples conceive. Procedures may involve hormone therapy, or they may be more invasive, such as in vitro fertilization.

assisted reproductive technology (ART) technologies and procedures that are designed to overcome or bypass certain types of infertility. Procedures may include egg retrieval, embryo transfer, and artificial insemination.

baby broker facilitator of black market adoption arrangements. A baby broker may be a doctor, lawyer, or an individual claiming to specialize in adoption arrangements, who arranges an adoption for profit. The individual may engage in adoption fraud or simply place a child without ensuring the suitability of the parents.

baby farmers individuals in the early 20th century who took in infants for a fee, usually from single mothers, and either neglected the infants until they died of starvation or sold them to adoptive parents.

bioethics the study of the ethical implications of certain biomedical procedures and technologies, such as genetic engineering, stem cell research, and assisted suicide.

birth parent a child's biological or first parent. In an adoption arrangement, the birth parent terminates parental rights in favor of the adoptive parent. The term *birth parent* was employed by the positive adoption language movement in place of natural or real parent.

caste system in Hinduism, the caste system refers to a hereditary hierarchy of social groups that are defined by economic status, occupation, and social rank. At the bottom of the caste system are the untouchables.

chaobao parents in China who adopt orphaned or abandoned children.

child abandonment the informal termination of parental rights by leaving a child to be found by someone else, or to die. Few children in orphanages around the world are true orphans, but have rather been abandoned by their parents.

child abuse the willful harm or endangerment of a child, which may include acts of violence or sexual exploitation. Generally, child abuse serves as grounds to remove a child from a home and forcibly terminate parental rights.

child neglect the willful refusal to meet a child's basic physical needs in providing such things as food, clothing, and shelter. Neglected children may become malnourished or ill.

children's rights the basic rights of all children to health, safety, nutrition, education, and life within a loving family. Many organizations have adopted the United Nations stance on children's rights as proposed in the United Nations Convention on the Rights of the Child.

child trafficking the kidnapping and transfer of children for the purposes of exploitation, such as prostitution, organ harvesting, child labor, or sale in black market adoptions. The purpose of child trafficking is to make a profit from the sale or exploitation of children.

child welfare the general well-being of children. Child welfare organizations conduct research and studies in specific regions to determine whether or not children's needs are being met through nutrition, health care, and education.

child with special needs a child with a physical or cognitive disability who requires attention and care in daily activities. In an adoption arrangement, children with special needs may include children with emotional disorders due to trauma and abuse, as well as children who were exposed to drugs and alcohol in utero.

closed adoption an adoption arrangement that emphasizes anonymity and no contact between the birth parents and the adoptive parents in the belief that this will allow all parties to move on with their lives. Until recently, closed adoption was the only arrangement available in the United States and Britain.

closed program a surrogacy arrangement in which the surrogate mother and contracting parents have no contact with one another. Few closed programs still operate, as surrogacy centers have found more success in open programs.

commercial surrogacy a surrogate pregnancy that is arranged for profit. While the surrogate mother may have altruistic motives, such as a desire to help an infertile couple become parents, she either cannot or will not carry a baby without payment.

contracting parents also called commissioning parents or intended parents, they contract with a surrogate mother who will gestate a child conceived through artificial insemination or in vitro fertilization and relinquish her parental rights upon delivery.

cryogenics the study of the effects of extremely low temperatures (-238°F) on materials. In assisted reproduction, eggs, sperm, and embryos may be cryogenically preserved for later use. Cryopreservation of embryos has sparked bioethical debates on reproduction and human dignity.

developed nation a nation with a developed economy and a high quality of life for its citizens, such as long life expectancy and a comprehensive education system. Former UN secretary-general Kofi Annan defined a developed country as "one that allows all its citizens to enjoy a free and healthy life in a safe environment." Also called an industrialized nation.

developing nation a nation with a weak economy, low levels of industrialization, and poor social programs, such as health care and education. A developing country may also have poor standards of human rights.

Glossary

domestic adoption   the adoption of a child within one's own country. In some industrialized nations, domestic adoption is complicated by a lack of adoptable, healthy infants due to the availability of contraception and abortion. Couples seeking to adopt a healthy infant may look to international adoption.

dowry   the money or land that a wife brings to her husband and his family upon marriage. In developing countries with high levels of poverty and lack of women's rights, the dowry system may make daughters a family liability.

egg donation   the process wherein a donor undertakes hormone injections and an egg retrieval procedure to supply an infertile woman with eggs. The process may be altruistic, to help a friend or relative conceive, or commercial, where the eggs are donated for a fee.

embryo donation   also referred to as embryo adoption. When a couple undergoes in vitro fertilization, excess embryos are created and stored for later use if a cycle is unsuccessful. If the cycle is successful, the parents may opt to donate excess embryos to other couples.

embryo transfer   the process during an in vitro fertilization procedure in which one or more fresh or newly thawed embryos are transferred to a woman's uterus. In a surrogate pregnancy, the resulting embryos are transferred to the surrogate's uterus.

eugenics   the belief that the human race can be improved through selective breeding. In earlier eras of western history, eugenicists often warned of adopting children, who they said were likely to be genetically defective.

exploitation   the utilization and/or abuse of a person, situation, or object for profit. Child exploitation may involve the selling of children into child labor, prostitution, or child pornography.

failure to thrive   a syndrome that manifests in infants who become depressed due to lack of affection or human contact. Symptoms include weight loss, unresponsiveness, and lack of appetite. Without intervention, the syndrome results in death.

family preservation   organized efforts through intervention programs to prevent unnecessary family separations. Family preservation programs may include drug and alcohol treatment programs, family therapy, parent education, and abuse and neglect prevention.

family romance   psychoanalytic theory developed by Sigmund Freud in which a young child fantasizes, first consciously and later unconsciously, that her parents are not her actual birth parents, but rather adoptive parents. The child may fantasize that her birth parents are actually nobility or royalty.

feeblemindedness   a theory popularized by eugenicists in the early 20th century that genetically unfit people are mentally or intellectually defective. Eugenicists also believed feeblemindedness included moral depravity, and

315

thus unmarried women who became pregnant were feebleminded by evidence of their actions.

fetal abuse   proposed charge against a woman who is caught abusing drugs and alcohol during pregnancy. The term is politically charged and highly contentious, as it threatens to encroach on abortion rights.

fetal alcohol syndrome   physical and mental disabilities caused by alcohol abuse during pregnancy. Children born with fetal alcohol syndrome tend to have visible facial deformities as well as problems with learning, communication, memory, and attention span.

feticide   epidemic of abortions, commonly used in reference to sex-selective abortion.

field studies   studies that aim to gather statistical information on adoption, including how many children are adopted, where adoptions occur, who is adopting, the ages of the children adopted, and the types of adoptions occurring. Field studies differ from outcome studies, which research the effects and experiences of adoption and foster care.

foster adoption   the process of adopting a child from foster care. In previous years, parents who wished to adopt were discouraged from taking in foster children, as the foster care system is designed to prioritize birth family reunification. Today, potential adoptive parents are encouraged to consider foster children.

foster care   the public care system for children who cannot safely remain at home with their parents. Foster care was designed as an alternative to orphanages and institutions, which could not provide individualized care or attention.

gender roles   the socially constructed traits and characteristics ascribed to individuals based on their sex. In many cultures, the feminine gender role includes a nurturing, maternal quality and greater emphasis on the home and family, while masculine gender roles tend to include a more public persona and an aggressive, protective quality.

gestational surrogacy   a surrogate pregnancy arrangement in which the surrogate mother is not genetically related to the fetus. Gestational surrogacy involves in vitro fertilization, using either the contracting mother's eggs or donated eggs. The embryos conceived are then transferred to the surrogate's uterus.

home study   steps in the adoption process that include education and parent training, interviews to determine how to match the parents with a child, home inspections, references, and background checks.

hukou   Chinese household registration. Similar to a birth certificate or social security number in the United States, a Chinese child must have a *hukou* to receive basic immunizations and enroll in school. Children who have been illegally adopted often do not have *hukous* and therefore are barred from many public programs.

illegitimacy   the event in which a child is born to unmarried parents. In many developed countries, unwed pregnancy and single parent homes have become more common and tolerated, but in past decades illegitimacy was considered a moral taint.

indentured servitude   the state of being an unpaid servant for a specific amount of time, often to pay off a debt. In early America and other nations, orphans were occasionally placed in homes as indentured servants.

independent adoption   also known as a private adoption, an independent adoption is arranged without the use of an agency. Adoptive parents may find a child to adopt on their own, or with the help of an attorney.

infanticide   the practice of willfully murdering an infant. In some cultures, particularly those that do not believe that an infant is fully human until a specific age, infanticide is practiced as a form of population control.

infertility   the inability to conceive naturally. In the United States, infertility is diagnosed if conception has not occurred after 12 consecutive months of having sex without using a method of birth control.

international adoption   the adoption of a child from a country other than one's own. In recent years, this has proven the most effective way to adopt an infant.

in vitro fertilization (IVF)   a procedure whereby a woman's eggs are retrieved (unless donated eggs are required), fertilized with sperm from the intended father or a donor, with the resulting embryos transferred to the intended mother's or a surrogate's womb.

kinship   familial relationships, which have traditionally been based on genetic relatedness in most cultures. With the advent of gamete donation, surrogate pregnancy, and various forms of adoption, the lines of kinship are being redrawn to include those who are not genetically related.

kinship care   the informal adoption or fostering of a child by relatives other than his or her parents. Kinship care arrangements commonly include grandparents, aunts, or uncles, and are arranged independent of a child welfare organization.

matching   the act of determining which children would do best with which parents. In previous years, matching included considerations of race, religion, and I.Q., and the process was viewed as one of finding the best child for a set of adoptive parents, rather than finding the best parents for a parentless child.

minimum standards   the basic standards of the adoption process as agreed upon after several decades of struggle between social workers, the government, and adoption agencies. Minimum standards include a basic investigation into the suitability of the adoptive parents, as well as a consideration for the rights of children.

missing females   the number of females around the world who should be alive, but, demographically, are not. These females are missing due to abandonment, sex-selective abortion, infanticide, unregistered births, malnutrition, disease, and maternal mortality.

ni ying   the ancient Chinese practice of female infanticide in which a midwife drowns a female child in a bucket of water.

open adoption   an adoption arrangement in which the birth mother or birth parents maintain contact with the child they placed for adoption. Levels of openness vary, but the open adoption process involves meetings between the birth parents and the adoptive parents, an exchange of information about one another, and sustained contact.

open program   a type of surrogacy arrangement in which the surrogate meets and develops a relationship with the contracting parents. Ongoing contact following the delivery of the baby is often sustained through yearly birthday cards, pictures, and letters.

orphanage   an institution that houses orphans. In previous years, particularly in United States and European history, an orphanage was distinct from a foundling hospital, where abandoned and destitute children were housed. Most developed countries have moved away from institutions and now place children in private family homes.

outcome studies   studies of the effects and successes or failures of adoption and foster care systems. Outcome studies differ from field studies, which survey trends and statistics within adoption and foster care systems.

over-quota birth   a birth that exceeds the maximum number of children allowed per family in China. This varies throughout the country, as different regions have different birth-planning policies. In rural areas, families are allowed to have two children, while urban families may have only one.

patriarchy   a community organization in which men guide and make decisions for the community. The social organization emanates from the family unit, in which the father heads the family. In a patriarchal society, men act as leaders and women are meant to be submissive.

patrilineal family   a family in which descent and heritage is based on the male line. Family names based on the father's last name is a visible reference to the historical tradition of tracing kinship lines through male relatives only.

patrilocal family   a family that is organized around a father and/or sons. Upon marriage, a woman relocates and becomes a member of her husband's family, which is headed by the eldest male. Women often play a subservient role in the patrilocal family, as their value is determined by the number of sons they, themselves, bring to the family.

Glossary

placing out   the act of placing children in private family homes rather than collecting them together in an institutional setting. The practice of placing out developed in response to overcrowding in orphanages and other institutions.

pro-natalist policy   political policy that encourages rampant reproduction to increase the population. At one time communist leaders evidenced pro-natalist positions. Upon proclaiming the People's Republic of China, Mao Zedong encouraged Chinese citizens to reproduce prodigiously. Former Romanian president Nicolae Ceauşescu once mandated a minimum birth rate of five children per woman.

receiving country   in an international adoption arrangement, the receiving country is the country to which the child relocates.

relinquishment   the act of pursuing legal channels to officially place one's child for adoption by another set of parents. In the past, relinquishment was referred to as surrendering or putting up for adoption.

reproductive tourism   refers to the trend of traveling to other countries to seek infertility treatments that are not offered or are too expensive in one's home country. Scholars have proposed different terms for such travel, such as *cross-border fertility treatment.*

reunification   the process of reuniting a family that experienced separation due to child endangerment. Reunification is the primary goal of the foster care system, and intervention programs are being developed to prevent unnecessary separation.

sealed records   an adopted child's confidential birth records, including the birth mother's name and information and the child's original birth certificate. Adult adoptees are not allowed to access their birth records in many states of the United States, while other countries, such as England, have passed legislation to open birth records.

selective reduction   the process of reducing the number of embryos or fetuses that have implanted during in vitro fertilization (IVF). This is often a painful process for parents who do not want to risk miscarriage or birth defects due to a multiple pregnancy, and one that can be avoided by transferring no more than two embryos at a time.

semi-closed adoption   an adoption arrangement whereby the birth parents and adoptive parents do not meet, but exchange limited information to develop an understanding of the child's background and future.

semi-open adoption   an adoption arrangement in which the birth parents and adoptive parents may meet and exchange limited information, but do not maintain future relationships outside of annual letters and pictures.

sending country   in an international adoption arrangement, the sending country is the country from which the adopted child originates.

sex ratio the corresponding number of boys to girls in a specific age group. The worldwide sex ratio at birth in 2008 was 1.7 males for every 1 female, which may be written 1.7:1, or 1.7/1.

sex-selective abortion the abortion of a fetus due to its sex. In India and China, sex-selective abortion refers almost exclusively to the abortion of female fetuses, a practice that is now illegal but poorly enforced in both countries.

sibling group in adoption arrangements, a sibling group refers to a set of siblings that have been removed from their home and must be adopted together. Child welfare organizations emphasize the importance of keeping siblings together, unless there is evidence of sibling abuse.

social work the professional field that addresses individual rights and protections for all members of the community. Once derided as women's charity work, early social workers struggled to professionalize their field, as well as the adoption and foster care systems.

son preference the tendency among patriarchal communities to favor sons over daughters, which may lead to sex-selective abortion, infanticide, abandonment, or the neglect, abuse, and malnutrition of female children in favor of male children.

Soviet bloc the former communist states of eastern and central Europe, including Russia (Soviet Union), Poland, East Germany, Czechoslovakia, Hungary, Romania, Bulgaria, Yugoslavia, and Albania.

special needs child any child waiting to be adopted who is older, a member of an ethnic minority group, part of a sibling group, mentally disturbed, or physically disabled. A special needs child is any child who is generally more difficult to place.

sperm donation the act of providing semen to a fertility clinic or sperm bank that will enable a couple experiencing male infertility to conceive. The donation may be altruistic and the donor may be a friend or relative, or it may be commercial and performed in exchange for payment.

stepparent adoption the adoption of a child by that child's stepparent. Stepparent adoptions now constitute a large portion of all adoptions in the United States, and adopters are usually stepfathers.

surrogate pregnancy an arrangement in which a couple experiencing infertility, usually due to the wife's inability to carry a pregnancy to term, contracts with another woman who will conceive and deliver a child for them. The surrogate may be artificially inseminated or undergo in vitro fertilization, and she may or may not be paid for her service.

traditional surrogacy a surrogate pregnancy that is established through artificial insemination. In this arrangement, the contracting father usually supplies the sperm, and the surrogate mother is genetically related to the child she produces.

Glossary

transracial adoption   an adoption in which the child is of a different racial or ethnic group than the adoptive parents. In the United States, the vast majority of transracial adoption arrangements involve white adoptive parents and children of color.

ultrasound technology   ultrasound is a cyclic sound pressure that penetrates the surface of a material to provide a reflection of the inside. The most common usage of ultrasound technology is in sonography, which provides images of fetuses in the womb.

waiting child   a child who is available to be adopted. The term was developed by the positive adoption language movement to replace the term *adoptable child.*

women's rights   humanitarian movement around the world to protect women's rights to education, health and reproductive care, freedom from domestic and sexual violence, vocational skill development, contraception, and abortion.

workhouse   an institution developed in 17th-century England to provide shelter for impoverished and destitute people. There, they were forced to labor intensively to earn their food and shelter, and life was intentionally designed to be less sustaining than that outside the workhouse.

Index

Page numbers in **boldface** indicate major treatment of a subject. Page numbers followed by *c* indicate chronology entries. Page numbers followed by *f* indicate figures. Page numbers followed by *g* indicate glossary entries.

A

AARP Grandparent
  Information Center
  229
abandonment 48,
  50–51
  in China 50–51, 55,
    57, 288*c*, 308*c*
  Christianity on 288*c*
  Council of Vaisons
    on 288*c*
  definition of 313*g*
  in India 50–51, 64
abortion
  legalization of 4, 10,
    34, 304*c*
  sex-selective 51
  definition of 320*g*
  in India 67, 307*c*
Abraham (biblical figure)
  16, 216*b*, 287*c*
abuses
  adoption ix, 51
  child
    definition of 313*g*
    drug use in
      pregnancy as 5

fetal 5
  definition of 316*g*
  v. women's
    reproductive
    rights 5
  in Great Britain
    306*c*, 309*c*
  in Guatemala 51–52,
    76, 77, 171–176,
    311*c*
  in Haiti 311*c*
surrogacy 20–21
Action Alliance for
  Children 229
Addams, Jane 295*c*
adoptable child 321*g*
Adopted Break Silence,
  The (Patton) 301*c*
adoptee rights 312*g*
adoption **6–16**
  in China 53–61,
    138–148, 294*c*
  cost of 22
  definition of 6
  ethics in **21–22**
  in Great Britain
    68–74, 165–167

in Guatemala 75–81,
  171–181
in India 61–68,
  152–158
international. *See*
  international
  adoption
language of 6–7
monetary
  reimbursement
  for 11
motivations for ix
no guarantee of
  success in
  15–16
participants in,
  characteristics of
  39–40
race and 7, 21–22,
  23, 32–34, 43, 79,
  204*f,* 300*c*, 303*c*
reproductive rights
  movement and
  34
types of 7–16
in United States
  28–35

323

children born to
single mothers
relinquished for
208*f*
demand for
206*f*–207*f*
percent of all, by
type 203*f*
preferences in
204*f*–205*f*
Adoption Act (Britain,
1926) 70, 71–72
"Adoption Agencies
Shun U.K.: Developing
Countries Brand
British Safeguards
as 'Unsuitable' for
Children Who Need
a Family" (Hill, 2006)
165–167
Adoption and Children
Act (Britain, 2002) 74
Adoption and Safe
Families Act (1997) 13,
307*c*
*Adoption and the Family
System* (Reitz and
Watson) 22
Adoption Assistance
and Child Welfare
Act (1980) 40, 42–43,
304*c*–305*c*
adoption fraud
definition of 312*g*
DNA tests for
preventing 77,
171–176, 306*c*, 310*c*
in Guatemala 51–52,
76, 77, 171–176,
311*c*
Hague Convention
and 51–52
Adoption Law of the
People's Republic of
China (1992) 60, 307*c*

Adoption of Children Act
(Britain, 1926) 298*c*
Adoption of Children Act
(Massachusetts, 1851)
28, 93–95, 293*c*
Adoptions Tracking
Service (ATS) 52
adoption triad 6, 312*g*
Adoption UK 74
adoptive parent(s) 6, 7,
312*g*
characteristics of 40
in China 57–58
in closed adoption
8–9
in Great Britain
71–72
in Guatemala 78–79
in independent
adoption 15
in India 64–65
in open adoption
7–8
in semi-closed
adoption 9–10
in semi-open
adoption 9
in U.S., perceptions
of 209*f*
Adult Survivors of Child
Abuse 230
advertisements, for
surrogates 22
African American(s)
adoption preferences
against 21–22, 43
adoption services
denied to 32
first adoption
endeavor for 301*c*
kinship adoption by
14, 32
transracial adoption
of 33, 34
age, U.S. adoptions by
202*f*, 204*f*

altruistic surrogacy 20,
38, 312*g*
Alvarado, Pedro de 290*c*
American Adoptions 22
American Association of
Social Workers 298*c*
American Federation of
Labor 295*c*
American Fertility
Association 230
American Foster Care
Resources, Inc.
230–231
Americanization
Indian Adoption
Project and 33–34
orphan trains and
29–30
American Society for
Reproductive Medicine
231
American Surrogacy
Center, The 231
American Youth
Congress 299*c*
amniocentesis 51, 312*g*
ancestor worship, in
China 53–54
Andrew, Clara
296*c*–297*c*
Annie E. Casey
Foundation 231–232
Arévalo, Juan José 299*c*
Aristotle 216*b*, 288*c*
Aristotle's Master Piece
290*c*
arranged marriage, in
India 64–65, 298*c*,
310*c*
ART. *See* assisted
reproductive
technology; *specific
types*
artificial insemination
36, 312*g*
Arzu, Alvaro 307*c*

Index

Asia, adoptions from 22
Assisted Human
  Reproductive Act
  (Canada, 2004) 52
assisted reproduction,
  definition of 313g
assisted reproductive
  technology (ART) 4–5,
  34–35, 313g. *See also*
  specific types
ATS. *See* Adoptions
  Tracking Service
Australia, as receiving
  country 50

B

baby broker 313g
Baby Cotton case 71
baby farmers 294c, 313g
Baby M case 21, **36–37,**
  42, 107–116, 305c
Baby P 310c
Bachrach, Christina
  39–40
Barnardo, Thomas
  216b–217b, 293c–294c
Bastard Nation 232
Belarus, as sending
  country 200f
Belgium, as receiving
  country 201f
Bentham, Jeremy 292c
Berger, Oscar 217b
Bernard, Viola 217b
Bharadwaj, Aditya 63–
  64, 152–158
"binding out" 288c
Binet Scale 30, 296c
biological parent. *See*
  birth parent(s)
birth control 4, 10, 34
birth parent(s) 6
  characteristics of
  39–40
  in China 57–58

in closed adoption
  8–9
definition of 313g
in Great Britain
  71–72
in Guatemala 78–79
in independent
  adoption 15
in India 64–65
in open adoption
  7–8
sealed records on
  30–31, 319g
in semi-closed
  adoption 9–10
in semi-open
  adoption 9
in U.S., racial
  differences in views
  of 210f
Blair, Tony 74, 308c
borstals 295c–296c
Brace, Charles Loring
  29–30, 95–99, 217b–
  218b, 293c
Brazil, as sending country
  200f
Brehon Laws 290c
Breo, Dennis L. 101–104
British Association for
  Adoption and Fostering
  232
broker, baby 313g
Brown, Louise 4, 35, 38,
  218b, 304c
Buck, Pearl S. 218b, 301c
Buffalo News 79
Bulgaria, as sending
  country 200f
Bureau for Information
  Exchange Among
  Child-Helping
  Organizations 297c
Bureau of Citizenship
  and Immigration
  Services 77

Bureau of Indian Affairs
  33, 302c
Buxton, Dorothy 297c

C

California, surrogacy in
  39, 43, 306c
Calvert, Crispina 39,
  218b–219b, 306c
Calvert, Mark 39,
  218b–219b, 306c
Calvert v. Johnson
  38–39, 306c
Cambodia
  kinship care in 13, 14
  as sending country
  49
  suspension of
  adoptions from 51
Canada
  Assisted Human
  Reproductive Act
  (2004) 52
  as receiving country
  50, 76
Cantwell, Nigel 80
CARA. *See* Central
  Adoption Resource
  Authority
Care Standards Act
  (Britain, 2002) 309c
Casa Guatemala
  232–233
Cassin, René 300c
caste system, definition
  of 313g
Castillo, Carlos 301c
Catholic Home Bureau
  295c
CCAA. *See* China Center
  of Adoption Affairs
Central Adoption
  Resource Authority
  (CARA, India) 64, 233,
  306c, 309c

Chamberlain, Neville 299*c*

Chang, P. C. 300*c*

chaobao, definition of 313*g*

Chapin, Henry Dwight 219*b*

child abandonment 48, **50–51**
  in China 50–51, 55, 57, 288*c*, 308*c*
  Christianity on 288*c*
  Council of Vaisons on 288*c*
  definition of 313*g*
  in India 50–51, 64

child abuse
  definition of 313*g*
  fetal 5

child health, Millenium Development Goals on 213*f*

child labor 290*c*, 292*c*, 295*c*

Childlessness Overcome Through Surrogacy (COTS) 233–234

child marriage 64–65, 298*c*, 310*c*

Child Marriage Prohibition Act (India, 2006) 310*c*

Child Marriage Restraint Act (India, 1929) 298*c*, 310*c*

child neglect
  definition of 313*g*
  drug use in pregnancy as 5

Children Act (Britain, 1948) 300*c*

Children Act (Britain, 1975) 71–72, 304*c*

Children Act (Britain, 1989) 306*c*

Children and Young Persons Act (Britain, 1933) 298*c*–299*c*

Children Now 234

Children's Bureau, U.S. 248–249, 296*c*, 297*c*, 302*c*, 303*c*

Children's Commissioner (Britain) 309*c*

Children's Defense Fund 234

Children's Partnership, The 234–235

children's rights
  in China 59
  definition of 313*g*

Children's Society (Britain) 305*c*

Child Rights Information Network (CRIN) 235

child trafficking 51–52
  in Cambodia 51
  definition of 314*g*
  in Guatemala 51–52, 76, 77, 171–176, 311*c*
  Hague Convention and 51–52

child welfare, definition of 314*g*

Child Welfare League of America (CWLA) 32, 33, 99–101, 235–236, 297*c*, 298*c*, 302*c*

child with special needs 7, 12, 314*g*

China **53–61**
  adoption in 53–61, 138–148, 294*c*
  adoption rules of 12, 307*c*
  adoptive parents in 57–58
  birth parents in 57–58

child abandonment in 50–51, 55, 57, 288*c*, 308*c*

children's rights in 59

contracting parents in 58

documents of/on 138–151

foot-binding in 289*c*, 301*c*

gender inequalities in 50–51, 55, 56, 308*c*

global role of 54–55

one-child policy of 49, 55–56, 58, 60–61, 304*c*, 310*c*

as sending country 49, 54–55, 76, 200*f*

standardization efforts in 60–61

surrogacy restrictions in 18, 55, 56–57, 58, 148–151, 308*c*

surrogate mothers in 58

unique circumstances in 59–60

women's rights in 59–60

China Center of Adoption Affairs (CCAA) 60, 145–148, 307*c*

"China Grapples with Legality of Surrogate Motherhood" (2006) 148–151

China.org.cn 148–151

Chinese Agrarian Reform Law (1950) 301*c*

Christianity 288*c*

Clarke, Kim 10

Climbie, Victoria 309*c*

Clinic of Child Development, Yale 296*c*

Index

closed adoption **8–9**
  advantages of 8
  definition of 314*g*
  disadvantages of 8–9
  as obsolete term 9
closed program
  (surrogacy) **20–21**, 36,
  314*g*
Code of Hammurabi 6,
  287*c*
Colombia, as sending
  country 200*f*
color-blindness 33
commercial surrogacy
  43, 314*g*. *See also*
  reproductive tourism
Concerned United
  Birthparents (CUB)
  236
confidentiality
  open adoption v.
  7–8
  sealed records and
  30–31, 319*g*
Confucian patriarchy 56
Conroy, Stephen 219*b*
consent for adoption,
  revocation of 11, 15
contracting parents
  characteristics of
  41–42
  in China 58
  in closed program
  20–21
  definition of 314*g*
  in gestational
  surrogacy 18–19
  in Great Britain
  72–73
  in Guatemala 79–80
  in India 65–66
  in open program
  19–20
  in traditional
  surrogacy 17–18

Corpus Juris Civilis
  288*c*–289*c*
cost
  of adoption 22
  of surrogate
  pregnancy 18–19
  of in vitro fertilization
  18–19, 53
Cotton, Kim 71,
  162–165, 167–171,
  219*b*
Council of Vaisons 288*c*
CRIN. *See* Child Rights
  Information Network
cross-border fertility
  treatment 319*g*
cross-racial adoption. *See*
  transracial adoption
cryogenics 314*g*
CUB. *See* Concerned
  United Birthparents
custody battles
  Baby M 21, **36–37**,
  42, 107–116, 305*c*
  Calvert v. Johnson
  38–39, 306*c*
  Great Britain 73–74
Custody of Infants Act
  (Britain, 1839) 293*c*
CWLA. *See* Child
  Welfare League of
  America

D

Daly, Laura Beth 81
Damelio, Jennifer 43
*Dangerous Classes of New
  York and Twenty Years'
  Work Among Them, The*
  (Brace, 1872) 95–99
day nurseries 293*c*
"Declaration of the
  Rights of American
  Youth" (1935) 299*c*

Declaration of the Rights
  of the Child (1923)
  298*c*
Declaration of the Rights
  of the Child (1959)
  302*c*
De Donis 289*c*
Deng Xiaoping
  219*b*–220*b*, 304*c*
Denmark, as receiving
  country 50, 62, 201*f*
developed nation 314*g*
developing nations 314*g*
Dickens, Charles 292*c*
DNA tests, for
  Guatemalan adoptions
  77, 171–176, 306*c*, 310*c*
domestic adoption 315*g*
domestic infant adoption
  10–11
Doss, Carl 33, 220*b*
Doss, Helen 33, 220*b*,
  301*c*
dowry
  definition of 315*g*
  in India 67
drug exposure, prenatal
  5

E

eastern Europe. *See also
  specific countries*
  adoptions from 22
economic disparities, and
  international adoption
  49
Edwards, Robert 35,
  220*b*
egalitarian approach, in
  surrogacy 42
egg donation 315*g*
Elementary Education
  Act (Britain, 1870)
  294*c*

Elementary Education
Act (Britain, 1880)
295c
Elizabethan Poor Laws
70, 290c, 291c, 292c
Embassy of United
States, Guatemala 176
embryo donation 315g
embryo transfer 35, 315g
*Essay on the Principle
of Population, An*
(Malthus) 291c
ethics **21–23**
of adoption 21–22
of surrogate
pregnancy 18,
22–23
Ethiopia, as sending
country 49, 200f
eugenics **30**
definition of 315g
post–World War II
rejection of 32
Europe. *See also specific
countries*
international
adoptions to 201f
Evan B. Donaldson
Adoption Institute 11,
236
Evangelical Child and
Family Agency 22
Every Child Matters
(Britain) 309c
exploitation 315g
exposure 288c

F

Factory Acts (Britain,
1802) 291c
failure to thrive 315g
Families USA Foundation
236–237
Families with Children
from China (FCC) 237

family
definition of 3–6, 16
as institution of social
organization ix
family adoption 13–14,
32
Family Equality Council
237
*Family Nobody Wanted,
The* (Doss) 33, 301c
family preservation
315g
family romance 315g
fathers. *See* adoptive
parent(s); birth
parent(s); contracting
parents
FCC. *See* Families with
Children from China
feeblemindedness 30
definition of
315g–316g
Goddard and 30,
222b, 296c
female(s)
fate of infants 50–51,
55, 56, 66–67, 307c,
308c
missing 66, 308c,
318g
rights of. *See* women's
rights
female feticide 51, 67,
307c, 320g
Ferre Institute 237–238
fertility drugs 35
fertility rates, total world
(1998) 211f
fertility tourism. *See*
reproductive tourism
fetal abuse 5
definition of 316g
v. women's
reproductive rights
5

fetal alcohol syndrome
316g
fetal rights 5
feticide
definition of 316g
female 51, 67, 307c,
320g
Fielding, Henry 29
field studies 316g
50/50 rule, in India 62
financial incentives, for
hard-to-place children
42–43, 304c–305c
First Mothers Action
Group 7
Fletcher, Samuel, Jr.
294c
Florida
race and adoption
in 32
surrogacy in 36
foot-binding, in China
289c, 301c
For Love and Money
(Cotton and Winn)
162–165
Forrest, Derek
220b–221b
foster adoption **12–13**
definition of 316g
infant adoption v.
10–11, 12
foster care 30, 316g
foundling hospitals 291c
France, as receiving
country 49, 201f
fraud, adoption
definition of 312g
DNA tests for
preventing 77,
171–176, 306c, 310c
in Guatemala 51–52,
76, 77, 171–176,
311c
Hague Convention
and 51–52

Freud, Anna 221*b*
Freud, Sigmund 221*b*
Freudian theory 30, 31
Frick surrogacy center
   21, 36–37

G

gay couples
   in Great Britain 74
   Guatemalan
      definition of family
      and 75, 177–181,
      310*c*
   surrogacy issues for
      19, 23
*Gay Couple's Journey
   through Surrogacy:
   Intended Fathers, A*
   (Menichiello) 19, 23
gender inequalities
   50–51
   in China 50–51, 55,
      56, 308*c*
   female feticide 51,
      67, 307*c*, 320*g*
   in India 50–51,
      66–67, 307*c*
   missing females 66,
      308*c*, 318*g*
   son preference
      50–51, 55, 56, 67,
      307*c*, 320*g*
gender roles, definition
   of 316*g*
genetic fitness (eugenics)
   30
   definition of 315*g*
   post–World War II
      rejection of 32
Gentleman, Amelia
   158–162
Germany, as receiving
   country 76, 201*f*
Gesell, Arnold
   221*b*–222*b*, 296*c*

"gestational carriers" 38
gestational surrogacy
   18–19, 38–39
   definition of 316*g*
   first successful 38,
      305*c*
   IVF costs in 18–19
   success rate of 18
Ghana, as sending
   country 200*f*
globalization 48
Goddard, Henry Herbert
   30, 222*b*, 296*c*
Graham, James 291*c*
Great Britain 8, 10,
   68–74
   abuse in 306*c*, 309*c*
   adoptive parents in
      71–72
   birth parents in
      71–72
   contracting parents
      in 72–73
   documents of/on
      162–171
   global role of 69–70
   as receiving country
      69, 76, 165–167,
      201*f*
   standardization
      efforts in 74
   surrogate mothers in
      72–73
   unique circumstances
      in 73–74
Growing Generations
   238
Guatemala **75–81**, 292*c*
   abuses in 51–52, 76,
      77, 171–176, 311*c*
   adoptive parents in
      78–79
   birth parents in
      78–79
   contracting parents
      in 79–80

DNA tests in 77,
   171–176, 306*c*,
   310*c*
documents of/on
   171–181
global role of 76–77
Hague Convention
   and 51–52, 76,
   80–81, 309*c*, 311*c*
Integral Protection
   of Marriage and
   Family Act (2007)
   75, 177–181,
   310*c*
reproductive tourism
   in 53, 76–80
as sending country
   49, 76, 200*f*, 311*c*
standardization
   efforts in 80–81
surrogate mothers in
   79–80
suspension of
   adoptions from
   51, 76, 81, 309*c*,
   311*c*
unique circumstances
   in 80
"Guatemala Adoption
   Fraud: Couple Pursues
   Baby's Identity/
   California Pair Wanted
   Girl but Decided to
   Expose 'Horrifying'
   System" (Llorca, 2008)
   171–176
Guatemala Adoptive
   Families Network 238
Guttmacher Institute 75,
   238–239

H

Hagar (biblical figure)
   16, 216*b*, 287*c*

Hague Complaint
  Registry 52
Hague Conference on
  Private International
  Law (HCCH) 239
Hague Convention on
  Protection of Children
  and Co-operation in
  Respect of Intercountry
  Adoption (1993) ix,
  12, 48, **51–52,** 82,
  117–133, 307*c*
    and Guatemala
      51–52, 76, 80–81,
      309*c*, 311*c*
    U.S. ratification of
      310*c*
Hague Evaluation 239
Haiti
  earthquake aftermath
    in 311*c*
  as sending country
    49, 200*f*
HAMA. *See* Hindu
  Adoption and
  Maintenance Act
Hammurabi, Code of 6,
  287*c*
Hands of Help 240
hard-to-place children 6,
  7, 12, 42–43
HCCH. *See* Hague
  Conference on Private
  International Law
Head Start 303*c*
Health and Human
  Services Department
  (HHS) 40
Health and Morals
  of Apprentices Act
  (Britain, 1802) 291*c*
"healthy infants" 21–22
heihaizi ("illegal" child)
  59

HHS. *See* Health and
  Human Services
  Department
Hill, Angela 165–167
Hindu Adoption and
  Maintenance Act
  (HAMA, India, 1956)
  62, 64, 301*c*, 303*c*
history
  China 55–57
  Great Britain 70–71
  Guatemala 77–78
  India 63–64
  United States 28–39
*History of Tom Jones, a
  Foundling, A* (Fielding)
  29
Holland, as receiving
  country 62
Holt, Bertha 81–82,
  222*b*, 301*c*
Holt, Harry 81–82, 222*b*,
  301*c*
Holt International 76,
  240
home study
  definition of 316*g*
  first law on
    (Minnesota) 297*c*
Horlock, Carole 70
*How Foster Children
  Turn Out* (Theis) 298*c*
hukou (household
  registration) 59,
  316*g*–317*g*
Hull-House 295*c*
human rights ix–x,
  59–60
Human Rights Watch 59,
  177–181, 240–241
HumanTrafficking.org
  241
Humphrey, John Peters
  300*c*

I
ICMART. *See*
  International
  Committee Monitoring
  Assisted Reproductive
  Technologies
illegitimacy
  concept of **28–29,**
    31, 32
  definition of 317*g*
  psychoanalysis and
    32
  race and 32
  sealed records and
    30–31
ILRC. *See* Immigrant
  Legal Resource Center
Immigrant Legal
  Resource Center
  (ILRC) 241
Immigration and
  Nationality Act (1961)
  302*c*
Immoral Traffic
  (Prevention) Act (India,
  1956) 301*c*
"In a Chinese
  Orphanage" (Thurston)
  138–145
indentured servitude 30,
  317*g*
independent adoption
  15
    definition of 317*g*
    as high-risk activity
      ix
    legality of 15
Independent Adoption
  Center 9
India 9, 18, **61–68**
  adoptive parents in
    64–65
  arranged/child
    marriage in 64–65,
    298*c*, 310*c*

Index

birth parents in
64–65
child abandonment in
50–51, 64
contracting parents
in 65–66
documents of/on
152–162
gender inequalities in
50–51, 66–67, 307c
global role of 62–63
reproductive tourism
in 53, 62–63, 66,
158–162, 309c
as sending country
49, 62, 67–68,
200f
standardization
efforts in 67–68
surrogate mothers in
65–66
unique circumstances
in 66–67
Indian Adoption Project
33–34, 302c, 303c
Indian Child Welfare Act
(1978) 34, 304c
Indian Council of
Medical Research
241–242
Indian Medical Council
68
"India Nurtures
Business of Surrogate
Motherhood"
(Gentleman, 2008)
158–162
individualism, extreme
x
Industrial Schools Act
(1857) 293c
infant adoption
domestic 10–11
international. See
international
adoption

infanticide 50–51, 55, 57
infertility 3–6
Integral Protection of
Marriage and Family
Act (Guatemala, 2007)
75, 177–181, 310c
intercountry adoption 7.
See also international
adoption
international adoption 7,
11–12. See also specific
countries
economic disparities
and 49
Hague Convention on
ix, 12, 48, 51–52,
82, 117–133, 307c
and Guatemala
51–52, 76,
80–81, 309c,
311c
U.S. ratification of
310c
receiving countries
in 48, 49–50, 201f,
319f
sending countries in
48, 49–50, 200f,
319g
as social injustice 5
suspension of,
countries under 51,
76, 81, 309c, 311c
UNICEF position on
133–135
International Committee
Monitoring Assisted
Reproductive
Technologies
(ICMART) 242
International Society for
the Prevention of Child
Abuse and Neglect
(ISPCAN) 242–243

International Surrogacy
Partners (Ukraine)
135–138
International Year of the
Child 304c
in vitro fertilization (IVF)
4, 35, 73, 304c
cost of 18–19, 53
definition of 317g
reproductive tourism
and 52–53. See
also reproductive
tourism
in surrogate
pregnancy 16–17,
18–19, 38–39
I.Q. testing 30, 296c
Ireland, as receiving
country 201f
ISPCAN. See
International Society
for the Prevention
of Child Abuse and
Neglect
Italy, as receiving country
50, 201f
IVF. See in vitro
fertilization

J

Jamaica, as sending
country 200f
Jebb, Eglantyne 297c,
298c
Jewish children, in World
War II 299c
Jigsaw 72
Johnson, Anna 39,
222b–223b, 306c
Johnson, Kay 58
justice x, 5
Justinian I (Byzantine
emperor) 223b,
288c–289c

Juvenile Justice Act
(India, 2000) 308c

K

Kallikak, Deborah 223b
Kallikak Family: A Study
in the Heredity of
Feeble-Mindedness, The
(Goddard) 30, 223b,
296c
Kazakhstan, as sending
country 49, 200f
Keane, Noel 21,
35–36, 101–104, 223b,
305c
kidnapping
in Guatemala 76,
171–176, 311c
Haitian charges of
311c
kinship, definition of
3–6, 16, 317g
kinship care **13–14,** 32,
317g
Kyrgyzstan, as sending
country 200f

L

labor, child 290c, 292c,
295c
language, positive
adoption 7
Lathrop, Julia 296c
Latin America, adoptions
from 22
Latin American Network
for Reproductive
Medicine 243
Latin American Parents
Association 243
law. See also specific laws
China 55–57
Great Britain
70–71
Guatemala 77–78

India 63–64
United States
28–39
Law on Maternal and
Infant Health Care
(China, 2004) 309c
"Letter to the
Guatemalan Congress
Regarding Marriage
and Family Law" (2007)
177–181
Levin, Richard 36,
223b–224b
Liberia, as sending
country 200f
Llorca, Juan Carlos
171–176
Los Angeles County
Bureau of Adoptions
303c
Louise Wise Services
(LWS) 243–244
Louisiana, race and
adoption in 32
Love Basket 21–22
LWS. See Louise Wise
Services

M

Madonna 69
Make Poverty History
(Britain) 309c
Malawi 69
Malik, Charles 300c
Malleus Maleficarum
290c
Malthus, Thomas Robert
291c, 292c
Manning, Barbara 224b
Mao Zedong 55, 224b,
300c, 301c, 302c, 303c,
304c
Massachusetts

Adoption of Children
Act (1851) 28,
93–95, 293c
Board of State
Charities 30, 294c
matching 317g
maternal health,
Millenium
Development Goals
on 213f
Maternity and Child
Welfare Act (Britain,
1918) 297c
MBL. See Mother's
Bridge of Love
"Measures for
Registration for the
Adoption of Children
by Chinese Citizens"
(2005) 145–148
Medical Tourism
Corporation 244
Menichiello, Michael
19, 23
Mexico, as sending
country 200f
Michigan
first adoption
standards in 295c
surrogacy in 35–36
Millenium Development
Declaration 308c
Millenium Development
Goals 213f
"Minimum Safeguards
in Adoption" (1938)
99–101
minimum standards
317g–318g
Minnesota
adoption law 297c
sealed records law
30–31
missing females 66, 308c,
318g

mixed-race adoption. *See*
transracial adoption
Moll Flanders (Defoe) 29
Monckton, Sir Walter
224*b*
monetary reimbursement
for adoption 11
for surrogate
pregnancy 11,
35–36, 38
moron, use of term 30
Moses 224*b*–225*b*, 287*c*
mothers. *See* adoptive
parent(s); birth
parent(s); contracting
parents; surrogate
mothers
Mother's Bridge of Love
(MBL) 244
Mother's Clinic, London
297*c*
Muhammad 225*b*, 289*c*
Multiethnic Placement
Act (1994) 34, 104–
107, 307*c*
Murdoch, Bob 11
Murdoch, Candy 11

N

NACAC. *See* North
American Council on
Adoptable Children
Namibia, kinship care
in 13
Napoleonic Code 292*c*
National Association of
Black Social Workers
34, 303*c*
National Black Child
Development Institute
(NBCDI) 244–245
National Center for State
Courts 14

National Children's
Adoption Association
(NCAA) 296*c*–297*c*
National Children's
Advocacy Center
(NCAC) 245
National Council for the
Unmarried Mother
and Her Child (Britain,
1918) 297*c*
National Education
League (Britain) 294*c*
National Family
Preservation Network
(NFPN) 245
National Society for the
Prevention of Cruelty
to Children (Britain)
295*c*
National Survey of
Family Growth 39–40
National Urban League
Foster Care and
Adoptions Project
301*c*
Native Americans,
adoption of **33–34,**
302*c*, 303*c*, 304*c*
NBCDI. *See* National
Black Child
Development Institute
NCAA. *See* National
Children's Adoption
Association
NCAC. *See* National
Children's Advocacy
Center
neglect, child
definition of 313*g*
drug use in
pregnancy as 5
neocolonialism 79
Nepal
adoption abuses in
51

as sending country
200*f*
Netherlands, as
receiving country 76,
201*f*
New England
Association of Farmers,
Merchants, and Other
Workingmen 292*c*
New Jersey Supreme
Court, Baby M ruling
of 37, 107–116
New Life Children's
Refuge 311*c*
New York, surrogacy
in 43
New York Children's
Aid Society 29–30,
293*c*
New York School of
Applied Philanthropy
295*c*
New York Society for
the Prevention of
Cruelty to Children
294*c*
New York State Charities
Aid Association 32,
295*c*, 298*c*
NFPN. *See* National
Family Preservation
Network
Nigeria
adoption abuses in
51
as sending country
200*f*
Nixon, Richard 303*c*
ni ying 56, 318*g*
North American
Council on Adoptable
Children (NACAC)
246
Norway, as receiving
country 10, 50, 62,
201*f*

notarios 76
Notification of Births Act (Britain, 1907) 296*c*, 297*c*
"Now I Realise How Hopelessly Naïve I Was to Become Britain's First Surrogate Mother, Admits Kim Cotton" (Weathers, 2008) 167–171

O

Odofredus 289*c*
Oettinger, Katherine 302*c*
Office for Standards in Education, Children's Services, and Skills (OFSTED, Britain) 310*c*
Office of Child Development 303*c*
OFSTED. *See* Office for Standards in Education, Children's Services, and Skills
Oliver Twist (Dickens) 292*c*
one-child policy, in China 49, 55–56, 58, 60–61, 304*c*, 310*c*
open adoption **7–8**
    advantages of 7–8
    definition of 318*g*
    disadvantages of 8
open program (surrogacy) **19–20,** 318*g*
Operation Babylift 82
OPTS. *See* Organization of Parents Through Surrogacy
Oregon, access to birth records in 308*c*

Organization of Parents Through Surrogacy (OPTS) 246
orphanage
    definition of 318*g*
    "In a Chinese Orphanage" (Thurston) 138–145
orphan trains **29–30,** 293*c*
outcome studies 318*g*
out-of-wedlock pregnancy (illegitimacy)
    concept of **28–29,** 31, 32
    definition of 317*g*
    psychoanalysis and 32
    race and 32
    sealed records and 30–31
over-quota birth
    Chinese restrictions on 49, 55–56, 58, 60–61, 310*c*
    definition of 318*g*

P

Pandey, L. K. 225*b*, 305*c*
parent(s). *See* adoptive parent(s); birth parent(s); contracting parents; surrogate mothers
parental rights, termination of 13
Parents for Ethical Adoption Reform (PEAR) 246–247
Parliamentary Select Committee on the Protection of Infant Life (Britain) 294*c*

participants. *See also specific participants*
    characteristics of **39–42**
Pate, Maurice 300*c*
Patel, Nayna 225*b*
patriarchy
    in China 50, 56
    definition of 318*g*
    in India 50, 66–67
patrilineal family 318*g*
patrilocal family
    in China 50
    definition of 318*g*
    in India 50, 66–67
Patton, Jean 301*c*
PEAR. *See* Parents for Ethical Adoption Reform
Pearce, Jonathan 74
Philippines, as sending country 200*f*
P.L. 103-382 (1994) 34, 104–107, 307*c*
placing out 319*g*
Poland, as sending country 200*f*
Polier, Justine Wise 226*b*
Poor Law Amendment Act (Britain, 1834) 292*c*
Poor Laws, Elizabethan 70, 290*c*, 291*c*, 292*c*
Population and Family Planning Law (China, 2004) 309*c*
population control, in China 49, 55–56, 58, 60–61, 304*c*, 309*c*, 310*c*
positive adoption language 7
pragmatic approach, in surrogacy 42
pregnancy, surrogate. *See* surrogate pregnancy

Index

Prenatal Diagnostic
Techniques Act (India)
67, 307*c*
Prevention of Cruelty to
Children Act (Britain,
1904) 295*c*
privacy rights 38
private (independent)
adoption **15**
definition of 317*g*
as high-risk activity
ix
legality of 15
private v. public life 3
privilege, cultures of ix
procreative tourism. *See*
reproductive tourism
pro-natalist policy 319*g*
psychoanalysis **31–32**
public v. private life 3
"put up" for adoption 29

R

race **32**
and adoption 32–34
denial of services
to African
Americans 32
Doss family and 33,
301*c*
first adoption
endeavor
for African
Americans 301*c*
of Guatemalan
children 79
Indian Adoption
Project **33–34,**
302*c,* 303*c*
kinship 14, 32
National
Association of
Black Social
Workers on 34,
303*c*

preferences in
21–22, 23, 43, 74,
204*f*
transracial adoption
7, **33,** 300*c,* 321*g*
and views of birth
parents in U.S.
210*f*
Ragoné, Helena 18–21,
23, 41, 42
Rajchman, Ludwik 300*c*
receiving countries 48,
49–50, 201*f,* 319*g. See
also specific countries*
records, sealed **30–31**
definition of 319*g*
first law on
(Minnesota)
30–31
open adoption v.
7–8
Reitz, Miriam 22
"Relation of Personality
Study to Child Placing"
(Taft) 297*c*
relative adoption **13–14,**
32
relinquishment 319*g*
reproductive rights
v. fetal abuse 5
impact on adoption
34
reproductive rights
movement **34**
Reproductive Science
Center 18
reproductive technology
4–5, 34–35. *See also
specific types*
reproductive tourism 48,
52–53
definition of 319*g*
in Guatemala 53,
76–80
in India 53, 62–63,
66, 158–162, 309*c*

in Spain 52–53
in Ukraine 135–138
"rescue" x
RESOLVE: The National
Infertility Association
247
reunification 319*g*
Rights of Infants, The
(Spence) 291*c*
Ritchie, Guy 69
Rock, John 35, 226*b,*
299*c*
Roe v. Wade 304*c*
Romania
reproductive tourism
in 53
as sending country
22, 54
Roosevelt, Eleanor 300*c*
Roosevelt, Franklin
Delano 299*c*
Russia
reproductive tourism
in 53
as sending country
49, 54, 76, 200*f*

S

St. Vincent de Paul
Society 295*c*
Sarah (biblical figure) 16,
216*b,* 287*c*
Save the Children 247,
297*c*
Schechter, Marshall 302*c*
sealed records **30–31**
definition of 319*g*
first law on
(Minnesota)
30–31
open adoption v.
7–8
selective reduction 319*g*
semi-closed adoption
9–10, 319*g*

semi-open adoption **9,**
319*g*
sending countries 48,
49–50, 200*f,* 319*g. See
also specific countries*
sex
    preferences/
    inequalities in
    50–51
    in China 50–51, 55,
    56, 308*c*
    female feticide 51,
    67, 307*c,* 320*g*
    in India 50–51,
    66–67, 307*c*
    missing females 66,
    308*c,* 318*g*
    son preference
    50–51, 55, 56, 67,
    307*c,* 320*g*
    U.S. adoptions by
    202*f,* 204*f*
sex ratio
    in China 51, 55
    definition of 320*g*
    in India 51, 66, 67
sex-selective abortion
51
    definition of 320*g*
    in India 67, 307*c*
Seymour, Susan C. 61
Shute, Nancy 10
sibling group 320*g*
Sierra Leone, adoption
    abuses in 51
Silber, Kathleen 9
single adoptive parents
22
social responsibility x
Social Security Act
    (1935) 299*c*
social work 295*c,* 298*c,*
320*g*
Society for the
    Prevention of Cruelty
    to Children 294*c*

Society for the
    Promotion of Christian
    Knowledge 290*c*
"soft law" on surrogacy
43
son preference 50–51
    in China 50–51, 55,
    56
    definition of 320*g*
    in India 50–51, 67,
    307*c*
Sorensen, Kelly 43
South Africa, kinship
    care in 13
South Korea, as sending
    country 22, 49, 81–82,
    200*f,* 301*c*
Soviet bloc 22, 54, 320*g.*
    See also Romania;
    Russia
Spain
    as receiving country
    49, 76, 201*f*
    reproductive tourism
    in 52–53
special needs, child with
    7, 12, 314*g*
special needs adoption
12
special needs child 12
    definition of 6, 320*g*
    financial incentives
    for adopting
    42–43, 304*c*–305*c*
Speenhamland System
291*c*
Spence, Thomas 291*c*
Spencer, Marietta 226*b*
sperm bank 35, 303*c*
sperm donation 320*g*
standardization
    in China 60–61
    in Great Britain 74
    in Guatemala 80–81
    in India 67–68
Stanley v. Illinois 303*c*

Starr, Ellen Gates 295*c*
State Department 12,
    51
state laws, on surrogacy
    43
Statute of Westminster II
    (Britain) 289*c*
stepparent adoption **14,**
    320*g*
Steptoe, Patrick 35,
    226*b*–227*b*
Stern, Elizabeth 37,
    107–116, 227*b,* 305*c*
Stern, Melissa 37
Stern, William 37, 42,
    107–116, 227*b,* 305*c*
Stopes, Marie 297*c*
subsidies, for hard-to-
    place children 42–43,
    304*c*–305*c*
Surrogacy and
    Fertility Law Center
    (Guatemala) 80
Surrogacy Arrangements
    Act (Britain, 1985) 71,
    74
Surrogacy in Canada
    Online 247–248
surrogacy programs,
    types of 19–21
Surrogate Mother, The
    (Keane and Breo) 35,
    101–104
*Surrogate Motherhood:
    Conception in the Heart*
    (Ragoné) 18
surrogate mothers
    advertisements for
    22
    characteristics of
    40–41
    in China 58
    in closed program
    20–21
    in gestational
    surrogacy 18–19

in Great Britain
72–73, 162–165,
167–171
in Guatemala 79–80
in India 65–66
medical evaluation
of 17
monetary
reimbursement for
11, 35–36, 38
motivation of 41
in open program
19–20
pragmatic v.
egalitarian
approach toward
42
in traditional
surrogacy 17–18
Surrogate Mothers, Inc.
20
Surrogate Mothers
Online, LLC 248
Surrogate Parenting
Centre (Britain) 71
surrogate pregnancy
16–21
altruistic 20, 38, 312*g*
biblical story of 16,
287*c*
in China 53–61,
148–151, 308*c*
commercial 38, 43,
314*g*
cost of 18–19
custody issues in
Baby M 21, **36–37**,
42, 107–116,
305*c*
Calvert v. Johnson
38–39, 306*c*
Great Britain 73–74
definition of 320*g*
ethics of 18, **22–23**
federal regulations
on, lack of 16

first successful
gestational 305*c*
in Great Britain
68–74, 162–165,
167–171
in Guatemala
75–81
in India 61–68,
158–162
international laws on
215*f*
motivations for
pursuing ix
participants in,
characteristics of
40–42
reproductive tourism
and 48, 52–53. *See
also* reproductive
tourism
types of 17–19
U.S. history and law
35–39, 214*f*
suspension of adoptions,
countries under 51, 76,
81, 309*c*, 311*c*
Sweden, as receiving
country 50, 62, 201*f*
Switzerland, as receiving
country 62

T

Taft, Jessie 227*b*, 297*c*
Taiwan, as sending
country 200*f*
Tao Lai Po-Wah, Julia 59
TASC. *See* The American
Surrogacy Center
test-tube babies. *See* in
vitro fertilization
Thailand, as sending
country 200*f*
The American Surrogacy
Center (TASC) 231
Theis, Sophie van Senden
227*b*, 298*c*

Thurston, Anne F.
138–145
tourism, reproductive
48, **52–53**
definition of 319*g*
in Guatemala 53,
76–80
in India 53, 62–63,
66, 158–162, 309*c*
in Spain 52–53
in Ukraine 135–138
traditional surrogacy
17–18
definition of 320*g*
ethics of 18
success rate of
17–18
trafficking, child 51–52
in Cambodia 51
definition of 314*g*
in Guatemala 51–52,
76, 77, 171–176,
311*c*
Hague Convention
and 51–52
trains, orphan **29–30,**
293*c*
Trajan (emperor of
Rome) 227*b*–228*b*,
288*c*
transnational adoption.
See international
adoption
transracial adoption **33**
definition of 7, 321*g*
Doss family and 33,
301*c*
first recorded in U.S.
33, 300*c*
of Guatemalan
children 79
Indian Adoption
Project **33–34,**
302*c*, 303*c*
National Association
of Black Social

Workers on 34,
303c
Turski, Diane 7

U

Ubico, Jorge 298c, 299c
Uganda, as sending
country 200f
Ukraine
reproductive tourism
in 135–138
as sending country
49, 200f
ultrasound technology
51, 321g
UNESCO. See United
Nations Educational,
Scientific and Cultural
Organization
UNICEF. See United
Nations Children's
Fund
United Kingdom. See
Great Britain
United Nations Charter
299c
United Nations
Children's Fund
(UNICEF) ix, 66, 71,
76, 248
founding of 300c
Position on
Intercountry
Adoption (2007)
133–135
United Nations
Committee on the
Rights of the Child
306c
United Nations
Convention on the
Rights of the Child
306c
United Nations
Educational,
Scientific and

Cultural Organization
(UNESCO) 300c, 304c
United Nations Relief
and Rehabilitation
Administration
(UNRRA) 299c
United States
adoption in 28–35
children born to
single mothers
relinquished for
208f
demand for 206f–
207f
percent of all, by
type 203f
preferences in
204f–205f
adoptive parents in,
perceptions of 209f
birth parents in,
racial differences in
views of 210f
international
adoptions to 49,
62, 199f, 201f
by sending countries
200f
by sex and age 202f
surrogacy in 35–39,
214f
Universal Declaration of
Human Rights (1948)
300c
UNRRA. See United
Nations Relief
and Rehabilitation
Administration
Upanisad, Yogatattava 63
Urban Institute 14
U.S. Children's Bureau
248–249, 296c, 297c,
302c, 303c
*U.S. News & World
Report* 10
Utting, William 306c

V

Vaisons, Council of 288c
Victoria (queen of Great
Britain, empress of
India) 292c
Vietnam, as sending
country 49, 82, 200f
Vineland Training
School for Backward
and Feeble-minded
Children 30, 296c
Vishnu, legal codes of 63
vocation, surrogacy as 41

W

waiting child 6, 321g
Waldheim, Kurt 304c
"Warden Information:
Rumors of Child
Stealing" (2007) 176
Warnock, Dame Mary
228b
Watson, Kenneth W. 22
Weathers, Helen 167–171
welfare, child 314g
Westminster II, Statute of
(Britain) 289c
Whitehead, Mary Beth
37, 107–116, 228b, 305c
White House Conference
on the Care of
Dependent Children
(1909) 296c
white infants, preference
for 21–22, 23, 43, 74
WHO. See World Health
Organization
"Why Adoption Is Not
an Option in India: The
Visibility of Infertility,
the Secrecy of Donor
Insemination, and Other
Cultural Complexities"
(Bharadwaj, 2003)
152–158
Wilson, Mary Ellen 294c

Wilson, Pete 43
Winn, Denise 162–165
Wise, Louise Waterman
  228*b*
women's rights
  in China 59–60
  control over
    healthcare, lack of
    212*f*

definition of 321*g*
reproductive
  v. fetal abuse 5
  impact on adoption
    34
workhouse 290*c*,
  321*g*
World Child Welfare
  Charter 298*c*

World Health
  Organization (WHO)
  249

Z

Zimbabwe, kinship care
  in 13